The Universal Path to Enlightenment:

The Eastern Answers to the Mysteries of Life

VOLUME TWO

By
Stephen Knapp

Find out more about
The World Relief Network
Stephen Knapp and his books at:
http://www.Stephen-Knapp.com

Dedicated to all who are seriously searching for spiritual wisdom
and the path that leads to enlightenment of the Absolute.
May this book to you be a sign that helps show the way.

ISBN 0-9617410-2-3

Library of Congress Catalog Card Number
92-80273

PUBLISHED BY

PROVIDING KNOWLEDGE
OF
REALITY DISTINGUISHED FROM ILLUSION
FOR THE WELFARE OF ALL

The World Relief Network
P. O. Box 15082
Detroit, Michigan
48215-0082

Contents

Contents

Preface

Throughout the history of civilization there has been an undying inquisitiveness and search for understanding who we are, where we have come from, what our true identity is, what the purpose of life is, and what is the ultimate, Absolute Truth. This quest, whether open and obvious or subtle and secretive, continues day after day, year after year, generation after generation, in every millenia. It may manifest in many forms. Scientists and researchers look for the absolute origin of life, or the absolute cause of the universe. Others may take to a religion or study some of the many cultures of the world in hopes of finding philosophical answers. We may find this quest taking place amongst thousands or millions of people at a time, or only amongst a few who might be sparsely scattered across the face of the earth. But no one can stop it. Not rulers, politicians, governments, or armies have been able to completely stifle this ever-present curiosity that exists to some degree within us all.

The essence of the answers to this quest for purpose and identity have always remained as the seeds of all metaphysical and spiritual philosophies, whether they have grown to fully blossom and be understood by society, or only remained as sprouts that were overlooked by a civilization that was spiritually unaware. In either case, these seeds of universal knowledge are found everywhere, in every culture, and when compared together can assemble a puzzle of explanations that can bring the world closer to being a united society. Thus, what appears to be a variety of cultures, religions, legends, traditions, and viewpoints that do not support each other, may actually be different versions of what once was the originating culture many thousands of years ago.

Most people, due to family relations, are born into a religious culture and are raised to think that their religion is the best. This is to be expected, but thoughtful individuals will wonder where and how their religion began and developed. And the most thoughtful will wonder how it compares to other cultures or spiritual paths. Naturally, the superficial aspects of religions, such as the dress, the traditions, rituals, and even the legends, may have many variations and differences. Yet, the essence and ultimate purpose of most religions are often quite similar. However, religion is never meant merely to be a belief system or a number of concepts or ideas that are blindly accepted as truth. Religion is meant to be a process which enables one to reach the stage of fully realizing by direct perception and experience the nature of spiritual reality.

By taking to an authentic spiritual path, you begin to progressively change an inner part of you, particularly your consciousness. As your consciousness evolves, you can begin to perceive that which is spiritual. This is the difference between merely conceptualizing something and actually experiencing or realizing it. When one truly realizes his or her spiritual position, this is the sign of qualification. Without this qualification one remains on an elementary and inexperienced platform. This is why the spiritual customs and practices of foreign cultures, such as those of the East, often remain a mystery to many people of the West. They cannot perceive the essence or purpose of it, or they simply feel that there is no need for them to try and understand it. Lack of realization is also what separates the serious followers from the frivolous and commen men who are quick to criticize what seems odd to them. This provides a natural means by which the powerful spiritual knowledge is protected from those who are not serious or who would misuse it. Only those who are qualified are worthy of fully understanding the mysteries of spiritual knowledge. And if a religion or path does not bring one to full spiritual realization, then he or she should move on to explore one that does, if that is for what a person is sincerely looking. Although all spiritual paths are meant to lead one in the same direction towards spiritual enlightenment, not all paths are the same in terms of their capacity to bring one to full spiritual realization, which will become obvious as we move along through this volume.

Full spiritual realizations, however, are not likely to happen overnight. It may take some time to attain such higher levels of experience and understanding. As already mentioned, the seeds of universal knowledge are found in every culture, but if one studies them carefully he will see that this knowledge is especially elaborated within the Eastern philosophy, particularly in the Vedic texts of India.

One of the unique things about Vedic philosophy is that within the many texts it contains, it deals with all varieties of viewpoints, from impersonalistic atheism, outright materialism, to loving devotion to God. And you have room to discover and realize the knowledge at your own rate, whether it be many months, many years, or even lifetimes. You can establish and discuss your own reasonings by Vedic evidence and personal experience, and listen to others do the same in an attempt to better comprehend the truths of life. In other words, you may at first be of an impersonalist persuasion and believe that the Supreme is only a great unembodied force. Or you might believe that God is a person. Or you may worship Durga, Ganesh, Shiva, Vishnu, or Krishna, and still be considered on the Vedic path, though on different parts of the path. But this is the sort of freedom and opportunity you have in the Vedic philosophy for your growth and development. However, we find that in other religions, such as Christianity and Islam, if you question or doubt the local scriptures or authorities, or argue different points of view, or look for answers from another religion, your faith will be questioned, you may be called a heretic, and you may even be excommunicated from the Church, which is supposed to equate with eternal damnation. This is obviously a very closed-minded discipline to work in compared to the freedom of the Vedic system. After all, what kind of God would make a system in which you have only one life to live and only one chance to discover how to attain Him, and then follow all the scriptural demands and requirements or face eternal damnation? Only the kind of God you are taught to fear, not one with whom you easily could develop a loving relationship.

It is the Vedic path that allows and encourages you to pursue truth to the fullest degree by whatever means you find suitable. Thus, it is easy for a Vedic follower to recognize the pursuit of Truth in other paths as well as his own. But we find that the exclusiveness and holier-than-thou attitudes found in some religions make it difficult for the aspirants of these faiths to recognize or tolerate the pursuit of Truth in other spiritual processes. In fact, history shows that the three traditions of Judaism, Christianity, and Islam have, in their monotheistic theologies, developed patterns and traits of prejudice, intolerance, violence, and war against all other religions and cultures. Although fatricidal or tribal wars may have occurred amongst the people within any culture, the worst and most devastating of all "holy wars" were caused by these three religions. In fact, the history of these three religions show that they have spread primarily because of political intolerance for other religions, militant zeal, and through fear of persecution, rather than by spiritual purity. Hinduism, on the other hand, has not spread on the basis of fear, whether that fear be of political persecution or fear of a wrathful God. But it has spread primarily on the basis of people's inclination to increase their understanding of God, to devote themselves to God, or to become spiritually advanced and enlightened.

The Vedic attitude is that religion is a matter of personal realization, and that the aspirant uses the various processes or portions of Vedic knowledge as an instrument to realize different levels of spiritual truths with the most important goal being the realization of the Absolute Truth. This is why we see in India such a tolerance and respect for so many people who participate in a wide variety of spiritual processes, auterities, levels of contemplation, and forms of meditation.

Ultimately, if there is only one Supreme God and Creator, there can only be one religion, the essence of which is the process for re-establishing our loving relationship with Him. Thus, any process you take up, it does not matter, if it helps you attain love for the Supreme, then it is alright. That is the main point. But many people profess that their religion is the only one that does that. So what is the difference between the major religions like Christianity, Islam, Hinduism, Buddhism, etc? How did they originate? What are their goals and philosophies, and how do they compare with each other? What do they all have in common? What are the different levels of knowledge in the Vedic literature? And what path offers the highest levels of realization and is specifically recommended for this day and age? As you go through this book, you will find the information that answers these questions and much more.

Introduction

The purpose of this book is to supply the reader with information about the many different religious and philosophical paths that are available for understanding oneself, the universe, life in general, the Absolute Truth, and the purpose of it all. Many times people know that they are looking to find a means of understanding the spiritual nature of themselves and the world, but do not know exactly how to go about it or where to begin. Since there are so many religions or paths that claim to be the best, a person can easily become confused about what is the real goal of spiritual life. Or a person may simply not think about comparing different spiritual paths and might feel that all other religions but his or her own are strange and unacceptable. But intelligent people will make some comparisons and decide for themselves in which process or culture they wish to participate after they have understood the goals and differences between each religion. This book provides the kind of information that allows the reader to begin understanding what are the goals, differences, as well as similarities of each culture and spiritual path.

The secondary purpose of this book is to supply the reader with knowledge and references of spiritual topics that normally would be difficult to find, or would be reached only after many years of research and study. I recognize that in this age not everyone has time to do everything they would like. In light of this, I have tried to compile this book so that with a limited amount of time and expense one could still have access to some of the most elevated knowledge and spiritual realizations ever recorded and known to man.

In supplying this information, I have tried not to write too extensively, but only enough to make things clear for the reader without being vague. If there are specific questions the reader has, either about this book, or about the practice of yoga, or how to get other books on these topics, they may correspond with me at the following address and I will be glad to give further help:

The World Relief Network
P. O. Box 15082
Detroit, Michigan
48215-0082

Some of the chapters in this book may be more important to the reader than others. Chapter Two deals with the many levels of knowledge that the Vedic literature contains, and for some people may be a little too detailed. But it is nonetheless an essential chapter for understanding exactly what kind of information the Vedic literature provides about the world and the Absolute Truth. Chapter Three describes the different kinds of yoga processes, how practical they are, and what is the goal of each one. Chapter Four supplies information about the major philosophical systems of the East. It also covers several of the important religions, including Buddhism, Jainism, Shaivism, Sikhism, etc. Chapter Five discusses other major religions of the world. This will help increase our understanding of how these religions originated and what is the real authenticity of their culture. Chapter Six explains the basis of Christianity and how it has been greatly influenced by the early pre-Christian "pagan" religions that it has so adamantly opposed over the years. It also shows how many of the Vedic teachings and legends have been adopted by Christianity and provides a brief look at the bloody history this religion has left in its wake through the centuries. In spite of this, the chapter also points out how similar the teachings of Jesus are to the ancient Vedic teachings. Chapter Seven gives an analysis of how influential the early Vedic Aryan religion and culture was to the other societies of that era. Many age old traditions found in other countries can be traced directly to the early Vedic customs and beliefs. Chapter Eight discusses the real purpose of any spiritual path, from the elementary to the advanced level, and Chapters Nine and Ten provide information on the necessary and essential spiritual practices that are meant for this age. It is considered that without this knowledge no spiritual path is complete. Chapter Eleven provides information about the necessary qualifications of a spiritual leader, how to recognize a true spiritual authority and one who is not, and how to seek spiritual knowledge from a qualified teacher. Chapter Twelve puts it all together and points out how most of the religions in the world have essential similarities that make it possible for all people to worship the Supreme together, and bring about a much more understanding, harmonious, and united world.

To help make this book more authentic and complete, there is also a special section on seeing the spiritual side of India. This section takes the reader on a tour of the major holy places and temples from Madras up through the eastern portion of India and Nepal, and on to New Delhi. This area has some of the most important temples and holy places in the world that are related to several of the major religions, and where some of them originated. Though several of the towns I describe are known only to those pilgrims who are well-versed in this kind of information, other towns are quite popular for being the locations where many pastimes of great personalities have taken place, such as those of Buddha, Krishna, Vishnu, Rama, Shiva, as well as many saintly men who are related to the Hindu, Buddhist, Islamic, Jain, Sikh, and other religions. As we travel to these different towns, I will not only discuss the legends connected with them, but also describe what they are like today, the best way to reach them, and which temples or sites are the most important. Thus, in this section you will get a better idea of what spiritual life is like in India today, and, if you ever go to India, you will know where the best places are for spiritual pursuits. Many photographs are included of a variety of temples, holy sites, and people engaging in many different aspects of life. In other volumes of *The Eastern Answers to the*

Mysteries of Life series we continue our travels through other areas of the East.

Regarding my photography, I am basically a photojournalist photographing life as it happens without contriving the scenes or manipulating the photos in any way. It is my way of trying to share the experience of India and convey information about what life and the spiritual culture is like. I use 35mm cameras for the spontaneity that format allows and for getting into situations that would be difficult with bigger cameras. This is especially important when I take a sneak shot in areas where photography is prohibited, or in festivals where thousands of people are participating, or when I am in temples or situations where I want to photograph people doing things without them realizing that I am there.

Further information on the knowledge of the East has been provided in Volume One of *The Eastern Answers to the Mysteries of Life*, which is titled *The Secret Teachings of the Vedas*. This book gives some very important information for anyone who is trying to understand real spiritual knowledge. The chapters explain such things as our real spiritual identity, the science of the soul, reincarnation, the law of *karma* and destiny, the *karma* of a nation, how to determine what will be your future life, recognizing the existence of God, descriptions of the spiritual world, attaining the highest happiness, and much more. Plus, it has a special section on traveling to the important holy sites and temples in South India, and includes over 75 photographs of temples, Deities, art work, sculptures, and people.

Though this second volume of this series is complete in itself, it follows a systematic process from Volume One in explaining spiritual knowledge. Thus, there are certain topics that may be mentioned in this volume that are more thoroughly explained in the first volume. So you may also want to read *The Secret Teachings of the Vedas* to increase your understanding of this information.

I do not use footnotes in this volume, but all scriptural quotes are accompanied by text and verse references. All literary works that were referred to for the information used in this book are listed in the back. However, additional information and stories that are used were also heard from various people and *sadhus* while I was traveling in India. Furthermore, rather than using diacritical marks for the transcription of Indian names and terms, the standard English style is used for the convenience of the average Western reader.

One point I wish to make, however, is that spiritual knowledge is for everyone, men and women alike. So if it seems that I use the words "he" or "him" a lot in this book when referring to the aspirant or follower of a spiritual path, it actually means anyone, he or she.

Presently, we are also working on Volume Three of *The Eastern Answers to the Mysteries of Life* which will be another important book based on the ancient Eastern texts. This book will continue to provide explanations about such things as the Vedic predictions of the future, how the worlds are finally annihilated, how we fit into this cosmic plan, the reason for it all, and much more.

CHAPTER ONE

Everyone Must Choose a Path

If we are nothing more than a combination of material substances created by an evolutionary process, without any spiritual essence within us, then why do we bother to try to understand who we are and where we have come from, or what we are doing in this world? Of course, some may say that curiosity is a typical trait of human nature that makes us want to know these things, but why do some of us almost instinctively look within ourselves and have a sense of an internal spiritual nature? Why has the quest for spiritual truth and understanding gone on since prehistoric times if something significant is not there? Why do people go through political revolution, repression, and even torture by atheistic governments just to cling to their religion if nothing substantial is found in religious experiences? Surely by now, after all these thousands of years, we would have discovered that religion, mystical experiences, or faith in a supreme being is an empty illusion if that is what it is. After all, if we are no more than an accidental creation in a universe that has no purpose, we should be content to go through life simply eating, sleeping, mating, and working hard for our survival without wondering why. But, on the contrary, many people search out a purpose for life, if only on a very personal level, and cling to their faith as much as ever, and often feel an emptiness in life without it.

In any case, no matter what one decides to do in his life, in terms of either material or spiritual progress, he or she must choose a course of action or a path to follow. If a person decides to become a businessman, or computer programer, a doctor, lawyer, mechanic, or whatever, he must get trained in that field before he can actually start his practice. This means deciding what school to attend, what courses to take, where and how to get his internship if necessary, and then which places to apply for getting a job, or where to go to start a business. This all must be done properly to be successful.

Similarly, when a person wants to make spiritual progress, he must also

1

decide what results he would like to attain. If a person does not consider this, he may simply follow the faith of his parents and attend the local church or temple without thinking much more about it. But we must understand that each religion or spiritual path takes us to a different level of consciousness and spiritual awareness, just as a different trade or vocation will determine how much money a person can make, what the working conditions might be, in which community and in what kind of house he might live, and so on.

Some religions, by offering certain precepts, can help give a person hope for a better future, or happiness, patience, kindness, morality, forgiveness, and other good qualities that make living much more pleasant and worthwhile. Other spiritual processes may include higher aspects of spiritual advancement, like the attainment of mystic powers, the ability to control one's physical health and development, the perception of one's spiritual nature, or even the capacity to directly see and enter into the spiritual world at will. Thus, there are different levels of spirituality, from the fundamental to the very advanced. So, depending on what one wishes to accomplish in his or her spiritual progress, a person must compare the different processes and consider which one to take since they are not all the same.

We can compare the spiritual path to a long highway, like one leading from New York to Miami. Many people may get on the path, but they may get on at different points, go in different directions, travel at various speeds, or get off at different exits. So not everyone will take the path in the same way or reach the same destination. Thus, they may only attain small levels of spiritual understanding. That does not mean that they may not later get back on the path and finish the journey, but how long they take to complete it depends on them. Few people will get on at New York and travel all the way to Miami. But only by getting on the path and traveling at a steady pace with sincerety and determination will we be assured of reaching the goal.

A person, however, will not be able to fathom the deepest levels of spiritual knowledge if he or she does not engage in the spiritual practices that are prescribed. This is particularly true of the Vedic path, which explains that regardless of academic qualifications, or how great a scholar a person may be, if a person is simply an armchair philosopher and does not engage in the disciplines that are described in the highest levels of Vedic literature, as also explained by an authorized *acarya*, a person will remain spiritually inexperienced. The reason is that such spiritual practice purifies one from the limited conception of material existence, and, thus, prepares one's consciousness for realizing the unlimited nature of the spiritual atmosphere and the Absolute Truth, which is far beyond one's ability to analyze with the use of ordinary material logic. Such logic, to reach conclusions of analysis, depends on the material laws of nature that exist in this universe, but such laws of nature do not exist nor do they affect the spiritual strata. Therefore, one's consciousness has to be spiritualized in order to understand that which is spiritual. The spiritual realm consists of what is beyond the conceivability of ordinary human intellect. So to understand it, or experience and realize it, requires that one follow and engage in the discipline of the proper spiritual path. Trying to understand spiritual knowledge without engaging in the practice of the spiritual path is compared to trying to analyze a bottle of honey without opening the lid to experience the unique taste of the contents.

When we begin to study the various religions and philosophies in the world, we will see the many factors they have in common as well as their differences. Naturally, all bona fide spiritual processes are connected in various ways or, in some cases, are derivatives of one another. We will see this more clearly as we continue through this book. But what is it that makes a religion a true religion? How does one decide which process is right for him? How does a religion get its start? Are they initiated by God, a representative of God, or just some man that happened to have a different idea of things and was thus labeled a prophet? Or are religions simply remnants of ancient traditions that few people today can understand? And if all religions are part of the same path to Truth, why are some of them so different? And why do they sometimes seem to contribute to the disharmony of the world rather than to the unity of it? And why do some of them teach such different conceptions or contain different levels of understanding?

How a spiritual process can contain many levels of awareness can easily be seen in an analysis of the Vedic philosophy, the oldest and most developed spiritual philosophy in the world. In fact, many of the viewpoints contained in the Vedic literature have been handed down to numerous other religions and spiritual paths that have been accepted throughout the ages. So in the following chapter we will review the many levels of knowledge the Vedic literature contains and how it systematically deals with all aspects of thought and contemplation, and provides assistance for the aspirant to ascend towards the topmost level of spiritual knowledge and realization.

CHAPTER TWO

The Levels of Knowledge Contained in the Vedas

The Vedic philosophy contains the oldest spiritual texts of any religion in the world, and its more advanced concepts can be difficult for even the greatest scholars of the West to fathom. The Vedic literature discusses many types of philosophical viewpoints, and studying some of them will let us see that many of the concepts that we accept as new today are nothing more than parts of the ancient Vedic knowledge that had been dealt with and thoroughly understood thousands of years ago. Thus, there are not many ideas that are really new at all. The main purpose of the Vedic literature is to establish knowledge of the Absolute Truth and the process for attaining the highest levels of self-realization. To do that it must, and does, contain the elementary as well as most advanced forms of spiritual and material knowledge. So let us see exactly what kind of information is found within the many volumes of Vedic literature.

THE FOUR PRIMARY VEDAS

The Vedic literature is composed of many books. The oldest texts are the *Rig-veda, Yajur-veda, Sama-veda,* and the *Atharva-veda.*

The *Rig-veda,* the "Veda of Praise," contains 1,017 hymns, or 10,522 verses, arranged in ten books or *mandalas.* The first eight mostly contain hymns of praise to the various demigods, such as Indra and Agni, that are used in rituals for ensuring immediate material needs. The ninth book deals primarily with the *soma* ritual, which was the extraction and purification of the juice of the *soma* herb. The tenth book contains *suktas* or verses of wisdom and *mantras* which would cause certain magical effects to take place. However, it was generally only the *brahmana* priests who could be sure of chanting the *mantras* accurately to produce the desired result. If the *mantra* was chanted incorrectly by someone who was not qualified, the desired result would not take place and often

4

something undesirable or horrible would happen instead. The *Rig-veda* is also a mystical text that contains knowledge in its abstract imagery of what the seers had realized. It has information on yoga, the spinal current and the *chakras*, the planets and their orbits, and historical accounts of early Vedic kings. Many aspects of this mystical knowledge are also contained in the other *Vedas*.

The *Yajur-veda* contains verse-*mantras* containing different levels of knowledge and wisdom, many of which are similar to those in the *Rig-veda*. The *Yajur-veda*, however, has two additional *samhitas*, or collections of verses, known as the *Black Yajur-veda*, or *Taittiriya-samhita*, and the *White Yajur-veda*, or *Vajasaneyi-samhita*. These were primarily for the priests to use as a guide in performing sacrificial rituals since they also contain directions or formulas which the priests use along with the verses that are sung during the ritual.

The *Sama-veda*, the "Veda of Chants," contains 1549 verses meant to be used as songs in various ceremonies. Most of them are taken from the *Rig-veda* and arranged according to their use as utilized in particular rituals.

The *Atharva-veda* is a book of almost 6,000 verses containing prayers, spells, and incantations which in some respects resembles magical instructons found in the *Tantras* and even various magical incantations found in Europe. The *Atharva-veda* contains verses of instruction, wisdom, as well as rules for worshiping the planets, rules for oblations and sacrifices, prayers for averting evil and disease, incantations for the destruction of foes, etc.

These four primary *Vedas* represent the accomplishment of a highly developed religious system and encourage satisfaction of material desires through worship of the demigods. They contain many directions for increasing one's power and position, or for reaching the heavens in one's future by properly performing particular sacrifices in worship to the *devas* (demigods), and so on. For example, one could worship Agni for getting power, Durgadevi for good fortune, Indra for good sex life or plenty of rain, or the Vasus for getting money. Such instruction is the *karma-kanda* section of the *Vedas* which many people considered to be the most important part of Vedic knowledge.

According to the *Vedas*, the demigods are not imaginary or mythological beings, but are agents of the Supreme Will to administer different aspects of the universal affairs. A transcendentalist sees that behind every aspect of nature is a personality. For example, when you walk into a big factory, you see so many workers. More important than the workers are the foremen, managers, then executives, and finally a chairman or president of the company. You may not see the president right away, but his influence is everywhere since all the workers are engaging in projects according to his decisions. The managers and foremen act as his authorized agents to keep things moving accordingly. The demigods act in the same way concerning the functions of nature.

It is said that there are as many as thirty-three million different demigods, of which a small portion are the most important. They affect all levels of universal activities, including the weather, or who is bestowed with particular opulences such as riches, beautiful wife or husband, large family, good health, etc. The reciprocation between the demigods and society is explained in *Bhagavad-gita* (3.10-12). It is stated that in the beginning the Lord of all beings created men and demigods along with the sacrifices to Lord Vishnu that were to be performed. The Lord blessed them saying that these sacrifices will enable men to prosper and attain all desirable things. By these sacrificial duties the demigods will be pleased and the demigods will also please you with all the necessities of life, and prosperity will spread to all. But he who enjoys what is given by the demigods without offering them in return is a thief.

In this way, people can perform sacrificial rituals to obtain their desires, but by the performance of such acts they should understand their dependent position, not only on the demigods, but ultimately on the Supreme. As further explained in *Bhagavad-gita* (3.14-15), all living beings exist on food grains, which are produced from rain, which is produced by the performance of prescribed sacrifices or duties. These prescribed duties are described in the Vedic literature, which is manifest from the Supreme Being. Therefore, the Supreme is eternally established in acts of sacrifice.

Although the demigods may accept worship from the human beings and bless them with particular benedictions according to the sacrifices that are performed, they are still not on the level of the Supreme Lord Vishnu (who is an incarnation or expansion of Lord Krishna). The *Rig-veda* (1.22.20) explains: "The demigods are always looking to that supreme abode of Vishnu." *Bhagavad-gita* (17.23) also points out: "From the beginning of creation, the three syllables *om tat sat* have been used to indicate the Supreme Absolute Truth (Brahman). They were uttered by *brahmanas* while chanting the Vedic hymns and during sacrifices, for the satisfaction of the Supreme." In this way, by uttering *om tat sat*, which is stressed in the *Vedas*, the performers of the rituals of sacrifices for worshiping the demigods were also offering obeisances to Lord Vishnu for its success. The four *Vedas* mainly deal with material elevation and since Lord Vishnu is the Lord of material liberation, most sacrifices were directed towards the demigods.

In *Bhagavad-gita*, however, Lord Krishna points out that men of small knowledge, who are given to worldly desires, take delight in the flowery words of the *Vedas* that prescribe rituals for attaining power, riches, or rebirth in heaven. With their goal of enjoyment they say there is nothing else than this. However, Krishna goes on to explain (in *Bhagavad-gita* 7.21-23) that when a person desires to worship a particular demigod for the temporary and limited fruits he or she may bestow, Krishna, as the Supersoul in everyone's heart, makes that person's faith in the demigod steady. But all the benefits given by any demigod actually are given by Krishna alone, for without whom no one has any power. Furthermore, the worshippers of the demigods go to the planets of the demigods, but worshipers of Krishna reach Krishna's spiritual abode.

Thus, as one progresses in understanding, it is expected that they will gradually give up the pursuit for temporary material pleasures and endeavor for reaching the supreme goal of Vedic knowledge. For one who is situated in such knowledge, self-realized, the prescribed duties in the *Vedas* for worshipping the demigods are unnecessary. As *Bhagavad-gita* (3.17-18) explains, for one who is fully self-realized, who is fully satiated in the self, delights only in the self, there is no duty or need to perform the prescribed duties found in the *Vedas*, because he has no purpose or material desires to fulfill.

Although the four principle *Vedas* include the concept of spiritual perfection, it is not so thoroughly developed. Therefore, to help one understand what the goal of Vedic philosophy is, there are also other compositions along with the four *Vedas*, namely the *Brahmanas, Aranyakas,* and the *Upanishads*.

The *Brahmanas*, such as the *Aitareya* and *Kausitaki Brahmanas* that are connected to the *Rig-veda*, are compositions which accompany different portions of the *Vedas* with additional directions the *brahmana* priests use when performing the sacrificial rituals. These include such things as what to meditate on and how to chant the *mantras* while conducting the sacrifice, and so on. The *Brahmanas* also contain cosmogonic legends and stories that explain the reason for performing the Vedic rituals. The *Aranyakas* are sacred writings which are supposed to frame the essence of the *Upanishads* and are considered to be secret and dangerous to the uninitiated. They are meant only for the *brahmana* priests and *kshatriya* warriors who have retired to the solitude of the forests, renouncing all materialistic activities.

Next we come to the *Upanishads*, which constitute one of the most sacred portions of Vedic philosophy.

THE UPANISHADS

The *Upanishads* are essentially presented for the continued spiritual progress of the individual. The name *upanishad* means to "sit down close" to one's spiritual master or guru to receive spiritual wisdom. It was considered the secret and confidential knowledge of reality. The *Upanishads* are a collection of 108 philosophical disertations, although there are over 100 other compilations if you also count the other so-called *Upanishads* which are not actually part of the primary group, making a total of well over 200. Out of all the *Upanishads*, the following eleven are considered to be the topmost: *Isa, Kena, Katha, Prasna, Mundaka, Mandukya, Taittiriya, Aitareya, Chandogya, Brihadaranyaka,* and *Svetasvatara*.

The *Upanishads* mainly focus on establishing the Absolute as nonmaterial and describe it as Brahman: the eternal, unmanifest reality, source and ultimate shelter of everything. The Brahman is said to be incomprehensible because it is without material qualities or form. The secret to understanding Brahman according to the *Upanishads* is that they describe the Absolute as having no material qualities or material personality, but has spiritual qualities.

The comparisons used in the *Upanishads* can be somewhat confusing to the beginner of Vedic study, but they are easy to understand for one who is self-realized. For example, when the *Upanishads* describe the Absolute as being unembodied, without veins, yet runs swifter than the mind, or as being able to walk yet does not walk, or as being within everything and yet outside of everything, how can we know what to think? Does the Absolute have any qualities that we can comprehend? The point is that the Absolute has spiritual legs to run or walk with and spiritual senses which are not limited like material senses. Therefore, though the *Upanishads* generally refer to the Absolute in an impersonal way, they also begin to establish that the Supreme Reality has form.

The *Isa Upanishad* in particular indicates that the Supreme Absolute is both impersonal and personal. Other *Upanishads* describe the Absolute as, "He who created the worlds," or, "Who is luminous like the sun," "beyond darkness," "the eternal among eternals," etc. In fact, the basic method used in most *Upanishads*, as explained in the *Hayasirsa Pancaratra*, is to first present the Absolute Reality in an impersonal way and then present the personal aspects.

Not only do the *Upanishads* begin explaining the impersonal Brahman and personal Bhagavan realizations, but they also speak of the Paramatma (Supersoul or Lord in the heart) realization. Especially in the *Katha, Mundaka,* and the *Svetasvatara Upanishads,* one can find statements explaining that within the heart of every individual in every species of life reside both the individual soul and the Supersoul. It is described that they are like two birds sitting in the same tree of the body. The individual soul, which is called the *atma* or *jiva*, is engrossed in using the body to taste the fruits of various activities which result in pleasure and pain. The Supersoul is simply witnessing the activities of the *jiva*. If, however, the *jiva* begins to tire of these constant ups and downs of material life and then looks toward his friend next to him, the Supersoul, and seeks His help, the *jiva* soul can be relieved of all anxieties and regain his spiritual freedom. This freedom is the spiritual oneness shared by the *jiva* and Paramatma when the *jiva* enters into the spiritual atmosphere by submitting to the will of the Paramatma. This is achieved by the practice of yoga and by being guided by a proper spiritual master. It is not said that the individual soul loses his individuality, but both the *jiva* and Paramatma remain individuals.

In any case, the *Upanishads* present a much clearer approach to understanding ultimate reality far in advance of the four primary *Vedas*.

Aside from the *Upanishads*, there are also the *Upavedas*, which are smaller compositions attached to the four main *samhitas* (*Rig, Sama, Yajur,* and *Atharva*). These are the eighteen principal branches of Vedic knowledge, which, according to the *Vishnu Purana*, are listed with their sources as:

The four *Vedas*, the six *Angas* (or subsidiary portions of the *Vedas*), viz., *Siksha*, rules of reciting the prayers, the accents, and tones to be observed;

Kalpa, ritual; *Vyakarana*, grammar; *Nirukta*, glossarial comment; *Chandas*, metre; and *Jyotish*, astronomy; with *Mimamsa*, theology; *Nyaya*, logic; *Dharma*, the institutes of law; and the *Puranas*, constitute the fourteen principal branches of knowledge. Or they are considered as eighteen with the addition of these four: the *Ayur-veda*, medical science as taught by Lord Dhanvantari; *Dhanur-veda*, the science of archery or military arms taught by Bhrigu; *Gandharva-veda*, or drama and the arts of music, dancing, etc., of which the Muni Bharata was the author; and the *Artha sastram*, or science of government, as laid down first by Brihaspati. (*Vishnu Purana*, Book Three, Chapter Six)

Each of these subsidiary portions of the *Vedas* mentioned above have additional texts that further explain that section of Vedic knowledge. For example, the *Kalpa-sutras*, which elaborates on the many kinds of rituals, are divided into the *Srauta-sutras* that explain the rituals the priests engage in, the *Grhya-sutras* that explain rituals performed by the householders, and the *Dharma-sutras* that deal with the customary laws. Beyond this are many other texts that include the *Sraddha-kalpa, Pitrimedhasutras, Parisistas, Prayogas, Karikas,* etc., all of which deal only with Vedic rituals.

A later text that also deals with the Vedic rituals is the *Rgvidhana*, by the sage Saunaka. This book gives explanations on the usage of many of the verses or hymns in the *Rig-veda*. The precise chanting of particular verses produces specific magical or quick results, such as overcoming one's enemies, getting rid of disease, protecting oneself from ghosts, and many other things. The *Rgvidhana* indicates which verses, and the procedure if necessary, to be used to accomplish their various effects.

Additional topics are also dealt with, such as alchemy, or architecture as found in the *Sthapatyaveda*, erotics as found in the *Kama Sutra*, and the *Manu-samhita*, which is the Vedic lawbook. Vedic mathematics is found in the *Shulba Sutras*, which means codes of the rope, since particular lengths of ropes were used to make exact measurements. These mathematical codes were compiled from the 8th to the 5th century B.C. The earliest Indian mathematical developments arose from the needs of their religious ceremonies that required altars of precise measurement. This started when the sages began to use external processes of worship and ritual as an additional means to attain internal awareness and spiritual progress. In other words, they were not interested in math outside of what it could do for them spiritually. The *Shulba Sutras* are supplements of the *Kalpasutras* which show the earliest forms of algebra as used by the Vedic priests. People in Arabia began using the Vedic system of numbers and mathematics, and its use continued to spread into Europe where it became known as Arabic numerals. Thus, the system of math which we all use today had its start in Vedic India.

THE VEDANTA-SUTRAS

After the *Upanishads* and the supplemental texts are the *Vedanta-sutras,* which are a systemization of *sutras* or codes for understanding Vedic knowledge. The *sutras* are like short, condensed bits of information used as reminders for the spiritual master in his discussions on Vedic philosophy with a student or disciple. Each line, therefore, is meant to be elaborated upon by the spiritual master for the understanding of the student.

Vedanta means "the end of knowledge," or final conclusion of the Vedic philosophy. The *Vedanta-sutras* are also called the *Brahma-sutra, Sariraka, Vyasa-sutra, Vedanta-darshana, Uttara-mimamsa,* as well as *Badarayana-sutra.* Vyasa and Badarayana are two names for the same person who is considered to be the author and compiler of the major portions of Vedic literature.

The *Vedanta-sutras* are divided into four chapters with four divisions each. In each division the theme within is stated, reasons for it are given, examples are supplied to uphold the presented facts, the theme is then explained further for clearer understanding, and finally authorized quotations from the *Vedas* are supplied to support it. In this way the information is given in a format meant to show the authenticity and reliability of the Vedic viewpoint.

The first two chapters discuss how the material world manifested from the Supreme and the relationship between the living entity and the Supreme. The third chapter explains how one engages in the prescribed duties to perform and how to act according to the relationship we have with the Supreme. The fourth chapter describes the result of such service, which is to ultimately return to the spiritual world.

The first verse of the *Vedanta-sutras* states: "*athato brahma-jijnasa,*" which means, "Now is the time to inquire about the Absolute Truth." Why is it time? Because we are presently in the human form of life and should utilize it properly since only in the human form do we have the intelligence and facility to be able to understand spiritual reality. In animal forms, the living entities cannot understand such things because they do not have the brain power. So we should not waste this human form of life by pursuing only the animalistic propensities, such as eating, sleeping, mating, and defending. Therefore, the *Vedanta-sutras* begin by stating that now is the time for us to understand the Absolute Truth.

The *Vedanta-sutras,* however, being written only in codes, can be somewhat vague and requires a commentary to elaborate and explain the aphorisms. Practically speaking, some of the codes are fairly unclear for anyone who is not experienced in Vedic philosophy. And since Vedanta comprises the purport of the *Upanishads* which contain knowledge of both the personal and impersonal aspects of the Absolute, which commentary on the *Vedanta-sutras* you read can make a big difference. Some commentaries sway toward the impersonal understanding of the Absolute, while other commentaries sway toward the personal realizations. Obviously, to reach a mature understanding in this regard, we need to comprehend both of these viewpoints. In fact, it is stated that unless one understands all the features of the Absolute Truth, namely, the impersonal Brahman, the localized Paramatma or Supersoul, and ultimately the Supreme Personality of God, Bhagavan or Krishna, one's knowledge is imperfect.

There have been many commentaries written on the *Vedanta-sutras*. The most influential were by such famous *acaryas* as Shankara, Bhaskara, Ramanuja, Nimbarka, Vallabha, Madhva, and Baladeva. So let us review a few of these.

Shankara (A.D. 788-820) was a follower of Shiva born of a South Indian *brahmana* family in the town of Kaladi, on the banks of the Periyar river. His two major works are *Vivida-cudamani* and *Sariraka-basya*. When Shankara appeared, Buddhism had spread throughout India because it had been patronized by Imperor Asoka in the third century B.C., and the followers of Buddhism had given up the *Vedas*. The Buddhist philosophy is that the material creation is the only manifestation of the Absolute Truth, which itself is temporary and brought on by egoistic desires. It is asserted that these desires must be eliminated for one to enter back into the void. The void itself is said to be all that is real and eternal, and the source from which everything manifests. Shankara's purpose, therefore, was to reform and purify religious life by re-establishing the authority of the Vedic scriptures. His interpretation of the *Vedas* is known as *advaita* or nondualistic because he taught that the individual *jiva* or soul is identical with God, and that there is ultimately no variety, no individuality or personality in spiritual existence. The individuality of both the Supreme Being and the *jiva*, according to him, is false.

In order for Shankara to teach like this, he had to ignore the many statements in the *Vedas* which assert that the Absolute Truth is the Supreme Person and the *jivas* are His subordinate parts. Therefore, by word jugglery, he developed a twofold theory that Brahman consists of the pure impersonal Brahman, and that any incarnation of God within this universe is simply a manifestation of that Brahman. This was a complete rejection of some of the Vedic literature, such as *Bhagavad-gita*, and in this way he differed with all orthodox Vedic schools. Like Buddha, he also refused to answer questions about the origin of the cosmos and said that *maya*, the illusory energy, was inexplicable.

This Mayavadi philosophy teaches that the material world is false and the impersonal Brahman, or great white light, is truth. One merges back into the Brahman, where there exists no activities or spiritual characteristics after giving up the ego or bodily consciousness. Therefore, we find that impersonalists generally do not study the *Vedas* beyond the *Vedanta-sutras* because as we progress through the Vedic literature up to the *Puranas*, it becomes more specific about the personal characteristics of the Absolute Truth which contradicts the impersonal viewpoint.

We must point out, however, that Shankaracarya was an incarnation of Lord Shiva who had been ordered by the Supreme Lord to cheat the atheists. The *Shiva Purana* quotes the Supreme Lord as ordering Lord Shiva: "In Kali-yuga mislead the people in general by propounding imaginary meanings from the *Vedas* to bewilder them." To do so, Shankara gave up the direct method of Vedic knowledge and presented an indirect meaning which actually covered the real goal of Vedanta. This is confirmed in the *Padma Purana* where Lord Shiva addresses his wife, Parvati:

> My dear wife, hear my explanations of how I have spread ignorance through Mayavada philosophy. Simply by hearing it even an advanced scholar will fall down. In this philosophy which is certainly very inauspicious for people in general, I have misrepresented the real meaning of the *Vedas* and recommended that one give up all activities in order to achieve freedom from *karma*. In this Mayavada philosophy I have described the *jivatma* and Paramatma to be one and the same. The Mayavada philosophy is impious. It is covered Buddhism. My dear Parvati, in the form of a *brahmana* in Kali-yuga I teach this imagined Mayavada philosophy in order to mislead the entire population toward atheism by denying the personal form of God.

Herein, Lord Shiva himself points out that to believe God has no form is impious and equal to atheism. Even though this Mayavada philosophy was not good for pious people to hear because it would sway them toward an impersonalistic viewpoint, we should note that Shankara's philosophy was just right for the time and circumstance. The Buddhists, who had spread throughout India and neglected the *Vedas*, believed in neither a soul nor a God and that, ultimately, the essence of everything is the nothingness or void wherein lies *nirvana*, freedom from all suffering. So considering how the Buddhists had followed a philosophy of complete atheism for hundreds of years and would never have accepted a viewpoint which advocated a supreme personal God, Shankara's was the only philosophy they would have considered. It was like a compromise between atheism and theism, but Shankara used the *Vedas* as the basis of his arguments. As Shankara traveled throughout India his arguments prevailed and Buddhism bowed. Therefore, his purpose was accomplished, so much so that his *Sariraka-bhasya* is considered the definitive rendition of Vedanta even to the present day.

Several times, however, Shankara revealed his true beliefs, that he was actually a devotee of Lord Krishna. For example, in his birthplace of Kaladi there is a temple near the *samadhi* tomb of his mother that has a Deity of Lord Krishna that was installed by Shankara himself. Furthermore, in his *Gita-bhasya*, the first verse explains that Narayana (another incarnation of Lord Krishna), or Bhagavan, is transcendental to the material creation. In *The Bhagavad-gita with the Commentary of Sri Sankaracarya*, Dinkar Vishnu Gokhale establishes that Lord Shiva writes in his "Meditations on the Bhagavad-gita": "Salutations to thee, O Vyasa [the incarnation of Krishna who compiled the *Vedas*]. Thou art of mighty intellect, and thine eyes are as large as a full-blown lotus. It was thou who brightened this lamp of wisdom, filling it with the oil of the *Mahabharata*." Shankara also readily points out that it is Bhagavan Krishna "whose glories are sung by the verses of the *Vedas*, of whom the singers of the *Sama* sing, and of whose glories the *Upanishads* proclaim in full choir."

This would seem to indicate that Shankara was encouraging everyone to read *Bhagavad-gita* and *Mahabharata* as written by Srila Vyasadeva to understand the conclusion of spiritual knowledge. This would also give evidence that Shankara's own personal beliefs were different from the philosophy that he taught. There is no evidence that makes this more clear than texts eight and nine of his *Meditations on the Bhagavad-gita* as follows:

> I offer my respectful obeisances unto the Supreme Personality of Godhead, Krishna, the transcendental, blissful husband of the Goddess of Fortune, whose mercy turns the dumb into eloquent speakers and enables the lame to cross mountains. Let all obeisances be unto the Supreme Lord Sri Krishna, whom Brahma, Varuna, Indra, Rudra, the Maruts, and all divine beings praise with the divine hymns of the *Vedas* and their supplementary parts, such as the *Upanishads*, whom the followers of the *Sama-veda* glorify with song, whom great mystics see with their minds absorbed in perfect meditation and of whom all the hosts of demigods and demons know not the limitations. To Him, the Supreme Lord, let there be all obeisances.

Near the end of his life, Shankara wrote a verse which is often neglected by his followers, yet was for those who might miss the actual purport of the *Vedas*. He wrote, "Worship Govinda [another name of Krishna], worship Govinda, worship Govinda, you intellectual fools. At the end of your life all your grammatical arguments will not help you."

Ramanuja (A.D. 1017-1137) did not accept Shankara's Mayavada interpretation of the *Vedanta-sutras* and sought to expose Shankara's contradictory arguments which were actually in defiance of the real Vedic conclusions. The three major commentaries for which Ramanuja is most known is his *Vedanta-sangraha*, which is on the *Vedas*; *Sri-bhasya*, on the *Vedanta-sutras*; and *Bhagavad-gita-bhasya*, which is on *Bhagavad-gita*. His prominent theme is his opposition to impersonal monism, especially of Shankara, and the support of Vaishnavism, worship of the one God Vishnu or Bhagavan Sri Krishna.

Ramanuja accepted that the Supreme and the individual living entities are one in spiritual quality, but the individual souls are very small and God is unlimited, and between them is a relationship based on *bhakti*, or spiritual love. By logical reasoning, he taught that just as the *jiva* controls his own body and uses it as an instrument, God controls the whole material creation as well as the *jiva* souls within. The soul is eternal and after being liberated from material entanglement lives in an eternal spiritual body.

Madhva (A.D. 1239-1319) was also a Vaishnava and worked to combat Shankara's impersonal philosophy. Madhva taught pure dualism and that there are three energies: the spiritual, marginal, and inferior. The Lord is of the superior spiritual energy and controller of all other energies. The living entities are the marginal energy since they can be engrossed spiritually or materially. And the material energy is inferior due to its temporary nature. The Lord and the living entities are eternal and always distinct, but the Lord is always completely transcendental to the material world. The Lord is the ultimate cause of the creation, maintenance, and annihilation of the material manifestation, thereby being completely independent while the living entities are completely dependent on the Lord. They remain bound up in material energy by the result of their own *karma* or activities based on their fruitive desires. But Madhva pointed out that through *bhakti*, devotion to God, they could eliminate their *karma* and return to their position in the spiritual world.

Sri Caitanya Mahaprabhu (A.D. 1486-1534) also strongly opposed Shankara's philosophy and established the principle of *acintya-bhedabheda-tattva*. This specified that the Supreme and the individual soul are inconceivably and simultaneously one and different. This means that the Supreme and the *jiva* souls are the same in quality, being eternally spiritual, but always separate individually. The *jivas* are small and subject to being influenced by the material energy, while the Supreme is infinite and always above and beyond the material manifestation.

Sri Caitanya taught that the direct meaning of the Vedic *shastras* is that the living entities are to engage in devotional service, *bhakti*, to the Supreme, Bhagavan Sri Krishna. Through this practice there can develop a level of communication between God and the individual by which God will lovingly reveal Himself to those who become qualified. In this understanding the theistic philosophy of Vaishnavism reached its climax.

Sri Caitanya Mahaprabhu, who is considered and was established by Vedic scripture as the most recent incarnation of God, did not become much involved in writing. In fact, He only wrote eight verses, but His followers compiled extensive Sanskrit literature that documented His life and fully explained His teachings. However, it is one of His followers, Baladeva, who wrote a commentary on the *Vedanta-sutras* called *Govinda-bhasya*. It is said that Baladeva had a dream one night in which Lord Krishna appeared and explained the *Vedanta-sutras* to him. Upon awakening, he wrote this powerful commentary and called it *Govinda-bhasya*, signifying that it was the words of Sri Krishna.

There is one more commentary on the *Vedanta-sutras* which we cannot neglect. Srila Vyasadeva, the original author of the *Vedanta-sutras*, was still not satisfied after writing it. After explaining this perplexing situation to his spiritual master, he was advised to write the *Srimad-Bhagavatam*. After doing so, Vyasadeva considered it his own commentary on the *Vedanta-sutras* and the complete explanation and conclusion of all Vedic philosophy. This is why Sri

Caitanya never cared for writing a commentary on the *Vedanta-sutras*, because He considered *Srimad-Bhagavatam* to be the topmost commentary which had already been written. This *Srimad-Bhagavatam* (also called the *Bhagavat Purana*) is part of the Vedic literature called the *Itihasas*.

THE ITIHASAS

The *Itihasas*, or supplementary Vedic literature, helped explain the rituals of the *Vedas* and the highly compressed philosophy of the *Vedanta-sutras* by using historical events of the universe and factual stories of many great sages, demigods, and so forth.

Included in the *Itihasas* is the *Mahabharata*, which is an historical epic about the great kingdom of *Bharatavarsa*, or the region of India. It contains 110,000 couplets making it the longest poem and greatest epic in world literature. It is a treasure house of Indian lore and holds within it a code of life for ethical, social, and spiritual relations. Throughout this great epic every sort of human situation is described and every kind of emotion is aroused. There is a saying, if it is not in the *Mahabharata* then it is not to be found.

The *Mahabharata* explains a great variety of historical incidents, mainly consisting of the story of how the demoniac Kuru dynasty cheated the family of pious Pandavas time and time again out of its rightful heritage of the kingdom of upper India. Finally, after the Pandavas are exiled to the forest and then attempt peaceful means to gain their right to the throne, the epic centers around the eighteen day battle at Kuruksetra, a place which is still found in Madhyadesa, a three hour train ride north of Delhi. There the Pandava army defeated the Kurus and their soldiers. This is also where Sri Krishna speaks the *Bhagavad-gita* to His friend Arjuna just before the battle takes place.

The *Bhagavad-gita* is from chapters 25 to 42 of the *Bishma-parva* section of the *Mahabharata*, and is a classic of Indian literature and considered the essence of all Vedic knowledge. It is especially good for those who do not have much time for reading or who cannot go very deeply into studying the Vedic literature. It contains knowledge of the soul, law of karma, reincarnation, attaining the Supreme, knowledge of God, and the essential purpose of life. The *Mahabharata* is especially meant to draw the attention of people to the *Bhagavad-gita* through the format of an exciting, historical adventure, which is certainly found in the *Mahabharata*.

A similar epic is the *Ramayana*, consisting of 24,000 verses written by the great poet Valmiki, which describes the life of Lord Ramacandra, an incarnation of God, and His wife Sita. This is also a touching and exciting adventure which explains how Lord Ramacandra lived in the forest and fought against and killed the great demon Ravana and his armies in order to rescue His wife, Sita, who had been kidnapped. Many other stories are included in this storehouse of wisdom which has been an inspiration for thousands of years to all people who have read it. In the incarnation of Lord Ramacandra, God appears as the perfect king and ruler, and inspires all His subjects with the greatest love for Him.

Even though the *Itihasas* are accepted as supplementary Vedic literature, the *acaryas* such as Shankara, Ramanuja, and Madhva have all presented the *Itihasas* as valid Vedic evidence and wrote commentaries on *Bhagavad-gita*. Actually Shankara thought the *Gita* was in fact the epitome of the essentials of the whole Vedic teaching. Madhva, commenting on the *Vedanta-sutras* (2.1.6), quotes the *Bhavisya Purana*, which states, "The *Rig-veda, Yajur-veda, Sama-veda, Atharva-veda, Mahabharata, Pancaratra*, and the original *Ramayana* are all considered Vedic literature. The Vaishnava supplements, the *Puranas*, are also Vedic literature." The *Chandogya Upanisad* (7.1.4) mentions the *Puranas* and *Itihasas* as the fifth *Veda*. The *Srimad-Bhagavatam* (1.4.20) also states, "The four divisions of the original sources of knowledge [the *Vedas*] were made separately. But the historical facts and authentic stories mentioned in the *Puranas* are called the fifth *Veda*." Therefore, the *Vedas* themselves accept not only the four *Vedas*, the *Upanishads,* and *Vedanta-sutras*, but also the *Mahabharata, Bhagavad-gita*, the *Ramayana*, and the *Puranas* as being authentic Vedic literature.

The point is, to be accepted as Vedic a literature must present the same purpose as the original texts. But if it deviates from the Vedic conclusion or is a hodgepodge of various concocted philosophies, as are many viewpoints which one will find merged under the name of "Hinduism," then it cannot be relied upon. Therefore, to be sure something is authorized, we only accept the established Vedic teachings which are supported in the many Vedic texts. In this way, Buddhism, Jainism, and Sikhism are considered non-Vedic, although outgrowths of Vedic philosophy.

Actually, in considering the word *hindu,* there is no such name in any of the Vedic literature. The Muslims from such places as Afganistan and Persia introduced the word *hindu* to describe the inhabitants of the tract of land in the northwestern provinces of India where the Sindhu river (the modern Indus) is located. Because the Sanskrit sound of "s" converts to "h" in the Parsee language, the Muslims called it *hindu*, even though the people of the area did not use the name *hindu* themselves. This word was used by foreigners to identify the people and the religion of those who lived in that area. Otherwise, the word is useless except for those who use it out of convenience, which the British did with the effect of focusing on the differences between the Muslims and Hindus with the intention of creating friction amongst the people of India. This was in accord with their divide and rule policy to make it easier for their continued dominion of the country.

The word *hindu* was gradually adopted by everyone and is applied in a very general way, so much so, in fact, that now "Hinduism" is often used to describe anything from religious activities to even social or nationalistic events. Many of these Hindu events are not endorsed in the *Vedas* and, therefore, must be considered non-Vedic. The *Vedas* describe its followers with the term *Aryan*, which refers to those advancing toward spiritual realization. Thus, not just anyone can call themselves a Hindu and be considered a follower of the *Vedas*.

THE PURANAS

Another important part of the *Itihasas* include the *Puranas*. The *Puranas* are the histories of the universe and contain many stories in which superhuman powers are common place and include descriptions of life on other planets. As we pointed out earlier, Vedic knowledge often consists of information about things from beyond our own sense perception or experience. We can be assured of its authenticity because of the fact that many Vedic scholars such as Sukadeva, Maitreya, Madhva, Ramanuja, and others have reached spiritual perfection with the help of information found in the *Puranas*.

Each *Purana* is supposed to contain five basic subjects and in some cases ten, which include the creation of the world, its destruction and re-creation, the genealogy of the patriarchs and the demigods, the reigns of the Manus (who are the *avataras* in each duration of time known as a *manvantara*), and the history of the Solar and Lunar dynasties. Many of them also include descriptions of the activities of the incarnations of God, as well as the great sages and devotees of God. One thing that may seem somewhat confusing is that the stories are not in any particular chronological order and may be related at any time according to need. This is primarily due to the fact that the *Puranas* are generally related in a dialogue format of questions and answers between sages and saints, or masters and disciples.

Other subjects included in various *Puranas* are geography, astrology, use of military weapons, organization of society, duties of different classes of men, characteristics of social leaders, predictions of the future, law of reincarnation and *karma*, analysis of the material elements, symptoms of consciousness, how the illusory energy works, the practice of yoga, meditation, spiritual experiences, realizations of the Absolute, etc.

The *Puranas* are meant especially for all classes of people. Since all men are not on the same level of consciousness and are spread over many different types of thinking, feeling, and desiring, the *Puranas* are divided so that any class of people can take advantage of them and utilize them to get out of the material entanglement either gradually or rapidly. So, depending on their position in life, people may use the particular *Puranas* that are most suited for them.

The *Puranas* are divided into two groups consisting of the primary *Mahapuranas* and the secondary *Upa-puranas*. The *Upa-puranas* consist of eighteen, entitled: *Sanatkumara, Narasimha, Naradiya, Shiva, Durvasasa, Kapila, Manava, Ausanasa, Varuna, Kalika, Samba, Nandi, Saura, Parasara,*

Aditya, Mahesvara, Bhagavata or *Bhargava,* and *Vasistha.*

The eighteen *Mahapuranas* are divided into three groups. One group considered to be related to the mode of ignorance or darkness consists of the *Linga, Skanda, Agni, Matsya, Kurma,* and *Shiva* (or sometimes the *Vayu*) *Puranas.* These are usually related to Lord Shiva. The next group is usually related to Lord Brahma and is considered connected with the mode of passion. These consist of the *Brahma, Brahmanda, Brahma-vaivarta, Markandeya, Bhavisya,* and *Vamana Puranas.* The third group relating to Lord Vishnu with the mode of purity or goodness prevailing are the *Vishnu, Bhagavata, Narada* or *Naradiya, Garuda, Padma,* and *Varaha Puranas.*

Out of all the *Puranas,* many scholars seem to agree that the *Vishnu Purana* seems to conform most closely to what a *Purana* is expected to be. It contains the five essential subjects that a *Purana* is supposed to relate and also contains many other topics that are dealt with in detail. The central theme is praise of Vishnu and it describes many aspects and incarnations of Lord Vishnu, and contains many stories of Lord Krishna in Vrindavana and Mathura. This *Purana* is quite similar to the contents of the *Bhagavata Purana,* otherwise called *Srimad-Bhagavatam,* which is also centered around the theme of praise of Lord Krishna, the source of all other incarnations of God.

THE SRIMAD-BHAGAVATAM

The *Bhagavatam* is held to be the most significant of all the *Puranas.* It is the most widely read and one of the greatest works of devotion ever written. Sri Caitanya, five hundred years ago, along with other scholars of the *Vedas,* relied on and researched the *Bhagavatam* extensively for information on the Absolute Truth and became emersed in many stories about Sri Krishna in their spiritual ecstasies.

The *Bhagavatam,* being Sri Vyasadeva's own commentary on all the Vedanta philosophy, brings to light all the different aspects of the Absolute Truth, but especially the personal characteristics of Bhagavan Sri Krishna as the final conclusion of all Vedic understanding. This is why those who are impersonalists or monists, believing God has no form and, therefore, performs no activities, never reach the *Bhagavatam* in their Vedic studies. But if they do read the *Bhagavatam,* they are sure to interpret it in an impersonalistic way and, thus, deprive themselves of the truth and purity which they could derive from it.

Srimad-Bhagavatam is considered the postgraduate study of the *Bhagavad-gita.* The *Bhagavatam* does not elaborate on worship of the other demigods or on rituals which award various temporary material benedictions as do some of the other *Vedas* and *Puranas.* Therefore, the *Bhagavatam* completely transcends all other philosophical viewpoints of the *Vedas.* This is confirmed in the *Garuda Purana (Brahma Kanda,* 1.45) where it states: "The wise declare knowledge to be manifold, consisting of various grades--high, low, and middling. All that knowledge is found in the *Bhagavat Purana*. Hence, *Bhagavat* is the highest of all *Puranas.*" Furthermore, in the "*artho 'yam brahma-sutranam*" verse, it fully states: "The *Srimad-Bhagavatam* is the authorized explanation of *Brahma-sutra*, and it is a further explanation of *Mahabharata*. It is the expansion of the *gayatri mantra* and the essence of all Vedic knowledge. This *Srimad-Bhagavatam*, containing 18,000 verses, is known as the explanation of all Vedic literature."

In fact, the second verse of the *Srimad-Bhagavatam* explains what this *Purana* consists of and who can understand it:

Completely rejecting all religious activities which are materially motivated, the *Bhagavata Purana* propounds the highest truth, which is understandable by those devotees who are fully pure in heart. The highest truth is reality distinguished from illusion for the welfare of all. Such truth uproots the threefold miseries. This beautiful *Bhagavatam*, compiled by the great sage Vyasadeva, is sufficient in itself for God realization. What is the need for any other scripture? As soon as one attentively and submissively hears the message of *Bhagavatam*, by this culture of knowledge the Supreme Lord is established within the heart.

As it is stated, this knowledge can be understood by those who are pure in heart. This means that those who are envious, atheists, or who read it with some ulterior motive will never be able to comprehend it. But for those who listen submissively and sincerely with an open mind, all the mysteries of the highest truth will gradually be revealed. That highest truth is "reality distinguished from illusion for the welfare of all." Not that we can make up our own reality, but we must understand what is actually reality.

Many quotations regarding the importance of the *Bhagavatam* can be found in several *Puranas*, such as the *Bhagavat-Mahatmya* section of the *Padma Purana*, wherein we find such verses as the following:

The holy scripture known as *Srimad-Bhagavatam* was expounded in this age of Kali by the sage Sukadeva Gosvami [Vyasadeva's son] with the object of completely destroying the fear of being caught in the jaws of the serpent of time. There is no means other than this conducive to the purification of the mind. One gets to hear *Srimad-Bhagavatam* only when there is virtue earned in one's past lives. (1.11-12). . . All the evils of Kali-yuga [this present age of quarrel and confusion] will surely disappear at the very chanting of *Srimad-Bhagavatam*, even as wolves take flight at the very roar of a lion. (1.62). . . If you seek the highest destiny, read even yourself daily one half of a quarter of a verse of *Srimad-Bhagavatam*. (3.33). . . Indeed, this is the righteous course prescribed in the Kali age for washing away all agony, poverty, misfortune and sin as well as for the conquest of passion and anger.

Otherwise the illusory energy of the Lord is most difficult to get rid of even for the gods. How then can it be set aside by men? Hence, the course of hearing *Srimad-Bhagavatam* has been recommended. (3.64-65). . . Like bubbles appearing in water or mosquitoes among living beings, those who remain deprived of hearing an exposition of *Srimad-Bhagavatam* are born only to die. (5.63)

There are many other verses in the *Padma Purana* which point out the potency and importance of the *Bhagavatam*. The importance of the book is also described in the *Bhagavatam* itself:

This *Bhagavata Purana* is as brilliant as the sun, and it has arisen just after the departure of Lord Krishna to his own abode accompanied by religion, knowledge, etc. Persons who have lost their vision due to the dense darkness of ignorance in the age of Kali shall get light from this *Purana*. (*Bhag*.1.3.43.)

Another example (*Bhag*.12.13.15) is where Suta Gosvami emphasizes its significance, stating that the glorious *Bhagavatam* is considered to be the cream of all the *Upanishads*, and a man who is satisfied with tasting the nectar from it will not find such pleasure anywhere else. Suta Gosvami also says:

Let me offer my respectful obeisances unto him [Sukadeva], the spiritual master of all sages, the son of Vyasadeva, who, out of his great compassion for those gross materialists who struggle to cross over the darkest regions of material existence, spoke this most confidential supplement to the cream of Vedic knowledge, after having personally assimilated it by experience. (*Bhag*.1.2.3)

The *Matsya Purana* says that which contains many narrations of spiritual instructions, begins with the *gayatri mantra,* and also contains the history of Vritrasura, is known as the *Srimad-Bhagavatam*. Whoever makes a gift of this great work on a full moon day attains to the highest perfection of life and goes back to the spiritual world.

All these references conclude that *Srimad-Bhagavatam* is the most ripened fruit of the tree of Vedic knowledge consisting of the highest realizations and understanding of ultimate reality--the Absolute Truth. Over and above that it is also considered the incarnation of God in the form of sound vibration as confirmed in the following verse: "This *Srimad-Bhagavatam* is the literary incarnation of God, and it is compiled by Srila Vyasadeva, the incarnation of God. It is meant for the ultimate good of all people, and it is all-successful, all-blissful and all-perfect." (*Bhag*.1.3.40)

From this verse it is made clear that *Srimad-Bhagavatam* is meant for the benefit of everyone, regardless of their background, who is sincerely interested in the highest truth. Furthermore, it is compiled by Srila Vyasadeva who was an incarnation of God who appeared in this world in order to give people this knowledge for the highest good. After all, who can explain the characteristics of the Supreme better than the Supreme Himself? This is also confirmed in *Bhagavad-gita* (15.5) in which Krishna explains that He is seated in everyone's heart and from Him comes remembrance, knowledge, and forgetfulness. He is the knower and compiler of the *Vedas*, by which He is to be known.

This is further elaborated in the *Vishnu Purana*, Book Three, Chapter Three:

> In every Dvapara [or third] age, Vishnu, in the person of Vyasa, in order to promote the good of mankind, divides the *Vedas*, which is properly but one, into many portions: observing the limited perserverance, energy and application of mortals, he makes the *Veda* four-fold to adopt it to their capacities; and the bodily form which he assumes, in order to effect that classification, is known by the name of Vedavyasa.

> Know, Maitreya, the Vyasa called Krishna Dvaipayana (Vedavyasa) to be the Deity Narayana; for who else on this earth could have composed the *Mahabharata*. . . That form of Vasudeva. . . composed of the *Rig, Sama,* and *Yajur Vedas*, is at the same time their essence, as He is the soul of all embodied spirits. He, distinguished as consisting of the *Vedas*, creates the *Vedas*, and divides them by many subdivisions into branches: He is the author of those branches: He is those aggregated branches; for He, the eternal Lord, is the essence of true knowledge." (*Vishnu Purana*, Book 3, Chapter 4)

These verses clearly explain that it is none other than the incarnation of the Supreme Being who has appeared in this world to compile and divide the *Vedas* so that people of all levels of intelligence can understand them. It is explained that no ordinary person can do such a thing. How can people who are limited and finite understand the Unlimited and Infinite unless that Supreme Being descends to explain this knowledge Himself? Therefore, as stated in the above mentioned verses, the essence of the Absolute Reality is to be found in the Vedic literature, especially within the *Srimad-Bhagavatam*.

DIFFERENT PATHS IN THE VEDAS

Even though Vyasadeva had worked for the welfare of all by writing the Vedic literature, before he wrote *Srimad-Bhagavatam* he had still felt dissatisfied. This is a great lesson. Naturally, we all desire freedom from the problems that material life causes us, but only by engaging in direct spiritual activities does the spiritual living entity, the soul, within these temporary material bodies begin to feel any real relief or happiness. How to do this by engaging in service or *bhakti-yoga* to the Supreme Being is what the *Vedas* are ultimately meant to establish. Because this had not yet been prominently presented in the literature Vyasadeva had written, he was still feeling dissatisfied. Now he was trying to understand the cause of his dissatisfaction.

In all the literature compiled by Vyasadeva, there are many descriptions of the temporary universe, prayers to the demigods, the process for attaining one's material necessities, information about the soul, the Brahman, the Supersoul, and the process of yoga for attaining spiritual realizations. There is also information about the Supreme Lord, Bhagavan Krishna. But the detailed descriptions of God, His form, His incarnations, names, activities, potencies and energies, and how He is the source of everything, including the ever-increasing spiritual bliss for which we are always looking, had not yet been fully described. Therefore, although the spiritual truths are presented in different degrees, it could be asked why the Vedic literature seems to also recommend different processes for people to achieve various levels of material and spiritual perfection.

This question was also asked by Uddhava in his conversation with Krishna in *Srimad-Bhagavatam* (11.14.1). He asked whether all the processes, recommended by the learned sages who know the Vedic literature, are equally important or if one process is superior.

As is revealed shortly there is one process that is more effective than others, but why there are different methods and rituals included in the Vedic literature is explained first. So in answer to Uddhava's question, as related in *Srimad-Bhagavatam* (11.14.3-8), Sri Krishna replied that the Vedic knowledge disappeared during the annihilation of the universe. Then after the subsequent universal creation took place, He spoke the Vedic knowledge to Brahma. Brahma in turn taught this knowledge to his eldest son Manu, along with the seven great sages and Bhrigu Muni and other sons of Brahma who are associated with the creation of the universe. From these fathers of creation came many descendents who took the forms of demigods, demons, human beings, Guhyakas [spirits who have secret powers], Siddhas [a class of beings with all mystic abilities], Gandharvas [angel-like beings], Vidyadharas [inhabitants of the heavenly planets], Caranas, Kindevas [demigod-like humans on another planet], Kinnaras [similar to human beings but with a horse-like body], Nagas [a race of extraordinary serpents], Kimpurusas [a race of extraordinary monkeys similar to humans], and so on. All of these species of beings had different desires and natures. To accomodate these different characteristics, there are many kinds of Vedic rituals, *mantras,* and rewards. And due to the great variety of desires and goals among human beings, there are so many different theistic as well as atheistic viewpoints. Therefore, with their judgement clouded by the illusory energy, they all speak their own whimsical ideas of what is good for people without knowing the truth.

From this we can understand that as various kinds of living entities evolved with different natures and desires, the Vedic literature also expanded to accommodate the different levels of consciousness. The *Vedas*, of course, are to provide the means by which the living beings can regulate their activities and thus be materially happy while simultaneously making spiritual progress. In this way, a variety of theistic philosophies have been handed down through tradition according to the level of illusion people are influenced by.

Everyone is essentially spiritual in nature, but as people forget their spiritual identity they become motivated by material desires for mental or sensual pleasure. Thus, people become engaged in a particular type of activity according to the mode of nature they are influenced by. Then they pursue a lifestyle or religious process which is conducive to the mentality they have developed. This is further explained in *Bhagavad-gita* (17.2-4): depending on the nature the embodied soul evolves, he develops a faith characterized by goodness, passion, or ignorance. Men in the mode of goodness worship the demigods, those in passion worship demoniac beings, and those in darkness worship the departed and ghosts. *Bhagavad-gita* (9.25) continues to explain that those who worship demigods take birth among them, those who worship ghosts take birth as such, those who worship the ancestors go to them, but those who worship and meditate on Krishna return to Him.

Herein we can understand that whatever mode of worship or activity we engage in brings particular results. Some may strive for happiness simply by filling their belly full of food and are content to work hard for no other reason. Others are satisfied by the pursuit for sex life, or by political power, or by religious activities, or by giving charity, or by achieving peace of mind. But if this is somehow or other based on pleasing the temporary body and mind of yourself or others, then all such happiness, being material, is temporary. The results are very meager, like trying to be satisfied with one drop of water while living in a desert. People who struggle to achieve one drop of happiness here and another drop there are busy running around, working very hard, and yet miss the real goal of life. This is explained in the *Bhagavatam* (11.21.28) by Sri Krishna that people dedicated to pleasures of the body that are obtained through the performance of Vedic rituals, or any other process for material happiness, cannot know Him, though He is situated in their hearts and the whole universe emanates from Him. Such people are like persons whose eyes are covered by mist and cannot recognize what is right in front of them.

In this way, according to the Vedic texts, people remain blind and cannot understand how to reach the real happiness that exists within them since they always focus on external comforts. Processes for attaining such things as external pleasures, heavenly bliss, a good future birth, or different levels of mystic awareness are included in the *Vedas* for those who want them. But such people miss the essence of the Vedic teachings which emphasizes the need to reach the ultimate spiritual perfection.

THE ULTIMATE PATH TO THE ABSOLUTE

Ultimately, the Vedic system is to engage everyone in a process that will elevate them from whatever position they are in to a higher mode of living. But without coming to the highest level of knowledge and realization, they will continue to engage in activities resulting in different degrees of anxiety and lamentation. Being concerned about this problem, the great sages 5,000 years ago, foreseeing the troubled times ahead, requested Suta Gosvami to explain the *Srimad-Bhagavatam* after having learned it from Srila Vyasadeva and others.

O learned one, in this iron age of Kali men have but short lives. They are quarrelsome, lazy, misguided, unlucky, and, above all, always disturbed. There are many varieties of scriptures, and in all of them there are many prescribed duties, which can be learned only after many years of study in their various divisions. Therefore, O sage, please select the essence of all these scriptures and explain it for the good of all living beings, that by such instruction their hearts may be fully satisfied. (*Bhag.*1.1.10-11)

In this way, the sages pointed out that in Kali-yuga, this present age, men are easily distracted by so many things and their lives are very short, so now let us not waste time but hear only the essence of all spiritual knowledge so that everyone can be satisfied and know the real goal of life and not remain confused. It was also for this reason that Srila Vyasadeva was feeling dissatisfied, even after compiling all the Vedic knowledge into written form. The essence of all spiritual and metaphysical understanding and realizations had not yet been put into a concise and conclusive format.

Vyasadeva, while questioning his unexpected dissatisfaction, was at that very moment greeted by the sage Narada Muni who had just arrived at Vyasadeva's cottage. Suta Gosvami, in *Srimad-Bhagavatam*, Canto One, Chapters Five and Six, relates the story in this way:

Narada Muni asked Vyasadeva whether he was satisfied after having written the great *Mahabharata*. Sri Vyasadeva answered that in spite of all he had done, he was not content and, accepting Narada Muni as his spiritual master, questioned him about the root cause of the dissatisfaction he felt. Narada replied that the cause was that Vyasadeva had not written about the sublime characteristics of the Supreme. The philosophy that does not satisfy the transcendental senses of the Supreme is considered worthless, but that literature which is full of the transcendental descriptions of the name, form, and pastimes of the unlimited Supreme can bring about a revolution amongst the misdirected civilization of the world. Even though improperly composed, such literature is heard and accepted by saintly and intelligent men.

This is exactly what is missing in the earlier Vedic texts as well as most other religious scriptures found in the world today. Narada is recommending that to include the topics he mentioned will certainly bring about a revolution to help all those who are living in a misguided civilization. The reason for this is simple; one may defend the science of religion or engage in so many philosophical conversations, but there will never be any final conclusion to such talks without practical experience of the Supreme. Without this genuine experience, all religious or philosophical talk is just mental speculation. It is another way of passing time for the armchair philosophers because anyone, simply by juggling words or taking things out of context, can steer various controversial topics towards any conclusion they want. This is the way some so-called religious leaders or propagandists use things like religion to justify their own selfish intentions.

More light is shed on these points in the *Bhagavatam* (11.22.5-6) wherein Krishna explains to Uddhava that when philosophers cannot agree on the way they view things, it is simply the interaction of Krishna's illusory energies that motivate their disagreements. But for those who have fixed their minds in Krishna, the Absolute Truth and ultimate conclusion of all spiritual realizations, the cause for argument and differences of opinion disappear.

Just as when you may have several hungry people in a room discussing the various causes of and means to extinguish their pains of hunger, no one has to tell them that the process of eating a nice meal has worked when, after having done so, they automatically feel their hunger subside. The experience is universal and, after eating and feeling satisfied, leaves no room for argument. Similarly, after having reached the platform of experiencing the Absolute Truth, what need could there be for further argument or disagreement? The experience is universal for those who have reached it. And for those who have, participating in a religion or faith which condones the idea of deliberately quarreling or fighting wars with members of other faiths is utterly absurd. Indeed, such fighting only shows the gross ignorance of one's real spiritual identity and the animalistic qualities of such people, though they may claim strong allegiance to a particular religion. Of what use to the world is such a religion or philosophy? As pointed out in the *Manu-samhita* (12.95-96), such a religion is simply based on darkness and is worthless, producing no good reward after death. Therefore, Narada Muni, to help avoid further quarrel and confusion among the people in this age, encouraged Vyasadeva to write and describe the eternal spiritual truths in a more direct manner.

Narada explained to Vyasadeva that spiritual knowledge, though free from material faults and connections, is still incomplete if devoid of an understanding of the transcendental characteristics of God. But Vyasadeva, who is completely perfect, can meditate on the Lord's pastimes for the liberation from material existence of all people. Only one who has retired from activities for material happiness deserves to understand such spiritual knowledge and experience spiritual bliss. Therefore, Narada emphasized that by Vyasa's mercy, those who are attached to material existence should be shown how to attain spiritual realization. Those who are truly intelligent will endeavor to reach this goal.

Vyasadeva knew all about spiritual knowledge and the transcendental qualities of the Supreme Being because he is a plenary portion of the Lord. Though he is birthless, he appeared in this world for the welfare of all. And to teach a lesson, he displayed dissatisfaction when he had still not engaged himself in writing the glories of the Supreme's spiritual qualities, and then accepted Narada as a spiritual master to learn the reason for his discontent. Thus Narada continued to explain to Vyasadeva that learned men have concluded that the actual purpose for engaging in austerities, sacrifices, studying the *Vedas*, chanting the hymns, etc., is to advance in the knowledge of the transcendental characteristics of the Supreme, which is the only way to remove all difficulties.

This is the ultimate process for perfecting one's life and for attaining full spiritual realization. This is the answer to Uddhava's question about whether a particular process in the Vedic literature is superior. Without understanding the Absolute Truth, one's knowledge of his real identity, or the universe, the purpose of life, and everything else in one's experience, is incomplete. So the conclusive purpose of the Vedic process is to increase one's knowledge of the Supreme, which will encompass all other forms of knowledge. The most direct way of doing that is through the practice of hearing about the Supreme Being from the Vedic literature, such as *Srimad-Bhagavatam*. Simply hearing or studying this literature is a part of the process of *bhakti-yoga*. As explained in *Bhagavad-gita* (11.54), only through *bhakti-yoga* can one enter into the mysteries of understanding the Supreme as He is. Similarly, *Srimad-Bhagavatam* (1.2.20) points out that only by *bhagavat-bhakti*, devotion to the Lord, can one get positive scientific knowledge of the Supreme Personality. Therefore, Narada requested Vyasadeva to describe the spiritual activities and qualities of the Supreme to satisfy inquisitive and learned men, and mitigate the sufferings of the people in general. After all, by engaging in ordinary yoga people may attain some peace of mind and freedom from desire and lust, but to give satisfaction to the soul requires the performance of devotional service, *bhakti-yoga,* to the Supreme. This is what Vyasadeva had yet to do. And the perfection of this would be to compile the great devotional work of *Srimad-Bhagavatam.*

At the time when Sri Krishna had left this planet 5,000 years ago after performing His various pastimes by which He attracts the conditioned souls, and at the beginning of the present age of Kali-yuga, which started in the year 3102 B.C. according to the Vedic scholars, the great sage Vyasadeva had heard all this from Narada Muni. The conclusion of this story, as related in the *Bhagavatam* (1.7.2-6), is after Narada Muni had explained all these points, he took leave of Vyasadeva. Then Vyasadeva, in his cottage at Samyaprasa on the western bank of the River Sarasvati, sat down to meditate. He fixed his mind, perfectly engaging it in devotional service, *bhakti-yoga,* without any tinge of materialism, and thus he saw the Absolute Personality of Godhead along with His external energy, *maya,* which was under full control. Deluded by *maya,* the living entities think they are a part of the material world and thus undergo the reactions of material miseries. However, such miseries, which do not really touch the soul, can be counteracted by engaging in devotional service, *bhakti-yoga*. But the mass of people do not know this, so to dispel their grief, materialistic infatuation, and fear, the learned Vyasadeva compiled this Vedic literature, *Srimad-Bhagavatam*, which is in relation to the Supreme Truth.

CHAPTER THREE

A Comparative Study of the Yoga Processes

Yoga is for developing one's finer qualities and expanding one's consciousness from material to spiritual awareness. When you progress in yoga you can feel the unwanted burdens of the mind fall away, such as anxiety, anger, greed, envy, hate, discontent, etc. Then other qualities like peacefulness, tranquility, contentment, and blissfulness will be felt. These are things everyone is trying to find and are some of the many things that can be accomplished with yoga, at least on the elementary level. As you make further progress, you may enter into the deeper levels of understanding the mind and gradually go so far as to attain realizations as to what your own spiritual identity is and what your relationship is with the Absolute. Becoming free from material life and regaining one's spiritual identity is the goal of all yoga. The Sanskrit word *yoga* means to link or unite with the Supreme, and the word religion, which comes from the Latin word *religio*, means to bring back or bind to God. Thus, there is no difference between the goal of yoga and the goal of religion.

The main kinds of yoga are *astanga-yoga, jnana-yoga*, and *bhakti-yoga*, but there are other systems as well. By understanding what is involved with each discipline, you will know how practical they are and what is the goal of each process. So this chapter analyzes and explains each of the important yoga systems.

RAJA-YOGA

Raja-yoga, sometimes called *astanga-yoga* or *sankhya-yoga*, is the eightfold path leading to liberation. It is sometimes called the royal (*raja*) way. The process involves calming all mental agitation, which gradually allows the meditator to fuse with the objects of meditation by supraconscious concentration. The process is divided into eight basic steps.

28

The first step is *yama*, the essential moral commandments. This includes nonviolence, celibacy, truthfulness, as well as avoiding such things as stealing, greed, and possessiveness.

The second step is *niyama* or preparation and discipline for self-realization. This involves austerity, or undergoing physical hardships for a higher result, along with study of scriptural texts, purity of mind and body, contentment, and devoting all one's activities to God. *Yama* means the things to avoid and *niyama* means the practice one must do. Together they help keep the yogi's passions quiet and stilled and keep him in harmony with nature.

The third step is *asana*, or posture for meditation, often used in *hatha-yoga*. *Asanas* help steady the mind and promote health. *Asanas* are exercises, some simple and some quite advanced, that can be performed alone with minimal equipment, like a blanket, fresh air, and room to move around, preferably outdoors. Different *asanas* develop and affect different nerves, muscles, and organs of the body and keep the system strong, limber, and free from disease. Thus, the body becomes a fit instrument for spiritual development. Learning *asanas* can also help in other systems of yoga, too, and helps keep the body in a good, healthy condition. We will not elaborate on the different kinds of *asanas* one can learn since there are many books available that explain these.

The fourth step is *pranayama*, breath control for fixing the mind in concentration. *Prana* means life or energy, and also can mean spirit. *Ayama* indicates the length and retension of breath. This also means the retension and control of the *prana* within the body. Since it is considered that a person is born with a certain number of allotted breaths in a lifetime, the yogi learns breath control to strengthen the respiratory system, soothe the nerves, and steady the mind for meditation, and prolong one's life. Simply by controlling one's breathing a person can steady the beating of his heart. When one's breathing is not smooth, the mind is also usually unsteady and easily agitated. So as one learns *pranayama*, the mind becomes equipoised and free from the pulling of the senses.

The fifth step is *pratyahara*, control of the senses and checking the mind's attraction to external objects. It is necessary to control the senses to advance in yoga, and in *pratyahara* the yogi analyzes the mind's attraction for external objects. By the use of his study and cultivated knowledge he recognizes that sensual delights lead to one's destruction, and the path of sense control leads to his salvation. By intelligently adjusting his consciousness, the yogi gives up sensual desires in order to achieve the proper frame of mind and freedom from the modes of nature to pursue successfully the goal of yoga.

The sixth step is *dharana*, concentrating on the object of meditation. When the mind has been completely stilled by the previous steps, the yogi can totally concentrate on a single object of meditation. The seventh step is *dhyana*, when the mind is in a state of undisturbed flowing meditation. In this stage the mind takes on the likeness of the object being meditated on, and in his contemplation of the Supreme Brahman the yogi remains in that state of supreme bliss.

The eighth and final step is *samadhi*, in which, according to the eightfold path, the yogi becomes one with the Supreme. At this stage the knower and the known, the seer and the seen, the soul and the Supersoul, become one. Thus, the yogi loses all individuality and merges into the Supreme. This is the result of reaching perfection on this path.

We should point out, however, that the path to *samadhi* through this eightfold system is arduous. Each of the eight steps calls for its own rigorous discipline. As in any science, if you do not follow the procedure, you do not get the results. For example, perfection in *pranayama* means that ultimately the yogi has to reach the stage of stopping his breathing entirely. Only after this is accomplished can the yogi withdraw his senses from all material engagements. By considering this we can understand why the Vedic sages who taught this yoga system in a previous age many hundreds of years ago tell us not to waste our time with it now in this age of Kali-yuga. Such practices of trying mechanically to subdue the mind and senses by long, difficult exercises in sitting, breathing, sense control, etc., are nearly impossible for anyone in this age. Besides, this yoga system required many years of meditation. This was not something that was done for twenty minutes a day, but was practiced all day, day after day for years on end. And in these modern times we can see that people are so restless that they find it difficult to sit still even for ten minutes.

Furthermore, this form of yoga is generally a path accepted by the impersonalists. Most of them do not meditate on the Supersoul or Supreme Being while practicing this process, but try to meditate on the void or the impersonal Brahman. This means that when the yogi experiences bliss, it is the bliss within the shelter of the Brahman effulgence and of being free of the pain of material existence, but not the supreme bliss of spiritual activities which are found on the spiritual Vaikuntha planets that are floating within the Brahman. Such yogis do not get a spiritual body but remain only a spiritual spark drifting in the great White Light of the Brahman. Thus, such yogis fail to reach the highest stage of self-realization which comes from understanding the spiritual nature of the Supreme Personality of God, the source of all spiritual and material worlds.

If, however, the yogi did meditate on God while performing this type of yoga, as explained in the *Yoga Sutras* of Patanjali, he usually meditated with the intent of merging into the body of God or to become God or equal to God. This idea again comes from a lack of knowledge of one's true spiritual identity as an eternal, individual servant of the Supreme with an eternal, spiritual relationship with the Supreme that must simply be reawakened. Such a relationship is not reawakened by attempting to merge into the body of God. That is only another way of disregarding or even trying to nullify this relationship. Thus, to practice yoga with such a desire does not lead to the highest level of self-realization.

Although many books are written about this form of yoga, the majority of books one may find do not discuss the above mentioned points and generally only describe the most elementary levels of yogic practices that must be done. Therefore, one may at first be encouraged to pursue this form of yoga and may experience some initial benefits, but the elementary stage is usually as far as one gets. Otherwise, many people who begin to practice it later give it up due to boredom or being frustrated at not achieving the expected results. In any case, if one wants to pursue this eightfold form of yoga, the *Bhagavad-gita* contains some important instructions on how this yoga process is actually meant to be performed. Many parts of the following instructions, however, can be applied towards any kind of yoga process.

It is explained in the Sixth Chapter of *Bhagavad-gita* that a transcendentalist should be free from desires, live alone, control his mind, and always concentrate on the Supreme. He should remain in a secluded and sacred place. He should arrange a seat, neither too high nor too low, with kusa-grass on the ground, covered with a soft cloth and deerskin, which is used to help keep away snakes. Sitting on the seat the yogi should keep his body erect and stare at the tip of his nose, control the mind and senses, purify the heart, and subdue the mind to keep it unagitated and free from fear. Thus, completely free from sex life, the yogi should meditate on the Supreme as Paramatma, Supersoul in the heart, and make Him the ultimate goal of life. By this process of controlling the body, mind, and activities, the mystic attains the spiritual strata by ending his material existence.

Furthermore, the yogi attains the goal of yoga after he becomes situated in Transcendence. This is possible only if he is temperate in his eating, sleeping, working, and recreation, and becomes devoid of all material desires. As steady as an unwavering lamp in a windless place, the yogi must meditate on the Supreme with his mind. This perfectional stage of yoga is *samadhi* or trance, when the mind is free from all material engagement. The characteristic of this is that the yogi can see the self and experience boundless spiritual happiness through his transcendental senses. The yogi realizes the ultimate spiritual truth and feels nothing is greater than this. Even amidst the greatest difficulties the yogi does not give up his spiritual consciousness. Thus, he is never shaken from his position of freedom from material miseries. In this way, one should practice yoga with steady determination and abandon all varieties of material desires. Gradually, step by step, one should intelligently practice yoga until he can enter the trance of thinking of nothing but the Supreme.

Although the above intructions can be used in any form of yoga or religion, the yogi on the path of *raja-yoga* is also supposed to raise his life energy up through the different *chakras* and fix it between his eyebrows and in full devotion remember the Supreme Lord. The yogi must practice constant celibacy, chant *om* properly, and remain detached from all sensual thoughts. By performing such meditation for many years, even hundreds of years if necessary, the yogi would gradually purify and control the mind until he could quit his body at will without any mental agitation or physical disturbance. Of course, in this age no one can practice this form of yoga for hundreds of years. Neither are there many who have the mental strength to meditate properly with a singularly focused mind for hours at a time. But thousands of years ago, when this form of yoga was meant to be practiced, people could do that and actually reach perfection. Thus, the yogi would quit his body when he was ready and at the proper time. *Bhagavad-gita* (8.24) states that those who know the Supreme leave this world during the day, during the bright lunar fortnight, and during the six months when the sun travels to the north (summer).

In this way, the yogi who practices the *raja-yoga* system should be so powerful that he can control the time when he will leave his body. Or if a proper time is present, he can raise his life air to the top of the head and, while meditating on the Supreme, immediately quit his body and enter the spiritual world. However, *Bhagavd-gita* (8.25) states that those who leave this life during the night, the moonless fortnight, or in the six months of the southern course of the sun, or those who attain the lunar planet, again take birth in the material world. Therefore, if the yogi happened to leave his body at the improper time, or was thinking of life in the heavenly planets, or of achieving mystical perfections, then he would not enter the spiritual world, but would be transferred to the region of the universe on which he was meditating. On some of the higher material planets, in the heavenly region, the residents are born with all mystic abilities and can travel through space at will. The yogi may evolve through such higher planets lifetime after lifetime, but until the mind is pure and the consciousness spiritualized, he cannot enter into the spiritual region and will be confined to the material universe.

It is significant to note that Arjuna, having heard about this yoga system from Lord Krishna in *Bhagavad-gita* (6.33), at first rejected it as being too difficult. He said the system of yoga which has been described appears impractical and unendurable, for the mind is too restless and unsteady. Later, Krishna went on to explain the process of *bhakti-yoga*, devotional service, as being much more practical and direct.

Five thousand years ago, when this conversation took place, Arjuna was a much more capable man than any of us are today. Even then he could not see how he could truly reach perfection through this process of *raja-yoga*. We are not stronger, nor do we have better mental faculty in this day and age to think we might be able to perform this type of yoga successfully. Therefore, only a very few may ever be found who can be completely successful at it, although many may try and reach elementary levels of progress. Such levels of expertise may be exhibited in the form of mystic powers and might look impressive at first, but these are not the end result. Of course, many people may be fooled by those who display mystic powers and think that such yogis are indeed great saints, but such mystic abilities are nothing more than by-products of one's austerities, and are not necessarily a sign of spiritual consciousness or purification. Some yoga students, especially in the West, may be attracted by these mystic powers and engage in yoga in the hopes of attaining them. But the number of Westerners who have ever displayed such mystic abilities is practically nil.

Yogis who have any of these powers may do something that seems very amazing to common people who then worship these yogis. Some yogis produce ashes or coins or other things like watches in their hands, but this is like a cheap magic show. Once one knows the principle by which it works, it is not so impressive. Yogis do it for adoration from cheap followers who like to be tricked by such people. In this way, they get money and make a living for themselves while posing as greatly advanced holy men. Other yogis can control the thoughts of people while speaking in front of large audiences and influence people in this way.

In any case, the point to remember is that these mystic powers are nothing more than added attractions that one may attain as they advance along the path of yoga. But it is advised that these mystic powers must be ignored or they will become obstacles in one's spiritual advancement. They are like toys or playthings that can cause one to be distracted from the real goal of yoga. Therefore, if a yogi or guru makes an open display of various mystic abilities in order to attract people and make disciples, this should be taken as a warning that he may only be a fraud, like a magician performing some tricks simply to get adoration and distinction.

MYSTIC POWERS

Yogis generally become attracted to the mystic powers that they may develop. What these yogic powers are and what they do is described in *Srimad-Bhagavatam* (11.15.3-8). There the Supreme Personality, Sri Krishna, says that master yogis have established eighteen types of mystic perfection, eight of which are primary, having their shelter in Him, and ten secondary, appearing from the material mode of goodness. The eight primary powers consist of *anima*, making one's body very small; *mahima*, becoming very big; *laghima*, becoming as light as air; *prapti*, acquiring whatever one desires; *prakamya-siddhi*, experiencing any enjoyable thing; *isita-siddhi*, controlling aspects of material energy; *vasita-siddhi*, overcoming the modes of nature; and *kamavasayita-siddhi*, obtaining anything from anywhere.

The ten secondary mystic powers that arise from the material mode of goodness through yoga are freedom from hunger and thirst, the ability to see and hear things far away, to move with the speed of mind, to assume any form, to see the pastimes of the demigods, to attain whatever one is determined to do, to hold influence over others, to have power to know past and future, to be immune from heat and cold and other dualities, to know the thoughts of others, to be invincible, and to halt the influence of fire, sun, water, and poison.

Although these yogic powers may seem impressive, many of them have also been accomplished by the advancement of materialistic technology. For example, the *Yoga Sutras* of Patanjali states that by controlling the nerve-currents that govern the lungs and upper body, the yogi can walk on water or thorns and similar objects. To reach this perfection, the yogi may have to struggle and meditate for twenty or thirty years. Or a common man may go to the boatman and pay a small fare to immediately cross the river. What is the advantage of practicing yoga for so many years simply to walk on water?

Similarly, from the *anima-siddhi* one can become so small he can enter into a stone or atom. But modern science has made tunnels through hills and mountains and have analyzed such small molecules as atoms, accomplishing similar results as the *anima-siddhi*. By scientific advancement we can also fly through the air, travel under water, or see and hear things from far away as on television or radio. Of course, there may be some things science cannot do, like the *laghima-siddhi*, which enables one to go to the sun planet by entering into the rays of the sunshine. Or *prapti-siddhi* which enables one to get anything by extending his hand and taking what he wants from anywhere. Although it may appear like he is magically producing the object himself, actually he is just stealing it from someone else.

By the yogic power of *isita-siddhi* one can create or destroy an entire planet. This power is much stronger than the atomic bombs that can only blow up a small portion of this planet and never recreate it. The *prakamya* power allows one to perform wonderful acts within nature, while the *kamavasayita* power enables one to control nature. And there are many other forms of these mystic powers.

Through these mystic perfections one can derive many kinds of material happiness, but such power is still material. They are not spiritual. Therefore, yogis who are absorbed in the use of these abilities or the happiness derived from such yogic powers cannot get free from the material creation. They may be able to perform so many wonderful miracles, but this is not the business of those who are actually spiritually advanced. Saints and sages who are pure in heart have no interest in displaying their mystical abilities, though they may have many. These yogic powers signify only a preliminary stage of spiritual advancement. Therefore, in Patanjali's *Yoga Sutras* (3.51), it is advised that by giving up these powers the seed of evil is destroyed and liberation follows. There is a similar statement in *Srimad-Bhagavatam* (3.27.30) in which Sri Krishna states that a perfect yogi no longer considers using mystic powers, which then makes the yogi's progress towards Krishna unlimited and causes death to lose its influence over him.

From these descriptions we can begin to understand that yogic powers, or other supernatural abilities one may possess by other means, such as from witchcraft, Tantraism, etc., are nothing more than another snare of the illusory energy. It is a trick of *maya* to keep one bound up in the material world. And using such mystical powers is another way of lording over and trying to control material nature for one's own enjoyment. They can cause one to become proud and to lose sight of what we are meant to accomplish in this life.

Patanjali describes in his *Yoga Sutras* (3.56) that perfection is attained only when the mind becomes as pure as the soul itself. In *Srimad-Bhagavatam* (3.27.28-29), Lord Kapiladeva (an incarnation of Lord Krishna) explains that His devotee actually becomes self-realized by His causeless mercy, and, when freed from all misgivings, steadily progresses towards his destined spiritual abode and never returns to material existence. That is the ultimate perfection one can achieve.

In this way, we can realize that although there are those who advance in yoga to the point of displaying wonderful powers or miracles, these powers do not help them or their followers to advance spiritually. But if one continues on the path of the real yoga process, regardless of whether one attains various mystical powers or not, he will still reach the perfectional platform in which everything else is automatically achieved. This is described in *Srimad-Bhagavatam* (11.15.33-34) by Lord Krishna where He tells Uddhava that those who are expert in devotional service claim that these mystic abilities are useless and impediments on the path of the topmost yoga, by which one attains all the perfections of life, including mystic powers, directly from Krishna. Not by any other means but devotional service can one attain the actual goal of yoga.

HATHA-YOGA

Hatha-yoga is not a separate system of yoga as many people seem to think, but is one of the eight steps of *raja-yoga*. It involves maneuvering the body through different *asanas* or exercises, and controlling the life airs within the body (the *prana*, the incoming and outgoing breath; *apana*, which expels bodily waste; *vyana*, assists in the power of physical movement; *samana*, distributes nutrition through the body; and *udana,* the air in the sushumna channel). *Hatha-yoga* has no goal other than helping to keep the body in shape and free from disease, and the mind peaceful and steady for spiritual pursuits. This, however, is very useful in whatever spiritual process we pursue because if our body is too diseased, and if our mind is too restless and unsteady, they become a hindrance in our quest for spiritual perfection. Thus, with the practice of *hatha-yoga*, the body and mind become healthier and our spiritual practice can continue with fewer impediments.

KARMA-YOGA

Karma-yoga is a system for attaining perfection through action. Such action is based on religious texts for one's purification and future happiness as in entering heaven after death. These activites may include ritualistic worship of the demigods, as well as a variety of other things, such as avoiding the causing of any harm to all other living beings, and doing activities for the good of others who may be less fortunate. The main interest of one practicing *karma-yoga* is for himself and in achieving good future results rather than transcendence. In other words, this path is for one who is too attached to materialistic fruitive activities. He works for himself but the results of whatever he does are meant to be offered to God, as regulated by the rules in the Vedic literature. When one gives the fruits of his work to God, the work becomes yoga, or linked to the Supreme. Without dovetailing one's work for God in this way, all activities simply cause one to accumulate more *karma*, not to be free of it. By giving the results to God, one becomes freed from the reactions of such work and also begins to make advancement on the path of yoga. *Karma-yoga* is considered to be the transitional stage between material and spiritual life. Nonetheless, one's *karma* (as we have explained in Volume One of this series, *The Secret Teachings of the Vedas*) should be a major concern for everyone.

JNANA-YOGA

Jnana-yoga is the path to enlightenment through the process of mental speculation and the study of empirical knowledge. The aspirant of *jnana-yoga* engages in long hours of study and discussion in the attempt to understand the highest truth. One following this path must also accept the authority of the great sages and study in their association, which is not always easy to find. Without proper guidance along this path one can easily become confused about what is actually the Absolute Truth. By merely involving the cognitive intellect, which is the main activity of the *jnana-yogi*, one simply remains on the mental platform. Therefore, it is very difficult for the *jnana-yogi* to rise above material existence and enter the spiritual realm. The reason for this is that knowledge alone does not purify the consciousness, although it can help one understand the proper path to be taken. One should not forever remain a seeker of truth, but should reach a stage of following the path that will give one realization of what the Absolute Truth is and enable him to reach the spiritual strata.

KUNDALINI-YOGA

Kundalini-yoga is a system in which those who practice it must understand a good deal about their body, subtle body, and the *chakras* and channels of energy within. One also must thoroughly understand the disciplines that help the yogi control his bodily functions and internal states. The term *kundalini* is hardly mentioned in any of the Vedic texts, and not at all in any of the *Upanishads*.

Thus, *kundalini-yoga* is not very much regarded as a valid process for spiritual purification or self-realization by the Vedic sages.

Kundalini-yoga is generally practiced by those who are followers of the *Tantras*. This process is similar to the *raja-yoga* system in which one must sit in the proper place and posture, control the breathing, and discipline the mind and senses. With practice, the yogi tries to awaken the *kundalini*, the "coiled one" or primal force, which is compared to a tiny snake or spiral of fire-energy lying asleep and coiled three and a half times at the base of the spine. The yogi performs certain exercises and techniques to arouse the *kundalini* and raise it through the *Sushumna* channel to the highest *chakra* at the crown of the head, called the *Sahasrara* or lotus of a thousand petals. The *kundalini* is female, or Shakti, while the *Sahasrara* is male, or Shiva. When the *kundalini* or Shakti energy unites with the universal Shiva force, the yogi is then considered to be united with the universal soul. The way this works is that as the *kundalini* energy ascends the spine through the *Sushumna* nerve, it pulls the yogi's life energy and soul up to the *Sahasrara* at the top of the head. The skull then fractures and the yogi leaves the material body and merges into the great white light. This is the ultimate goal of *kundalini-yoga*.

The various experiences that a person sometimes has when the *kundalini* begins to awaken can be quite profound. As the *kundalini* rises to the different *chakras*, one may have many physical sensations and psychic experiences or acquire different mystic powers. A person may even have visions of other realms or view events of the future, or may mystically travel to the planets of hell or heaven or the subtle realms of existence that are described in the Vedic *Puranas*. When the *kundalini* rises to the heart *chakra*, the heart and emotions open and one can be flooded with waves of great bliss. At the *Ajna chakra*, the mind becomes quiet and steady. As it rises towards the *Sahasrara chakra*, one can hear cosmic sounds described as the inner harmonies of the celestial spheres. These experiences can be caused by the energy within or from simply opening oneself to the subtle realm or astral plane beyond the physical dimension. However, this does not mean a person is making spiritual progress. The subtle realm has many levels, both high and low, or awesome and horrible. Opening channels that allow us to experience these subtle energies does not mean we are in control of them. A person may have fantastic mystical experiences, or undergo nightmarish encounters, depending on the level of energy and consciousness with which one comes in contact. One may also encounter various entities from these subtle levels, both benevolent or intimidating. Once the channels to the lower levels of the subtle realm have been opened, harmful entities may come through and cause trouble in a number of ways. Other stages of *kundalini-yoga* are described in the next section on the *chakras*.

The ways through which the *kundalini* can be properly awakened include intense devotion to God, repetition of particular *mantras*, or by yogic exercises under the guidance of an empowered guru. Rarely is it spontaneously aroused because of one's progress in past lives, but it can happen, which may create confusing experiences if the person does not understand what is taking place. It can also be aroused when the guru transmits his energy to the disciple through touch. This causes the disciple to have an awakening of superconsciousness, but only to the degree to which the guru is empowered. This also happened with Sri Caitanya Mahaprabhu in Bengal 500 years ago. Whomever came in contact with Him or heard His ecstatic chanting of the Hare Krishna *maha-mantra* would be imbibed with His potency and become emersed in ecstatic love of God. Some people relate this form of God-realization to the arousal of the *kundalini*, while others refer to it simply as being a spiritual reawakening of one's spiritual position. Even though Sri Caitanya gave this powerful ecstasy to many people, He never put any emphasis on rousing the *kundalini*. He only taught that the goal is to reawaken one's spiritual love of God through the process of *bhakti-yoga* by absorbing oneself in the chanting of the *maha-mantra*, which can bring complete spiritual enlightenment and transform one's vision on every level.

To master the *kundalini* energy may take many years. One must take instruction from a guru who is well experienced in this practice because the aspirant must know how to handle the *kundalini* force when it is awakened, otherwise negative reactions can be expected. If the *kundalini* is not controlled properly once one is able to begin raising it, or if it is awakened forcibly by one who is improperly trained, it can be more than the person can handle. The *kundalini* may become active, but in an irritated manner. In such a case, it can cause serious damage, both physically and psychologically, up to the point of mental agitation, confusion, illusion, or insanity. Thus, the practice of *kundalini-yoga* can be dangerous if one has not been thoroughly trained by an expert guru.

I have personally seen the damage this form of yoga can do if one does not know what he is doing. One boy who used to visit a yoga center I was staying at years ago also practiced *kundalini-yoga*. He started becoming good at awakening this force. He could raise it a little, but never learned what to do with it. At one point the force went up his spine and all the way to his brain. What exactly happened I cannot say, but it obviously affected him psychologically and damaged some of the nerves in his brain. From then on he acted very peculiar, as if he was mentally retarded. Before that he was very normal and enthusiastic. But afterwards, you could not even carry on a decent conversation with him. He simply lost his ability to communicate well, even though he would try to. So a neophyte must not rush in and begin trying something for which he is not prepared.

You first have to ask yourself why you are engaging in yoga. Are you sincerely trying to attain spiritual enlightenment, or are you just trying to see some white light or hear some cosmic sounds? Are you actually longing for a purified consciousness, or do you simply want a little excitement, another cheap thrill? If all you want is some new sensation, then what is the difference in your pursuit of yoga and your desire for sex? Sex can produce a thrill, too, although very temporarily. But if such is the case, then your practice of *kundalini-yoga* is no different than your search for sex. It is only for a little stimulation and sense gratification. The real goal is missed. Engaging in yoga for such purposes is like undergoing the struggle of digging a deep well in order to find water to satisfy your thirst while residing on the banks of a clear, fresh water lake. In other words, it will reward you with only shallow results after much work, while, on the other hand, attaining the real goal of yoga through the purification of your consciousness allows you to experience the bliss within, which is like an ocean of joy.

THE CHAKRAS AND KOSHAS

If you are interested in *raja-yoga* or *kundalini-yoga*, you must know the science of the *chakras* and *koshas*. Within the gross physical body there is the subtle or *sukshma* body, which is divided into layers. As *Bhagavad-gita* (3.42) explains, the working senses are superior to dull matter; mind is higher than the senses; intelligence is higher than the mind; and the soul is higher than the intelligence. This describes the way the body has layers or sheaths called *koshas* which cover the living entity and become decreasingly dense as one goes inward.

The physical body is called the *annamaya-kosha* which is made from food. Then there is the *pranamaya-kosha* made of the vital air circulating within the gross body. Deeper is the *manomaya-kosha*, or mind body, and the *vijnanamaya-kosha*, or intelligence body. Finer than all these is the *anandamaya-kosha* wherein one attains bliss.

Within the subtle body are *chakras* which are the psychic centres of energy situated along the spinal column. Each of the *koshas* are connected with the different *chakras*. The *annamaya-kosha* is made up and connected with the elements of earth, water, and fire, which are centered respectively in the *Muladhara chakra* at the base of the spine, the *Svadhisthana chakra* along the spine near the genitals, and the *Manipura chakra* at the level of the solar plexus. Composed of air and ether is the *pranamaya-kosha* which is centered in the *Anahata chakra* near the heart, and the *Vishuddha chakra* along the spine behind the throat. The *manomaya-kosha* and *vijnanamaya-kosha* are centered in the *Ajna chakra* situated between the eyebrows. And the *Sahasrara chakra*, or lotus of a thousand petals, is located just above the crown of the head.

These subtle sheaths have particular connections with the physical body at numerous points that are linked with many subtle energy channels known as *nadis* that flow through the whole body. (These points also correspond to acupuncture points.) But the most important *nadi* is the *Sushumna*, the central channel that runs from just below the *Muladhara chakra* and extends up the spine to the forehead. On the left side of the *Sushumna* is the white lunar *nadi*, called *Ida*, and on the right side is the red solar *nadi* called *Pingala*. Two currents of psychic energy flow through the *Ida* and *Pingala nadis* in opposite directions, spiraling around the *Sushumna* from the base of the spine and up to meet at the forehead. Within the *Sushumna* are three more channels called *Vajra*, *Chitrini*, and *Brahmani*. It is the *Brahmani* or *Brahma-randhra* in which the *kundalini* travels upwards.

As one raises the life energy or *kundalini*, there will be a transformation of awareness from the physical to the subtle. This can be understood in the way each *chakra* corresponds with one of the elements. The *Muladhara* relates to earth or solidity, *Svadhisthana* with water or liquid, *Manipura* to gaseous or fire, *Anahata* with air, and *Vishuddha* with ether or space. At the *Ajna* center one becomes merged in divine consciousness; yet, the identification with a separate ego remains and keeps the practitioner from attaining perfect unity with Brahman. Only after reaching the *Sahasrara chakra* is there perfect *samadhi* and unity with the void.

In this way, the practitioner or yogi passes through progressively elevated planes of consciousness. This means that one not only acquires new realizations as each *chakra* becomes opened and the blockages along the path are broken down, but he must also give up attachments or hangups on the plane of consciousness related to the *chakra* he has reached for complete unfoldment to take place. In other words, one has to leave their habitual and preconceived conceptions of things behind before full perception of the realizations at the next *chakra* can begin. And when one is very inclined toward activities related to the *annamaya-kosha*, the physical body, it is very difficult to go inward to the more subtle bodies or raise the *kundalini* to higher *chakras*. Basically, consciousness goes no higher than the first three *chakras* if one is absorbed in worldly thoughts. Thus, the aspirant must penetrate these lower levels of consciousness if he expects to make any progress at all. And getting past the *Muladhara*, the *Anahata*, and the *Ajna chakras* are the most difficult.

For the average person in the West, this is a very difficult path to attempt and takes serious determination to be successful. Of course, there have been reports of those who have been able to raise the *kundalini* Shakti to some degree, but there is more to reaching perfection in this system than raising the Shakti and experiencing whatever mystic powers, bliss, or other feelings that come along. You must also finally completely release the *jiva*, or your soul, from the body.

This is done by sitting in the proper *asana* and restraining your breathing, and leading the *jivatma*, your individual soul, into the heart of the *Muladhara chakra*. Then by contracting the anus and following the rules for this yoga process, you awaken the *kundalini*. As the *kundalini* awakes, you merge the Paramatma in the impersonal form of the *prana* or life-force into the *Sushumna nadi* and raise it up along with the soul through the different *chakras* to the *Ajna chakra*. There you merge all the diverse elements, from the gross to the subtle, into the *kundalini*, along with the *jivatma*. Then you merge the *kundalini* with the universal Shiva and pierce the *Brahma-randhra* and leave the body altogether and finally become merged with the Brahman. If, however, you cannot accomplish this last step, then all of your efforts on this path remain incomplete.

This science of *chakras* is, essentially, a part of the mechanical yoga process. If you follow it properly, certain mystic powers or other results will be achieved as the *chakras* become open, but it is not necessarily in relation to the Supreme Personality. In fact, some aspirants do not care about occult powers or opening the *chakras*. They are only interested in realizing God. Thus, they learn to meditate, and when they make progress through meditation the *chakras* open automatically. The opening of the *chakras* has nothing to do with God-realization, regardless of what anyone may tell you. Opening the *chakras* or raising the *kundalini* is done primarily for achieving mystical powers or to satisfy one's desires for mystical experiences or amusement. But many times the achievement and distraction of mystical powers has taken sincere seekers away from the path toward the Absolute Truth. Such powers are often a curse rather than a blessing, as previously explained.

The science of *chakras*, at the ultimate stage, is used mostly for merging into the void or Brahman effulgence. As we have established in *The Secret Teachings of the Vedas*, the Brahman effulgence is simply the spiritual rays that emanate from the body of the Supreme, which consists of innumerable spiritual sparks or souls. These sparks, the liberated living entities, indefinitely drift in the eternal spiritual sky without any spiritual engagement. But when there is some tendency for activity, they must return to the material world for engagement since they have no knowledge of, nor did they develop the inclination for, devotional service to the Supreme Being on the eternal spiritual planets that exist within the eternal spiritual sky. After returning to the material world by their own free will, they again start over and proceed through the rounds of birth and death, going up and down throughout the various levels of planetary systems within the material cosmos. Thus, it is considered by the topmost sages that even if one does fulfill all the requirements to reach complete perfection on the path of *raja* or *kundalini-yoga*, he has not reached the ultimate stage of spiritual realization.

LAYA-YOGA

Laya-yoga is very similar to *kundalini-yoga*, but as one raises the feminine energy at the base of the spine through the *chakras* towards the crown of the head, the emphasis is on meditating on the inner sounds that one experiences at each *chakra*. The final goal is to raise the feminine energy up to the crown *chakra* and merge with the Supreme.

KRIYA-YOGA

Kriya-yoga is a system for those who are inclined towards the mystic process. Among its purposes is to provide a method for recharging the blood with oxygen through its recommended exercises. From this extra oxygen, the atoms are turned into life energy to rejuvenate the *chakras* and brain. By reducing the toxins in the blood, the yogi is able to reduce the decay of tissues and improve his health and prolong his life. One who is advanced is able to get energy from his cells or turn the cells into energy. By mastering it a yogi's body can dematerialize or materialize at will.

Kriya-yoga can also help clear and purify one's consciousness from unwanted or regressive thought patterns. As the yogi continues to advance, he can turn the energy used for bodily maintenance, such as for breathing and heart action, and use it for higher purposes such as raising inner subtle energies to higher levels. Thus, the goal is ultimately, by breath and mind control, to unite the mind with divine realms, allowing the yogi to concentrate on the cosmic consciousness or Supersoul within.

Kriya-yoga is also outlined in the *Garuda Purana*. It is stated there that any person who in gladness sees the worship of the Deity in the temple will obtain the results of *kriya-yoga*, which are described in the *Pancaratra* scripture. In other words, one can learn to concentrate on the Supreme in the heart by years of practice of *kriya-yoga*, or one can simply walk into the temple and immediately absorb oneself in seeing the Deity form of the Lord and obtain a similar result. *Kriya-yoga* is a system much like devotional service, or *bhakti-yoga*, but it is especially meant for those who are attached to the performance of mystic yoga.

MANTRA-YOGA

Mantra-yoga is one of the oldest forms of yoga and an easy system for enlightenment. It is recommended as the best means for focusing the mind on the Supreme in this age of Kali. The word *mantra* literally means to deliver the mind. The instrument used to accomplish this is the secret power of vibrations arranged in a particular formula, called a *mantra*. Different *mantras* have different purposes. Some bring happiness, some fulfill material desires, some are used in the worship of various demigods, some simply focus and steady the mind, some help raise the life energy up through the *chakras*, while others are incantations for casting spells and so on. But *mantras* used for spiritual enlightenment release vital energy, strengthen the mind, and prepare the consciousness for perceiving higher realms of existence. By concentrating on the *mantra*, the mind associates with the energy within it and takes on the characteristics found within the sound vibration. In this way, the mind can be purified by the spiritual vibrations within the *mantra*. One who chants a *mantra* generally repeats it a particular number of times each day while using a string of beads like a rosary. Further descriptions of the benefits and procedures for practicing *mantra-yoga* are described in Chapter Ten.

BHAKTI-YOGA

Bhakti-yoga is a system which is highly recommended for this age and is generally practiced by the followers of Vedanta called Vaishnavas, or worshipers of Vishnu or Krishna. It is by far the easiest of all the yoga processes and has fewer requirements for the practitioners than any other process. *Bhakti* is the yoga that begins, continues, and ends with love and devotion to the Supreme. Attaining this sentiment holds the sum and substance of all other yoga processes and religions. This path is so powerful that even married people may practice it successfully, while in other systems one must be celibate. There are no extreme austerities to undergo; yet, the results are sublime. It is a scientific method of expanding one's consciousness to perceptions of unlimited joy and inner peace. *Bhakti-yoga* brings complete fulfillment to those who seriously practice it, and gives realizations of one's real identity and what one's relationship is with the Absolute. It can be practiced anywhere at anytime.

In *bhakti-yoga* there is not much concern about the *chakras* and the practice for raising the life energy up the *Sushumna nadi* or freeing oneself of the subtle body. The reason for this is explained in *Srimad-Bhagavatam* (3.25.33), which states that *bhakti*, devotional service, dissolves the subtle body of the living entity without separate effort, just as fire in the stomach digests all that we eat. In other words, being fixed in devotional service, which itself is a direct way of engaging in eternal spiritual activities, the yogi burns up the five coverings of the gross and subtle body as he becomes more and more spiritualized. Thus, there is no need to struggle in the separate endeavor of trying to open the various *chakras* within the subtle body or becoming free of it if the subtle body is automatically dissolved. The *bhakti-yogi* naturally becomes free from ignorance, attachment to the body, false egotism, and material consciousness, and can rapidly reach the spiritual platform. This is confirmed in *Bhagavad-gita* (14.26) where it states that one who engages in full devotional service and does not fall down transcends the material modes and reaches Brahman.

The way this works is that within our material body and senses are our spiritual senses, which are lying dormant. They have no spiritual engagement, being covered by matter. Devotional service, and the ultimate goal of any other yoga or religious system, involves freeing our real senses from the confines of matter and material consciousness and engaging them in direct spiritual activities to the Supreme. When the contamination of materialistic consciousness has been removed and the senses act in purified God consciousness, we then have reached our eternal sensory activities, which are spiritual and in relation with our real identity as an eternal spiritual servant of the Supreme Spirit. Eternal spiritual activities means to engage in serving the Supreme, our natural occupation, while temporary material activities means to engage in the attempt to satisfy our dull mind and senses, which keeps us a prisoner within matter.

While the yogis of other processes are struggling hard to control artificially their mind and senses, the senses of the *bhakti-yogi* are automatically controlled and purified by engagement in devotional service. One example of this from the Vedic literature is of Visvamitra. He was a great yogi, seriously practicing and performing many austerities. However, even though in meditation, simply by hearing the tinkling ankle bells of a beautiful woman walking nearby, named Menaka, he fell from his yogic position and had sex with her. After many years of living with Menaka he realized the futility of his position, angrily gave up married life, and again took to his yogic practices. However, when Haridasa Thakura was tempted by a prostitute while engaged in *bhakti-yoga* and chanting the *maha-mantra*, he did not fall down. In fact, while the woman waited for hours in hopes of having sex with Haridasa, she became purified by hearing his chanting. She then gave up her interest in sex and also took up *bhakti-yoga*. Therefore, by experiencing a higher taste, Haridasa Thakura was successful. This is the advantage of engaging in *bhakti-yoga*. This is confirmed in *Srimad-Bhagavatam* (3.25.43-44), which states that those yogis who have spiritual knowledge and have renounced material interests engage in devotional service to the lotus feet of the Supreme Being for their eternal happiness. With their minds fixed in such devotional service, they are easily able to enter the spiritual kingdom. This is the only means for one to attain the final perfection of life.

Therefore, those yogis or mystics who engage in devotional yoga are considered first-class because, while living in this material universe, they engage in the same devotional activities that are going on within the spiritual planets in the spiritual sky. Thus, they have already attained their natural spiritual position. There is no higher perfection than this. More is explained about this process in Chapter Nine.

CHAPTER FOUR

The Main Philosophical Systems of the East

Besides the philosophy writtien in the Vedic literature, there are still seven other major philosophical systems of the East that are connected with Vedic thought. These are known as Buddhism, Nyaya, Vaisesika, Sankhya, Yoga, Mimamsa, and Vedanta, and were founded by Buddha, Gautama, Kanada, Kapila, Patanjali, Jaimini, and Vyasadeva respectively. All but Buddhism belong to the orthodox school of thought in that they accept the authority of the *Veda*. Buddhism, Jainism, and Carvaka, belong to the heterodox school and do not accept Vedic authority.

The purpose of these philosophical systems is to help a person comprehend the nature of reality. From Nyaya to Vedanta there is a continuous development of thought and philosophical understanding. Thus, one system may use portions of another in the way it establishes its analytical principles of reasoning and debate. To help you clearly understand the difference in each system and how they culminate in Srila Vyasadeva's Vedanta philosophy, a brief description is given of each.

BUDDHISM

It was several hundred years before the time of Lord Buddha that his birth was predicted in *Srimad-Bhagavatam*: "In the beginning of the age of Kali, the Supreme Personality of Godhead will appear in the province of Gaya as Lord Buddha, the son of Anjana, to bewilder those who are always envious of the devotees of the Lord." (*Bhag*.1.3.24)

This verse indicates that Lord Buddha was an incarnation of the Supreme who would appear in Gaya, a town in central India. But some historians may point out that Buddha, Siddhartha Gautama, was actually born in Lumbini, Nepal, and that his mother was Queen Mahamaya. Therefore, this verse may be inaccurate. But actually Siddhartha became the Buddha after he attained spiritual enlightenment during his meditation under the Bo tree in Gaya. This means that his spiritual realization was his second and most important birth. Furthermore, Siddhartha's mother, Queen Mahamaya, died several days after Siddhartha's birth, leaving him to be raised by his grandmother, Anjana. So the prediction in the *Bhagavatam* is verified.

When Lord Buddha appeared, the people of India, although following the *Vedas*, had deviated from the primary goal of Vedic philosophy. They had become preoccupied with performing ceremonies and rituals for material enjoyment. Some of the rituals included animal sacrifices. The people had begun to sacrifice animals indiscriminately on the plea of Vedic rituals and then indulged in eating the flesh. Being misled by unworthy priests, much unnecessary animal killing was going on and the people were becoming more degraded and atheistic.

The rituals that included animal sacrifices, according to the *Vedas*, were not meant for eating flesh. An old animal would be placed in the sacrificial fire and, after the *mantras* were chanted, it would come out of the fire in a new and younger body as a test to show the potency of the Vedic *mantras*. However, as the power of the priests deteriorated, they could no longer chant the *mantras* properly and, therefore, the animals would not be brought back to life. So in the age of Kali all such sacrifices are forbidden because there are no longer any *brahmanas* who can chant the *mantras* correctly. Thus, Lord Buddha appeared and rejected the Vedic rituals and preached the philosophy of nonviolence. In the *Dhammapada* (129-130) Buddha says, "All beings fear death and pain, life is dear to all; therefore the wise man will not kill or cause anything to be killed."

The Vedic literature also teaches nonviolence, but Buddha taught the people who used the *Vedas* for improper purposes to give them up and simply follow him. Thus, he saved the animals from being killed and saved the people from being further misled by the corrupt priests. However, he did not teach the Vedic conclusions of spiritual knowledge but taught his own philosophy.

Buddha (560-477 B.C.) was born in the town of Lumbini in Nepal as the son of a king of the Shakya clan. His mother, Queen Mahamaya, before she conceived him, saw him in a dream descending from heaven and entering her womb as a white elephant. After his birth his father sheltered him from the problems of the world as much as possible. Later, Buddha married and had one son. It was during this time that he began to be disturbed by the problems life forced on everyone, especially after he had seen for the first time a man afflicted with disease, another man who was decrepit with age, a dead man being carried to the cremation grounds, and a monk who had dedicated himself to the pursuit of finding a release from the problems of life.

Soon after this, at the age of 29, he renounced his family and became a wandering beggar. For six years Buddha sought enlightenment as an austere ascetic. He would eat very little food, sometimes only one grain of rice a day, and his bones would stick out as if he were a skeleton. Finally giving that up, thinking that enlightenment was not to be found in such a severe manner, he again became a beggar living on alms. When he started to eat more regularly, the five mendicants who were with him left him alone, thinking that he had given up his resolution. During this time he came to Gaya where he determinedly sat in meditation under the Bo tree for seven weeks. He was tempted by Mara, the Evil One, with many pleasures in an effort to make Gautama Buddha give up his quest. But finally he attained enlightenment. It was then that he became the enlightened Buddha.

Buddha at first hesitated to teach his realizations to others because he knew that the world would not want them. Of what use would there be in trying to teach men who were sunk in the darkness of illusion? Nonetheless, he decided to make the attempt. He then went to Benares and met the five mendicants who had deserted him near Gaya. There in the Deer Park, in present day Sarnath, he gave his first sermon, which was the beginning of Buddhism.

Buddha taught four basic truths: that suffering exists, there is a cause for suffering, suffering can be eradicated, and there is a means to end all suffering. But these four noble truths had previously been discussed in the Sankhya philosophy before Buddha's appearance, and had later been further elaborated upon in Patanjali's *Yoga Sutras*. So this train of thought actually was not new.

Buddha also taught that suffering is essentially caused by ignorance and our own mental confusion about the purpose life. The suffering we experience can end once we rid ourselves of this confusion through the path of personal development. Otherwise, this confusion and ignorance causes us to perform unwanted activities that become part of our *karma* that must be endured in this or another existence. When *karma* ceases, so does the need for birth and, naturely, old age, sorrow, and death. With the cessation of birth, there is the cessation of consciousness and entrance into *nirvana* follows. Thus, there is no soul and no personal God, but only the void, the nothingness that is the essence of everything to which we must return. Although this was the basic premise from which Buddha taught, this theory was mentioned in the *Nasadiya-sukta* of the *Rig-veda* long before Buddha ever appeared.

Buddha refused to discuss how the world was created or what was existence in *nirvana*. He simply taught that one should live in a way that would produce no more *karma* while enduring whatever *karmic* reactions destiny brought. This would free one from further rebirth.

In order to accomplish this, Buddha gave a complete system for attaining *nirvana* that consisted of eight steps. These were right views (recognizing the imperfect and temporary nature of the world), right resolve (putting knowledge into practice or living the life of truth and nonviolence toward all creatures, including vegetarianism), right speech (giving up lies, slander, and unnecessary talk), right conduct (nonviolence, truthfulness, celibacy, nonintoxication, and nonstealing), right livelihood (honest means of living that does not interfere with others or with social harmony), right effort (maintaining spiritual progress by remaining enthusiastic and without negative thoughts), right mindfulness (remaining free from worldly attachments by remembering the temporary nature of things), and right meditation (attaining inner peace and tranquility and, finally, indifference to the world and one's situation, which leads to *nirvana*).

However, because of Buddha's lack of interest in discussing any metaphysical topics, many interpretations of his philosophy were possible, especially after his disappearance. The two main divisions of Buddhism that developed were the Hinayana, or lesser vehicle, and Mahayana, or greater vehicle. The Hinayana was more strict and held onto Buddha's original teachings and uses Pali as the language of its scriptures. It also accepts reaching *nirvana* as the goal of life. Hinayana stresses one's own enlightenment and puts less emphasis on helping others, and Mahayana emphasizes the need of enlightenment for the good of others while overlooking the need to realize the truth within. The Mahayana accepts Sanskrit as the language for its texts and integrates principles from other schools of philosophy, making it more accessible to all varieties of people. Gradually, as followers came from numerous cultural backgrounds, Mahayana Buddhism drastically changed from its original form.

The ideal of the Mahayana system is the *bodhisattva*, the person who works for enlightenment for all other living beings. The personification of this enlightened compassion is Avalokiteshvara, who is represented in a variety of forms. The *mantra* that is the sound representation of this enlightened compassion is *om mani padme hum*, which is chanted on beads by aspiring Buddhists. The vibration of this *mantra* evokes compassionate qualities and feelings in the heart and consciousness of a person who chants it.

A third division of Buddhism is the Vajrayana sect. This has the same principles as the Mahayana, but the Vajrayana bases its process for achieving enlightenment on the Buddhist *Tantras*, which are supposed to reveal a quicker path to enlightenment. The Vajrayana path is one of transforming the inner psychological energy toward enlightenment by the use of various types of yogic techniques. First they try to change their conventional perceptions of this world by identifying themselves as the deity they feel affinity for, and to view the *mandala* of the particular deity as the world.

Ultimately, this form of meditation, as well as other techniques used in this system, is meant to give one the experience of what is called the "clear light." This clear light is said to be experienced by everyone shortly after death, but most people hardly notice it because they are not prepared for it. The idea is that if one is prepared for it before death, it can help one to be ready to merge into it when he sees it after death.

As Buddhism flourished, the Hinayana spread through the south in Ceylan, Burma, and Thailand, while the Mahayana spread to the North and East and is now found primarily in Tibet, China, and Japan. The Mahayana school still uses knowledge of *kundalini* and the *chakras* in its teachings. It is this school which has now developed more than twenty sects with a variety of teachings that, in some cases, especially in the West, have become so distorted that it is impossible to distinguish the original principles that were established by Buddha.

There are basically nine principles of the Buddhist path: (1) the creation is eternal and has no creator, (2) the cosmic manifestation is false, (3) consciousness is aggregate without individuality, (4) there is repetition of birth and death, (5) Lord Buddha is the only source of understanding the truth, (6) *nirvana* or annihilation is the ultimate goal, (7) the philosophy of Lord Buddha is the only philosophical path, (8) the *Vedas* are compiled by human beings and therefore faulty, and (9) pious activities, mercifulness, etc., are advised. However, the *Vedanta-sutras* refute many of these points as we will discuss in the following paragraphs.

If one thinks about it, there are obvious limitations in this philosophy. For example, the first principle that the creation is eternal and without a creator contradicts the Buddhist theory that the highest truth is void, or the dissolution of everything. If everything is ultimately void, then what is the source of our consciousness and of the material world? Anyone can easily see that anything material has a beginning, middle, and end. Everything has a source or a cause. If everything has a source, then the material world also has a source. It also has an end. But if the material world is eternal, as the Buddhists say, then there is no question of dissolution or everything returning to a state of void. In this case, the Buddhist goal of dissolving the body, mind, and consciousness to become nothing is absurd. If the Absolute Truth is void, then how could something, such as the material world and living beings, come from nothing? How can you get numbers (like 1, 2, 3, etc.) if all you have is zero? Buddha never explained this, so Buddhists have no answer.

The second point, that the creation is false, is also not quite accurate. The world is not false, but it is temporary and therefore illusory. If the Buddhists originally considered the creation eternal, how could they turn around and say it is false? If the world was actually false, why would anyone have any interest in it? But we see everyone has an interest in this material creation. Everyone has goals they want to accomplish or things they are concerned about. Therefore, the material world is not false, but it is temporary like a dream.

The third point that consciousness is aggregate without individuality is also not accurate. If there is no individuality, then there would be no different points of view and no need for argument or debate. Everyone would think and feel the same. Yet, an integral part of establishing Buddhist philosophy is through argument and debate, which many Buddhists practice. For this there must be two people or individuals with different viewpoints, which is based on the fact that everyone is an individual spirit soul. Therefore, we are not all part of an impersonal aggregate consciousness, but are separate souls expanded from the Supreme Soul. In other words, we are small independent energies from the Supreme Energetic, the source of all energy. Thus, we are able to view and experience things differently and express our thoughts from various perspectives on an individual basis.

The fifth principle, that Lord Buddha is the only source of knowledge, is also unacceptable. Lord Buddha rejected the Vedic knowledge and established his own philosophy by intellectual speculation. Anybody can do the same thing and we often find in these modern times that many people like to interpret everything their own way. Therefore, many people may claim their own philosophy and change the meaning of scripture by word jugglery. But nothing is accomplished by such means. It only adds to the confusion in society. Yet, we should remember that Lord Buddha was an incarnation of God with a specific purpose for rejecting the *Vedas* at the time. Only by his personal influence could he have been successful in spreading a faulty philosophy such as Buddhism. Therefore, those who were envious of the followers of the *Vedas* or used them for duplicious means were tricked into giving up the *Vedas* and worshiping Lord Buddha. And let us remember that there were many topics which Buddha simply refused to discuss at all, such as the science of the soul and the creation of the universe. So, if Buddha is the only source of knowledge, the information he provides is far from complete.

The Buddhists also claim that reaching *nirvana* is the ultimate goal. This kind of *nirvana* of which the Buddhists speak is simply freedom from material existence and all the pains and pleasures therein. This means that those who become perfect in this system and actually attain *nirvana* merge into what is known as the Viraja River, which is an area located just beyond the material creation and separates the material and spiritual worlds. Thus, they enter into a realm which is neither material nor spiritual. Such existence, or nonexistence as the Buddhists would say, is far from any level of authentic spiritual realization that one can get by studying the Vedic literature.

The Buddhists also say that the *Vedas* are compiled by ordinary human beings, but this is not the case. The truth is the *Vedas* are eternally existing in the form of spiritual sound vibration. Traditionally, Lord Brahma was originally instructed in the *Vedas* and passed the knowledge on to other great sages who, by practicing the Vedic instructions and attaining spiritual realization, expanded the Vedic information for the benefit of everyone. If Brahma, the original living being in the universe, was instructed, then who was his instructor? Therefore, Vedic knowledge came from someone else, someone more elevated than he, and was not originally formed by ordinary men by means of their mental speculation, even though such has been the beginning of many religions and philosophies we find today. Furthermore, the *Vedas* were compiled primarily by Srila Vyasadeva who has been recognized as an incarnation of God whose purpose was to put the Vedic literature into written form. Many instructions of Lord Krishna are also included in the Vedic literature. And through the years, many sages and transcendental scholars have attained spiritual realization by studying and following these Vedic instructions and have written their own enlightening commentaries that have been referred to by society for hundreds of years. Therefore, we cannot accept that the *Vedas* are nothing more than the compilations of ordinary men.

The Buddhists also believe in being merciful. There is no doubt that everyone should be merciful to others, but mercy is a relative thing. For example, one may be merciful to hungry people by giving them food. But if the food is chicken, beef, or something similar, then what kind of mercy is that? So many chickens and animals must be killed to become food for others, and you, along with those who slaughter them and the people who eat them, become implicated in such violent actions. This kind of violent activity produces violent reactions which cause further suffering. Therefore, such mercy does not really improve the situation. In fact, unless there is absolutely no other kind of food to give, like vegetables, grains, fruits, etc., giving slaughtered animals away as food is not mercy at all. Similarly, since the Buddhists are advocating a faulty philosophy for others to follow, this is not mercy. The Buddhists do not acknowledge the existence of the soul or of God, so their mercy is defective.

Recognizing these various flaws, we cannot accept that the Buddhist philosophy is the only way. Although Buddhism has many beneficial points that one can utilize for uplifting one's consciousness, a perfect philosophy does not have the defects that are discussed here. Therefore, after the disappearance of Lord Buddha, the authority of the *Vedas* was reinstated by such scholarly personalities as Shankaracarya, Ramanujacarya, Madhvacarya, Nimbarka, Baladeva Vidyabushana, Sri Caitanya Mahaprabhu, and others.

NYAYA

This is a school of logic which regards doubt as a prerequisite for philosophical inquiry. All other Indian systems of philosophy use the Nyaya system of logic as a foundation for reasoning and debate.

The five principles of the Nyaya system are: (1) to present the proposition, (2) the reason for presenting the proposition, (3) an example of it, showing that it is realistic or unrealistic, depending on the instance, (4) apply the example of the proposition presented, and (5) establish the conclusion of the proposition.

The ultimate purpose of the Nyaya system, which is closely linked to the Vaisesika system, is to achieve liberation from *karma* and material existence by properly understanding reality, or the difference between matter and spirit. Nyaya accepts that the only way to liberation is to obtain knowledge of the external world and understand its relationship with the mind and self. Through logical criticism, one can dicriminate between truth and illusion and, applying such understanding in daily life, rid oneself of suffering and attain liberation. Additionally, this system of logic was developed to prove the validity of its principles by analysis and argument to counter the criticism of the Buddhists,

Jains, and Carvakas. However, the Nyaya system was empirical and mostly relied on perception, inference, comparison, and testimony as its means of acquiring knowledge.

VAISESIKA

The *Vaisesika-sutra* was the first work written on this philosophy by Kanada. Prasastapada later wrote a definitive commentary on this *sutra* entitled *Svartha Dharma Samgraha*. The name Vaisesika comes from *visesa*, which means uniqueness or particularity. Therefore, the Vaisesika system is a study of the uniqueness and qualities of existence, such as the elements, atoms, their interactions, as well as the soul. But it accepts only two independent sources of knowledge, which are perception and inference.

The *Vaisesika-sutra* contained several ideas: (1) that everything is composed of atoms bearing the qualities of either earth, water, light, or air; (2) that the individual souls are eternal and pervade a material body for a time; (3) there are nine basic elements, consisting of earth, water, light, air, ether, time, space, soul, and mind, which are all eternal; and (4) there are seven categories of experience, which are substance, quality, activity, generality, particularity, inherence, and non-existence. God is not mentioned in the *sutra*, but later commentators included knowledge of God to complete the system.

Vaisesika attempted to integrate philosophical theories with moral and spiritual attitudes or *dharma* which would lead people to good in this life and the next. However, it did not bring the Supreme Being to the point of ultimate reality, but as merely an agent of release from *karma* and repeated birth and death. Therefore, the Vaisesika philosophy is not complete in its understanding of the Absolute Truth or of material nature.

The Vaisesika theory, that merely by interactions between atoms the elements are formed and, thus, the world and all objects within appear, is refuted by the *Vedanta-sutras*. If atoms are simply inert matter, then atomic combinations could not properly take place without some higher directional force. The Vaisesikas say this is the unseen principle but fail to explain fully what it is, where it resides, or how it works. They also say that atoms and relationships between the atoms of the elements as earth, water, air, etc., are eternal, but this would mean that any form composed of atoms would also be eternal, such as the material world and all that is in it. However, anyone can see that this is not the case since everything is always changing and breaking apart. Even the Vaisesikas accept the fact that all bodies and forms composed of atoms are temporary. In this way, we can recognize the contradictions in the atomic theory of the Vaisesikas, which is, therefore, unacceptable.

SANKHYA

The principal aim of this system is to analyze the distinctions between matter and spirit. The study of the twenty-four material elements was originally developed as a complex science by Lord Kapila, as elaborated in *Srimad-Bhagavatam*. But later, there was another Kapila who presented an atheistic Sankhya system. Therefore, in other schools of this system, the existence of God is considered irrelevant. This is because the universe is regarded as a system of cause and effect. In other words, the cause of the universe is that which is eternal but ever-changing, or *prakriti*, the ever-changing material energy. God is eternal and non-changing, so, within this atheistic view of Sankhya, it is considered that God cannot be the cause of the universe. Obviously, there are limitations in this analysis, such as not defining where *prakriti* came from and how could *prakriti*, which is inert, form the material universe without any guidance, and so on. So, gradually, there were additional arguments that again led to an acceptance of God in the philosophy of Sankhya.

The original Sankhya system, as explained in *Srimad-Bhagavatam*, acknowledges matter and spirit as two separate principles of reality. Thus, Sankhya introduces a dualistic philosophy more developed than the previous three systems discussed so far. Sankhya analyzed such factors as *purusha* and *prakriti* (spirit and matter), the creation and development of matter through excitation of the *purusha*, how the world evolved, how the modes of nature operate and affect us, how *ahankara* (false ego) causes our identification with matter and bondage to the material world, the five organs of action and five senses of perception, the subtle elements, the gross elements, etc.

The goal of this system is to understand that the real self is eternal and free, but because of ignorance the soul identifies with what is temporary and, therefore, suffers. Through this kind of analysis of the material world it is expected that one will realize the difference between matter and spirit and attain freedom from false identification. After this stage is attained, release from existence in the material world is reached through spiritual training, meditation on the real self and Superself, and the practice of yoga.

YOGA

Yoga is the application of the Sankhya system. Sankhya is the theory, and yoga is the practice. Yoga, which is essentially theistic, was known many years before Patanjali. Although he is often given the credit for it, he merely codified it in his *Yoga Sutras*. The complete system of yoga is very complex and has many steps to it, each of which must be perfected before one can go on to the next step. Although the basis of this system may be quite popular, few people can actually reach the higher levels of self-realization through this process in this

day and age. The different levels of this process and the different yoga systems
are explained in the previous chapter.

MIMAMSA

Mimamsa means solutions by means of critical examination, and was
expounded by Jaimini in the twelve chapters of his *Mimamsa-sutra*, written
around 400 B.C. This system was traditionally called Purva Mimamsa, meaning
the early revered thought. This is in relation to the study of Vedanta since
Mimamsa was considered the preliminary understanding of Vedanta philosophy.
On the other hand, Vedanta is also called Uttara Mimamsa, meaning the
conclusion and higher teachings of Mimamsa philosophy, because the *Vedas*
are regarded as self-evident scriptures that reveal divine knowledge.

The Mimamsa system emphasizes the importance of action in terms of ritual,
worship, and duty or *dharma*, as the means of reaching liberation from *karma*
and the cycle of repeated birth and death. *Dharma* is considered to be those
moral activities that harmonize individual life with cosmic life. Mimamsa is
basically a systematized code of rules for rituals and worship used along with the
Vedas and explains the purpose and meaning of rituals. It is especially meant
to help householders regulate and spiritualize their daily lives, while Vedanta
is meant more for those who had grown tired of materialistic existence and are
ready to retire and seriously engage in spiritual pursuits.

VEDANTA

Vedanta means the conclusion of the *Veda* or end of all knowledge. Vedanta
is also known as Uttara Mimamsa, or later examination, and is a companion to
the Purva Mimamsa, or preliminary examination. The Purva Mimamsa deals
with the early portions of the *Vedas* and the Uttara Mimamsa deals with the
latter portions. The Vedic tradition, unlike other religions and philosophies, is
rooted in such remote antiquity that its origin cannot be fully traced. The Vedic
literature explains that it exists in the form of eternal spiritual vibrations, and is
present both within and outside the universal creation.

Vedanta has been the most influential of the seven main systems of Eastern
philosophy. Though the name Vedanta is often taken to mean the impersonalist,
nondual or Mayavada school of thought, it is essentially dualistic theism, but
various commentaries have interpreted it to mean different things. The *Sariraka-
Bhasya* commentary by Shankara established the Vedanta as a nondualistic
philosophy, meaning that the ultimate reality is but one. In this regard, the
Brahman and the Atman (individual souls) are identical, and the Brahman is the
Absolute Reality from which everything manifests and back into which

everything merges. This interpretation has gained much respect and influence, but is not the correct viewpoint of the *Vedas*, as explained in Chapter Ten of *The Secret Teachings of the Vedas*.

Ramanuja's interpretation of Vedanta, as related in his *Sri Bhasya* commentary, establishes the soul as a part of God, but that it remains individual in nature even after liberation from the body, rather than merging into the Absolute. He also explains that the process for liberation includes surrendering to the personal form of God.

Madhva's interpretation of Vedanta, as found in his *Tatparya Nirnayas,* also presents Vedanta philosophy as dualistic, similar to Ramanuja's but more developed. Nimbarka also delivered a commentary based on the dualistic idea, but establishes that God is one with yet separate from each soul. This means that God and the individual souls are spiritual in quality; yet God is infinite, and the living entities are infinitesimal. Baladeva Vidyabushana also establishes the individual nature of the soul in his *Sri Bhasya* commentary. But Srila Vyasadeva, the compiler of the original Vedic literature, wrote his concluding commentary on Vedanta in the form of *Srimad-Bhagavatam*.

In the *Bhagavatam*, Srila Vyasadeva very clearly establishes that real Vedanta, or the ultimate end of all knowledge, is to understand the Supreme Personality of Godhead, Lord Sri Krishna:

In the revealed scriptures, the ultimate object of knowledge is Sri Krishna, the Personality of Godhead. The purpose of performing sacrifice is to please Him. Yoga is for realizing Him. All fruitive activities are ultimately rewarded by Him only. He is supreme knowledge, and all severe austerities are performed to know Him. Religion [*dharma*] is rendering loving service unto Him. He is the supreme goal of life. (*Bhag.*1.2.28-29)

In this way, Vedanta emphasizes *sanatana-dharma*, the real religion or eternal nature of the soul, which is to surrender with love to the Supreme Soul. The Vedic path for this is called Vaishnavism, which is the worship of Sri Krishna and His expansions, such as Vishnu, Narayana, Rama, etc. The process of spiritual realization practiced by all Vaishnavas is *bhakti-yoga*, which is more fully explained in Chapter Nine. Elements of this devotional process are easily recognized in all other religions of the world, but *bhakti-yoga* is the most developed of these spiritual processes. Thus, all systems of philosophy and religion reach their culmination in Srila Vyasadeva's Vedanta, as described specifically in *Srimad-Bhagavatam*.

The science of Vedanta is extensive and thorough. It not only includes the knowledge of the Absolute Truth, but also explains the path by which one can attain their own individual realization of the Absolute. This in itself separates it from most religions we find today that usually do not include higher principles of spiritual self-realization, but depend mostly on basic moral doctrines and the blind faith of the followers for the continuation of such religions. Since we have been explaining the Vedic knowledge in *The Secret Teachings of the Vedas* and now *The Universal Path to Enlightenment*, we will not try to summarize it here.

VAISHNAVISM

Vedanta is essentially the doctrine of Vaishnavism, and the path of Vaishnavism is, basically, *sanatana-dharma*, which is the practice of acting according to the eternal nature of the soul and reawakening our consciousness to our spiritual identity and the loving relationship we have with the Supreme.

A Vaishnava is a person who worships Sri Krishna or any of His expansions or incarnations, such as Vishnu, Narayana, Rama, etc. The main difference between the Vaishnava philosophy and all other philosophies of the world is that the goal is also the means of attaining the goal. In other words, *bhakti*, devotional service to the Supreme, is attained by engaging in devotional service to the Supreme. This devotional process purifies one to the level where he or she becomes completely spiritually realized, at which time a person knows his or her real spiritual identity. The Supreme also reveals Himself to such a pure soul, and his or her relationship with the Supreme becomes awakened. Then *bhakti* is no longer merely a process to be followed, but it becomes a spontaneous flow of emotion and attraction for the Supreme who reciprocates such love. Then the eternal, spiritual, loving activities and pastimes, along with a person's spiritual realizations and ecstasy, knows no limits.

The Vaishnava sect is one of the three major divisions of Hinduism, the others being Shaivism and Shakta. Vaishnavas have four major sects: the Ramanujas founded by Ramanujacarya; the Madhvas founded by Madhvacarya; the Vallabhas founded by Vallabhacarya; and the Gaudiya *sampradaya*, founded by Sri Caitanya Mahaprabhu, who is regarded as an incarnation of Krishna Himself. The various aspects of this Vaishnava philosophy are found in Volumes One and Two of this series.

OTHER RELIGIONS

Besides these systems of philosophy, there are also other forms of religion located in the vicinity of India. Some of these are outgrowths of the *Vedas* and may hold many similarities, but are not completely supported by Vedic authority. Others rejected the Vedic teachings and started something new. These philosophies are worth taking a look at to understand their views and authenticity. So basic reviews of a few of them are supplied.

JAINISM

The ideas behind Jainism can be traced to the *Yajur-veda* and were originally started by Lord Rishabhadeva, as described in *Srimad-Bhagavatam*. It is explained that when giving up family life and renouncing the world, Rishabhadeva took to the practice of a particular kind of yoga system wherein He completely neglected caring for His body. Wandering about naked, He simply absorbed His mind in always thinking about the Supreme in a mood of love and devotion. In this way, He showed people how to become free of the illusory energy. However, Arhat, who was at that time the King of Konka, Venka, and Kutaka, imitated Rishabhadeva's activities and started a new system of religion. He gave up the *Vedas* and concocted a new philosophy that was opposed to Vedic principles. Other atheistic religions also followed this system. Thus, unworthy men without any conception of God or spiritual reality could wander the countryside and gain respect and adoration, though having no qualifications. This was the beginning of what became known as Jainism.

The Jains believe the universe is eternal, having no beginning or end, but goes through innumerable cycles. Each cycle has two phases of rise and fall of civilization. Within each cycle twenty-four saintly teachers, Tirthankaras (those who lead the way over a crossing), appear and attain liberation and then show others the way. In this age of decline, Rishabhadeva was the first. The twenty-second Tirthankara was Nemi, a cousin of Sri Krishna, and much later the twenty-third was Parsvanatha of Benares. The twenty-fourth was Vardhamana (599-527 B.C.), who became known as Mahavira (Great Hero), who systematized this philosophy. However, he claimed to merely be the coordinator of the teaching of Parsvanatha who lived in the eighth century B.C.

According to Jain tradition, Mahavira is believed to be the last of the twenty-four great personalities who appear in this world to show others the way to salvation. He was born in a village (present day Vaisali) twenty-seven miles north of Patna and lived in the eastern provinces of India during the sixth century B.C. According to one tradition, Mahavira was a lifelong bachelor. Another tradition says he married and had a daughter. Whatever the case, it is accepted that on the death of his parents when he was twenty-eight years old he renounced his family and became a mendicant following the path of Parsvanatha. For twelve years he wandered about completely naked and silent. During the thirteenth year, after engaging in the most severe austerities and fasting, he reached the supreme enlightenment while in meditation near the town of Jrimbhikagrama. Thus, it is said, he liberated himself from the cycle of repeated birth and death.

As an acclaimed Tirthankara, a teacher who knows the way, he spent the remaining thirty years of his life teaching and organizing his followers. At the age of seventy-two he entered complete *nirvana* in the small town of Pava, present day Pawapuri, twenty-five kilometres from Nalanda.

Like Buddhism, Jainism was also a protest movement against the animal sacrifices that followers of the *Vedas* were performing at that time. The Jains similarly do not believe in God, but believe that those who become liberated from material existence through the Jain tradition attain a God-like status. For this reason, Jains build temples to the liberated predecessors, treating them as divine beings. Rejecting gods, the *Vedas*, and the *brahmana* priests, Jainism places man in charge of his own salvation, but establishes that by following the path of the liberated Tirthankaras, one is assured of liberation from birth and death and the attainment of a God-like position as achieved by the Tirthankaras.

Jainism accepts that there is no personal god or universal ruler from whom we can seek help. Man is the only one who can help himself, and that is accomplished through the Jain process. Jainism explains that due to *karma* formed by our desires, the soul is placed and entangled within a body. To be released from the body, one must stop all activities that produce *karma*. This is done by right belief (in the Jain philosophy), right knowledge, and right conduct. Right conduct consists of nonviolence, truthfulness, celibacy, non-stealing, and renunciation of worldly attachments. Through this process one can free himself from the bodily condition and enter the pure state of eternal bliss and knowledge.

The formal rules amongst the laity for following Jainism are twelve in number: (1) never deliberately kill a living entity and be vegetarian; (2) never lie; (3) never steal; (4) be celibate or never be unfaithful in marriage; (5) never possess more than a certain amount of money; (6) never travel beyond set limits; (7) never possess more than one needs; (8) never think evil of others; (9) meditate a certain length of time each day; (10) live and act in certain areas only; (11) be a monk or nun for a certain portion of life; (12) and help support other Jain ascetics. Further rules include not engaging in any business that involves killing or the destruction of any living entities. Jains feel that safety is the greatest gift one can make to others. Jains are also expected to abide by the laws of the country and follow the established customs, but must not gamble or indulge in excess. Jains are also supposed to read the scriptures every day.

Vows for monks or nuns are more strict, such as limiting food intake to thirty-two mouthfuls a day and being celibate. When one is ready to become a monk, he renounces everything, including his family, possessions, and sometimes all clothing as with the Digambara sect. Then he takes initiation at a Jain temple under the auspices of a senior monk. After the formalities, he lives by begging for his food and wanders from place to place, and only engaging in study, penance, and meditation. It is recommended that when he is near the end of his life that he fast until death and die like a saint. Nonviolence is the essential principle of Jainism; yet, since injury to other entities cannot always be avoided, doing good for others and practicing death by starvation in old age atones for it.

Jainism rejects the authority of the *Vedas* and substitutes logic and experience in place of it. The idea is that knowledge of any object is subject to critical consideration before any conclusions can be made. From this premise the Jains developed a system of determining what is knowledge and reality by various types of perception. It views that all knowledge is partial or only probable, and reality is relative to the way we perceive it. Everything is both eternal yet perishable, or real and unreal, depending on how it is analyzed. The doctrine of the Jains states that there are two types of substances, namely soul and non-soul, or consciousness and unconsciousness. Unconscious substances include matter or bodies, *dharma* or merit (which causes motion or progress), *adharma* or demerit (which causes regression or immovability), and time and space. All are considered to be everlasting and have form, but time has no form.

This philosophy obviously holds some contradictions. First of all, how can things be of an ambiguous nature, such as being eternal yet perishable, or real and nonreal at the same time? It must be one or the other. No one sees an object that is hot and cold at the same time. If objects are similar to other objects, then, for example, what is dry may also be wet or vice versa. In such a case, a person may quench his thirst not only by drinking water but also by eating dirt. This kind of logic, which states that something is different yet nondifferent, or real and nonreal, has a very fragile level of reasoning and will not be able to withstand much argument. Nothing can be understood with certainty in such a process. This means that the followers of this kind of philosophical system will never understand anything beyond their mental speculation.

The Jains also hold the view that the soul has the particular size of the body it inhabits. This would mean that the soul of a baby would not fill the body of a grown man later on. But if the soul expands or contracts to suite the body, this would indicate that the soul is changeable and no more permanent in nature than other material substances that change with time, such as the physical body. If the soul has a particular unchangeable size upon being released from the body, as the Jains proclaim, then the soul actually would have no different size while in material existence. But this is not reconciled in the Jain philosophy. Therefore, this philosophy does not present a clear understanding of the soul or of the difference between reality and illusion.

Jainism began to decline when Ramanujacarya converted the Hoysala king Bittiga into a worshiper of Vishnu in the 12th century. Bittiga was formerly a Jain and upon being converted he adopted the name of Vishnuvardhana. Corruption among the Jain priests also contributed to its decline. Furthermore, Ramanuja publicly defeated the Jain texts on the basis of Vedic knowledge, taking away much of its credibility.

CARVAKA

This philosophy is completely materialistic with roots traceable to ideas discussed in the *Rig-veda*. It is said to have been propagated by Carvaka, the early leader of the movement. But the founder of this school is traditionally believed to be Brihaspati. The *Brihaspati Sutra*, written around 600 B.C., is the main work embodying this philosophy, although it no longer exists.

Carvaka accepts that the principle of reality is merely composed of combinations of earth, air, fire, and water. Otherwise, if something cannot be perceived, it does not exist. Thus, according to this philosophy, perception is the only means of knowing the truth. The soul is considered to be merely one's personality which is developed by the total activity of the living person.

Like modern materialistic science, it considers the universe to be a product of cause and effect originating with an accidental cause that began combining the basic elements of matter into various forms. But the existence or nonexistence of anything could not definately be established in this philosophy.

The goal of the Carvaka philosophy is nothing more than the continued enjoyment of sensual pleasure and happiness. But it also accepts that good actions lead to happiness and bad actions produce suffering. Beyond this, heaven and hell are considered myths, and the practice of religion is useless and foolish.

PASUPATAS OR SHAIVISM

Shaivism centers around the worship of Lord Shiva, one of the prominent demigods. Its origin predates recorded history, but references to the worship of Shiva can be found in the *Vedas* and *Puranas*. The philosophy of Shaivism covers a wide range of Hindu thought, from idealistic monism to pluralistic realism, depending on the locality. As it changed through the years, a number of Shaivite sects were established, and the Pasupatas are considered the earliest.

The Shaiva cults have had great popularity with village people throughout India, and use a form of asceticism for their means of spiritual advancement. This includes rising above anger and greed, engaging in deep meditation, and concentrating on the repetition of the sacred syllable *om*. The initiates often smear their bodies with ashes from crematoriums, chant *mantras* to become free from the bondage of material existence, and dance and sing to induce trance-like states. Some of their practices are very unorthodox and peculiar. Thus, the cult has met much opposition at various times. Much information about the practices of Shaivism is given in the *Shiva Purana*.

The Pasupatas based their ideas on two works by Kaundinya: the *Pasupatasutra* (written around 100-200 A.D.) and the *Pancarthabhasya* (400-600 A.D.). The Pasupatas accept the idea of a Supreme controller, but do not use the *Vedas*. They establish the existence of the Supreme through inference and say that the Supreme, who they accept as Lord Shiva, is not the original cause of the material world, but is the operative cause in that he simply used the material ingredients which already existed to form the cosmic manifestation. Therefore, through a combination of the potency of Lord Shiva and the material energy, generally regarded as Shakti or Mother Durga, the universe is created.

This teaching goes against the Vedic philosophy which establishes that Lord Narayana, Krishna, is the creator of the material worlds and all ingredients thereof. The Vedic literature also maintains that demigods such as Lord Brahma and Lord Shiva are created by and subordinate to Lord Narayana. The *Varaha Purana* specifically states that Narayana is the Supreme Personality of Godhead, and from Him Brahma was born, from whom Shiva was born. Therefore, the demigods are not the Supreme but only dependent agents of the Supreme who work under His direction. This is confirmed in many other verses throughout the Vedic literature. Although in some places we may find that demigods like Shiva, Ganesh, Surya, Indra, etc., are described as the ruler and creator of all, we should understand that almost all prayers to the demigods use such terms. But the words should be taken in their etymological sense referring to Narayana, or Vishnu, who is the source of the power that the demigods have. The name Pasupati means "Lord of all souls," Ganesh means "Lord of all beings," Surya means "the goal of the wise," Indra means "the supreme ruler," all of which ultimately refer to the Supreme Lord and not any lower beings.

The *Vedanta-sutras* point out many contradictions in the philosophy of the Pasupatas or Shaivites and conclude that if one is serious about attaining spiritual enlightenment and liberation, he must avoid this questionable philosophy, for in spite of the uncommon austerities and lifestyle of the Shaivites, their destination after death is not certain. The reason is that, though they may worship Shiva as the Supreme (which in itself is incorrect), they generally believe that God is an unembodied void with which they try to merge. They accept Shiva or any other deity as simply being a material manifestation of the void or Brahman. Thus, their understanding of the Absolute Truth is faulty, and the process they use for spiritual realization is misdirected.

We should point out, however, that the Vedic literature establishes Lord Shiva as one of the topmost devotees of Lord Vishnu or Krishna. Shiva is often pictured in meditation, and many verses from the *Puranas* explain that he is always meditating on the Supreme, Sri Krishna. This means that Shiva is a Vaishnava. Furthermore, he is also one of the most important demigods in the universe. Therefore, as long as one understands Lord Shiva's real position and avoids the impersonalistic philosophy that most Shaivites follow, there certainly is no harm in worshiping or offering respects to Lord Shiva or visiting the temples dedicated to him. In this case, worshiping Lord Shiva is simply offering respects to a superior devotee of God.

SHAKTAS AND THE TANTRAS

Another form of worship that appeared was the Shakta cult. The original ideas of the Shakta belief can be traced back to the *Rig-veda* and other later works. The Shaktas are those who believe that the active and creative principle of existence is the divine energy called *shakti*. Shakti is the feminine energy inherent in everything throughout the universe and is oftentimes considered the companion of Lord Shiva in her personified form. However, to consider that Shakti or energy alone can be the independent cause of the world is a faulty understanding. The reason is that energy alone cannot create without the cooperation and direction of the energetic, which, in this case, is the Supreme.

The Supreme is the energetic or source and controller of the energy, just as the powerhouse is the source of the electrical energy that is controlled to illuminate so many light bulbs. Thus, energy cannot exist without the energetic. Therefore, the followers of the Shakti cult who have imagined that energy is the cause of the world are not supported by Vedic authority. It is not possible that merely by energy all the elements of the universe can be produced. In the same manner, we do not see a woman produce children without the contact of a man. Only through the energy given by the seed of a man can there be conception in a woman. Similarly, only if Shakti or nature is controlled and directed by the contact of the *purusha*, God, can there be the organized formation of the material elements. In this way, everything proceeds from the Supreme Being, as explained in the Vedic literature, and Shakti is not independent.

The Shaktas are divided into two groups, one called the Right-hand, the other called the Left-hand group. The Right-hand or *dakshinacara* are the ascetic group, while the Left-hand or *vamacara* are those who combine their yogic practices with wine drinking, meat-eating, ritual songs, and sex. In most cases, the drinking of wine, eating meat, and sexual activities are meant to be used as part of a sacrificial ritual used in the worship of goddess Kali or Durga.

The *Tantras* are the texts studied by those, especially amongst the Shaiva and Tibetan Buddhist Vajrayana cults, that worship Goddess Shakti, the personification of the universal feminine energy. Scholars have not been able to determine whether Tantrism originated in Buddhism or Hinduism, but evidence suggests that Tantrism was first systematized by particular Buddhist schools. This systematization seemed to have resulted in dividing Buddhism into several major and minor groups because of philosophical differences. All such groups assisted in laying the groundwork for various radical ideas, among which was Tantrism. Tantrism greatly influenced the Vajrayana and Mahayana sects.

The *Tantras* generally accept Shakti as the creative force, worshipable as an aspect of the Divine but inseparable from the masculine principle, which is called Brahman by some and Shiva by others. Tantraism is linked with yoga and the magical formulas of the *Atharva-veda*. The ascetic process of the Tantric path is very similar to the *raja-yoga* and *kundalini-yoga* systems. But before going on to the advanced stages, one must perfect the basics, such as simplicity, kindness, devotion, prayer, and self-analysis, along with the *yama* and *niyama* principles as described in *raja-yoga*. However, the *Tantras*, in order to allow only the initiates to understand its meaning, used much erotic symbolism and esoteric terminology. This has led to a misunderstanding of its ideology as well as of its practices.

Tantra is a path meant to utilize all the sciences to develop psychic power, understand reality, and expand one's awareness in all states of consciousness. In this way, all levels of consciousness are to be explored by performing various kinds of exercises and techniques. However, the training and procedures that some Tantric yogis may have to do as a sign of advancement can be a dreadful experience for one who is psychologically unprepared. Detachment from the body and advancement on the path is attained by the performance of what most people would consider unusual if not bizarre practices. In Tantrism, particularly the Left-hand path, progress and liberation are achieved primarily through direct experience rather than through meditation. Once the Tantric yogi has mastered all the basic requisites of yoga, such as the sitting postures, controlling his external and internal organs, and keeping his mind from all material attractions and repulsions, then he can continue with more arduous austerities. He may be instructed to go to the cremation grounds and search through the ashes to find and eat particular parts of a corpse which do not burn. He must do this without the slightest disgust. He may also make a human skull into his eating bowl, or the top of a monkey skull as a drinking cup. The human thigh bone is also often used as a horn for calling spirits.

Some of the Tantric followers also practice magic and alchemy in their techniques. It is well known that Tantrics who know the art of magic can possess amazing but dark powers. The apparel of such sorcerers usually include items like flayed animal or human skin as coverings, necklaces of teeth or bone, a girdle of snakeskin, and they sometimes cover themselves with the ashes of cremated bodies or the dirt from an exhumed corpse. Elements used in their rituals may consist of charred bones, eyeballs, fat, marrow, and even excrement from corpses, along with *mantras* addressed to demons and ghouls. With such items they perform ceremonies such as the black ritual that is a secret and dangerous short path to attaining occult power. One ritual in Tibetan is called the *chod*, in which the Tantric practitioner goes to the crematorium and invites spirits to feast on his body, which symbolizes destruction of ego, pride, selfishness, fear, etc. After the spirits have dined and departed, the Tantric, recovering from the ordeal, mentally reassembles his bones and organs until he is whole again. Another aspect of this black ritual is known in Tibet as *rolangs*, in which the Tantric, through occult powers, animates a dead corpse by calling spirits to possess it and then asks it questions or uses it for magical purposes.

If the yogi remains sane and continues on the Left-hand Shakta or Tantric path, he may also try to perform the sex ritual. In this case, the Tantric yogi worships the woman as a representation of Shakti and accepts the role as Shiva and has intercourse with her, but does not ejaculate any semen. The tantric controls his mind and senses, and during intercourse constricts his stomach muscles in particular ways so that he takes in the fluid and energy released by the woman. Thus, he keeps the combination of his male energy and the female energy at the base of his spine. By combining the male and female energy in such a way, the practitioner is said to get special power and enlightenment. This is also supposed to help awaken the *kundalini* at the base of the spine when it is time for the yogi to begin meditation. However, some descriptions of these sex practices are very strange, and the texts that describe them are quite graphic. It has also been said that even Marco Polo, while witnessing these Tantric practices and acts of sorcery during his explorations of the world, did not consider it fit to give a full account of what he saw. This, however, is only one aspect of the Tantric cult. Other techniques include *mantra, pranayama,* meditation, etc.

Now in the West people use certain Tantric practices as an excuse to simply engage in sex in the name of so-called religion or yoga. Although they hardly know anything about the real Tantric practices or bother to reach any of the initial yogic qualifications one must attain, they are very eager to engage in so-called Tantric sex with the hopes of increasing the duration of their orgasm. This, however, was the exact opposite of the real purpose of the ritual. Extended orgasm is considered to deplete the yogi of his mystic powers and mental and psychic capacity. Even Buddhist texts mention that keeping the seed (semen) is life, while the falling of the seed is death. In this way, by retaining one's semen, a man can become very powerful.

There are, however, different *Tantras* for different people. There are specific *Tantras* for those who are in the mode of darkness (as described above), those in the mode of passion, and those in the mode of goodness. There are the Shaiva *Agamas*, the Shakta *Agamas*, and the later Tibetan Buddhist *Agamas*, as well as the *Linga, Kalika,* and *Devi Puranas.* The *Agamas* are divided in four parts: metaphysical knowledge, yoga, ritual practices, and conduct. There are also the Vaishnava *Tantras,* which include the *Narada-pancaratra, Pancaratra,* and *Vaikhanasa.* These contain rules and regulations for engaging in the process for purifying the mind of the stumbling blocks of material attachments and for fixing the consciousness on the qualities and spiritual pastimes of the Supreme.

The difference in the Vaishnava *Tantras* from the *Tantras* of the Left-hand Shaktas is that they remove the illusion that the physical body is the self, while the Left-hand Shaktas are attached to magical powers, wealth, high position, or quick liberation. To be successful on the Left-hand path is very difficult and the aspirant can rarely persevere to the end. As we can easily see from our partial description of the Tantric Left-hand path, such philosophy and activities are deeply imbedded in the mode of darkness. By tampering with this path, one usually increases his illusion, selfishness, pride, or it can bring disease, evil-mindedness, insanity, and sometimes sudden death. This is not surprising since whatever is associated with the dark modes produces dark results.

The Vaishnava *Tantras,* on the other hand, brings one to a higher state of being, a loftier awareness of our real identity and our relationship with God. It enables one to feel an inner joy and happiness. Soon the obstacles that seemed insurmountable have no effect. A serious follower can feel himself progressing very rapidly. As he attains a higher spiritual taste, he becomes less concerned for bodily attractions and is content in any situation, whether it be in gain or in loss. His unity with God increases and he becomes perfectly satisfied. In this way, he soon leaves material consciousness behind and through his spiritual realizations reaches the perfectional stage of life.

SIKHISM

Sikhism now has about thirteen million followers. The word "Sikh" is derived from the Sanskrit word *shishya*, meaning "disciple." This signified that a Sikh lives a life of continued learning and practice of moral values and virtue in everyday life for spiritual development. Qualities like honesty, compassion, generosity, patience, humility, etc,. are integral in the life of a Sikh.

Sikhism started with the intention of harmonizing Islam and Hinduism. The founder of Sikhism was Guru Nanak (1469-1539 A.D.) who was born in a *kshatriya* family in rural Punjab in a town now called Nankana Sahib southwest of Lahore. There he grew up, married at the age of 14, and had two sons. Thereafter he moved to Sultanpur. Near the year 1500, he had a vision of God. In this vision, God told him to chant His name, cause others to repeat it, practice charity, perform worship, and meditate. Guru Nanak would be the guru of those who followed these instructions. Thus, from this vision, Sikhism began as Guru Nanak became a wandering mendicant, traveling throughout India, chanting the names of God, and teaching those who became his followers. Later, a piece of land along the Ravi River was donated to him where he started the village of Kartarpur, which is also where he died.

Guru Nanak taught strict monotheism and rejected idols and incarnations of the Divine, yet retained the principle of reincarnation of the living entity. The religion also rejects hypocrisy, the eating of meat, the performance of austerities, fasting, pilgrimages, rituals, as well as the use of intoxicants like tobacco, wine, and drugs. The religion rejects all forms of caste and proclaims that God is the Father of all and that mankind is a universal brotherhood. Sikhism also gives equal status to women. During the time of Guru Nanak womanhood was considered a low position of life. But the Sikh gurus gave women social equality and religious freedom, allowing them to participate fully in the religious functions.

Guru Nanak believed in the fundamental spiritual truths of all religions and stressed spiritual discipline, loyalty to Sikhism, gratitude, impartiality, honesty, compassion, generosity, humility, and meditation as a means of advancement. He also taught the unity that both Muslims and Hindus shared under the one true God, and that by chanting and hearing God's names people could become free from sin and purify the mind and attain enlightenment.

His conception of God was taken from Islam as a Being who created all, one without a second, who is not subject to time, space, cause, and effect. God is the Creator, Sustainer, and Destoyer of the universe. Guru Nanak also accepted the Vedic conception that God created *maya*, illusion, and that illusions cause the false notion of one's separateness from God. Guru Nanak felt that the mystery of God could not be fathomed by the mind of man, but enlightenment in this regard could be attained by cutting through one's imaginary separateness from God and understanding that man is fully dependent on God. Although God is unknowable in His completeness, God can still be perceived by the limited mind of one who is spiritually awakened. Through inward meditation one can understand that God is present everywhere in all creation. Through this perception, one can determine what is reality and what in this world is *maya*, unreality. Those who seek fulfillment in worldly pleasures are victims of *maya* and bound to the cycle of repeated birth and death. Therefore, man is responsible for his actions and must be vigilant in what he does. But by perceiving the divine nature that exists within the universe and striving to work in harmony with it can bring salvation. Then one can reach his true position in glorifying God's name and rendering service to God. This is the goal of Sikhism.

The Sikh process for salvation is a devotional discipline meant to be engaged within oneself, not through external processes such as temple worship, pilgrimages, asceticism, etc. And when the soul attains mystical union with God, blissful salvation is reached. Thus, one's attitude toward God should be devotional rather than simply submissive in the way the Muslims are in their awe and reverence toward God. The devotional process in Sikhism is the harmonizing of one's consciousness with the sacred syllable or divine name of God through meditation and chanting. The name of God is considered unimportant, whether it be Shiva or Allah, yet Nanak settled for Sat Nam, which is not really a name of God but simply means True Name.

Guru Nanak was followed by nine other gurus. The second guru was Angad Dev, a most obedient follower of Guru Nanak who spent much of his time wandering and preaching. Angad created a modification of the Punjabi alphabet that was used for the transcriptions of Guru Nanak's hymns and the beginning of the Sikh sacred literature. Angad died in 1552 and appointed Amar Das as his successor.

Amar Das was a serious propagator of Sikhism and was greatly respected by Emperor Akbar. He created the foundation of the great lake, called Amritsar (Lake of Nectar). He was followed by his son-in-law, Guru Ram Das, who continued the work on the lake and laid the foundation of the Golden Temple. Ram Das died in 1581 and chose one of his sons as his successor.

Guru Arjan Dev, the youngest son of Ram Das, was the fifth Sikh guru. He developed Amritsar as the center of Sikh culture, and in 1603 and 1604 collected the hymns of the first four gurus and various Muslim and Hindu saints, along with some of his own hymns, and compiled the *Adi Granth*, the original Sikh scripture. Arjan Dev was a highly influential man, but his prestige roused the jealousy of the Muslim Emperor Jehangir, the son of the tolerant Emperor Akbar. Jehangir summoned Arjan Dev to Delhi and ordered him to remove particular verses from the *Granth*. Arjan refused and was placed under the charge of Chandu, who tortured the guru by pouring boiling water and hot sand on him, causing Arjan Dev to die the death of a martyr in 1606.

Guru Hargobind was the sixth guru, and surrounded himself with bodyguards and ordered the use of weapons for his followers. He was guru for 39 years and died in 1645. His son, Guru Har Rai, followed him and upheld the Sikh cause for 16 years, and died in 1661. Har Rai's eldest son was a prisoner of the Emperor, so Harkrishan Ji, a boy of only five years, became the next guru, but he died of smallpox only three years later. So Harkrishan's great uncle, Teg Bahadur Ji, was then persuaded to accept the position as the ninth guru. He was a courageous man for his old age and criticized the persecutions of the Hindus by the cruel Emperor Aurangzeb. The guru was then summoned to Delhi and imprisoned. He was offered freedom if he converted to Islam, but he refused and in 1675 was martyred by the Muslims in public where now stands the Gurdwara Sis Ganj Sahib on Chandi Chowk Road in Delhi. The story is that some Kashmiri Hindus who had been told to accept Islam came to Teg Bahadur for help, and he agreed. The Hindus sent a message to the Emperor that if Teg Bahadur accepted Islam they would follow. So the Muslims asked him to accept Islam or show a miracle. Teg Bahadur refused to do either since he felt a forceful change of religion was a direct interference with one's life, and showing one's supremacy over others by a display of a miracle would be against the wishes of God. Thus, he gave his life for the preservation of Hinduism. Thereafter the military spirit of the Sikhs became even more prominent.

The tenth and last guru was Govind Singh (1666-1708) who was installed as guru at the age of nine years soon after the death of his father, Teg Bahadur. He realized that difficult times were ahead, especially in regard to the Moghul imperialism. Therefore, he began training his disciples in the art of warfare. In this way, Govind Singh diverted from the original pacifistic idealism of Sikhism and created a warrior fraternity. But the militarization of the Sikhs was for self-protection and to oppose Islam, not for conquering people or forcing the expansion of Sikhism. Govind Singh also introduced the Sikh practices of wearing a turban and never cutting the hair. He was a patriot who opposed the tyranny and fanaticism of the Muslim Aurangzeb. In fact, his victories in the battles of Bhangani in 1687 and Nadaun in 1689 undermined the power of the hill Rajas and the Moghuls. Even his four sons and mother died for the sake of upholding religious freedom.

The Sikhs later moved to the Punjab after conflicts with the British and fought a fierce war there with the Muslims. Soon afterward as many as two and a half million Sikhs moved from East Punjab to West Punjab in India.

Govind Singh established the Khalsa in 1699 in order to bring Sikhs into a tighter organization. He also made the Sikh scripture, the *Granth*, the eternal guru of the Sikhs in 1708, which was set in the center of the Golden Temple. Thus, no longer is there a place for a living guru in Sikhism. The *Granth* is a compilation of 5894 instructional hymns consisting of writings by the first five Sikh gurus, such as Guru Amar Das, Guru Ram Das, Guru Teg Bahadur, with as many as 2216 of the hymns contributed by Arjan Dev. There are 937 hymns by Muslim and Hindu saints like Kabir, Namdev, and Ravidas. Thus, the *Granth* is an attempt to be the scripture for all nations.

In daily practice, passages from the *Granth* are recited after one's morning bath, or the family may gather in the morning to read verses from the *Granth*. There may be temple worship consisting primarily of singing passages from the *Granth*, which everyone does together at certain appointed times. The Sikhs are friendly and allow everyone of any faith to visit their temples.

Sikhism believes that family life is no barrier to salvation, and that it is possible to live amidst the world's problems and temptations and remain detached. But man is responsible for his actions and their results; so, he must be vigilant in what he does. In this way, the goal of life is God-realization by following the teachings of the guru, which is the *Granth*, and by performing acts of charity, and by meditation of the holy name of God.

One requirement to be a Sikh is surrender and devotion to guru and God. Death in the service of truth, justice, and country is considered a part of their character. The Sikhs believe in democracy, but they also feel man's duty to society is to help the less fortunate through acts of charity.

Sikh baptism, called *Amrit*, is the ceremony wherein those accepting Sikhism are given a new name ending with "Singh" for males, and "Kaur" for females. Being baptized means following the Khalsa discipline, which has specific rules. These include: (1) belief in one God, ten gurus, and the *Granth*; (2) acceptance of the *Mul-mantra* of the *Granth* as the basic creed; (3) daily recitation of the morning and evening prayers; (4) maintenance of the five symbols, which are not cutting the hair, keeping the comb for the hair, wearing of the knickers, the possession of the sword, and wearing the iron bracelet; (5) no plundering or exploiting of the poor; (6) no coveting of another's spouse or wealth; (7) no use of intoxicants like drugs, alcohol, tobacco, etc.; (8) no violation of these codes, nor eating of meat or committing adultery, (otherwise one becomes fallen and must do penance and take baptism again); (9) performance of only Sikh ceremonies at the time of birth, weddings, or death; (10) no worship of images, graves, ancestors, etc.

Some Sikhs follow these rules more strictly than others, and some claim to be Sikhs without taking baptism. Younger Sikhs, especially those living outside India, are more inclined not to follow all these rules strictly nor to wear the external symbols of Sikhism. And although Sikh scripture advocates a vegetarian diet, because of Muslim influence many Sikhs no longer strictly observe it.

Sikhism basically started as a reform movement to correct various social injustices of the time. It also tried to unite various Muslim and Vedic principles, but it is not considered Vedic. In fact, Sikhism rejects some of the basic Vedic principles, such as God being able to incarnate and appear within this world to re-establish principles of religion when need be. Certainly God can appear as often as He likes to guide society at large and protect His devotees. Yet Sikhs reject this but still keep the idea of reincarnation for the individual soul. How can the infinitesimal soul do something that God cannot? This is not very good logic. This is certainly an aspect of limiting and misunderstanding the infinite potency of the Supreme. Although there are many positive points about the Sikh religion--and it certainly advocates a devotional process similar to the Vedic teachings--but this uncertainty about the nature of the Supreme shows the defects a religion or philosophy can have if it originates from a religious leader who has not fulfilled the necessary requirements of complete spiritual development and full realization.

This issue may be considered a small point of controversy for some people. After all, Sikhism stresses the importance of the chanting and praising of God's name, which is especially recommended in the Vedic literature and in many other religions as the essential process for God-realization in this age. But the very fact that God has a name means that God must be personal, with a form that can appear whenever and wherever God wants. But Sikhism, by eliminating the worship of the Deity form of God, also de-emphasizes the personal aspect of the Supreme and presents no clear understanding of God's personal nature in its philosophy. And Guru Nanak was not clear on what the real names of God are or what name to use for chanting. He simply chose Sat Nam, meaning True Name, which is not really a name of God at all but merely a title. Therefore, the words Sat Nam offer the chanter little if any spiritual benefit, although the process may help one think of God in a devotional mood. And Guru Nanak's view that the name itself made little difference, whether Shiva, Allah, or whatever, shows that he was swayed toward impersonalism. Therefore, we can see that Sikhism, though preserving many principles that people should endeavor to maintain, still may not be a complete path for attaining a full understanding of the Absolute Truth.

From this chapter we can understand that many of the philosophies of the East are based on or have their roots within some part of the Vedic scripture. No matter whether it is the idea of complete materialism as with the Carvaka philosophy, which is mentioned in the *Rig-veda*, or the philosophy of Buddhism, as is mentioned in the *Nasadiya-sukta* of the *Rig-veda*. The Vedic literature may at first dicuss many kinds of viewpoints, but ultimately Vedanta reaches the conclusion that *bhakti*, devotional service, is the most dependable and direct means of attaining the fullest realization of the Absolute Truth.

CHAPTER FIVE

Other Major Religions of the World

Other religions of the East have also affected and influenced the lives of many people, both past and present, in India and elsewhere. It is important to review some of these major religions to not only understand the other spiritual paths one might participate in and what the goal is of these paths, but also to get a view of how they appeared in the world and what is the basis of their authority.

ZOROASTRIANISM

Zoroastrianism is a religion that still has some effect in the East, although it is slowly diminishing. It was started by Zoroaster, but there were three men known as Zoroaster. The first, said to have lived about 7000 years ago, was a Sumerian philosopher who combined all the traditions of the sun worshiping cultures that had existed four to five thousand years earlier. The second Zoroaster (Zoroaster Spitama) lived 2000 to 3000 years later and is said to have been a Persian teacher who wrote a volume that explained all the traditions the first Zoroaster had taught. The third Zoroaster, also called Zarathustra (his Persian or Iranian name), was born in Afghanistan and lived from 628 to 551 B.C. Some scholars say he lived around 1200 B.C., but most acknowledge that certainty of dates is impossible. In any case, he is the one who actually started Zoroastrianism by bringing together the same teachings of the previous Zoroasters in the form of what is now the *Zend Avesta*.

He began preaching in northeast Iran after he had a vision on a mountain top of a great being of light who told him to give the people a new religion based on good thoughts, good words, and good deeds. His preaching at first aroused anger toward him so that he had to flee his homeland. However, he did find one follower, Vishtaspa, who was a local ruler that allowed Zoroaster to

70

become somewhat influential. It is said that Zoroaster had married and begot two sons and one daughter. While in his seventies, he was murdered.

Zoroaster felt he should help deliver society. He had many spiritual visions and felt he was directly conferring with God. He thought that the end of the last period was upon earth and that he and his followers might see the end of the devil and attain the kingdom of God.

This religion espoused the idea that God, Ahura Mazda, the god of light, is the all-good and wise creator of all things. There is no evil in God. All evil is because of the devil who has always existed. The devil, in Zoroastrianism, is not presented as having a physical form, but remains as a force which attempts to destroy the work of God. This force, however, is called Ahriman or Angra Mainyu and is also depicted as a personality who, during creation, breaks through the sky and descends to earth to spread disease and death to the created beings. The universe was created with virtue and good, but Angra Mainyu, a god of darkness and corruption, brings in evil and malice. The first man, Gayomat, was swayed by Angra Mainyu towards darkness; thus, mankind has a fallen tendency which must be avoided. God has a host of helpers, holy ones, who do His bidding, and so does the devil.

In Zoroastrian tradition, the history of the world is the story of God's conflict with the devil and is divided into four periods of three thousand years each. In the first two periods the forces of good and evil, God and the devil, increase. There is conflict between them in the third period, and then in the final age, Saoshyant, the incarnation of the prophet Zarathustra will again be born of a virgin and battle and destroy the lord of darkness, Angra Mainyu, and his influence. The universe will be restored to the nature of light and goodness, and the dead will be resurrected as radiant beings.

The idea of a devil or Satan, the prince of darkness, does not appear before this time in any other religion. There may have been gods or spirits who roamed the earth and were known for their evil intent or were considered inauspicious, but there was no ultimate devil. So this concept of a devil or Satan seems to have originated in Persia, possibly with Zoroastrianism, and later developed into the concept we see today, especially as found in Christianity, Judaism, and Islam. In Judaism, Satan was introduced to help explain evil and the fallen condition of man after being tempted by the devil in the garden of Eden. But could this God, in the Jewish conception, not have given man more sense to avoid these temptations, or simply forgive him for his mistake if God is so all-loving and powerful, and rightly put the blame on the devil? Evidently not, because we are told that Adam and Eve were deceived by this devil and were then forced to leave the garden. And now we are still paying for their mistake by having to sweat and toil for our survival, all because of this devil.

In Christianity, the devil is depicted as a fallen angel who is the cause of evil. But there is no explanation of where evil first arose. How could God create a being that would become the source of evil and ruin? Or does God have limited power over the creatures He creates? Otherwise, why should the all-powerful Jewish, Christian, or Islamic God not be able to do away with this devil and get him out of the way? We fallen humans have enough trouble as it is without some devil on the loose making things worse, or creating temptations that cause us to go to hell. Actually, this concept of the devil simply shows the faulty understanding people have of God's real position. It displays the imagination the Zoroastrians had for their legends and theology, and shows that they were not spiritually self-realized. Nonetheless, this faulty concept of a powerful deity of evil fighting with a God who has limited power over His creation was adopted by Judaism, Christianity, and Islam.

Zoroastrians feel that the body and soul are united and that the world is God's world, good and just, and that men should work rightly and enjoy life and help others. Death is considered the work of the devil and a corpse is an abode for demons. To bury or burn the body would contaminate the elements, so it is taken to the "Towers of Silence" where it is eaten by vultures. Fire is considered the son and symbol of God; so, many ceremonies include fire. Their basic religious principles are good thoughts, words, and deeds.

The *Zend Avesta* explains how the 16 forces of good are created by Ahura Mazda, which form the Kingdom of Light, and how the 16 forces of darkness are created by Ahriman. By following the process of good words, good deeds, and good thoughts, a person can work in harmony with the forces of good and avoid the forces of darkness. At death every thought, word and deed are weighed in the balance to see if good outweighs the bad. If it does, the person passes into heaven; otherwise, one enters hell for a fitting punishment, which a person creates by his own evil deeds. But hell is not eternal. After being reformed in hell, a person will be able to face the final judgement day when all entities will become pure and worship and live with God in His creation, while the devil and his influence will be completely destroyed.

The majority of the Zoroastrian scripture, the *Zend Avesta*, had been burned by Alexander in the fourth century B.C. During the Mohammedan book burnings in the tenth century, more of the scripture disappeared. From what was left, the present *Avesta* was put together and consists of the *Gathas*, songs of Zoroaster; *Vispered*, rituals; *Yashta*, the hymns of the angels; *Vendidad*, the story of creation; and the *Khorda Avesta*, a compilation of short prayers.

The Zoroastrian beliefs that include such concepts as the devil, hell, the resurrection of the body, afterlife, and the end of the world, are thought by many biblical scholars to have strongly influenced the development of Judeo-Christian beliefs, which included or adopted many of these concepts. Other aspects of Zoroastrianism that were adopted by these religions are the emphasis on man's free will to choose between right and wrong in a single life on earth, and the final judgement after death in which the good and the sinful are separated for either punishment in hell or bliss in heaven.

At one time Zoroastrianism was found in an area from the Mediterranean to India, but now it is primarily located in scattered parts of Iran, Pakistan, and India. There are only about 125,000 Zoroastrians at present. In India, they are called Parsis because after being persecuted in Persia, many of them fled to India from the province of Pars. They are now primarily located near Bombay.

JUDAISM

Judaism is said to have originated with a compact between God and Abraham. This began in the city of Ur, where the nomadic tribes that had captured the town from the Sumerians worshiped nature spirits and made many deities of them in their temples. Terah, a man who made such deities, had a son, Abraham, who had many dreams and visions that made him feel that deity worship was wrong. So he would smash the deities his father made. He also had a dream in which God instructed him to take his people west to Canaan, which he did around 2100 B.C. when they began many years of wandering. This is described in *Genesis*, Chapter 12, in which God instructs Abraham to leave his father's house and go to the land God would show him, and He would make him a great nation and bless him. However, there have been some doubts amongst scholars as to whether Abraham was actually a historical figure or simply a character in the Jewish myths.

Some of the stories in the Old Testament relate some rather strange qualities of the Jewish patriarchs. For example, in *Genesis*, Chapter 12, when Abraham entered Egypt he was afraid the Pharaoh would kill him because of his beautiful wife, Sar'ai. So he tells the Pharaoh that Sar'ai is his sister, and the Pharaoh takes Sar'ai into his house as his wife. To close the deal for taking Sar'ai, the Pharaoh gives Abraham sheep, oxen, asses, men-servants, maid-servants, and camels. So now Abraham is quite wealthy. But God becomes angry, not at Abraham for deceiving the Pharaoh, but at the Pharaoh for taking Abraham's wife. So God sends great plagues onto the house of the Pharaoh who then realizes what he has done and asks Abraham why he lied to him about Sar'ai. So the Pharaoh sends them on their way. If Abraham was afraid the Pharaoh was going to kill him, this would have been the time the Pharaoh's anger should have been aroused.

The strange thing is that Abraham does the same thing in *Genesis*, Chapter 20. Abraham, who is now 100 years old, tells Abim'elech, the king of Gerar, that Sar'ai, who is now called Sarah and is 90 years old, is his sister. Then Abim'elech takes her into his place. Fortunately, he does not touch her, but the biblical God becomes angry at Abim'elech and tells him he is a dead man for having taken the wife of another and to give her back to Abraham. Abim'elech does so and asks Abraham why he did this to him, "What were you thinking of that you did this thing to me?" Abraham explains that for some odd reason he thought he would be killed on account of his wife, and that, indeed, Sarah is his half-sister, the daughter of Abraham's father, but not of his mother.

Now this is another odd thing because in *Leviticus* (20.17) we find that God explains to Moses that if a man takes his sister, a daughter of his father or mother, and sees her nakedness, it is a shameful thing, and they shall be cut off from their people and he shall bear his iniquity. So this is a very shameful thing in the eyes of God, but Abraham not only got away with it, he also sold, more or less, his wife to other men for a very nice profit. In this case, Abim'elech gave Abraham sheep, oxen, male and female slaves, and a thousand pieces of silver, and sent them on their way. And still this God was pleased with Abraham. Now what kind of standard is this?

Furthermore, when Isaac lived in Gerar, he also told the people that his wife, Rebekah, was his sister. But King Abim'elech could tell by the way the two were acting that Rebekah was Isaac's wife. So he scolded Isaac for having said she was his sister since someone may have lain with her and brought guilt upon the people of Gerar.

In *Genesis*, Chapter 19, we find that when Lot traveled to the city of Sodom, many men came from the city to the house of Lot and surrounded it and asked Lot to bring out the men who came with him so they could *know* them. But Lot replied that they should not act so wickedly, and that he had two virgin daughters that he would bring out for them to do as they pleased with if they would leave the men of his family alone. Now this is a very strange situation. After all, what kind of father would send his two young daughters out to take their chances with a mob of sexual deviants? If Lot had any heroism or good qualities, he and the men with him would have done whatever they could to protect the women. It seems that women were not very much valued by the early Jewish men. But the men always seemed to have women if they wanted them. Even after Sarah died, Abraham, who was very old at the time, took many wives and concubines and had many sons by them.

In the *Second Book of Samuel*, Chapter 11, we find that King David also had a lust for women. On one occasion after he had sent many of his troops to engage in war with the Ammonites, he was on the roof of his house and saw a beautiful woman taking a bath. Being attracted to her, he sent for her and lay with her, even though he knew she was Bathsheba, the wife of Uriah the Hittite who was off fighting in David's war. After their union, Bathsheba became pregnant and David conspired to hide his crime. He called Uriah from the war and encouraged him to go home to the comforts of his wife, then Uriah would think he made Bathsheba pregnant. But due to his feelings of loyalty to his king, Uriah slept on the steps of David's house. Even after David got Uriah drunk, Uriah would not go home. So the next morning David sent Uriah back to the war with a note to his commander, Joab, which contained instructions from David to send Uriah to the forefront of the hardest fighting so he will surely die. In this way, the great King David had his loyal and faithful servant killed in battle to hide the crime of adultery that he committed with Uriah's wife.

Thereafter, David took Bathsheba as his wife which displeased the Lord, but the only thing He did to punish David was to cause the new son of Bathsheba to die, although in *Leviticus* (20.10) it states that a man who commits adultery shall be put to death. But David simply went on with his life and again laid with Bathsheba who became pregnant with Solomon.

King Solomon was known for his vast riches and wisdom, but he was also a lover of many women. *The First Book of Kings*, Chapter 11, describes how he had many foreign women for his wives, including the daughter of the Pharaoh, and Moabite, Ammonite, Edomite, Sidonian, and Hittite women, even though the Jewish God had ordered that they (the Jewish people) must not enter into marriage with foreign women because they would come to worship foreign gods. Anyway, Solomon went on to collect 700 wives and 300 concubines.

According to tradition, the beginning of the Jewish nation started with Abraham who had a son, Isaac, who also had a son, Jacob. It is said that God appeared to Isaac as well as Jacob and gave Jacob the name Israel and told him to give up all strange gods. Jacob, or Israel, had twelve sons whose names were the names of the twelve tribes of Israel. The word *Judah*, from which came the name *Judaism*, originally comes from the name of Jacob's fourth son. Judaism later meant those people who lived in the southern half of Palestine when it was divided into the two kingdoms of Judah and Israel. After some time, Judaism was known as the faith of all who worshiped Yahweh or Jehovah.

It is said that when the first Jewish people went south to Egypt to live in Goshen for 400 years, they greatly multiplied. They kept to themselves, but the Egyptians became fearful of their growing population and enslaved them. Nonetheless, they continued to multiply until one Pharaoh, trying to curb this growth, ordered that the oldest male child of each family should be cast into the Nile. It was during this time that one Hebrew woman placed her son in a small reed basket and let it float down the river. The daughter of the Pharaoh found and adopted the baby, naming him Moses.

Moses lived in the palace for 40 years, learning the highly regarded wisdom of Egypt. But after killing an Egyptian in a fit of rage, he fled to the desert. After 40 years of living as a shepherd, it is said that he saw God as a burning bush who instructed him to deliver his people from Egyptian slavery and take them to the promised land of Canaan after leaving Egypt. It took another 40 years of wandering before they returned to Canaan to capture the land from the Semite people who were living there.

As the Jewish people traveled to Canaan, they conquered and killed many people in the cities they encountered. The reason is that they felt they had a God-given right to do so, as explained in *Deuteronomy* (20.10-18) where the Jewish God instructed that when they came near a city they should offer terms of peace, and if the people accept, then the Jews could put the people to forced labor. And if the people make war, then everyone should be killed except for the women and children, which could be enjoyed as the spoils of the enemy. Thus, they should utterly destroy the Hittites, Amorites, Perizzites, Hivites, Jebusites, and Canaanites. Even after the Jewish people had settled, they waged war and killed many others amongst the neighboring cultures while their nation expanded.

Moses also gave the quarreling Jewish people the God-given law that he received on Mount Sinai. This is one of the most significant incidents in Jewish history. The Jews feel that since God revealed His law to them through Moses, they must be the chosen ones to play an important part in the coming of God's kingdom, which will be preceded by the arrival of a personal Messiah.

This written law forms the essence of the Hebrew Bible, which is a collection of books written over a period of 1,000 years, in which Judaism has its roots. The commandments are a part of the written law. We know the biblical story of how Moses went up to Mount Sinai and communed with God who appeared to him in the form of a great dark cloud that covered the Mount. It was there that God gave Moses the stone tablets that contained the commandments. However, the ten commandments that were traditionally given by God to Moses were in fact not given by God, but were simply a summary of laws that had been known in the area for years long before Moses' time. Although Hebrew tradition relates how Moses received the law from God on top of a mountain, this is said to have also happened to Zoroaster many years previous. Zoroaster had ernestly prayed on the mountain, was given enlightenment by God, and then descended with the book of law, which developed into the *Zend Avesta*. It is said that even Minos, the law-giver of the Cretans, climbed a mountain and received the law from Zeus. In fact, the proposal that the laws for mankind were given by God has been propagated in a variety of cultures in order to give them more authority. This is also seen with Mohammed, who said he was called by God to be the prophet for the Arabs and was given the *Koran* by mental telepathy, or by channeling the angel Gabriel and then writing what was said.

A vastly different description of how the Jewish law was originally developed is given in the *Book of Jasher*, a lost book of the Bible. Jasher was the son of Caleb, one of the close associates of Moses, who is said to have written a simple book that records many of the incidents that took place during the wanderings of the early Jewish people. The *Book of Jasher* is also mentioned in *Joshua* and *The Second Book of Samuel* in the Bible. Therefore, even though the *Book of Jasher* is not well-known, it has authority.

In the *Book of Jasher*, it is related that long before Moses went onto Mount Sinai he had a meeting with Jethro, his Midianite father-in-law, in which Jethro described the commandments for the people of Israel to follow and how they should be judged accordingly. Moses wrote down all these rules. When Moses wanted to establish these customs, he was met with resistance by Miriam, his sister, and the people who felt they did not need the customs of the Midianites. Moses became very angry with Miriam and had her arrested. But the people demanded that she be released.

Miriam had become highly respected by the people because it was she who found water for the tribes of Israel when they were dying of thirst during their sojourn from Egypt. The Bible describes how Moses struck a rock with his staff and the people drank the water that flowed from it, but in the *Book of Jasher* this does not occur. Instead, what is described is that Miriam discovered a spring under the shade of a tree. When Moses and a few others dug out the spring, it turned into a small rivulet leading them to a place where there were 12 wells. The people all went there and drank and praised Miriam for having found the water needed to refresh them.

So upon the demand of the people, Moses released Miriam after arresting her, but after some time she died and the people greatly mourned over her death. Then Jethro, seeing the opportunity, visited with Moses again because Moses could now carry out the intructions of Jethro without anyone's intervention. First, as Jethro had instructed him, Moses made the people of Israel choose 70 elders. Then he placed Aaron and Hur in charge of the people while he took Joshua, Nadab, Abihu, and the 70 elders up on Mount Sinai to stay for 40 days and nights. There he met Jethro who instructed Moses and the others how to build a tabernacle to their God and establish priests. Moses then decided to let Aaron and his sons, the Levites, be set aside as the priests of the tribes of Israel. During the remaining 40 days, Jethro, Moses, and the elders decided on all the statutes and ordinances that were to be observed. Then they wrote them all down in a book for remembrance.

During this time the people of Israel at the foot of the mount murmured against Moses, speculating that he was cunningly trying to set himself up as a king of all the people. Aaron sent messengers to Moses and the elders to tell them of this disturbance among the people. After hearing the news, Moses became very angry, sent the messengers away, and suggested to the elders that they tell the people that they had seen and communed with God on the mount and that the commandments are actually from God as He had spoken them. All the elders agreed to accept this plan except for Nadab and Abihu who were then cut off from the assembly and returned to the people below.

When Moses and the elders came down from the mount, they were greeted with rebellion. Then Moses met with Aaron to tell him that God had chosen Aaron and his sons to minister before the Lord in the tabernacle and that they should separate themselves from the rest of the people. The next day, Moses told the sons of Levi to take up swords and kill all those who were rebellious to Moses' plans. So they went through the camp and killed Nadab, Abihu, and another 3000 people. After the slaughter, the rest of the people became humble and promised to follow Moses.

Under Moses' instructions, a tabernacle was built and Aaron and his tribe were established as the priests. From the tabernacle Moses read the book of commandments before the congregation, saying that these were the laws given by God. In this way, many rules were given, prefixed with the words, "Thus saith the Lord." This was completely misleading and deceitful on the part of

Moses since most of the rules had originally been set forth by Jethro and then agreed upon by the council of elders. The group had not actually seen God on the mount, nor had there been a dark cloud that covered the mount, nor had God ever given Moses the commandments on a stone tablet as the Bible describes.

After Moses had established the priesthood in Aaron's house, Korah, Dathan, Abiram, On and 250 other renowned and respected men of the congregation objected to this. They asked why only the tribe of Levi should be favored with doing little work, being clothed in soft raiment, and eating sumptuously everyday from the remnants of the sacrifices. After all, were not all people holy? And should not all people help till the ground? So, the next day Moses ordered these men to appear before the tabernacle and then commanded the Levites to slay them with fire. Thus, all 250 respected men were burned to death in front of the tabernacle by the Levites, and because of this slaughter great fear fell on all of the people. This is the way Moses used force and fear to stabilize his rule. However, in the book of *Numbers* this incident has been written to describe that Korah, Dathan, Abiram, and their families were swallowed up by a pit that opened in the earth. After that it is explained that a fire came from the Lord that burned up the other 250 men. In this way, the Hebrew writers described the event to appear like a supernatural occurence.

Thereafter, according to Jasher, Moses established many types of animal sacrifices, saying that they were ordained by the authority of the Lord. Moses made it so that the sacrifices had to be performed by the people in order for them to become cleansed of various sins. Oxen, bulls, rams, and even doves would often be sacrificed to God in the tabernacle as a means of atonement. Even a woman who gave birth to a child was expected to offer a lamb for sacrifice in order to become cleansed. Of course, this is totally illogical when viewed with knowledge of *karma* and the soul. The killing of animals does not cleanse the soul, but only implicates one more deeply in sinful reactions. This only displays the ignorance of the customs and the mentality of the people, and how little they understood of anything really spiritual. Later, the Bible indicates that God condemned such sacrifices:

> To what purpose is the multitude of your sacrifices unto me? Saith the Lord: I am full of the burnt offerings of rams, and the fat of fed beasts; and I delight not in the blood of bullocks, or of lambs, or of goats. . . When ye spread forth your hands, I will hide Mine eyes from you: yea, when ye make many prayers, I will not hear, for your hands are full of blood. . . If ye be willing and obedient, ye shall eat the good of the land. But if ye refuse and rebel, ye shall be devoured with the sword: for the mouth of the Lord hath spoken it. (*Isaiah* 1.11,15,19-20)

The son of Shelomith, showing a little spiritual understanding, accused Moses in front of the congregation of misleading the people. He said all these sacrifices and things that Moses had established were not actually said by God, but were imaginations of evil. Moses obviously knew the man was correct, but, again calling on the Levites, Moses commanded that the son of Shelomith be taken from the camp and stoned to death, for the Lord hath spoken. And so they did. Obviously, Moses was not a man with much tolerance, nor did he exhibit much spiritual purity or any inclination for philosophical debate. Force was the medium by which Moses established himself as the voice of the Lord.

In any case, these are the stories that are provided about the characteristics and qualities of the original patriarchs of Jewish culture. And we can see that the *Book of Jasher* gives a very different perspective of how the sacrifices and commandments were established when compared with the description found in *Exodus* and *Leviticus*. If the *Book of Jasher* is correct, we can see how the rabbis who originally compiled the books that are attributed to Moses included many embellishments to make the Bible stories more extraordinary. And we can only guess how many other stories were also given special treatment to make it appear as if God had directly conferred with Moses or shown special favor when actually such incidents may never have taken place at all.

Another example of this is in the story of the exodus. In *Prickard's Historical Records*, it is explained how Choeremon the historian recorded that while the Jews were living in Goshen, Egypt was infested with a disease. In order for Egypt to be rid of this disease, using the advice of Phritiphantes the scribe, the Pharaoh had the Jews driven out of the country.

Further elaboration is given in S. F. Dunlap's *Vestiges of the Spirit History of Man*. It is said that the Jews hated and did not worship the Egyptian gods, and the Egyptian people considered the Jews to be dirty and unclean foreigners, which is, for all practical purposes, confirmed when one regards the laws given in *Leviticus*. But it is known that the Egyptians practiced a high level of cleanliness. The priests bathed every day, shaved their bodies, practiced circumcision, and wore clean white linen. They looked on the Jews as being worth only the most menial of tasks. Leprosy was rampant among the Jewish people, and the disease was considered to be displeasing to the Egyptian gods. So, the Oracle of Ammon ordered the Pharaoh to purify the land by driving the Jews out into the wilderness. The more noble of Jews are said to have followed Cadmus and Danaus to Greece, while the rest of them followed Moses to Palestine.

In *Exodus* we read how the Egyptian Pharaoh pursued Moses and his people out of Egypt to the sea where the water magically divided to let the Jews pass through. Then while the Egyptians were in the midst of the sea, the water came together to drown all the Egyptians. But, historically, there is no Egyptian record of any Pharaoh taking his army to chase after the Jews, nor of any Pharaoh drowning in the Red Sea. Neither is there any record of any Pharaoh killing all the eldest sons of the Jews while they were in Goshen. Such events surely would have been recorded somewhere if they had actually happened. But why would an army chase after a group of people who had been ordered to leave the country because they were considered dirty and diseased? Thus, it is quite unlikely that this episode happened the way the Hebrew writers depicted. Furthermore, the mummy of the Pharaoh who reigned during the Jewish captivity in Egypt, King Ramses II, the third king of the 19th dynasty, was found in a cave near Thebes in August of 1881 in a state of near perfect preservation. So, obviously, he did not drown in the Red Sea. Therefore, the stories in *Exodus* must have been written in a way that would fit more closely with other extraordinary legends that the writers wanted to include in their scripture. After all, it is known amongst those who have studied the history of Jewish religion that the Hebrew writers borrowed from many traditions and legends of neighboring cultures.

For example, in *Exodus* it is described how Moses performed many miracles. But many of these are the same as those of Bacchus, one of the early Greek gods who is described in the hymns of Orpheus, the earliest of Greek poets. Bacchus also had a staff which could change into a serpent. He also passed through the Red Sea without getting wet. He also drew water by hitting a rock with his staff, and he was led by a light during the night, similar to the pillar of fire that is said to have led Moses and his people. Bacchus was also the law-giver of his people and the laws were written on two tables of stone, just as it is said to have happened later on with Moses. And as a bably, Bacchus was also put into a boat on a river and was discovered by a woman who adpoted him. Thus, there are significant parallels between the early legends of Bacchus and Moses which could not be merely coincidental.

Another legend was that of the great flood with Noah and his ark, which was supposed to have taken place near 2348 B.C., although histories of that period in Egypt and elsewhere make no mention of any great flood. The biblical flood was copied by the Hebrews from the Chaldean version, as was written by Berosus, the Chaldean historian, with the later biblical version having only a few differences. The Hebrews did the same with the story of the creation. The account of the creation found in *Genesis* is very similar to not only that described in the *Zend Avesta* of Zoroastrianism, but also to the Etruscan and Persian legends, as well as the Babylonian legend of creation which existed 1,500 years before the Hebrew version. Without such duplicating, the Jews were bereft of these histories in their own tradition.

Although the Pentateuch is often referred to as being written by Moses (consisting of *Genesis, Exodus, Leviticus, Numbers,* and *Deuteronomy*), Moses actually had little to do with its writing, especially its present form. Though Moses was Hebrew he had been raised as an Egyptian in his youth and was known to have been an adept in the ancient Egyptian mysteries. It is said that he used Egyptian hieroglyphics when he wrote the original portions of the Pentateuch, but the meaning of the hieroglyphs was soon lost. So when the Jews first compiled the Pentateuch and needed to translate it into Hebrew, it was an almost impossible task. Many errors were made, not only in the translation but also in the attempt to understand the highly esoteric meaning of the message itself. Thus, many things that were expressed in the language of the adepts, which the Jews were not, were misunderstood. So how were these books written and from where did the writers get their ideas and adaptations of legends to include in the Pentateuch?

Dr. Knappert, in his book *The Religion of Israel*, gives some indication of how this developed. First of all, there were three different periods in which the books of the Pentateuch were written and modified. The first period of writing was around 722 B.C. It was during this time that many of the Jews had been captives of Salmanassar, King of Assyria, when they learned the legends of the Babylonians, Persians, and others, and adopted many of these accounts into their own recorded history. But before this time the Jews had no divine or sacred scripture since the early tribes of Israel did little writing.

Nothing changed until 620 B.C. when a priest wrote another book of law that was included in *Deuteronomy* and labeled authoritative by King Josiah. It was Hilkiah who was probably the writer of the book he claimed to have found in the temple. To add authority to it, he said it was somehow written by Moses 800 years earlier. However, the phraseology was that of a recently written book, not of one 800 years old. Nonetheless, objections to this were ignored since Josiah had been won over by the Jews of the period. Thus, the book became part of the Pentateuch.

The third period of biblical writing was done by Ezra around 444 B.C. when he made additions to the Pentateuch in the form of various stories and laws that he had learned from the priests of Babylon. When he finished adjusting the Pentateuch, it stayed in that form and is what we find today. It is Ezra who is said to have rewritten the books of the Old Testament and claimed them to be Holy Scriptures, books given by the inspiration of the Spirit of God. Only from that time on were they considered divine. The Apocryphal book of *Esdras* has an account of this. But the Pentateuch underwent a few more changes when the King of Egypt, Ptolemy Philadelphus, ordered that it be translated into Greek in 287 B.C. In any case, the Pentateuch as we find it today was not written by any one writer.

Most scholars agree that the Old Testament books were written by a wide variety of people and sometimes describe contradictory accounts of the same events. Thus, it becomes very difficult to separate factual history from embellished legends. The books of the Old Testament are divided into three sections. The section called the Earlier Prophets consist of *Joshua, Judges, Samuel,* and *Kings.* The Later Prophets include *Isaiah, Jeremiah, Ezekiel,* and twelve minor books. The Writings consist of *Psalms, Proverbs, Job, Song of Songs, Ruth, Lamentations, Ecclesiastes, Esther, Daniel, Ezra, Nehemiah,* and *Chronicles.* These books are said to have already been in existence before this period near 287 B.C. in the forms of songs, letters, and prophetic books of the

Persian kings that had been collected by Nehemiah. And according to Professor Breasted, a number of *Psalms* and the *Book of Proverbs* are based on the older Egyptian texts. Anyway, the followers of Ezra, the scribes in Jerusalem, collected and edited these texts and then added them to the other sacred books. Thus, by understanding how these books were put together, we can see that the Old Testament, rather than being the embodiment of Jewish history and law, is actually the retainer of much of the ancient Chaldean theology and many Babylonian legends, although it was embellished and molded in a Jewish fashion.

Looking at the history of Jewish society, during the 11th through the 8th centuries B.C., it was under kings Saul, David, and Solomon, that the kingdom of Israel reached its zenith. But after Solomon's death in 977 B.C., the society broke in two. Ten tribes, calling themselves Israel, went to the north and made Samaria their capital. They gave up the law that was supposed to have been given by Moses and again worshiped the Canaanite gods. This kingdom lasted until 722 B.C., when the people were conquered by Assyrians and were taken away.

The tribes of Judah and Benjamin stayed in Palestine and made Jerusalem their capital. This kingdom lasted until 586 B.C. when Nebuchadnezzar came, destroyed Solomon's temple in Jerusalem, and took the people as captives to Babylon. During the time of their captivity and the destruction of the First Temple, they began to anticipate the coming of a Messiah descending from the house of David, who would reorganize their nation and bring the kingdom of God to earth. Some of them returned to Jerusalem after Cyrus freed them when he conquered Babylon in 538 B.C. Those who returned rebuilt the temple, but Greek thought with its more abstract concepts of God was already present then and political and religious factions developed. It was while the Jews were in Babylonia that they incorporated such ideas as the resurrection of the body and belief in Satan, and it was only after the conquests of Alexander the Great (323 B.C.) did they begin to accept the precept of the eternality of the soul.

The slow transition of Judaism began after the completion of biblical writing (150 B.C.). Many controversies arose concerning various issues about the Pentateuch, and many sects evolved and debated with one another. Such sects included the Sadducees and Pharisees, while the Samaritans and Essenes seemed to keep more to themselves and developed their own opinions and practices.

When Jesus appeared, many Jews considered him to be the Messiah who would bring the Jewish nation to its appointed destiny, and Jesus certainly seemed to indicate this in his teachings. Yet his death at the hands of the Romans was accepted as a sign for the majority that he had not actually been the expected Messiah. Thus, the Jews claimed that Jesus was not the Messiah and that it was not they who killed him, but that he was crucified by the Romans as a political offender. Nonetheless, as Paul introduced new ideas about the life of Jesus, specifically as being a divine incarnation, the controversy increased within the Jewish community until the followers of Jesus started a new religion called Christianity. At first the Christians, being Jews, continued to go to the Synagogue to worship, but the Jews regarded Christians as a heretical cult. The Jews did not accept that God had sent His only begotten son, who was also a Jew, to deliver them. In fact, the Jewish people never believed any of the New Testament which was supposed to have been written by Christ's Jewish disciples. The Christians later considered the Jews as a cursed society since they had not been able to recognize Jesus as their true Messiah, and they separated themselves completely from Judaism when the Romans abolished the Jewish nation.

Rome destroyed the Jewish nation in 70 A.D. because of the continual disturbances within it, and the fact that the Jews believed a Messiah would come to bring them world domination. Thus, the Jews scattered throughout the world, being persecuted, driven out of countries, and settling wherever they could survive. But hundreds of thousands of Jewish people returned to Israel when it was finally established as a nation in 1948.

After the Second Temple was destroyed by the Romans in 70 A.D., the main place of worship became the local synagague which was overseen by the rabbi. This also marked the end of the elaborate sacrificial system along with the temple priesthood that had been a part of the temple. This opened the way for a new process of sacrifice through individualistic acts of charity and prayer service.

To validate these changes, the *Mishna* was written about 200 A.D., which was said to be the oral tradition of Moses as given by God on Mount Sinai along with the written law, the Torah or Pentateuch. The oral law had been handed down by Moses' successors up to this time and was put into writing by Rabbi Judah ha-Nasi. The *Mishna* was a compilation of the customs and concepts of Jewish tradition to protect them from destruction.

Over the years, emphasis was placed on study of the Bible and a variety of new concepts or interpretations were developed and examined. As new traditions invariably sprang up, the *Mishna* was also consulted, bringing about another book called the *Talmud*, which was the study and commentary on the *Mishna* that presented civil and religious laws not found in the Torah. This was of two versions, the Palestinian and Babylonian. The Palestinian *Talmud* was completed by the 5th century, and the Babylonian *Talmud* in the 7th century.

These *Talmuds* contained a sizeable amount of theological thought as well as the conclusions that resulted from such thinking. Topics dealt with included life after death, immortality, the will of God, destiny of man, Jewish laws, details about Jewish holy days and festivals, marriage, and relations between Jews and the Gentiles. Parts of the *Talmud* have instructions for weakening or destroying the Gentiles and non-Jews, which some people feel the Jews still take very seriously. The word *goi* (the derogatory term for cattle or beast) is used in the *Talmud* to refer to the Gentiles, particularly the Romans, since some of the *Talmud* was written when the Roman Empire was still somewhat strong. The Holy Roman Empire existed from 27 B.C. with Augustus Caesar to 395 A.D.

with Theodosius I, the last ruler of the united empire. It continued to 474 in the East with Leo II, and until 475 with Romulus Augustulus in the West.

Many additional commentaries and codifications of Jewish tradition appeared as time went on. Moses Maimonides (1135-1204) produced *Moreh Nevukhim*, "Guide for the Perplexed," a philosophical treatise, and *Mishnah Torah*, a code of Judaism meant for the student. This at first created much criticism of the work, and Maimonides was accused of writing his opinions without supplying references. But later it was accepted as a very scholarly book.

Another code was written by Rabbi Joseph Karo (1488-1575) called *Shulchan Arukh* or "Prepared Table." It was also at first criticized but has since been universally accepted after additions had been made by Moses Isserles (1525-1572). As these controversies went on, the philosophical conflicts amongst Jewish sects and the connection the Jews had with other faiths, such as Christianity and Islam, forced the rabbis to re-examine their philosophy and traditions and confirm their conclusions from a new point of view. In fact, not only were many commentaries and interpretations on the Bible written, but even interpretations of the commentaries were developed, all with the hope of explaining the word of God and justifying Judaism.

The path of early Judaism contains the belief in one eternal, all-loving God who created everything. It is accepted that man can commune with God through meditation and prayer, and that God reveals the law to people through revelation. God has provided the Torah which holds the law which must be carried out for God to establish His kingdom on earth. Besides living by the rules of the Torah, one is expected to live by right conduct, which includes acting with justice, mercy, tolerance, compassion, and believing in freedom and human rights for all. Since everyone is created by God, all people are equal. Doing good deeds, using one's profits and the gifts of the world to worship God and make the world a better place, along with attaining love of God, are the ways man shows his cooperation in the process for purifying himself to reach salvation. Salvation is found in this world and will take place when the kingdom of God appears on earth and brings with it eternal peace. Yet, in the meantime, everyone has inherent inclinations toward good as well as evil, but it is up to the individual to control his evil desires. Thus, as free agents, mankind can choose between good and evil, and everyone is responsible for his or her own righteousness, which is the means for slavation. In this way, man is directly responsible to God for redeeming his own soul.

The Jews also believe in the resurrection of the body after death and the eternality of the soul. However, the beliefs of physical resurrection and the appearance of a personal Messiah have undergone significant changes by the recent Reform movement and are no longer accepted by everyone. Judaism also presents the concept that God is impersonal, a power and force without form. However, this has been a controversial issue at various times in Jewish history. It was Maimonides who concluded that God had no form, which was generally accepted. However, he did have his critics, such as Abraham ben David who considered God to be a person, and who cited other philosophers and biblical verses that also presented the personal form of God. But Judaism swayed toward the incorporeality of God. One reason for this was to distinguish Judaism from the non-Jewish religions which did accept that God could have a form. Nonetheless, there is a book written by two mishnaic rabbis called *Shi'ur Komah* which establishes the mystical form of God by presenting various biblical texts. Unfortunately, this book was completely rejected by Maimonides as well as orthodox Judaism simply to accomodate the concept of God's inconceivability by man. Thus, Judaism does not provide for a means of developing a loving relationship with the personal form of God. Though Judaism advocates love and surrender to God, you cannot love something that is merely a force or a power. It is like trying to love the sun. At best, you can simply have respect, admiration or awe for it, but you cannot have a personal loving relationship with it. Therefore, as we have discussed earlier in this volume, this impersonalistic concept of God is far from the highest level of spiritual realization, but it is all that Judaism has to offer.

There are also some extensive laws about diet in Judaism which give directions on such things as the types of animals that may or may not be eaten, how the eatable ones are to be prepared, and how all blood must be drained from the meat. This was because eating fat and blood was forbidden, as stated in *Leviticus* (3.17): "It shall be a perpetual statute for your generations throughout all your dwellings, that ye eat neither fat nor blood." So the logic is that if the blood is drained and the meat becomes "kosher," then one can eat it, which is a tradition that has gone on for hundreds of years, but is nonetheless very questionable. After all, how can one eat meat without blood regardless of how much blood is drained from it? Blood helps maintian and form flesh and, thus, permeates it.

Furthermore, *Leviticus* (17.10 & 14) explains:

And whatsoever man there be of the house of Israel, or of the strangers that sojourn among you, that eateth any manner of blood; I will set my face against that soul that eateth blood, and will cut him off from among his people. . . For it is the life of all flesh; the blood of it is for the life thereof: therefore I said unto the children of Israel, Ye shall eat the blood of no manner of flesh: for the life of all flesh is the blood thereof: whosoever eateth it shall be cut off.

Genesis (9.4-5) also explicitly states, "But flesh with the life thereof, which is the blood thereof, shall ye not eat. And surely your blood of your lives will I require; at the hand of every beast will I require it." This simply means that if you eat meat, God will require payment for it with your own blood. This certainly seems to encourage a vegetarian diet.

Another aspect of Judaism was the path of the mystic, which has as its goal union with God. This was to be attained through meditation, prayer, and spiritual exercise. The *Sepher Yezirah* or "Book of Creation" is one of the first and most important books on Jewish mysticism. It is said to have been written sometime before the sixth century and describes how the world was created on the basis of the twenty-two letters and ten numbers of the Hebrew language. It is also considered one of the main sources that went into the making of the *Kabbalah*.

The origins of the *Kabbalah* are not certain, but it was in the early Middle Ages when the name Kabbalism was used to designate this form of theosophy. The *Kabbalah* discusses topics that include the nature of God, divine emanations, angels and man, how man cannot conceive God, how God created the universe, how the angel Metatron guides the planets, descriptions of the levels of heavenly and hellish planets, how the evil spirit Samael "the Beast" lives in the lowest region, and other things, such as reincarantion. Although reincarnation is generally not discussed in Judaism, it is a topic found in the *Kabbalah*, specifically in the section entitled "Sefer Ha Gilgulim." In the Torah are 613 commandments (365 negative and 248 positive) that a Jew must follow to perfect his life. In the Kabbalistic writings it is mentioned that a person who does not perfect himself according to these 613 rules will have to reincarnate to continue his progress.

The *Kabbalah* is believed to have originally been taught by God to a certain group of angels. After the fall of man the angels gave this heavenly knowledge to man so he could return to heaven. From Adam it went to Noah, then to Abraham who emigrated to Egypt where the Egyptians and other Eastern countries learned some of it. Moses was initiated into the *Kabbalah* and later expressed some of it in the first four books of the Pentateuch. Also David and Solomon are said to have been deeply initiated into it. Later, Simeon ben Yohai compiled it.

Upon studying the *Kabbalah*, obvious similarities to Zoroastrianism are found in it, and one will readily find that it is full of speculations and assumptions. It has also been linked with medieval magic. Oddly, it has received the strongest criticism from the Jews themselves. But one sect, Hasidim, is based on the *Kabbalah* and stresses communion with God through joyful prayer, study, and service to God.

The *Zohar* is another important work which contained eleven dissertations that were a mystical commentary on the Pentateuch, the best known of which are the *Book of Secrets*, the *Secret of Secrets*, the *Mysteries of the Pentateuch*, and the *Hidden Interpretations*. This was the fundamental basis of the *Kabbalah* or mystic tradition, and is said to be authored by Simeon ben Yohai in the second century who used the traditional conversations between God and Adam in Paradise as the basis of his writing. It has also been said that the *Zohar* had been discovered in a cave in Galilee after being hidden for 1,000 years. But it has been proved that it was mainly composed by Moses de Leon in Spain at the end of the thirteenth century.

The essence of Judaism, which is based on devotion to and dependence on God, is highly recommended and uplifting, especially for this age. And those who follow this path tend to be very devotional with a strong faith in God. Yet, as we can see, Judaism is another philosophy that produced its theology not through the process of spiritual purity and self-realization, but through confrontations with new problems that forced it to re-evaluate its viewpoints in order to present newer conclusions and justify its purpose. Presently, it is a religion that is based primarily on tradition, whether the traditions are fully understood or not. The ultimate goal of perfectly following Judaism is not always made clear. If you ask the layman what the goal is, he will say to love and serve God, or become one with God. But what exactly does this mean? If God is not a person, which is the understanding of Judaism, then how can you serve or actually love God? Actually, the Jewish people have placed more concern with the fate of their nation than for a future life in heaven or hell with rewards or punishments. The book of *Daniel* presents the first references regarding those who are resurrected to an eternal life, while the wicked are given punishment. And Jewish scholars do not agree on the meaning of the few references that comment on this topic. The Jews generally never gave as much thought to this as people of other religions. Their main interest is to have a nation in which they are responsible to no one but God who rules all and who delivers the promised land to them in this world.

As we can see from its history, Judaic theology has continually changed, sometimes dramatically, through the years since its origin and still keeps changing in various ways. How much it will continue to change because of reforms, or divisions within it because of fundamental differences, or because of political or nationalistic considerations remains to be seen.

ISLAM

The word *Islam* means surrender or commitment, signifying one's proper relation to God. Islam demands total surrender to the one God, Allah. The path of Islam is straight and narrow, contrasting sharply with the Vedic way, which is broad and allows one to progress from whatever station of life one finds themselves. Islam demands its followers to have complete faith in the *Koran* and the prophets. There are 28 prophets in Islam, 18 of whom are of the Old Testament. The prophets include Abraham, Moses, Jesus, John the Baptist, and Mohammed, the founder of Islam. Mohammed said that all the prophets teach the same essential truths. But Mohammed established himself as the last and most important of the prophets, and that belief in and obedience to him were necessary for salvation.

Muslims are prohibited from gambling, stealing, killing, committing adultery, eating pork, and drinking alcoholic beverages. Islam forbids the worship of images or idols; yet, some exceptions to this can be found in India where some Muslims still take care of deities. They must also honor their parents, give help to those who are helpless, protect widows, be honest, look on all men as brothers, especially other Muslims, and treat servants and animals kindly.

One of the reasons for treating animals nicely is that Mohammed had a love for animals and did not approve of anyone ill-treating camels or other kinds of animals. As noted by his biographers, Mohammed preferred to eat vegetarian foods, living mostly on a diet of barley, bread, dates, water, and sometimes milk and honey. He instructed those who ate meat to wash out their mouths before praying. He also encouraged his followers to be vegetarian, but did not force the issue. So, presently, most Muslims have forgotten about this issue and eat the flesh of many kinds of animals, except when they are on pilgrimage when, according to the *Koran* (9.1), all Muslims are forbidden to eat meat.

The Five Pillars of Islamic faith are the basic elements that make up Muslim worship. The first is *shahadah*, confession of one's faith by which the Muslims declare, "There is no God but the one God, and Mohammed is His prophet." This is repeated several times a day. The second pillar is *salat*, the prayer said while bowing towards Mecca five times a day: at dawn, noon, late afternoon, sunset, and after dark. The third pillar is *zakat*, alms given to the needy based on a percentage of the kinds of property a Muslim owns. The fourth is *sawn*, the fast during the month of Ramadan in which no food is taken between dawn and sunset. The fifth pillar is *haji*, the pilgrimage to the Kaaba in Mecca which every good Muslim is expected to do at least once in a lifetime.

Mohammed was born between 570 and 580 A.D. in the Bani Hashim, a poor but noble clan of the Quraysh tribe of Arabia. His father had died before his birth and his mother died shortly thereafter. Mohammed was raised an orphan by his uncle Abu Talib. Mohammed's education was very basic, and what he learned mostly came from his uncle. While he and his uncle were on a journey to Syria when he was 12 years old, he came in contact with Christianity for the first time, which left a philosophical impression on him. Yet his direction in life was not clear. He was a shepherd and a camel driver for a time, and learned business and trade from his uncle. When he was 25 years old he led a caravan to Syria for the wealthy widow Khadijah who soon offered to marry him, which he did. She was 15 years older than he, but it was a good marriage and they had two sons and four daughters. However, the boys died at a young age. He continued to work until he was 40 when his interest in religion and meditation became quite strong. He often retired alone to Mount Hira near Mecca for meditation. During this time he had also been influenced by Jewish and Christian teachings.

It was after Mohammed's fortieth birthday, said to be in 610, while in meditation, when an angel appeared and commanded him to recite in the name of God. According to tradition, Mohammed did not respond, so the angel grabbed him by the throat and shook him, repeating the command. When Mohammed still did not respond, the angel choked him until Mohammed did as he was told. Thus began Mohammed's prophethood and the writing of Muslim scripture, the *Koran*.

For a long time Mohammed felt unsure about the vision or from where the channeled revelations of the *Koran* were really coming. Finally, however, Mohammed gained a clear understanding of what his mission was and then determinedly began preaching the divine message.

For over ten years Mohammed preached in Mecca but was mostly ignored. His earliest followers were his family, Khadijah, and others from the lower classes who formed a small sect. During this time Mohammed once entered the Kaaba and announced, "There is but one God," which immediately angered the Meccans who were used to worshiping a number of gods and goddesses. Mohammed could have been killed, but his uncle protected him. His followers fled the place and sought refuge in Abyssinia. After the incident, his uncle tried to make him give up his preaching, but he continued anyway. Hostility and opposition to Mohammed increased until Mohammed entered Yathrib where he, in 621, was able to find a place for himself and his followers. Later, Yathrib became known as Medina, the city of the prophet. This emigration became the starting point of the Islamic calender. And by this time his faithful wife, Khadijah, had died.

At Medina, Mohammed occupied himself with strengthening his position. The continuing revelations that were being compiled in the *Koran* began to provide answers to criticism of Mohammed, and it also condemned as hypocrites those people of Medina who remained non-Muslim. Mohammed became especially angry with the Jews of the area for refusing to accept him as a prophet and for criticizing him, claiming that he distorted the stories in the Bible of former prophets. Eventually, most of the Jews were either banished or massacred by him and his followers. Mohammed also condemned the theory of the Christian Trinity on the grounds that it made God appear like He had partners in His Divinity. He also proclaimed that Jesus was not the Saviour nor a part of the Divine Nature. For this reason Christians sometimes consider Islam a heresy.

As his position became stronger, he displayed his military force to bring alliances with the Bedouins and other tribal groups. He also took as many a 15 wives, though he had preached that a Muslim should take no more than four. Several of these marriages served to strengthen his relations with various tribes. He also began attacking the Meccan caravans that were a source of wealth and strength to Mecca. Mohammed soon engaged in armed conflict with the Meccans in 624, who saw him as a threat to their city. But they were not good fighters, and Mohammed was victorious.

Mohammed gained possession of Mecca without a fight due to his military strength and diplomatic abilities in 630. He then destroyed the deities and forced the people to stop worshiping the goddesses and worship only Allah, and accept him as Allah's prophet. Mohammed also declared that the black stone in the sacred shrine had been given by God to Abraham, and it has been worshiped to this day, though the real origin of this stone is not clearly known. There is an interesting story that explains that the stone is a Shiva *linga*, or a part of one, and if ever anyone goes into the shrine and pours Ganges water on it (as is the usual process for worshiping a Shiva *linga*), the incident will cause the decline and gradual end of Islam. In any case, this victory in Mecca gave Mohammed enormous gain in prestige and Bedouins and Arabs from all over came to pledge their allegiance to him.

Just before his unexpected death in 632, he was easily the most powerful man in Arabia and he demanded that everyone bow to the Islamic ideals. After Mohammed died, Abu Bakr, the first caliph or successor of Mohammed, continued to use military force in attempts to hold together the tribes who had entered into Islam. For the next ten years, the Muslims attacked Syria, Palestine, Damascus, Jerusalem, Iraq, and Egypt. Through the years they continued their attacks into other areas such as across North Africa and Spain in 711, which was later lost in the 15th century. They were stopped in France in 732. In the 11th century Sultan Mahmud of Ghazni started attacking into the mountainous regions of Afghanistan and continued into India. Mohammed Ghori, 150 years later, kept up the conquest of North India to bring that area under Islam rule, an area where political and religious unrest has continued ever since. When the Muslims entered India, they slaughtered thousands and thousands of Hindus and Buddhists alike, and took pride in destroying many hundreds of temples.

As the Muslims expanded, they faced new problems with new and often much more sophisticated people who had religious systems that were much more developed than their own. They found that the conquered people did not quickly agree that the Muslims were bearing a new and superior religion. Thus, to solve these additional problems, the Muslims began to resort to the old traditions as the best examples to follow. However, as old customs could not always be cited to solve various issues, they often concocted new traditions in order to justify their needs or actions.

It became obvious that the *Koran* needed to be further expanded with additional authority to handle the new problems with which Muslims had to deal. Thus, new books were compiled from the traditional practices of the prophet that were called *sunnah*. The *sunnah* was known according to oral descriptions of the prophet's activities and sayings. This oral tradition was known as *hadith*. Several collections of *hadiths* were made during the first few centuries of Islamic history. The *hadiths* are accepted as an accurate authority by the more conservative and fundamental Muslims; yet, modern scholars point out contradictions in the *hadiths* and say that they are not a reliable source of information about Mohammed and merely reflect the general attitude of Muslims during the third Islamic century. Some modern Muslims have now rejected the *hadiths* and their usage in Islamic tradition and rely only on the *Koran* as their authority.

For the Muslims, the *Koran* is the infallible word of God and said to be a transcript of a tablet found in heaven. The *Koran* is traditionally considered to have been given to Mohammed by the angel Gabriel and was gradually revealed over a period of twenty years. It was thought that earlier prophets had been given portions of this heavenly tablet who had then written it for mankind's guidance in the form of scripture, such as the *Injil* or Gospel of Jesus, *Psalms* of David, Torah of Moses, and so on. The reason for Mohammed to reveal another book was that the Arabs needed a prophet of their own and a scripture in their own language dealing with their own spiritual needs rather than through the Christian and Jewish books. It was also considered that Mohammed was the last of all prophets. Even though Mohammed had been influenced by Jewish and Christian teachings, the *Koran* accuses the Jews of distorting the scripture and the Christians of worshiping Jesus as the son of God rather than directly worshiping God as God had commanded. And all such people, as is so often the message in the *Koran,* go to hell.

The name *Koran* means that it must be recited. Every Muslim is expected to read the entire *Koran*. It is divided into 114 chapters, which all begin with the phrase, "In the name of Allah, the Compassionate, the Merciful." The *Koran* as we find it today was put together only after Mohammed's death. It was Zayd ibn Thabit who gathered all the various writings from the many people in the community who had copied or collected them. An official version of the text was then produced under the order of Uthman, the third caliph or head of Islam.

Ultimately, the *Koran* demands surrender to the one supreme God. This is actually the basis and conclusion of any bona fide religion, as especially enunciated in the Vedic literature. Although the *Koran* primarily considers the impersonalist conception of God, in the end it refutes impersonalism and establishes the personal form of the Lord. According to the *Koran*, the Lord has a spiritual, blissful body and is the all-pervading, eternal being from which everything originates. The *Koran*, although seeming to prescribe various methods, briefly describes what are aspects of *karma-yoga* and *jnana-yoga* and acknowledges that the ultimate position of everyone is to worship and offer prayers (or *bhakti*) to the spiritual form of the Lord, the Supreme Person. Thus, though not always recognized, devotional service to the supreme spiritual form of the Lord is actually the perfection of correctly following the *Koran*.

As anyone who reads the *Koran* will see, in comparison with other scripture, it is not a book which focuses much on theology or spiritual doctrine. It does not dwell on describing our eternal spiritual identity, the characteristics of the soul, or the spiritual nature of God. In fact, it provides a harsh view of God, when compared to other religious texts like the Vedic literature. It presents God,

Allah, as a God who gives out much punishment with no mercy for those fallen ones who do not follow the Islamic path.

Actually, the deity of Allah was known to the Bedouin Arabs long before the appearance of Mohammed, but Allah's function at the time was not clear; so, he did not play a prominent role in their religious practice. Even then, the Kaaba in Mecca was an important place of pilgrimage, and Hubal was the principal god. Other deities were also established there since each clan would place their own deity in a sacred area of the shrine. Although Mohammed destroyed these "idols" later on, still many of the religious functions at the time were incorporated into modern Islamic practice, but with a more religious view.

The fact of the matter is that Islam and the *Koran*, as presented by Mohammed, provides guidance for daily practice, but no practical spiritual philosophy. The *Koran* is mostly a book that intructs what is expected of a Muslim and warns of what can happen to those who do not follow it. It is a book which leaves many matters unclear and incomplete. Whatever Islamic theology we find today was developed after Mohammed's death and has, more or less, been added to it. Even as theological premises were developed, many thousands of sects appeared, and many disappeared, which accepted or rejected various portions of this theology and thus modified their lifestyles, worship, meditation, and zealous attitudes accordingly. Sometimes these sects became locked in dispute with other sects for many years. Some sects that appeared were the Sunni, Wahhabi, Sufi, Shiah, while the no-longer existing Assassin sect and the present Druze sect are Ismailis, which are subsects of the Shiah.

The real development of theology in Islam did not start until the third Islamic century with the appearance of a small group of Muslim philosophers called the Mu'tazilah, who tried to convey a rational understanding of Islam. They taught that there was only one God and no evil force or Satan, although there are verses in the *Koran* that refer to Satan. They also said that the *Koran* was created and was not a transcript of an eternal tablet in heaven. They also denied that God could be perceived by man or that God had human attributes, as was referred to in the *Koran*. The Mu'tazilah school eventually passed out of existence sometime after it lost the favor of the Abbasid rulers. But from that time, Islamic theology has continued to transform and evolve as different people tried to present a variety of views to solve the various philosophical problems with which Islam had to deal. In this way, we can see how Islam has continually changed in its attempt to justify itself through tradition and philosophy, and develop a theology which can show its superiority to other societies.

Islam does, however, have a developed mystical tradition, beginning with Mohammed's experiences that are now incorporated into the Sufi sect. Up to the present, Sufism is considered the real meaning of Islam for most Muslims. According to tradition, Sufism was developed by Mohammed through Ali Ibn Abi Taleb, the fourth caliph. Some say the word *sufi* means one whose heart is pure. Others say *sufi* comes from *saff*, meaning one who is close to God through spiritual development. Others say it comes from the word *suf* (wool), meaning to wear simple woolen garments, which was begun as a protest against the theological forms and worldliness of the Muslims at the time.

It was Hasan al-Basri of Iraq who first engaged in the asceticism that was taken up by others, later known as Sufis, who wanted to experience the presence of God as Mohammed did by performing mystical practices. They believed that all being is one, all entities emanate from the divine, and before being created they exist in Allah's mind as ideas and are, therefore, eternal with God. They also accept, like the Islam faith in general, that there is one God, there are angels, there are prophets, there is a day of resurrection when one is judged by God, and there is fate. They also accept that the universe is primarily good, but evil comes from selfishness or desires which separate oneself from God.

The Sufi process of development is broken down into stages, of which the first is practice of asceticism and detachment to worldly affairs and the body and bodily possessions. Silent meditation is an important practice. The second stage consists of studying with a teacher to acquire the esoteric knowledge that accompanies mystical experience. The worship usually consists of chanting the 99 names of Allah on the 99 beads of their rosary. The third stage consists of attaining enlightenment of the experience of love between God and man, which leads to ecstasy. This is very similar to the element of *bhakti* found in Vaishnavism. This is why many Sufis who had been persecuted as heretics in Arabia moved east into India where their lifestyle was better received.

Presently, there are over 700 million Muslims in the world, and the expansion of Islam is making gains by peaceful means, especially into sub-Saharan Africa and other areas of the world. But for many years, as we can historically see, the expansion was based on zealous military strength rather than spiritual purity and goodness. Except for some of the sects like the Sufis, much of Islam has been a fighting religion and continues to be so to this day. This certainly seems to go against some of the basic tenets of Islam, such as treating others with kindness, helping those who need it, etc. Yet, such recent leaders as Ayatollah Khomeini announced that Islam was a religion of fighters for freedom who must comply or be obliterated. This outlook does not seem to leave the followers of Islam much choice in how to conduct their lives. And pity the person who does not comply, as was seen by all the executions and torture of those who opposed Khomeini, such as the Bahai sect which has a much more humanitarian philosophy. Many had to flee the country to avoid this repressive Islamic government. Thus, not all Muslims are so extreme in their attitude. In fact, many of them are content with simply trying to live in harmony with God and their fellow man as best they can in following the Muslim path.

Since the death of Khomeini in June of 1989, countries like Iran are becoming more liberal with new reforms under way. This provides the means for increased individual and social freedoms, but there is still a very long way to go. Artists, writers, and musicians still fear censorship and imprisonment if they should incur the wrath of any Muslim cleric or government official. Obviously, this is still a religion that is evolving and going through dramatic changes, depending who its leaders are and how mature is their spiritual understanding, and in which countries the followers are located. And, as previously stated, as long as the foundation of a religion is not based on real spiritual knowledge that can be realized by its followers on a practical level, such a religion is bound to remain in flux, ever-changing along with everything else that cannot rise above the influence of temporary material nature.

CONFUCIANISM AND TAOISM

Confucianism and Taoism, which are both outgrowths of an earlier religion, have existed some 500 years before Buddhism entered China. The earliest religion in China included such practices as worship of the ancestors, fertility rituals, and worship of the various nature deities. Some of these have remained in Chinese culture while some have faded. Confucianism and Taoism are, more or less, philosophical teachings to consider and not necessarily religious dogma that one must follow if they are a member of that school of thought. The basic foundation of these religions were laid from the sixth to the third centuries B.C.

Confucianism was started by Confucius (551-479 B.C.) who was born in the State of Lu in the Shang-Tung province. Confucianism was further developed by Mencius (390-305 B.C.) and Hsun Tzu (312-238 B.C.). Confucius relied on the policies of the early Chou kings and also the *Book of Songs* as his guide, which was a compilation of early Chinese poetry. He essentially preserved and restored the earlier traditions found in the old chronicles and formed an ethical and moral system. Confucius made this knowledge available in five great volumes which are now accepted as Chinese classics. These are (1) the *I-Ching, Book of Changes*; (2) the *Shu-Ching, Book of History*; (3) the *Shih-Ching, Book of Poetry*; (4) the *Li-Ching, Book of Ritual*; and (5) the *Ch'un Ch'iu, Spring and Autumn Annals*. Although he died disheartened and quite unrecognized for his efforts, except for a few loyal followers, it was hundreds of years later in the second century B.C. when his teachings gained wide acceptance.

Confucianism hardly deals with anything spiritual. It is mostly a code of living taught to the princely order. Much of Confucius' sayings are recorded in the *Lun Yu* or "Analects." This contains contributions from his various disciples wherein they discuss Confucius' life, character, and teachings. Confucius did not talk about the will of heaven or of spirits. The goal of his teaching is to establish a good society by virtuous social behavior as determined by individual development of character. A person was to live a virtuous life; the way of a true gentleman. This is accomplished by having respect for elders, along with the study of poetry and music, and developing righteousness, neighborly love, respect, truthfulness, generosity, and so on.

Taoism was founded around the sixth century B.C. by Lao Tzu who, it is said, was dissatisfied with Confucian principles and wanted to find something better. When Lao Tzu retired and was traveling to his place of retirement he met a gatekeeper who asked him to write something about his philosophy. Thus, he stopped long enough to write the famous *Tao-Te Ching*. However, this account is not upheld by all scholars, some of whom say the *Tao-Te Ching* was compiled by a group of Chinese mystics rather than a sole author. To substantiate this some refer to the name of Lao Tzu, which means old philosopher or philosophers.

The *Tao-Te Ching* is divided into 81 chapters, which is further divided into two parts that are *Concerning Tao*, the way, and *Concerning Te*, its power. The *Tao-Te Ching*, the *Chuang Tzu* and *Lieh Tzu* are the core of Taoist scripture, although much more writing was compiled through the years.

Taoism was originally similar to yoga in ways. It was a religion of mysticism in which knowledge was gained in trance. At one point Taoism became associated with magic, divination, and other mystic powers. The *tao* is considered to be the nameless invisible, formless and infinite reality behind all things. The *tao* is also regarded to be the source of the *yin* and *yang* or positive and negative forces of nature. From these forces the heaven and earth and all created beings become manifest. This reality of the *tao* is that with which man must learn to relate. The *tao* is beyond all words and names, but enlightenment can be attained through tranquil and complete mental stillness and voidness. Through this practice one associates with the *yin* principle, the inactive female basis of things, rather than *yang*, which is the active male principle. By being receptive, one becomes master and remains in harmony with the natural flow of things. Thus, nature itself helps propel one toward his rightful position, the place one is meant to be as an agent of the *tao*, and rise above the limitations of time and space and transcend the physical plane.

Confucianism had risen in popularity on account of being thoroughly studied under the early Han emperors and later established as the state religion. In the meantime, the people in general, regardless of religious connections, believed in personal gods, and, therefore, magicians and shamans abounded. It was believed they could help one to establish a relationship with the gods and ensure immortality after death. Taoism believed in the continuation of the personality after death. This aspect of religious belief was often neglected by the official state religions like Confucianism.

The rise of the Church of Taoism can be traced back to Chang Ling who emigrated to West China and gathered a large number of followers. By the second century A.D. a Taoist church with Chang Ling's surname had already been established by his descendants. The church had divided into two regions, that of the East and that of the West. The Eastern Church is said to have had as many as 360,000 followers. In both churches, large organizations extending down through priests and laity had been developed.

Taoism gradually changed from a philosophy based on mysticism to an organized church that propagated salvation through rites and services for atonement of sin. Entrance into paradise could be attained through a variety of ways, which may include yogic exercises, abstinence, taking drugs, charity, service to the priestly community, and so on.

As Confucianism gained wide acceptance among the rulers and Taoism was becoming the popular religion among the masses of China, another religion entered China, which was Buddhism. Buddhism was initially considered a foreign form of Taoism and over the years actually absorbed various aspects of Taoism into its practice. Although the spread of Buddhism was difficult at first, it continued to make greater inroads into the culture of China and thus became a serious challenge to Taoism in the fourth and fifth centuries. As Buddhism developed, it produced a number of Chinese sects, of which the most prominent were the Ch'an school, which taught enlightenment through meditation; the Ch'ing T'u school, which taught that even without enlightenment it could be attained through faith in the Buddhas; and the T'ien-t'ai school, that taught salvation was attained through a balance of several practices, including meditation, study of scripture, discipline, and ritual. Another school was also the Chen-yen or tantric sect which employed worship of the many deities of the Tantric tradition along with magical and secret ceremonies, many of which had already been a part of Taoism.

SHINTO

Before Buddhism was introduced in 539 A.D., the earlier religious tradition in Japan was Shinto. Shinto refers to the way of the *kami*, which are the spirits or gods. It is based primarily on the attempt to experience divinity. This is done through traditional rituals often pertaining to the respect of the ancestors, as well as participating in festivals and visiting shrines that house the *kami* or supernatural beings who may be cosmic creators, the moon (*Tsuki*), the sun (*Hi*), ghosts of the dead, wandering spirits, or other undeterminable beings of the subtle realm. By practicing Shinto, one hopes to become a *kami* when they die. The Shinto path does not aim for personal salvation.

Shinto beliefs were passed on orally long before Chinese writing was introduced in Japan in 405 A.D. Before this, there had been no written history of Japan. There is, however, the *Kojiki*, "The Record of Ancient Things," written in 712 A.D., and the *Nihongi*, "The Japanese Chronicles," of 720 A.D., both written in Chinese. They are said to describe the early history or mythology of Japan. These books also give an indication of how many deities are included in the Shinto pantheon. They describe the number as eighty myriads or as eight hundred myriads of deities. The *Yengishiki*, 927 A.D., contains the ancient ritual prayers. Due to Chinese influence the practice of worshiping the ancestors and various aspects of Taoist magic were incorporated into the Shinto religion.

The experience of divinity within Shinto can be that of feeling the presence of a Supreme Being that gives care and love, and who may also appear to be present within parents or political superiors, such as the Emperor or Empress. It may also be in experiencing the influence or power of the nature spirits or ghostly beings of the subtle realm. The other aspect of experiencing the divine is perceiving the inner essence of reality, or the *buddha* nature within all.

This religion lacks emphasis on theology or spiritual knowledge. Even trying to understand what the *kami* or gods actually are can be difficult, for the name can be referred to anything supernatural, either dreadful or revered. Though Shinto makes the attempt for one to experience or be aware of the divinity, or *kami*, the concept is so vague that it becomes impossible to have an accurate understanding of what it is. Perhaps a better description of Shinto may simply be the way of the incomprehensible.

CONCLUSION

We could discuss other religions or philosophical systems of the East in this chapter, such as Zurvanism, Mithraism, or the Mandeans and Manicheans, or even the new religions of Japan that have cropped up over the past several hundred years, such as Tenrikyo (The Religion of Heavenly Wisdom), Konkokyo (The Religion of Metal Lustre), or Hito no Michi (The Way of Man). But many of these systems, some of which have already declined in influence, have only recently originated in the last several hundred years with the appearance of a founder or prophet who presented certain new ideas or compiled new scriptures. Thus, with such a beginning, they take the same course as many other philosophical theories that have appeared, stayed for some time, produced some by-products or offshoots, and then dwindled and vanished by being overpowered by other philosophical ideas that gained popularity.

Of course, all systems of religion or philosophy have their advocates as well as opponents who want to change things or start separate groups. But the foundation of any religion's scripture must be completely spiritual and beyond the susceptibility of being changed upon public demand. This has been one of the major problems with the religions discussed in this chapter. Knowledge or truth which needs continual revision or updating is not truth at all, but merely relative fact, or fact as long as the situation stays the same. In other words, a philosophy or religion must be able to answer all questions regarding spiritual topics in a sound and reasonable manner at all times throughout history. Otherwise, people who are advanced in science and philosophy will not have faith in such scripture, just as scientists now cannot accept the simplistic theory of creation as found in the Bible. But we must often look carefully to see the essential truth within.

A real and authentic religion must not only describe the truth, it must also provide the path or process for one's individual attainment and understanding of the Absolute Truth. It must give the means for a person's own spiritual realization, which must be the developed results of properly following the path. Of course, if someone claims to be a member of a religion but does not properly follow the process, failing to attain the complete results is to be expected. But the point is that a real religion cannot simply give theological dogma or duties for practice and expect its followers to act merely on blind faith in its scripture or its leader. If such is the case, then the religion is incomplete.

It is natural, however, to see many kinds of religious sentiment take on various methods of expression, but each one should be analyzed to see whether it has any practical authenticity or not. Authenticity in this case means that it perfectly establishes what the Absolute Truth is and provides an effective means for the initiate to attain and realize it in accordance with spiritual authorities, as in the case of the Vedic literature, the experienced sages, and the spiritual masters. If its precepts are upheld by these three kinds of spiritual authorities, then it may be considered a genuine spiritual process. Otherwise, it will prove faulty and produce only temporary results, being incomplete and not based on the absolute platform.

Even in the few religions we have looked at in this chapter, we can see that most of them offer almost nothing in the way of true spiritual knowledge. They do not explain the nature of God, what is the spiritual realm, or the science of the soul. Nor do they explain who we are, where we have come from, where we are actually going in this universe, what is the purpose of it, or so many other things. They primarily deal with nothing more than rules for moral standards. They may give a little theology when they are pressed for answers, but offer no practical spiritual experience. Thus, they hardly touch upon the higher principles of spiritual realization. So where can these religions actually take us? How much progress can we really make from them even if we follow them perfectly?

Any religion's fundamental principles for spiritual advancement, such as self-control, peacefulness, truthfulness, austerity, wisdom, knowledge, meditation or faith in God, may be quite laudable at first glance. But we still must be informed to know the difference between lip service and engaging in real spiritual activities. Such knowledge has been provided for the well-being of society in general in such books as *Bhagavad-gita* and *Srimad-Bhagavatam*. This is the kind of spiritual knowledge we are trying to explain in this volume, as well as the previous volume, *The Secret Teachings of the Vedas*.

By utilizing complete spiritual knowledge, one gains full understanding, not only of one's position on the spiritual platform, but also of how to direct one's life on the material level. Thus, one knows how to live to reach the perfectional stage of life and not be distracted or cheated by useless goals, false prophets, or imperfect systems of religion. In the material world, simply finding a source of complete spiritual knowledge and being able to discern between a genuine process of spiritual development and one that is not fully mature in its teachings is half the battle. If one can do that and then begin progressing on the right path, he will gain much enlightenment and insight concerning every aspect of life.

Without this kind of spiritual advancement, everything else becomes frustrated, like building a castle out of sand. Without a proper foundation, everything we do is ultimately useless. Without knowing the purpose of life, society becomes like a blind man who is running in a hurry, but does not know where his running will take him. Such a society works to build a fool's paradise with so many attractions for cheap thrills, but for no useful purpose. In such a society, very few are found to be really happy, and most everyone is forced to work hard simply for the privilege of continuing to work hard in a never ending struggle for existence. But for a God-centered and spiritually uplifted civilization, everything changes.

When a person knows who he is, what is this universe, what is the purpose of life, what one's relationship is with God and his fellow living entities, and how to work according to that relationship, he knows what to do. And a real religion or philosophy has to provide this knowledge in order to be complete. Only by cultivating full spiritual knowledge will a person understand the real purpose of life. By participating in a genuine and authorized spiritual discipline, a person attains higher and higher levels of spiritual realization and will know he is making real progress in life. It is not that he is working so hard only to lose everything at the time of death. But by spiritual advancement one prepares for putting on the robes of immortality and gaining the qualities and assets that death can never take away. Thus, one is able to escape the repeated cycle of birth and death in the material world and go back home to the spiritual strata. This is the real goal of any true system of religion or yoga process and the completion of all philosophical understanding.

CHAPTER SIX

Christianity and the Vedic Teachings Within It

The major religion of the world at this point in history is Christianity, so it is important for us to review this path to understand what is the basis of this religion and what is expected of the follower of this path. This study will allow us to recognize many similarities between Christianity and the Eastern teachings that had already been in existence for many hundreds of years.

A BRIEF LOOK AT CHRISTIANITY'S BEGINNINGS

At the time of Jesus' appearance there were many cults in Judaism. There were the Pharisees, the Sadducees, and another was the Essenes who were very pure in their habits. They were very frugal and were strict vegetarians, eating no meat of any kind and drinking fresh fruit juices or water. They believed in working in harmony with nature and the forces that surrounded the world and all within it.

The name *Essene* is supposed to derive from a Syrian word meaning physician, and they would practice the healing of the sick in mind, body, and soul. They had two main communities, one in Egypt, the other in Palestine near the Dead Sea. Another was in Syria. Their origins can be traced to the Far East, and their methods of prayer, meditation, and fasting were quite similar to Eastern practices.

Their membership was open to all and they were a well respected order with many hundreds waiting to join. But their teachings were given only to members. To be a member of the Essene order, one had to pass a probationary period of one year and be able to fast for 40 days. Their school had three degrees, and few passed successfully through all. They divided themselves into two levels, consisting of those who were celibate and those who were married. The Essenes were a peaceful order of pious men and women who lived in asceticism, spending their days in simple labor and their evenings in prayer. They never became involved with political or military affairs. They never became merchants, or entered into commercial life in the cities, but maintained themselves by agriculture and raising sheep for wool, as well as by crafts like pottery and carpentry. (And we know Jesus was a carpenter.) Any profits or harvests were not kept individually, but were given to the community and then divided.

Jesus was a member of the Essenes and was apparently the head of one of the Essene temples. In all the Essene temples there was one leader and twelve assistants. When they had their ritual, which they had been doing many years before Jesus appeared, they would break bread and take wine. The leader would stand over the wine and bread and say, "This is my body, this is my blood," acting as a representative of God. Then he would distribute it. This is information from the Dead Sea Scrolls which were written long before Christ appeared. So we can see that this is a tradition previous to Christ that is still being carried on in the Christian churches today.

The philosophy of the Essenes was very exalted for that period of time. Traditionally, the Jewish doctrine for justice was an eye for an eye. But the Essenes, even before Christ, taught that one should simply turn the other cheek. So in many cases when Jesus taught, he was simply repeating the doctrine of the Essenes. It was not original. But considering the advanced level of the Essene philosophy in general, it would not be surprising if they had been influenced by the Vedic writings in some way. In fact, evidence of this can be seen when we consider that the school of the Essenes was originally conducted chiefly for the purpose of interpreting the Pythagorean symbols and teachings.

According to legend, Pythagoras was one of the many sages and saviors of antiquity for whom an immaculate conception is asserted. He was born between 600 and 590 B.C. and the birth was predicted by the oracle of Delphi. Pythagoras had traveled and learned the mysteries of the Greeks, Egyptians, Babylonians, Chaldeans, and even went through Media and Persia to Hindustan to study for several years under the learned *brahmana* priests. This is accepted by some to be the same areas where Jesus later traveled and learned the Eastern spiritual philosophy.

One of the things Pythagoras had declared was that meat-eating clouded the reasoning faculties, and that judges should refrain from eating meat before a trial to assure that the most honest decisions would be made for those who went before them. He also taught that mortals who, during their earthly existence, had become like animals in their activities would return to earth again in the form of the beasts they had grown to resemble or act like. Pythagoras also taught the medicinal properties of plants and how to heal by the use of color, vibrations, music, herbs, etc. He also taught how there was a Supreme World, spiritual in nature, which pervaded all things. The material worlds existed within the nature of this supreme sphere, and people should try to recognize the spiritual nature in their surroundings. The Essenes taught many of these same points. They also believed in the eternality of the soul and the philosophy of reincarnation, as did the Pythagoreans and other groups of that time, and taught that rewards of righteousness must be earnestly striven for.

Jesus' brother James was one of the leaders of the Essenes in Jerusalem and was a strict vegetarian. It is said that never in his life did he eat meat, nor did he drink liquor. He was an ascetic. So if these two brothers were stalwart preachers of the Essenes and one was a staunch vegetarian, it is hard to imagine that the other one would not also be. Of course, if a person wants to establish Jesus as a meat-eater, they can repeat the biblical story wherein he distributed many fish. But that was an emergency situation, and whether Jesus actually ate any fish is still in question. But, from an objective point of view, there is evidence that Jesus did not eat meat. For example, in *Isaiah* (7.14-15) it is stated: "Therefore the Lord Himself shall give you a sign; Behold, a young woman shall conceive and bear a son, and shall call his name Immanuel. Butter and honey shall he eat, that he may know to refuse the evil, and choose the good." This shows that Christ was a vegetarian.

The founding fathers of the early Christian church, such as Tertullian, Pliny, Origen, St. John Chrysostom, etc., were also strict vegetarians. In fact, St. John Chrysostom advised that saints are loving not only toward people, but also to the beasts because they come from the same God who created mankind. Other saints who were either vegetarian or who at least made friends with animals or protected them from hunters include St. Francis, and Georgian saints like St. David of Garesja, St. John Zedazneli, and early Celtic saints like St. Wales, St. Cornwall, and St. Brittany. Therefore, a real "Christian" who follows Christ's doctrines should also extend their love to all of God's creatures as Christ had done. Otherwise, how can they be considered real followers of Christ?

The fact of the matter is that the Bible, in *Genesis* (1.26), states: "And God said, Let us make man in our image, after our likeness: and let them have dominion over the fish of the sea, and over the fowl of the air, and over the cattle, and over all the earth, and over every creeping thing that creepeth upon the earth." Herein, dominion does not mean to do whatever one wants to with other creatures, but to have dominion as a ruler of a country has leadership over the people he rules. It is not expected that a leader will torture and eat the people who inhabit his country. That is no leader at all, but merely one who exploits others for his own interests. Furthermore, only a few verses after the one above we find that God expects us to be vegetarian: "And God said, Behold, I have given you every herb bearing seed, which is upon the face of all the earth, and every tree, in the which is the fruit of a tree yeilding seed, to you it shall be for meat." (*Genesis* 1.29) Therefore, meat-eating should be avoided.

Only after the Ecumenical councils at the time of Emperor Constantine, who was a meat-eater, did vegetarian Christians have to practice underground. It was either this or live in fear of having molten lead poured down their throat, which Constantine would do if he caught any vegetarian Christians. Of course, now this is no longer an issue in Christianity. Almost everyone considers that meat-eating is normal and that animals have no soul or feelings.

The idea that animals have no soul was started by Aristotle (384-322 B.C.). St. Augustine (354-430 A.D.) also supported this view because he favored meat-eating. Aristotle based his opinions on his speculations, but later Thomas Aquinas (1225-1274) unfortunately adopted Aristotle's philosophy, and the Church took Aquinas' teachings as dogma. And now most everyone in Christianity has followed suit. In fact, due to the expansion of Christianity in Ceylon and other parts of the East, meat-eating has spread, although the slaying of animals is forbidden in Buddhism and amongst those lamas, yogis, and *brahmanas* who are working to attain the highest spiritual development. Therefore, we can see how this destructive opinion that animals have no soul, which is based on a gross ignorance of spiritual knowledge, has spread.

The understanding that meat-eating is incompatible with spiritual progress can be seen more clearly in early Christianity and Eastern religious systems. In fact, such similarities between the Eastern and Western philosophies were more evident before the Ecumenical councils, which did away with many of the early Christian teachings that dealt with such things as reincarnation, *karma*, rebirth, and so on. Such Eastern influence was no doubt partly due to Jesus' travels through the Eastern countries, such as India, Ceylon, and a few of the Himalayan countries. But the modern Church often declines to dicuss the fact that early Christianity shows every evidence of being influenced by the East. And the East, specifically India, has always been viewed as the land of spiritual knowledge since time immemorial. So it should not be considered too unusual that many philosophical ideas of Christianity are rooted in the Vedic literature. However, if it is ever established beyond a doubt that Jesus was an initiate of the so-called "pagan" Asiatic teachings, it could certainly have a considerable effect on the members of the Christian faith. However, more and more people are gradually becoming aware of this Eastern influence.

PAGANISM IN CHRISTIANITY

The name *heathen* comes from the word *heath*, which is a common name for a variety of evergreen shrubs that live in swamps or along mountain slopes. Thus, the name *heathen* simply referred to those who lived in the country near such plants. The name *pagan* means a country man. Therefore, the use of the name *heathen* or *pagan* originally was not meant in a condescending way. To be a heathen or pagan simply meant that one followed those religions that existed prior to Christianity, or that he or she participated in the nature religions, which primarily meant demigod worship. And people throughout pre-Christian Europe worshipped a variety of spirits and demigods, known by different names according to culture and region. The Romans and Greeks of that time also worshiped demigods. The sun-god, Mithra, was apparently considered the most exalted of the demigods. Even King Constantine (280-337 A.D.) was originally a devotee of the sun-god. His famous vision of the cross that he had while marching on Rome came to him from the sun. In fact, even after he was converted to Christianity, he remained a devotee of the sun-god, and because of that he continued to hold the Sabbath day on Sunday, which traditionally was celebrated on Saturday.

According to Jewish tradition, the Sabbath was Saturday when God finished the creation and rested. So Saturday is the seventh day and Sunday is the first. Therefore, the Seventh Day Adventists, in a kind of protest, changed the Sabbath back to the original day. So even today the Sabbath is celebrated as a kind of pagan carry-over on the sun's day. In this way, each day was set aside for different demigods, who are the presiding deities of different planets. Thus, Sunday is for the sun, Monday is for the moon, Tues is the Greek name for Mars, Wednesday is for Mercury, Thursday for Jupiter, Friday for Venus, and Saturday for Saturn.

We can find many more similarities between Christianity and other cultures. The origin of one of the first stories in the Bible can be traced to Zoroastrianism. In Zoroastrianism we find where the Lord, Ahura Mazda, creates the world in six stages, and then creates the first man and woman and brings them to consciousness with the breath of life. Shortly afterward, Ahriman, the devil, convinces the man and woman to eat of the forbidden fruit, thus bringing sin and death into the world.

In other cases, the Jews, having such little information on their founders, borrowed ideas from the legends of neighboring cultures to make their own heroes look special. For example, the stories of Moses' activities are borrowed from the god Bacchus, who as a baby was found floating in a small boat in the water the way Moses was. Bacchus also emitted rays of light from his forehead, wrote laws on stone, crossed the Red Sea without getting his feet wet, and had armies that were led by pillars of fire. Other similarities can be found in the story of Lord Rama and in the activities of Zoroaster who is said to have lived many years before Moses. There are also events and miracles in the life of Jesus that were known to have happened to Buddha a few hundred years before.

Actually, Paul was the fanatic who took whatever was known of Jesus and, while misinterpreting Jesus' teachings, made Jesus out to be the incarnation of God, the Messiah, that Jesus never wanted to be. As described in *Mark* (8.29-30), when Jesus asked his disciples who they thought he was, Peter said that he was the Christ. And Jesus charged them that they should tell no man of him. In fact, the name *Christ* was first used in relation to Jesus by Paul when Paul first started preaching in the city of Antioch. The name *Christ* was simply the Greek word for Messiah.

Paul developed Christian theology and ritual and simply wrote in the Epistles his own ideas of Jesus while never referring to what Jesus actually said. Paul also put many threats into the philosophy of Christianity and created an image of a fearsome and jealous God rather than one that was merciful and loving. But, according to Paul's version of Christianity, salvation was granted by God alone who would save you if you simply became a Christian because Christ had already died on the cross as a sacrifice for your sins. In this way, faith was all that was needed, and faith outweighed the need for good works. This may be a simple and comfortable concept for Christians but is not a true one and was never presented in the real teachings of Jesus, who actually did emphasize the need for good works. So what we really find in Christianity are the teachings of Paul, which in some areas have little to do with what Jesus actually taught.

Paul also accepted Sunday as the day of rest from Mithraism rather than Saturday, the seventh day as found in the Hebraic tradition. Paul also took Easter from Mithraism as the day Jesus rose from the grave. Mithra is said to have died in battle on a Friday and was buried in a rock tomb from which, after three days, he rose on the festive occasion of the spring equinox, called Eastra, the Latin word for Astarte, the earth mother goddess. Interestingly, the 40 days before the spring equinox corresponding to Lent was the period for searching for the renewal of life in that tradition. Furthermore, the celebration for the resurrection of the Greek god Adonis is said to have taken place as late as 386 A.D. in Judea at the same time as the observance of Jesus' resurrection. And the use of dyed Easter eggs was widely known by such people as the Jews who used them in the Passover feast, and by the Egyptians and Persians who made presents of them. These were some of the non-Christian traditions that became incorporated into the Christian Easter holiday.

We can easily recognize many more outside influences in Christianity if we take a closer look. For example, one of the basic doctrines of Christianity is the Trinity of the Father, Son, and Holy Ghost. But the holy trinity existed many years prior to Christianity as an Eastern tradition. In the earliest form of it we find the *tri-murti* of Brahma the creator, Vishnu the maintainer, and Shiva the destroyer, often worshiped in a three-in-one Deity form or separated on individual altars in many temples of India. A variation of that is Lord Vishnu as the universal father, His incarnations as the sons, and His form of the omnipresent Supersoul as the Holy Ghost. And there were many other cultures that also worshiped a trinity. The Scandinavians worshiped Odin, Thor, and Frey. The Druids worshiped Taulac, Fan, and Mollac. The Romans' trinity was God, the Word, and the Spirit. Even the ancient Mayans had a trinity of Tezcatlipoca, Huitzlipochtli, and Tlaloc. The Persians worshiped a trinity consisting of Ahura Mazda as the creator, Mithras as the son or saviour, and Ahriman as the evil one, or destroyer.

Thus, the trinity was nothing new in the world when Christianity adopted it. But it was not until the 2nd century when the Christians claimed Jesus to be the son in their Trinity. This idea is traced back to Justin Martyr who simply stated that he realized this understanding by God's special favor rather than by using biblical references to verify it. In fact, though it had been proclaimed by Paul, the very idea that Jesus was God in human form, and, therefore, a part of the Trinity, was not settled until 325 A.D. during the Councils of Nicaea and Constantinople. Controversy had developed in regard to whether there was a time when the Trinity did not exist and whether the Trinity was formed only after the birth of the son, Jesus. Emperor Constantine was forced to summon the Council of Nicaea in hopes of solving this problem. During the council it was resolved that never was there a time when the Son of God did not exist, and those who thought there may have been were anathematized by the Church. They denounced the teachings of Arius, who had taught that the Son of God was a created human being who appeared once only and was secondary to the Father. Thus, by a majority vote, the Church pushed the resolution through and those who did not agree or believe it were expected not to oppose it and to keep their thoughts to themselves.

In fact, it was at this Nicaean Council that all the bishops gathered to discuss what interpretations of Christian theology the Church would teach. This was an attempt to calm the many disputes that had been going on within the Church about its varied teachings. Once this was settled, all other teachings were thrown out and considered heretical, and to teach or follow them was punishable by excommunication or death. To solidify these essential teachings, the Church compiled and edited the New Testament, ommitting that which was not acceptable and adding new material to justify its viewpoints and fill in what it did not know. Thus, the Church presented itself as the only source of truth and salvation.

There were as many as 50 gospels in circulation at the time when the New Testament was compiled, but the selection was limited to the ones presently found in the New Testament. These were chosen on the basis that they all maintained the conclusions the early Christians wanted to establish. One book that was left out was the *Gospel of Peter* because it did not accept the crucifixion as an act of atonement by Jesus for the sins of the people. And the *Acts of John* was also excluded because it denied that Jesus had a physical body, which is a concept subversive to the traditional Christian doctrine. This means that the Christian religion is not necessarily based on the Bible, but the Bible is based on the prevailing religion and ideas at the time the books of the Bible were compiled. Anything that did not meet the proper standard was thrown out.

As Christianity became stronger a few hundred years after Jesus' death, Constantine and the Pope, with the intention of suppressing all contradictory views of Jesus' divinity, commanded that all such "heretical" books should be found and completely destroyed. The authors of these works and their followers were all automatically excommunicated and declared eternally damned. Emperor Theodosius convened the second General Council at Constantinople in 381 and severely persecuted as heretics all those who did not accept the resolutions. Thus, the standard was set and was spread by force. Nearly 50 years after the death of King Constantine, the Church became the official religion of the Roman Empire and the position of the Church was then fixed. Nonetheless, many philosophical debates continued, as one did between Nestorius of Constantinople and Cyril of Alexandria in the fifth century. Nestorius accepted the humanity of Jesus and described Mary as the mother of Christ rather than the mother of God. Cyril, taking the view the Church propagated, that Christ was God, greatly opposed Nestorius. The third council of the Church at Ephesus, in 431, condemned the ideas of Nestorius and exiled him to the desert of Egypt in 435, but his theories continued to spread into Persia, India, and on into Central Asia and China. Such controversies in the Church continued, and lead to different conclusions and the formation of different sects. Even today we can see the almost unlimited variance of Christian sects and churches, each of which has its own ideas as to what is the nature of Christ, what is the soul, what is heaven, and so on. And each one thinking they are better than all of the others.

In light of these disputes over Christian philosophy, it has been found that more theologians and biblical scholars who understand the actual history of the biblical texts are less likely to blindly accept such concepts as the immaculate conception of Jesus or his death on the cross. It is this that forces the Church to continue to re-examine the foundations of the Christian religion and the idea that the Bible is composed by God, written by men who were "inspired" by the Holy Spirit. Not to be sure about such matters and yet preach as though the Bible is infallible is certainly a grave error, especially when the high-living preachers pose as the most righteous and truthful, concerned for the souls of all men, while demanding their followers to be righteous believers as well, and to show their faith by giving lots of money for the cause.

Another interesting point regarding pagan influence that may be very surprising to some is that the crucifix was not exclusively a Christian symbol. Prior to Christianity, history shows that the cross was an auspicious and mystical symbol amongst ancient Babylonians, Indians, Egyptians, Greeks, Romans, Druids, and even Laplanders and Scandinavians. For centuries, Indians used the cross in a variety of shapes, most notably as a swastika. For many years the Romans carried a cross with a dark skinned man on it as a standard. The crucifix was also known in ancient Mexico, as discovered by the Spanish monks who first went there. They were told that the Son of God, Quetzalcoatl, died on the cross for the sins of mankind. Even Tertullian, as late as 211 A.D., wrote that the Christians neither adored nor desired crosses, and criticized the pagans for doing so and for putting a man on the cross as well. For pagans, the cross was a sign of eternity.

In the first several centuries of Christianity, Jesus was represented as a lamb, or as a shepherd with a lamb over his shoulders. It was not until the 6th synod of Constantinople that it was decided that the symbol of Christianity, which was confirmed by Pope Adrian I, would be represented from that time on as a man crucified on the cross. In fact, the earliest instances of any artwork that illustrates Jesus on the cross can be traced back only to the eighth or ninth century. Thus, the Christians adopted the crucifixion as a symbol from the pagans.

It is also interesting to note that outside the New Testament there is no evidence that Jesus was crucified by the dictates of Pontius Pilate, nor do any of the historians of that time mention it. However, the *Talmud* refers to Jesus as having been a student of Joshua Ben Perachiah. The two of them went to Egypt where Jesus became learned in magic, and there died by being stoned, and then hung because of his blaspheming amongst the people.

Whether this is true or not cannot be verified, and many people may not want to try, but it is interesting to note that early historians and writers in Rome, such as Celsus, Lucian, Suetonius, and Tacitus, called Christianity a cult that was based on the principles of magic as taught by Jesus. The Christians were said to hate all outsiders as enemies. It has also been recorded that Jesus performed miracles by the use of magic and powers of the demons. Jesus was often considered a magician, one who had been initiated into the magical art while in Egypt. Thus, some accused him of performing miracles not as a Jewish prophet, but as a magician or necromancer, especially in the way he would cast out devils and his raising Lazarus from the grave. He was also supposed to have had special association with the powerful devil Beelzebul, and was even suspected of being possessed by demons. Some of these writers also asserted that Jesus took portions from the Jewish tradition, such as the idea that the Jewish messiah would appear from a virgin birth, and applied them to himself, thus misleading many Jewish people and directing them to worship foreign gods.

Another interesting point regarding pagan influence is within one of the first principles of Christianity: the virgin birth of Jesus from Mary. Chapter 19 of the *Koran* explains Mary's pregnancy, which some interpret to mean she was impregnated by an angel of the Lord, said to be Gabriel. But the idea of a virgin birth for a highly revered personality is not exclusive to Christianity. Those who are said to have had a miraculous birth, or were born from a virgin, include Buddha, the Siamese Codom, the Chinese Fo-hi (said to be born 3468 B.C.), Lao-tzu (604 B.C.), the Chinese sages Yu and Hau-ki, as well as Confucius. In Egypt, there is the god Ra, and Horus born of the virgin Isis. Also Zoroaster of Persia. The Greek Hercules, Bacchus, Amphion, Prometheus, and Perseus are all said to have been fathered by the gods and born of mortal mothers. There are also Romans, such as Romulus, Alexander the Great, Ptolemy, King Cyrus of Persia, Plato, Pythagorus, and others who have the reputation of being born of virgin mothers.

The celebration of Christmas is, of course, supposed to commemorate the birth of Jesus. However, we actually know from historical evidence that Jesus was born in the springtime. Some of the early churches observed the birth in

April or May, and some in January. Even today the Eastern Church celebrates Christmas on the seventh of January, while the Western Church celebrates it on December 25. Generally, no one is really sure of what day it was. But the birth of Jesus being held on the 25th of December can be traced back to the time of Emperor Commodus (180-192 A.D.), but it is earlier attributed to Telesphorus who had influence during the time of Antonins Pius (138-161 A.D.).

Other cultures also celebrated the 25th of December. The Persians celebrated it as the birthday of Mithras. The Greeks celebrated it as the birth of Bacchus. The Romans also celebrated the Saturnalia festival by feasting, stopping all business, holding public games, and exchanging gifts. The Scandinavians celebrated it as the birthday of Freyr, son of their god Odin and goddess Frigga. Here, too, there was much merry-making and exchanging of presents. The early Germans observed it as part of the Winter solstice, called the Yule feast. They spent time in jovial hospitality, made sacrifices, and worshipped their gods and burned the yule-log on the eve of the 24th. *Yule* was the old name for the 25th, which came from the word *Jul* used by the Scandinavians, while *Noel* in French came from the Hebrew word *Nule*.

Actually, the whole affair with the Christmas tree, the use of the mistletoe, hanging wreaths of flowers or evergreens on the doors, giving presents and so on, were all a part of the pagan celebration. The gift-giving we now observe on Christmas is a carry-over from the early pagan celebrations, and is not something that was started by Christianity. In fact, Tertullian, one of the early Fathers of Christianity, called such practices rank idolatry since it was associated with the "customs of the heathen." After all, the use of evergreens, Christmas trees, wreaths, etc., have nothing to do with Christianity, but they were used in the old traditions to signify the return of the sun, the longer days, and the regenerative power that was sure to follow the winter solstice. Thus, the 25th of December was a day of celebration and for showing respect to the gods long before the Christians adopted it for their purposes.

One of the purposes of the Christians was to change the pagan festivals into Christian holidays, and, hopefully, to attract the heathens to Christianity. For example, everyone knows that December twenty-first is the winter solstice, the shortest day of the year. For the next three days the length remains the same. But then on December twenty-fifth the day begins to get longer. So on this day the people celebrated in a very raucous manner. They took it that the sun-god was the redeemer and that on account of his birth there was the hope that everyone would be saved. Therefore, when the Christians wanted to establish their Christendom everywhere, they found some opposition to eliminate the birthday of the sun. People had become accustomed to enjoying themselves on that day. Of course, the Christians could not go on celebrating the birthday of the sun-god; so they simply replaced it with the celebration of the birth of Jesus. In this way, the Christians calculated that the pagans could go on with their celebrations but would simply change the meaning of it. But instead, Christianity incorporated and helped preserve many of the pagan traditions that were observed on the 25th.

Nowadays, the Christians are supposed to be religious people observing the day of Christ's birth, but they still celebrate in a very paganish way. They have kept many of the aspects of the pagan celebration that earmarks Christmas day; namely, drunkeness, revelry, spectator events like football, and feasting on slain animals. Each year so many advertisements go up claiming that amongst the best gifts on Christmas include a fifth of liquor or other useless items. So gradually, Christmas has deteriorated from what was meant to be an observance of a holy day to a mere display of devotion to commercialism.

Just as which day Jesus was born is not clear, neither is the year in which he was born known for sure. Some say he was born in 4 B.C., or 5 B.C., or even 15 B.C. According to statements made in the gospel of *St. Luke*, Jesus was born about 10 B.C. This is also verified by Eusebius, the first ecclesiastical historian. Both say that Jesus was born while Cyrenius was governor of Syria, and it is known that he was not governor until about 10 years after King Herod's death. Only the gospel of *St. Matthew* states that Jesus was born during the time of Herod. But this has been discovered to be due to the ignorance of Jewish history by the narrator because the gospel of *Matthew* also mentions the taxing of Cyrenius taking place during Herod's time. This is not true because Cyrenius could not impose taxation until he was governor. And let us not forget that, according to *Luke*, Joseph and Mary went to Bethlehem to be taxed when Jesus was born. In this way, we can see how contradictory statements exist in the biblical books about important points of Christian theology and history. This also indicates that everything the book of Matthew describes regarding Herod is false and that there was no killing of the children by Herod in his hopes of killing baby Jesus because Herod had been dead before Jesus was ever born. Therefore, this concept of the king killing all the children must have come from some other source and was included in the story of Jesus.

Another point about the birth of Jesus is that, historically, there was no direct account of it. Factually, all the gospels were written several decades after his death and there were no eye witnesses who had actually seen the birth. Traditionally, it is said that he was born in a stable with a few shepherds around, and supposedly some wise men also came from India, although in *Matthew* we find that Herod had sent them. However, the Christian Church never really agreed on how many wise men there were or where they came from. The Christian Church became divided in the 5th century into the Eastern division and Western division. The Eastern Church said there were sixteen wise men who came to see the birth of Jesus, and the Western Church said there were only three. They could never agree on where the wise men came from; so, they simply said from the East. Historically, however, there was never any record that any wise men came from anywhere to see the birth of Jesus.

Even the Bible is not clear on Jesus' birth. In *Matthew* (2.11) we find that Jesus was born in a house, but *Luke* (2.7, 12, 16) describes that Jesus was lying in a manger, or born in a stable. But in *Protevangelion*, the apocryphal gospel that is said to be written by James, the brother of Jesus, we find it described that Jesus was born in a cave near Bethlehem. This is also upheld by such early fathers of the Church as Tertullian (200 A.D.) and Jerome (375 A.D.). Furthermore, only in Matthew do we find Herod killing all the first-born sons in an attempt to kill Jesus; yet, the other gospels make no mention of such an atrocious crime, neither is it substantiated by any Roman or Jewish historical accounts. Also, there were many histories of that period, written by the contemporary historians of that time, and there is no record whatsoever of such a brutal killing of all the infants, except for one report made by the Essenes during Jesus' lifetime referring to the King as having killed both young and old. Although most Christians will naturally refer to the four gospels of the New Testament, namely, *Matthew, Mark, Luke,* and *John,* as the truth regarding Christ and the primary basis of Christianity, still it is not possible to determine accurately when these texts were written. It has been estimated that they were written between 50 and 100 A.D. in Greek or Aramaic, no earlier than several decades after the death of Christ. This means that there is no sure way of knowing who the authors were, and it is obvious that by the time they were written most of the data on Christ's life had already been lost.

It is also recognized that the gospels of the New Testament are not likely to have been written by those whose names are attached to them. Although several of them are written by Paul, the authorship of most of the books in the New Testament is unknown or highly questionable. Therefore, the authenticity of the information in these gospels are just as questionable. Even *Revelations* is accepted by many scholars to be merely a collection of works by unknown authors. In fact, though the gospels are said to have originally been written several decades after the disappearance of Jesus, the gospels as we find them today can be traced back only to the time of Irenaeus in the 2nd century. The gospel of *Matthew* is considered to be the oldest and does not seem to have existed in its present form until 173 A.D., when Apollinaris, Bishop of Hierapolis, accredits the book to Matthew. But earlier editions may have dated to 100 A.D. The gospel of *Matthew* seems to have been primarily taken from a previous text called *The Gospel of the Hebrews*, which gave the genealogy of Jesus back to David, yet did not contain a description of Jesus' virgin birth. Thus, some say the story of Jesus' birth was added later after the idea had been taken from other stories of significant personalities being born from pure virgins.

Many people feel that the gospels of the New Testament are written by the 12 apostles, so who could have been more authorized to write them? But the 12 apostles were Andrew, John, Bartholomew, Judas, Jude, James, another James, Matthew, Peter, Phillip, Simon, and Thomas. After Judas committed suicide he was replaced with Matthias. So Mark, Luke, and Paul, who are supposed to be authors of several of the New Testament books, were not apostles. And Paul never even met Jesus and became a Christian several years after Jesus had disappeared.

By careful study one can find many discrepancies between the gospels. The authors, whoever they were, wrote of things of which they had little knowledge and ascribed sayings to Jesus that do not conform to his faith. Thus, they obviously wrote their tales as they heard them from other reports or previously existing texts, and in this way included various inaccurate statements.

For example, *St. Mark* (7.31) states: "And again, departing from the coasts of Tyre and Sidon, he came unto the Sea of Galilee, through the midst of the coasts of Decapolis." It is known that Decapolis was on the southeast side of the Sea of Galilee, and northeast of Judea. So there were no coasts of Decapolis, which is a name that was not known prior to the time of Emperor Nero, who reigned 54-68 A.D. This indicates that the narrators knew little of what they were writing about, at least in regard to the local geography, what to speak of other things.

We also find where the narrator of *Matthew* has Jesus explain in chapter 24 the signs that will indicate the second coming of Christ. These include false Christs and false prophets, pestilences, earthquakes, famine, wars, nation against nation, the darkening of the sun and moon, the stars falling from the sky, etc., all described in verses that are often referred to by many. But finally in verse 34, Jesus specifically says: "Verily I say unto you, This generation shall not pass, till all these things be fulfilled." But we can plainly see that many, many generations have passed since the time this was said. Years later, the fact that these things had still not taken place was attempted to be justified in *II Peter*, Chapter Three, where it says that the Lord is not slack in His promise and the day of Jesus' return will come like a thief in the night. This may be true, but this is also a prime example of how one book of the Bible tries to justify mistakes made in another, and shows how convinced the early Christians were that Christ was expected to appear again very soon.

VEDIC INFLUENCE ON CHRISTIANITY

When we consider the story of how baby Jesus appeared in the heart of Mary by immaculate conception, as well as the bright star appearing in the night sky, we can discern a direct parallel to Lord Krishna's birth three thousand years earlier in Vrindavana, India, as recorded in the Vedic literature. It is also described how Krishna appeared in the mind of Vasudeva, Krishna's father, and was then transferred into the heart of His mother, Devaki. During Krishna's birth, the bright star Rohini was high in the sky, and the king at the time, Kamsa, actually ordered the killing of all the infants in an attempt to kill Krishna, similar to the way Herod was supposed to have done as described in the gospel of *Matthew*. And just as a multitude appeared among the shepherds in the hills praising God at the time of Jesus' birth, there were also many demigods who came and danced and sang about the glories of Krishna when He was ready to appear in this world. And as wise men were supposed to have presented Jesus with frankincense and myrrh, Krishna was also presented with gifts that included sandalwood and perfumes.

There was a darkness that descended when Jesus was crucified, just as there was a darkness and many calamities taking place when Krishna left this world. And as there is a discription of many ominous signs that are to signify the second coming of Christ, there are even more symptoms of the terrible age of Kali that we are going through that indicates the time before the coming of the Krishna's next incarnation as Kalki. There are many other parallels that we could refer to that are disclosed in the *Vedas*, which were written many hundreds of years before the Bible.

Practically speaking, what we find in the Bible regarding Jesus' birth is a description of the appearance of Lord Krishna, but only the names have been changed. Of course, there are different theories about how this happened. One theory is that when the Christians went to India, they found out that this story was there in the *Bhagavat-Purana*; so, they immediately had to change the date of when the *Bhagavat-Purana* was supposed to have been written. So now the historians generally say that it was written about 1400 years ago. Otherwise, how could they explain the story of Krishna's birth being so similar to the story of Christ's birth? They thought that the Vedic pandits must have heard about the story of Jesus and adapted the story to their own incarnation, as if the Vedic scholars would demean themselves by putting a story into their scripture that was heard from people who were considered low-born foreigners.

One archeological find that proved that knowledge of Krishna antedated Christianity by at least 200 years was the Heliodorus column built in 113 B.C. in central India by the Greek ambassador to India, Heliodorus. On it is an inscription commenting on the ambassador's devotion to Lord Vishnu (Krishna) and mentioning when the column had been erected. The column still stands near the town of Vidisha.

We must remember that when the Christians first came to India to preach, they were not very well received by the local people. There was very little penetration because the Christian priests and missionaries were seen for what they were: *mlecchas* and *yavanas*, more or less unclean cow-killers or untouchables in local terminology. So it is doubtful that the Vedic pandits spent much time even listening to them, what to speak of writing scripture or changing the story of Krishna's birth on account of hearing these missionaries. Of course, now as Indian society has deteriorated and become more attracted to Western values (partly due to being indoctrinated by the British rule years ago), Christianity is more easily accepted.

So, the conclusion we must arrive at is that the story of Lord Krishna's birth, along with numerous other parts of the Vedic philosophy, must have come to the mideastern part of the world because of the many trade caravans going back and forth at that time from India to the region of Palestine. Since there were no real witnesses of Christ's birth and hardly any history in the gospels of the life of Christ up to the age of thirty, it is likely they applied the story to Jesus' life. Otherwise, there is little historical evidence that any of it is factual.

There is evidence, however, as more facts are being uncovered, that contends that Jesus may have been nailed to the cross but did not die on it. After having been taken from the cross, he later recovered from the ordeal rather than rose from the dead. The Shroud of Turin, if it is authentic, seems to provide some evidence that Christ was not dead when taken from the cross since his body was still bleeding while wrapped in the cloth. Even if Christ did appear to die on the cross, being a yogic master, he could have put himself into trance to be revived later. This goes on even today with yogis in India or fakirs in Egypt who can appear to die, be buried for hours, days, months, or sometimes years, and then be uncovered and resurrected from their apparent death. Even the *Koran* claims that Jesus did not die on the cross.

There is also evidence that after the crucifixion Jesus traveled through Turkey, Persia, and then India. The Russian scholar Nicolas Notovitch discovered in 1887 Buddhist documents at the Hemis monastery in Ladakh that describe the life of Issa. Issa is the Arabic spelling of the name Jesus, and the name for Jesus commonly used in Islam. The ascension into heaven may have referred to his entrance into Kashmir, an area considered by many to have been like heaven or the promised land. One usually travels through Kashmir before going to Ladakh.

Furthermore, the *Bhavishya Purana*, dating back to 3000 B.C. and said to have been compiled by Vyasadeva, also describes the future coming of Christ and his activities. Dr. Vedavyas, a research scholar who holds a doctorate in Sanskrit, said that the *Purana* tells of how Jesus visited the Himalayas and did penance to acquire spiritual maturity under the guidance of the sages and *siddha-yogis* of India. Dr. Vedavyas says that besides describing the future events of Kali-yuga and the coming war of wars that could change the world near the turn of the century, the *Purana* predicted that Jesus would be born of an unmarried woman, Kumari (Mari or Mary) Garbha Sambhava, and would first go to India when he was 13 years old and visit many Hindu and Buddhist holy places. The actual burial place of Jesus is believed to be in Anzimar, Srinagar's old town in Kashmir, where thousands of pious pay homage to the tomb of Issa each year.

In any case, the Christian Church began with what Paul said about the resurrection of Jesus. Whether the resurrection actually happened or not cannot be proved. Nonetheless, a new faith was born. But through the years there has been much controversy about the nature of Jesus and whether he was actually God as some Christians seem to believe. None of his direct disciples believed that he was, and, indeed, there are many Bible verses which state directly that he was the son of God, such as *Luke* 1.35, *Matthew* 17.5, *John* 4.15, 8.28, 14.28, and others. Only Paul put forward the idea that Jesus was God. But he never met Jesus personally, and was converted to Christianity a few years after Jesus' disappearance. Other than that, most of Jesus' followers thought that perhaps he was the Jewish Messiah. But the Jewish Messiah, according to their prophecies, was not God but rather a Jew who was empowered by God. This actually fits into the Vedic view because there are many empowered living beings who appear from time to time who are sent by God to represent and disseminate His law. Furthermore, Bhaktisiddhanta Sarasvati, one of the great Vaishnava spiritual masters in the Madhava-Gaudiya line of disciplic succession, has stated that Jesus was a *shaktyavesha avatar*, or an empowered living entity meant to preach the glories of God.

People may say that Jesus walked on water, healed the sick, raised the dead, so he must have been God. But even today in India there are yogis who can walk on water or do other amazing things, like walking over hot coals. This is not like the Hollywood fad of fire walking, but the yogis let the coals burn for days and get so hot that you cannot even get near them without burning your clothes. Then, after spending one month in penance, praying to Durga, they walk across the fire and do not even burn their feet. But some people will say this is the work of the devil. However, is this not peculiar logic to say that walking across fire is of the devil, but if one walks across water he is God? This kind of thinking that is usually found amongst fundamentalists simply shows a great ignorance of yogic powers, which is all walking across fire or water is. Therefore, the miracles of Jesus are a sign of his knowledge of the mystical powers that come from practicing yoga. But it is not a proof that someone is God. In fact, the Dead Sea Scrolls prove more or less conclusively that the whole concept of Jesus Christ's divinity is a later addition.

One important part of Eastern knowledge that was present in early Christianity was the understanding of *karma* and reincarnation. I have already discussed this and pointed out some of the verses that showed the acceptance of reincarnation in the Bible in *The Secret Teachings of the Vedas*; so, I will not go into it so deeply here. But it is known that the Second Council of Constantinople in 553 A.D. threw out all references to reincarnation and stated that the idea of it was a myth, and anyone who believed in it would be excommunicated. Of course, this action would not be unexpected in light of the other things the Church has done throughout history in order to place itself as the only way to reach heaven and attain the mercy of God. By eliminating the possibility of reincarnation and the soul's existence prior to this life, there could be no chance for the soul to reach the state of spiritual perfection over a period of several lifetimes. There would only be this one lifetime in which the soul came into existence, and one chance for a person to reach either heaven or eternal hell, which would be determined by the intervention of the Church. In other words, the Church felt threatened by the fact that the soul has an eternal and personal relationship with God that must be rekindled either in one, two, or however many lifetimes it takes, and this relationship does not necessarily depend on one's good standing in any religious organization. Thus, people could try to re-establish their relationship with God by other means than the dictates of the Church, which is what the Church could not tolerate.

Unfortunately, by taking out the knowledge of reincarnation and *karma*, the Church has created huge gaps in its philosophy which leave questions it cannot answer. For example, the Christians cannot explain why one person may be born blind, poor, deformed, or sickly, while another may be born healthy and rich. They do not understand why reversals in life may happen to some, and others seem to have a life of ease. They cannot explain why these differences take place and, in fact, they sometimes blame God for such things, which only shows their ignorance of spiritual knowledge. Furthermore, they do not understand the science of the soul and our spiritual identity, the nature of the spiritual realm, the characteristics of the personality of God, nor the pastimes and incarnations of God, and so on. Thus, the spiritual knowledge that the Christians utilize in their philosophy is very elementary and incomplete. And as we have already established in a previous chapter, reaching complete spiritual perfection is not possible in such an incomplete spiritual process. At best, it promotes good moral values, detachment toward worldly life, attachment and devotion to God, and the possibility of reaching the heavenly planets, but the heavenly planets are still within the material cosmic manifestation and not in the spiritual realm. A real transcendentalist is interested only in reaching the level of spiritual self-realization that enables him to directly perceive his spiritual identity and enter the spiritual strata far beyond this material creation.

Actually, Christians still must accept the understanding of *karma* and reincarnation to some extent in order to explain logically how one can have a life after death in heaven or hell. According to the Christian doctrine, qualifying for heaven or hell depends on one's actions in this life. That is called *karma* in Vedic literature. And as one enters heaven or hell in his next life, he takes on or incarnates in a different form. This is reincarnation. So Christians must, at least to this degree, accept *karma* and reincarnation whether they fully understand it or not. But to understand it more completely, as explained in the philosophy of the Vedic literature, allows us to realize that our good or unpleasant situations in this life depends on our activities from past lives. And by our activities in this life we can cause our future existence to be good or bad, or we can reach the heavenly or hellish planetary systems to work out our *karma*. This understanding is accepted by many cultures throughout the world. In fact, the scholar Max Muller once remarked that the greatest minds humanity has produced have accepted reincarnation.

I could go on pointing out more Eastern traditions that influenced or were adopted and preserved in various levels of Christianity, but there are other topics that should be covered. So, in summary, let me say that it has been recognized by many men of the past, such as Bishop Faustas when writing to St. Augustine, Ammonius Saccus the Greek philosopher, the Epicurean philosopher Celsus, Eusebius the historian, and the early Christian writer Justin Martyr, that Christianity does not differ from the old traditions and customs that were called paganism, nor does Christianity hold anything that was not previously known to the ancients. If anything, through its attitude of exclusivety and general feelings of proud superiority, Christianity has lost the elaborate explanations of the once well known truths and now merely holds hazy reflections of the ancient wisdom. So many Bible stories are interwoven with tales borrowed from neighboring cultures, and numerous Christian rituals and symbols have been taken from previous ancient customs and traditions. So, Christians should look beyond the superficialities of modern Christianity to try and see the real religions and cultures from which it came. As Saint Augustine said hundreds of years ago: "The same thing which is now called Christian Religion existed among the ancients. They have begun to call Christian the true religion which existed before." And to quote T. W. Doane from his book, *Bible Myths and Their Parallels in Other Religions*, (page 413), he sums it up as follows:

We have seen, then, that the only difference between Christianity and Paganism is that Brahma, Ormuzd (Ahura Mazda), Zeus, Jupiter, etc., are called by another name; Krishna, Buddha, Bacchus, Adonis, Mithras, etc., have been turned into Christ Jesus: Venus' pigeon into the Holy Ghost; Diana, Isis, Devaki, etc., into the Virgin Mary; and the demigods and heroes into saints. The exploits of the one were represented as the miracles of the other. Pagan festivals became Christian holidays, and Pagan temples became Christian Churches.

THE DARK SIDE OF CHRISTIANITY

Let us not forget that the Church has a long and bloody history in its concern for the souls of all men. In the fourth and fifth centuries, the Church began to burn the huge libraries and close the schools of free thought in places like Alexandria and Athens. To push on Christian thought and control the philosophical views of people, it was Christianity, especially the rules established by the wicked King Constantine, that began what is called the Dark Ages. This was a time of intense prejudice, cruelty, and persecution against all who may not have been in complete agreement with the Christian doctrine. The early Christian leaders were cruel and looked on anything other than their own faith as heresy, just as we see today some modern fundamentalist Christians who view anything other than Christianity as being associated with the devil and worthy of being stamped out. This is the same kind of logic they use to say that it is the wrath of God on the heathen if a Hindu temple is damaged by a storm or something, but it is the work of the devil if a bolt of lightning strikes a church.

Once Christianity began to spread through Europe, it was often met with resistance, but the "heretics" were treated with torture and death. Christianity was a religion of the sword that compares with the organized terror of the Nazis. Anything the Christians did not like they destroyed, including academies and the books by the Greek poets and philosophers of the time. They went so far as to kill Hypatia, the great woman who was head of the School of Philosophy at Alexandria, by a mob attack on her in which they tore off her clothes, cut her body up into pieces with oyster shells, and burned her piece by piece, simply because she was a woman known to teach men in her lectures, and because Cyril, the Christian bishop of Alexandria, wanted to ruin her. Cyril hated her because of her many accomplishments and because she was a symbol of individual freedom and freedom from the fanatical and growing power of the Church. Quite obviously, the Church had no respect for women and, like barbarians that many of the men seemed to be, treated them so.

Later, in 1233, the Roman Catholic Church established the Inquisition as the forceful aspect of the Vatican for the purpose of eliminating heresy. In the thirteenth century it began its slaughter of heretics throughout Europe. In the cases of heresy that the Inquisition dealt with, charges could be brought up on anyone, and the offenders would not have to be told who accused them or what specifically were the accusations. If a neighbor simply did not like you, they could start rumors that would force you to be subjected to the torture of the Inquisition. If you were found guilty of any kind of heresy, you could face punishment of heavy fines or even death by being burned alive. In 1252, Pope Innocent IV authorized the use of torture while the accused was being interrogated. Once the torture started, it usually did not stop unless the victim confessed to whatever the charges were. The Spanish Inquisition was established in 1480 and was much more severe in the way it meted out punishment.

As this madness swept across Europe, things became totally barbaric and the Inquisition, which sometimes held its trials in secret, struck fear into the hearts of everyone. Thousands upon thousands were killed and burned alive as the Church and authorities grew rich by confiscating the property of the victims, all in the name of Christianity. Unfortunately, many of these so-called heretics were people or clerics who simply wanted to return to the basic piety and message of Jesus and distance themselves from the intrigues and excesses found in the Roman Church.

In time, the interest in the condemning eyes of the Church and Inquisition included not only wiping out heretics but also finding witches. In many cases, the charge of being a witch or heretic was the same. The witch hunts started in the 14th century and lasted more than 300 years and affected all of Europe. By the 17th century, as many as 200,000 or more people had been killed by the Christian-controlled courts.

For many years, being a witch was nothing extraordinary. It merely meant that one followed the old nature religions or respected the early demigods and goddesses, like Thor, Wotan, Herne, Mithra, etc., that were popular in various regions prior to Christianity. It might also have meant that someone was familiar with herbology and the old folk traditions of healing. Of course, there may have been those who could cast spells, but that was not the primary objective.

Over the years as the Roman Empire declined, the power of the Church rose. As it did, it began to incorporate the days of pagan celebrations into its holy days, like Christmas, as previously explained. As this did not always work to distract the people's attention from these pagan practices, the Church declared that these pagan gods were all demons. Thus, these demigods, along with the creatures of the subtle realm, like elves, gnomes, fairies, etc., and anyone recognizing or respecting them, were considered enemies of the Christian Church and all true Christians.

Later, the Church went so far as to say that witches were not merely practitioners of paganism, but were servants of the devil. This made them even more despised in the eyes of the Church. Thus, everything from reciting prayers to heal the sick, casting horoscopes, preparing charms, or wearing amulets, to using folk remedies for disease, was condemned as being the practice of a witch.

Large gatherings of witches performing their rites were called sabbats. The Church made up many disgusting activities that the witches were supposed to have performed at these sabbats. These would include such things as riding to them on a broomstick, worshiping the devil, kissing his genitals or anus, copulating with the devil, forming a pact with the devil, sacrificing babies and then roasting and eating them, engaging in wild orgies, or announcing to the other witches all the evil deeds thay had recently done. Anyone accused of being a witch would be charged with performing any or all of these activities, making them extremely wicked in the eyes of the Christians. And under enough torture, these poor men and women would confess to anything in hopes of having the torture end. Any people the Church did not like could be accused of being a witch: servants of the devil. Thus, their fate would be sealed.

Let us remember that in Christianity the concept of a devil or Satan, the ultimate god of evil and enemy of God, was carried over from Judaism, which had taken it from Zoroastrianism where it originated. Before Zoroastrianism, the existence of a mighty god of evil does not seem to be a concept that had been present in the early religions, though there may have been some demons or spirits of an evil nature. Even other religions at the time did not recognize any such god of evil or Prince of Darkness. So, if there really is no Satan, which many people still believe in, this would indicate that all of the charges against witches and their connection with the devil were false from the start. They had simply been a fabrication, a pretext for the Church to use in order to maintain power and control and to instill fear in the hearts of its subjects. The propaganda was that the Church was one's only salvation from the power of the devil and eternal damnation.

Unfortunately, a single person accused of being a witch could implicate dozens of others since victims under torture would often confess to anything or accuse anyone else that the torturers suggested. The torturers would demand that accomplices be named, otherwise the torture would become more severe. Many times the accused women would be raped before being tortured. The instruments of torture would be blessed by a priest before being used so that they would more effeciently perform the will of God. Some of these instruments were the rack, which could stretch and dislocate the joints of the body, pulling arms, knees, and hips from their sockets and increasing the length of the body by a foot; the knee splitter, a vise that could crush joints, shins, etc.; thumbscrews; the head crusher, which could put enough pressure on the skull to shatter it or make eyeballs pop out; a metal spiked chair; and other instruments used in much more sadistic ways, such as a simple wagon wheel. The wagon wheel would be used to hit and break all the major bones of the victim's body as he lay helplessly tied to the ground. Then the executioner would thread the victim's broken arms and legs between the spokes of the wheel. The wheel would then be raised up on top of a pole, under which a fire would be made to slowly roast the victim to death, or he would just be left for the vultures.

Obviously, a religion that can resort to such tactics of torture is no religion at all. It is an abominable and vengeful institution that is merely interested in maintaining political power and control rather than saving souls. Such an institution hardly has any understanding of mercy, compassion, kindness, or the law of *karma*, what to speak of the higher principles of real spiritual knowledge.

As the witch burnings increased, sometimes whole villages simply disappeared. And few individuals were bold enough to object to the proceedings since the Inquisition made it plain that only another witch would find fault with it. And those who tried to justify what the Inquisition did would cite the Bible verse, "thou shalt not suffer a witch to live," from *Exodus* (22.18). But it was not only the Roman Catholic Church who actively tried to kill anyone accused of withcraft, the Protestants did so as well. Martin Luther shared the same view of witches as the Roman Church, and went so far as to say that he would burn them all. Oddly enough, the Catholics and Protestants were engaged in much fighting with each other. To help destroy the Protestants, Catholics would start rumors about Protestant people being engaged in witchcraft, and they would soon be facing the Inquisition, and then death at the stake.

In time there were the most deceitful men known as the witch hunters who would be paid for discovering and obtaining confessions from heretical witches. One technique the witch hunters would use to discover who was really a witch was to find a patch of skin that would have no feeling, which was said to be the mark of the devil. The accused women would be forced to go to the quarters of the witch hunter and take off her clothes while he would search her body for the devil's mark. To help find such a mark they would use intruments resembling ice picks to poke the skin. Some of these allowed the blade to easily withdraw into the handle so the victim would feel nothing while it would look like it was poking the skin. Thus, an innocent woman would be implicated and tortured until she confessed and named others of being witches. In this way, a profitable career would be made by the witch hunters for finding so-called witches amongst innocent villagers.

Once a woman was accused of being a witch, her death was certain. During one period of 150 years, a total of 30,000 women had been burned at the stake, all in the name of Christianity. Gradually enough people began to speak out against the prosecutions and witch burnings that they began to subside. But for many years after they had ended, the prejudice, suspicion, and fear that the Church fostered about witches or witchcraft continued, even to the present day.

One of the reasons for this terribly callous attitude toward women was that the leaders of early Christianity were Jews, and in the Hebraic tradition they had little regard for women. Saint Augustine of Hippo went so far as to say women had no souls. This is certainly a ridiculous statement, but the real absurdity is that enough men thought it a serious possibility that it became an issue that was actually debated at a Council at Macon in the sixth century. Whether this attitude toward women helped explain the killing and cruel treatment of so many women who were labeled as witches later on, it is hard to say, but it probably contributed to it.

Even Paul taught that women should be silent and simply serve their husbands. After Paul, King Constantine was the chief exponent of male supremacy and women's inferiority. It was also Constantine, the first Christian Emperor, who slowly boiled alive his first wife under the suspicion of committing adultery. He also murdered his son Crispus and killed his brother-in-law Licinius, who had been more broad-minded about the pagans at the time. Constantine also had Licinius' son whipped to death for no reason. This paved the way for the cruel habits and attitudes of other rulers that followed over the next 14 centuries to murder their wives or those they did not like. Even Saint Thomas Aquinas in the Middle Ages placed women lower than slaves.

This type of idealogy comes from nothing more than an almost total lack of any kind of spiritual understanding. As we have explained in *The Secret Teachings of the Vedas*, consciousness in any living body is a symptom of the soul within. On the eternal, spiritual platform everything is absolute. So even though there may be any number of differences between one material body and another, how can one soul be superior to another, regardless of whether the body is male or female? Spiritually the only difference between any of us is the level of spiritual realization we have attained. Otherwise, to question whether women have souls or not is completely preposterous. Of course, let us remember that this form of ignorance is the same ignorance that causes many followers of these fundamental religions to remain convinced that animals have no souls and are meant simply to serve man in any way we choose. And, as we can see, this exploitation of animals spills over to the exploitation of women and the callous or cruel attitudes we have toward each other.

The dominating nature of the Church can also be seen in the early history of the Americas. In 1492 Columbus landed in America and many Christian missionaries soon followed. In many cases, the Europeans arrived hungry and in need of assistance. The Indians helped them at first, only to be treated later as any other pagan and heathen culture in the view of the Christian Church, which was that all non-Christian civilizations should either be converted or conquered and dominated in any way it saw fit. Rather than coming to the New World to understand a new culture and share in its knowledge and resources, the European conquerors preferred to take control of the land and dominate the native people. It was the Church that implemented campaigns to destroy all religions, languages, and histories of the native American Indians. With the condescending Christian attitudes toward the American natives, many Christian conquerors felt no pity for killing hundreds of thousands of American Indians in order to claim the territory and do their will with it. In addition, as many as 50 million Indians died from the diseases that the Christian Europeans brought with them, such as smallpox, measles, etc.

To justify their conquering of the American land and natives, the Christians adopted the concept of "Manifest Destiny," which proclaimed that the land was allotted to them by God to do as they wished. This is in accord with their ethnocentric philosophy that justifies their feelings that they are superior to every other race and culture.

The Christian Spaniards are known for their most bloody conquests in the 16th century of the Taino Indians of Hispaniola (present day Haiti and the Dominican Republic), Mexico's Aztec Indians, the natives of Panama, as well as the Incan Empire along the Andes Mountains in South America. Once again it was all in the name of Christianity and their desire to find gold and riches. "Santiago" was the battle cry, and the name would often be shouted out by the soldiers in their massacres of the Indians. Santiago Matamoros, St. James the Slayer of Muslims, was the patron saint of the Christian armies of King Ferdinand and Queen Isabella when they crushed Granada, the last Muslim community that was left in Spain in 1492. The cry "Santiago" became a call for the heavenly power to purge the earth of all non-Christian infidels, no matter if they were Muslims or Jews in Europe, or natives of the Americas.

Much of the money that Spain used for the military conquests in the New World had been obtained from the property and wealth confiscated from the Jews during the Inquisition. Although many of the civilians who came to America had hopes of finding religious freedom, the same bigotry they were fleeing they now directed toward the American Indians.

In order to find treasures, the Spaniards would torture the Indian chiefs for information, and both men and women were forced to carry heavy loads of valuables to the Spanish towns. And no pretty woman, married or not, was free from being raped as long as these Spanish barbarians were present. Thus, the Indians were forced to serve the new masters in the most demeaning ways. In this process, most of the Indian culture was gradually wiped out, primarily because of the disrespect the Christians had for any culture but their own.

Columbus originally came to America looking for a way to make money by finding a new route to India and an easy source of gold. After he arrived in America and learned that he would not be able to make his fortune from gold, he decided to try making a profit by capturing the local Indians to be sold as slaves in Europe. Most of the captives in his first load died on the way, so his venture of trading Indian slaves did not work. But his idea of slave trade was quickly picked up by others. In fact, it was the Spanish Catholic priest Bartolome de Las Casas who encouraged the enslavement of Africans instead of the native Americans who were dying in great numbers. In 1505 the first African slaves were shipped to the Americas by the Spanish Conquistadors, and as many as ten million slaves were brought during the next four centuries. The high point of the slave trade was in the 1700s and was primarily done by the British, French, Dutch, and Portuguese, who were all of the Christian persuasion. Most of the slaves went to the Caribbean and Brazil, and the rest went to North America. This is how the Christian tendency and desire for domination swept through the Americas and redistributed major portions of the world's population.

* * *

One of the reasons I have included this information on the dark history of Christianity is to show how inflexible the Church became in considering other paths of understanding universal truths. It did not matter whether it was the religions that had existed before Christianity, or folk healing, astrology, Roman demigod worship, Greek philosophy, Celtic mythology, Judaism, Hinduism, Islam, Buddhism, or whatever. They were all heretical in the eyes of the Church. This not only meant that these practices were not worth considering, but also that those who practiced them were automatically labeled as the lowest of mankind, heathens, pagans, idol worshipers, enemies of the Church who should be tortured and killed in the most sadistic ways. This is what can happen when a group or institution has such a divisive vision. Rather than increasing harmony, understanding, and God consciousness, the institution turns the land into a battlefield leaving scores of senseless deaths in its wake. So, after reading this history, we have to ask ourselves, who were the real barbarians? Who were the real enemies of all forms of understanding and philosophy? Who were the ones afraid of losing power and control to the point where they killed anyone who might be a threat? And did the devil really exist amongst all those so-called witches who were executed, or was he actually located in the hatred the Church exhibited toward hundreds of thousands of fellow human beings? And where was the mercy and forgiveness that the Church proclaimed to be a necessary quality to reach heaven? And though great reforms have been made, has the beast of such fanaticism and narrow-mindedness been vanquished, or is it only sleeping?

In the present times, we might not have witch hunts, but we still find what is called "the fear of cults." This fear is nothing more than irrational prejudice based on the ignorance of foreign customs by fundamentalists who feel that anything other than their own conventional religion or viewpoint is bad, is a cult, and should be viewed with suspicion. This prejudice and persecution can presently be seen in the courts of government that force different groups or less conventional religions to prove to a jury the legitimacy of their religious beliefs, and their constitutional right to practice freely the legal traditions of their religion. This cuts away at the religious and legal freedoms on which this country was founded. This is nothing more than a repeat of history in which fundamentalists try to enforce their own dogma on everyone else, some of whom, like Hindus or Buddhists, have far more experience and history in their culture, and a much further developed philosophy of spiritual topics than Christianity.

Of course, there may be some cults that are very secretive about what they do. These should be carefully analyzed to see if they practice something unlawful. But many so-called cults are nothing more than groups of people practicing spiritual customs that have been in existence for thousands of years. Let us not forget that Christianity was viewed as nothing more than a small cult of eccentric people in the beginning. And if it was not for cults like the Essenes, of which Jesus was a member and in which he first began his spiritual training, there may never have been any Christian religion. Even the Christians were known as nothing more than a radical cult in the beginning.

Let us also remember that the founding fathers of the United States did not start this country on the basis of any one philosophy or religion, Christian or otherwise. Ben Franklin, John Hancock, Joseph Hewes, Robert Payne, and 28 of the other 56 men who signed the Declaration of Independence were Masons, men interested in pursuing metaphysical understanding that might not necessarily be completely in line with Christianity. Even the date of July 4, 1776 was astrologically calculated as being a favorable time for initiating activities for the future well-being of this country. Also, when George Washington laid the cornerstone of the White House, he did so in full Masonic uniform, thus utilizing a 3,000 year old Egyptian ritual. In this way, you could say this country was founded on freedom of choice: the freedom for one to choose the philosophy and idealism most suited for him or her while living peacefully with others, and without forcing that idealism on those who may not feel the same. But any form of tyranny, whether religious or political, that works unjustly to force its views on others, will work against such freedom and will stifle the growth and development of the individuals who make up that country. When this is noticed, it must be corrected immediately.

Actually it does not matter whether this segment is about Christianity or some other religious or political institution. The point is that all people have to have the freedom to find themselves to the fullest extent on whatever path it takes, providing it is a bona fide path. So how do we make sure we can continue to have this freedom? By understanding each other, by understanding other cultures of the world and other paths of self-discovery, and by recognizing the value that they have to offer. We must also bury our preconceived prejudices that are based on our immature feelings of superiority because, spiritually speaking, we are all the same. We just have to attain that spiritual vision to see the reality of it. And the path we take to do that is the only difference among us.

Of course, by discussing the history of the Church we are not attempting to demean Jesus. We are simply showing to what extent a religion will go to maintain power and control, especially when it feels threatened by what it does not understand. Furthermore, the dark history of Christianity represents the small but fanatically narrow-minded side of it that has continued to the present day in the form of fundamentalists thinking that if a religion or culture is not Christian, then it must be of the devil. Christians are often ready to dismiss or criticize other religions and cultures without understanding them. They may see a ceremony or ritual of another religion and immediately say it is heathen or devil worship. But a similar misunderstanding can happen in Christianity. For example, in the Eucharist ritual they partake of drinking the blood and eating the body of Christ. Does this mean that Christians are cannibals, or have a cannibalistic mentality? Not if you understand that the blood and body of Christ is distributed *symbolically* in the form of wine and wafers. So proper understanding is needed in any religion.

In light of this it is interesting to point out that (at the time of this writing) a letter was recently released from the Vatican to the Bishops which criticized zen and such spiritual practices as yoga and meditation. The letter was written by Cardinal Ratzinger but was also approved by Pope John Paul II. The letter warned against the sensations of spiritual well-being that one gets from practicing yoga or meditation, and said that this could lead to schizophrenia, moral deviations, or even psychic disorders, and degenerate to a cult of the body. Now on what basis do they make these claims? Of course, if one improperly practices a complicated form of yoga, such as *kundalini-yoga* as described in a previous chapter, there may be some adverse results. But for the most part, yoga and real transcendental meditation means to fix the mind and become absorbed, at least for certain lengths of time, on that which is transcendent, which is God. This is real spirituality, as well as the original mystical tradition in Christianity. So what is wrong with this when this is the goal of any spiritual path? Why would they issue such a letter, unless they are once again simply trying to condemn every other form of religion? If this is the case, this signifies that they are not really interested in true spirituality or in helping people with spiritual advancement. Yoga and meditation have existed for hundreds of years before Christianity ever came along. Why should people not look at other cultures to get answers and experiences that are not found in conventional Western religions? Many Christians have risen to new levels of awareness of biblical teachings by practicing certain aspects of the Vedic path.

In any case, it does not take much study to understand that there was a great difference between the ways and teachings of Jesus and the methods and theocracy of the Church. Jesus was obviously a great master and an empowered preacher and guru sent by God who accomplished a great deal for spreading theism throughout the world. So, on that basis, we all should have great respect for Jesus. But people should recognize Jesus for what he is, as a Vaishnava, a devotee of the Lord. And those who call themselves Christians should worship him by following in his footsteps and take the time to understand the many aspects of God consciousness exactly as Christ did in his travels through India and Persia before he took up his work of preaching to his people. This does not mean that one must necessarily travel to the East, but the point is that if one looks closely, he can understand that the teachings of Christ are based on the same essential spiritual truths as found in the Vedic literature. Therefore, by understanding the essential spiritual teachings in the Vedic literature, one can more easily understand the teachings in the Bible and the real teachings of Jesus. So, let us take a closer look at what Jesus actually taught.

JESUS TAUGHT BHAKTI-YOGA

By studying the teachings of Jesus, we can easily recognize that the essence of what Jesus taught was an elementary level of *bhakti-yoga* and *karma-yoga*. He taught that everyone should love God with their whole heart and mind, which is the quintessence of *bhakti-yoga*. *Bhakti* means devotion and surrender to God. As stated in *Matthew* (22.36-40): "Master, which is the greatest commandment in the law? He answered, Love the Lord thy God with all your heart, with all your soul, with all your mind. That is the greatest commandment. It comes first. The second is like it: Love your neighbor as yourself. Everything in the Law and the prophets hangs on these two commandments." These two rules are the heart of the processes of *bhakti* and *karma-yoga*.

In this way, Jesus taught people the most basic portions of God's law and gave the most simple commandments, such as, "Thou shalt not kill," and "Thou shall not steal," and so on. These rules deal only with moral standards. They do not deal with any real spiritual discipline or transcendental philosophy. This is a sign of the kind of people Jesus was dealing with. They were very primitive and had to be taught the most basic of spiritual knowledge. Obviously, one cannot comprehend advanced spiritual topics if he does not have any understanding of simple moral values. Therefore, Jesus was very limited in what he could teach the people of that era. As Jesus said, (*St. John* 16.12-13, 25):

I have yet many things to say unto you, but ye cannot bear them now. Howbeit when he, the Spirit of truth, is come, he will guide you into the truth: for he shall not speak of himself: but whatsoever he shall hear, that shall he speak: and he will shew you things to come. . . These things have I spoken unto you in proverbs: but the time cometh, when I shall no more speak unto you in proverbs, but I shall show you plainly of the Father.

Thus, Jesus could not reveal the whole truth to the people of that era, but promised that there would be a time when the whole truth would be open to everyone. But whether the people accept it or not is another thing.

Jesus also taught that one is judged by his works and the way they behave. This is also the same process as found in *bhakti* and *karma-yoga*. Without good works and sincere devotion, one cannot enter into the kingdom of God. Yet, we find in modern Christianity an emphasis on faith, not on works. But this is not upheld in the Bible, as we can see in this verse: "But wilt thou know, O vain man, that faith without works is dead." (*James* 2.20) The way one works is a sign of his faith. And those that do claim allegiance to the faith and preach in the name of Christ yet do various duplicious activities in private are still bereft of attaining the favor of Christ, as stated in *Matthew* (7.21-23):

Not everyone that saith unto me, Lord, Lord, shall enter into the kingdom of heaven, but he that doeth the will of my Father which is in heaven. Many will say to me that day, Lord, Lord, have we not prophesied in thy name? And in thy name have cast out devils? And in thy name done many wonderful works? And then will I profess unto them, I never knew you; depart from me, ye that work iniquity.

Jesus never said that faith alone was all it took to enter the promised land. When Jesus was asked, "What shall I do to inherit the eternal life?" he answered, "Thou knowest the commandments. Do not commit adultery. Do not kill. Do not steal. Do not bear false witness. Defraud not. Honor thy father and mother." (*Mark* 10.19) So if one considers that they love God, he must show it by example. He must act accordingly because Jesus expected and taught that one must become perfect in this life. "Be ye perfect, even as your Father in heaven is perfect." (*Matthew* 5.48) If, however, people make excuses and continue with their sinful activities because they think that Jesus, being "the Lamb of God which taketh away the sins of the world" (*John* 1.29), died on the cross and suffered for their sins, which allows them to do whatever they want, then they are condemned. To think in this way is perverted, even though many people do so. The Bible explains that those who continue their sinful activities nail Christ back onto the cross. "If they shall fall away, to renew them again unto repentence; seeing they crucify to themselves the Son of God afresh, and put him to an open shame." (*Hebrews* 6.6) Thus, the only way to enter the kingdom of God is to uphold the law of God in all of one's actions, beginning with keeping the commandments. Therefore, Jesus specifically said, "If ye love me, keep my commandments." (*John* 14.15)

Furthermore, it is not possible to call oneself a Christian and remain engaged in sinful activities. One must do one or the other, as explained in *Matthew* (6.24): "No man can serve two masters, for either he will hate the one and love the other; or else he will hold to the one, and despise the other. Ye cannot serve (both) God and mammon."

Jesus taught that there were two paths a person could take, one leading to destruction and the other to life. The way of destruction is broad and easy, whereas the path leading to life is narrow and difficult to find. But each path can be seen for what it is according to the fruits it produces.

Enter ye in at the strait gate: for wide is the gate, and broad is the way, that leadeth to destruction, and many there be which go in thereat: Because strait is the gate, and narrow is the way which leadeth unto life, and few there be that find it. Beware of false prophets, which come to you in sheep's clothing, but inwardly they are ravening wolves. Ye shall know them by their fruits. Do men gather grapes of thorns, or figs of thistles? Even so every good tree bringeth forth good fruit; but a corrupt tree bringeth forth evil fruit. A good tree cannot bring forth evil fruit, neither can a corrupt tree bring forth good fruit. Every tree that bringeth not forth good fruit is hewn down, and cast into the fire. Wherefore by their fruits ye shall know them. (*Matthew* 7.13-20)

Further elaboration is given in *I John* (2.15-17):

Love not the world, neither the things that are in the world. If any man love the world, the love of the Father is not in him. For all that is in this world, the lust of the flesh, and the lust of the eyes, and the pride of life, is not of the Father, but is of the world. And the world passeth away, and the lust thereof; but he that doeth the will of God abideth forever.

In this way, we can see that regardless of what particular spiritual path people may claim to belong to, if they are attaining the qualities of the fruits of the spirit, then they are spiritually advancing in various degrees. And no matter how much faith in a religion one may have, if he clings to the deeds of the flesh, life in the kingdom of God will not be awaiting him.

This, therefore, is the essence of Jesus' teachings that, as we can see, include the same basic principles of *bhakti-yoga* and *karma-yoga* (loving God, upholding God's law in all our actions, and doing good for others), which is fully explained in the Vedic literature (and in Chapter Nine of this book). Jesus never presented anything new or invented, but taught what God had taught and gave all credit to God, as verified in the following quotes:

The son can do nothing of himself, but what he seeth the Father do. (*John* 5.19). . . When ye have lifted up the son of man, then shall ye know that I am he, and that I do nothing of myself; but as my Father hath taught me, I speak these things. (*John* 8.28). . . I go unto the Father, for my Father is greater than I. (*John* 14.28)

In these verses we have the words of Jesus from the Bible that explain that he taught only what God had spoken and was not himself God, but was the son of God the Father. Furthermore, in *Bhagavad-gita* (9.17), Krishna specifically explains that He is the Father of all living entities, and (*Bg.*7.6, 10.8) is the origin of all that is material and spiritual. Therefore, no contradiction exists in the understanding that Jesus was a son of God, and Krishna is the supreme Father and Creator.

DO ALL CHRISTIANS GO TO HEAVEN?

Regardless of whether or not Christianity is a complete spiritual process that can bring one to spiritual perfection, most Christians feel that they are bound to go to heaven because, as they say, Christ died for their sins. So even if they cannot give up their sinful habits, all they have to do is have faith and they will be saved. Yet this is a controversial point. Not all of the gospels that were in circulation when the New Testament was compiled agreed that the crucifixion was an act of atonement. Even the divinity of Jesus was added later, after he had already died, as the Dead Sea Scrolls indicate. And the Jews completely rejected him as a divine person or Messiah. And if Jesus is really not the messiah or of divine nature, that practically cancels the basis of Christianity, which is what Jewish people think.

Jesus was, however, a Jew whose message was primarily for the Jewish people. In *Matthew* (10.5-6), Jesus tells his twelve disciples to go and preach, but not to the Gentiles (non-Jews), nor to the Samaritans, but go to the lost sheep of the house of Israel. Again in *Matthew* (15.22-24), a woman besought Jesus and asked for mercy because her daughter was vexed with a devil. But Jesus said nothing to her. Even his disciples, who were Jews, asked him to send her away because she cried after them. Yet his answer was that he had come to this world only for the lost sheep of Israel. His intention was to help only the Jewish people. Only after much pleading from the woman did Jesus finally cure her daughter. So this seems to indicate that Jesus' main interest was with the Jews; yet, they completely rejected him. And when he was crucified by the Romans, this was taken as further indication that he was not the messiah that was described in the Jewish prophecies. Nonetheless, the Gentiles and non-Jewish people accepted the doctrine of Christianity and now believe they are saved by the blood of Christ, which is a concept that came primarily from Paul.

So do all Christians go to heaven? Not when you consider all the rules for exclusion. According to the books in the New Testament, Jesus left specific instructions that have to be followed or entrance into heaven may not be as sure as many Christians think. In *Matthew* (10.37), Jesus says that if anyone loves his or her father, mother, son, or daughter more than him is not worthy of him. But also in *Matthew* (15.4), God commands that a person must honor his father and mother, and he that curseth his father or mother must die the death. So you must honor your parents, but not more than you love Jesus or you will not get to heaven.

Jesus also explains in *Matthew* (12.36) that any idle words a man speaks will have to be accounted for on the judgement day. So you must also avoid idle words and gossip. That is not an easy task for many people. Jesus further explains in *Matthew* (16.23-28) that a person must deny himself the interests or pleasures of men and take up the cross and follow him if he expects to reach the kingdom of God. This certainly indicates that more than mere faith is expected of a Christian, but how many can deny themselves of the common pleasures of men and take up the cross?

In *Matthew* (18.34-35), Jesus says that the Lord will punish you if you do not forgive everybody of their trespasses against you. And again in *Matthew* (25.35-46) we find that it is expected that a good Christian must feed and clothe the poor, and take in the homeless, though they be strangers, for as much as you do this for them, you do it also for Jesus. And if you ignore such people, it is as if you ignore Jesus, and you will go into everlasting punishment.

Now we can see that the requirements for getting into heaven are getting more demanding. But wait, there is more. In *Matthew* (19.20-30), a man comes to Jesus and wants to follow him, but Jesus tells him to first sell everything he has and give the money to the poor. However, the man could not bring himself to do that and sadly went away. Jesus explained to his disciples that hardly any rich man can enter heaven; it is easier for a camel to go through the eye of a needle. Then his disciples were amazed and wondered, if this was the case, who could be saved. Jesus replied that all things are possible with God, but those who have forsaken houses, father, mother, wife, children, or property for his name's sake shall inherit everlasting life.

Similarly, in *Luke* (6.20, 24-30), Jesus says blessed are the poor, for they shall reach the kingdom of God, and woe to the rich, woe to those who are full for they will be hungry, and woe to those who laugh now for they will know sorrow. Plus, you must love and do good to your enemies and those that hate you, give the other cheek for those that hit you, do not forbid anyone to take your coat, and do not ask that your goods be returned from one who takes them.

In *Luke* (9.61-62), there is the story of another man who came to Jesus and asked to follow him, but first simply wanted to bid farewell to his family. But Jesus rejected him and said that no man, having once put his head to the plough and looks back, is fit for the kingdom of God. In another place in *Luke* (9.59-

60), Jesus orders a man to follow him, but the man requests that Jesus first allow him to bury his father. Jesus, however, says to let the dead bury their dead, and go preach the kingdom of God. In *Matthew* (5.21-22), Jesus explains that if a person kills another he shall be in danger of the judgement. But he further explains that simply getting angry at another without just cause shall also put one in danger of the judgement. And (*Matthew* 5.20) unless your own righteousness exceeds the righteousness of the scribes and Pharisees, you shall in no case enter the kingdom of God.

What all this seems to indicate is that anyone who wants to follow Jesus has to display a high degree of detachment and renunciation from the world and its material attractions and pleasures, and take up the cross. Otherwise, they are not true followers of Jesus, nor are they fit for the kingdom of God. Many Christians may feel that faith alone is all they need to be saved, but these biblical quotes of Jesus certainly indicate that he expected and required much more than that.

So what happens to all those who cannot measure up to the proper standard? In *Matthew* (13.41-42), Jesus says that the Son of man will send his angels who will gather out all the things that offend and the people who do iniquity and cast them into a furnace of fire where there will be great wailing and gnashing of teeth. If all these rules that Jesus explains must be followed perfectly, along with all the commandments, etc., in order for Christians to get to heaven, then that furnace must be a very big place. But what kind of God would create a hell where people eternally suffer? Especially if, according to Christian theology, they are given only one lifetime to have one chance at either becoming perfect and righteous or go to eternal hell. What is the value of eternal punishment if it never ends and the soul does not get the chance to rectify himself? Why would God create living beings who have a fallen tendency and then send them to suffer eternally if they cannot measure up to the proper standard? Threatening someone with eternal damnation is hardly an expression of love and mercy. Therefore, this Christian concept of God and hell makes little sense because this form of punishment is not a matter of rehabilitation, but is based on an attitude of anger and vengeance. What need does God have for this if He is a God of love, mercy, and compassion? Why would God spend His time acting like an angry tyrant? He certainly has better things to do.

The Christian concept of God is that He is a God we must fear. To verify this some people, of course, will point out that in *Exodus* (20.5) it is written that God says He is a jealous God. But a person exhibits jealousy or anger when he is afraid of losing something, feels insecure, or does not get what he wants. But why would God, who is the creator and controller of everything, feel insecure or fearful? Qualities such as jealousy, insecurity, anger, or vengeance are qualities found in the modes of passion and ignorance. And these modes do not touch the Supreme. But God is perceived differently by different cultures.

In the *Bhagavad-gita* (9.18), Lord Krishna says that He is the creation, the basis of everything, the sustainer, the goal, the refuge, the master, and the most dear friend. This is a much more appropriate understanding of God. Naturally, He must be our friend since we are all parts of His spiritual energy. The only thing that gives the appearance of our being in opposition with God, or being fearful of Him, is our ignorance of spiritual reality. This ignorance must be overcome, not compounded by the inadequacies of a religion that is lacking in spiritual knowledge and provides a deficient understanding of God. The goal of any complete spiritual path is to attain enlightenment of God, our spiritual identity, and our relationship with God. The goal of the Vedic path of *bhakti* is to develop love and devotion for God, but you cannot love someone when you are afraid of them. Love and fear are incompatible. Therefore, a spiritually realized person will find it difficult to accept that God is angry, jealous, or vengeful. Why should God be angry or vengeful with us when the universal laws that have been established automatically take care of whatever good or bad things we deserve? For one who is spiritually realized knows that God allows us the freedom to do what we want within the confines of the universal laws, such as the law of *karma*, and is always waiting for us to turn toward Him, and that He is a God of love, mercy, compassion, and unfathomable understanding. This is God as He really is and is the God we will know in our state of spiritual enlightenment.

THE BIBLE TEACHES THE CHANTING OF GOD'S NAMES

So how is a person supposed to become purified and advance spiritually in worshiping the Supreme in Christianity, aside from trying to follow the rules that are described by Jesus? The Bible has many verses that explain the process. The information in this section applies as much to the essential Jewish forms of worship and meditation on the Supreme as it does to the Christian tradition.

In one of the foremost prayers spoken by Jesus, it is said, "Our Father, who art in heaven, hallowed be Thy name." The value and holiness of the name of God, as well as being the primary way to meditate on Him, is stressed throughout the Bible. This is also taught in the Vedic literature, as explained in Chapter Ten of this volume. Many verses instructing people to sing praises to God and sing His holy name are found. Even in the books of Moses we find evidence of this: "Then sang Moses and the children of Israel this song unto the Lord, and spake, saying, I will sing unto the Lord, for He hath triumphed gloriously." (*Exodus* 15.1)

Furthermore, after delivering the ten commandments, Moses told his people:

Hear, O Israel: the Lord our God is one Lord: And thou shalt love the Lord thy God with all thy heart, and with all thy soul, and with all thy might... Thou shalt fear the Lord thy God; Him shalt thou serve, and to Him shalt thou cleave, and swear by His name. He is thy praise, and He is thy God, that hath done for thee these great and terrible things, which thine eyes have seen. (*Deuteronomy* 6.4-5, 10.20-21)

Thus, we find that Moses also set forth the basic principles for people to follow that were the same as those found in *bhakti-yoga*: that one should love and serve God completely and take shelter of Him through the process of singing praises to Him. Not only that, but one should also chant and tell others about the holy name of God just as Moses did, as stated in the following verses: "My doctrine shall drop as the rain, my speech shall distill as the dew, as the small rain upon the tender herb, and as the showers upon the grass: Because I will publish the name of the Lord: ascribe ye greatness unto our God." (*Deuteronomy* 32.2-3)

Further quotes can be given which show a similar sentiment. The fact of the matter is that the Old Testament, although describing the process within the context of Judaism, is full of the same essential teachings as found in the Vedic literature. Therefore, there is no surprise to find the following verses from various parts of the Bible which state that one should sing songs unto the Lord and praise His holy name: "Hear, O ye kings; give ear, O ye princes; I, even I, will sing unto the Lord; I will sing praise unto the Lord God of Israel." (*Book of Judges*) "Therefore I will give thanks unto Thee, O Lord, among the heathen, and I will sing praises unto Thy name." (*Samuel II* 22.50)

"Thus all Israel brought up the ark of the covenant of the Lord with shouting, and with sound of the cornet, and with trumpets, and with cymbals, making a noise with psalteries and harps." (*I Chronicles* 15.28) This description certainly sounds like a typical chanting (*kirtana*) party as you would find in the temples of holy cities in India and elsewhere. And the following verses sound exactly like some of the Vedic quotes that are included in the chapter on *mantra-yoga*. This indicates that chanting the holy names of the Supreme is definately the process for this age, regardless of what culture or tradition with which you affiliate:

Then on that day David delivered first this psalm, to thank the Lord, into the hand of Asaph and his brethren. Give thanks unto the Lord, call upon His name, make known His deeds among the people. Sing unto Him, sing psalms unto Him, talk yet of all His wondrous works. Glory ye in His holy name; let the heart of them rejoice that seek the Lord. Seek the Lord and His strength, seek His face continually. (*I Chronicles* 16.7-11). . . Sing unto the Lord, all the earth; shew forth from day to day His salvation. Declare His glory among the heathen; His marvelous works among all nations. For great is the Lord, and greatly to be praised: He also is to be feared above all gods. (*I Chronicles* 16.23-25)

And Jehoshaphat bowed his head with his face to the ground: and all Judah and the inhabitants of Jerusalem fell before the Lord, worshipping the Lord. And the Levites, of the children of the Kohathites, and of the children of the Korhites, stood up to praise the Lord God of Israel with a loud voice on high. And when he [Jehoshaphat] had consulted with the people, he appointed singers unto the Lord, and that should praise the beauty of holiness, as they went out before the army, and to say, Praise the Lord: for His mercy endureth forever. (*II Chronicles* 20.18-21)

And he [Hezekiah] set the Levites in the house of the Lord with cymbals, with psalteries, and with harps, according to the commandment of David, and of Gad the king's seer, and Nathan the prophet; for so was the commandment of the Lord by His prophets. And the Levites stood with the instruments of David, and the priest with the trumpets. And Hezekiah commanded to offer the burnt offering upon the altar. And when the burnt offering began, the song of the Lord began also with the trumpets, and with the instruments ordained by David King of Israel. And all the congregation worshipped, and the singers sang, and the trumpeters sounded: and all this continued until the burnt offering was finished. And when they had made an end of offering, the king and all that were present with him bowed themselves and worshipped. Moreover Hezekiah the king and the princes commanded the Levites to sing praises unto the Lord with the words of David, and of Asaph the seer. And they sang praises with gladness, and they bowed their heads and worshipped. (*II Chronicles* 29.25-30)

There was also the prophecy given by Isaiah who said: "And in that day shall ye say, Praise the Lord, call upon His name, declare His doings among the people, make mention that His name is exalted. Sing unto the Lord; for He hath done excellent things: this is known in all the earth." (*Isaiah* 12.4-5)

Another quote given in *Isaiah* (42.10-12) concerning the fact that everyone in the world should declare the Lord's glories was the following:

Sing unto the Lord a new song, and His praise from the end of the earth, ye that go to the sea, and all that is therein: the isles, and the inhabitants thereof. Let the wilderness and the cities thereof lift up their voice, the villages that Kedar doth inhabit: let the inhabitants of the rock sing, let them shout from the top of the mountains. Let them give glory unto the Lord, and declare His praise in the islands.

The Psalms of David put special attention on chanting the holy names of God, and practically instructs how congregational chanting should be performed.

Make a joyful noise unto the Lord, all the earth: make a loud noise and rejoice, and sing praise. Sing unto the Lord with the harp, and the voice of a psalm. With trumpets and sound of cornet make a joyful noise before the Lord, the King. . . O clap your hands, all ye people; shout unto God with the voice of triumph. (*Psalms* 98.4-6,47.1)

Praise ye the Lord. Praise God in His sanctuary: praise Him in the firmament of His power. Praise Him for His mighty acts: praise Him according to His excellent greatness. Praise Him with the sound of the trumpet: praise Him with the psaltery and harp. Praise Him with the timbrel and dance: praise Him with stringed instruments and organs. Praise Him upon the loud cymbals: praise Him upon the high sounding cymbals. Let everything that breath praise the Lord. Praise ye the Lord. (*Psalms* 150.1-6)

The Bible also indicates that as one continues to engage in this process, one becomes more and more fixed in understanding God; one's faith continually increases, as mentioned:

My heart is fixed, O God, my heart is fixed: I will sing and give praise. Awake up, my glory; awake, psaltery and harp: I myself will awake early. I will praise thee, O Lord, among the people: I will sing unto Thee among the nations. For Thy mercy is great unto the heavens, and Thy truth unto the clouds. Be thou exalted, O God, above the heavens: let Thy glory be above all the earth. (*Psalms* 57.7-11)

It is also established that if one expects to be successful in one's search for God, the Absolute Truth, one must relentlessly engage in chanting God's names and glories: "O give thanks unto the Lord; call upon His names: make known His deeds among the people. Sing unto Him, sing psalms unto Him: talk ye of all His wondrous works. Glory ye in His holy name: let the heart of them rejoice that seek the Lord. Seek the Lord, and His strength: seek His face evermore." (*Psalms* 105.1-4) And also the following: "Praise the Lord, O my soul. While I live I will praise the Lord: I will sing praises unto my God while I have any being. (*Psalms* 146.1). . . And they that know Thy name will put their trust in Thee: for thou, Lord, hast not forsaken them that seek Thee." (*Psalms* 9.10)

As one advances in one's self-realization and in one's faith in praising God, one will naturally feel much happiness and joy in doing so, according to the *Psalms*:

Sing unto the Lord, O ye saints of His, and give thanks at the remembrance of His holiness. Thou hast turned for me my mourning into dancing: thou hast put off my sackcloth and girded me with gladness: To the end that my glory may sing praise to Thee, and not be silent. O my God, I will give

thanks unto Thee forever. (*Psalms* 30.4,11-12). . . Make a joyful noise unto
the Lord, all ye lands. Serve the Lord with gladness: come before His
presence with singing. (*Psalms* 100.1-2). . . I will sing unto the Lord as long
as I live: I will sing praise to my God while I have my Being. My meditation
of Him shall be sweet: I will be glad in the Lord. (*Psalms* 104.33-34). . .
Praise ye the Lord: for it is good to sing praises unto our God; for it is
pleasant; and praise is comely. (*Psalms* 147.1). . . It is a good thing to give
thanks unto the Lord, and to sing praises unto Thy name, O most high.
(*Psalms* 92.1). . . Praise ye the Lord. Praise, O ye servants of the Lord,
praise the name of the Lord. Blessed be the name of the Lord from this time
forth and for evermore. From the rising of the sun unto the going down of
the same the Lord's name is to be praised. (*Psalms* 113.1-3)

In *The Revelations of St. John* it is pointed out that only those who have
perfected this path are the ones who will enter the kingdom of God, and the
people of all nations are expected to join in this process of glorifying the
Supreme.

And I looked, and, lo, a Lamb stood on the Mount Sion, and with him an
hundred forty and four thousand, having his Father's name written in their
foreheads [like Vaishnava *tilok*]. And I heard a voice from heaven, as the
voice of many waters, and as the voice of a great thunder; and as it were a
new song before the throne, and before the four beasts, and the elders: and
no man could learn that song but the hundred and forty and four thousand,
which were redeemed from the earth. And I saw as it were a sea of glass
mingled with fire: and them that had gotten victory over the beast, and over
his image, and over his mark, and over the number of his name, stand on the
sea of glass, having harps of God. And they sang the song of Moses the
servant of God, and the song of the Lamb, saying, great and marvellous are
Thy works, Lord God Almighty; just and true are Thy ways, Thou King of
saints. Who shall not fear Thee, O Lord, and glorify Thy name? for Thou
only art holy: for all nations shall come and worship before Thee; for Thy
judgements are made manifest. (*Revelations* 14.1-3, 15.2-4)

In this way, many verses throughout the Bible, only a few of which are
presented here, establish the chanting of the Lord's names as an integral part
of the Judaic and Christian traditions. However, those people who seriously
take up this path are likely to be met with opposition since this world is filled
with many who are faithless and have no attraction for the names of God. This
may be unfortunate, but is not to be considered out of the ordinary. Therefore,
Christ warned his disciples, "And ye shall be hated of all men for my name's
sake: but he that shall endure unto the end, the same shall be saved." (*Mark*
13.13) But Christ also pointed out that this is a sign and test of one's spiritual

advancement. The more spiritual one becomes, the more they begin to leave the material world behind, and the more difficult it is for one to participate in the mundane affairs within materialistic society. As Christ stated: "If the world hate you, know that it hated me before it hated you. If ye were of the world, the world would love its own; but because ye are not of the world, but I have chosen you out of the world, therefore the world hateth you." (*John* 15.18-19) But even if we may feel overwhelmed by such difficulties, or that we are all alone in this world with no one else to turn to, we can immediately be relieved simply by invoking or singing the name of God. By doing so we instantly come in contact with God's presence. Or as Christ explained it: "For where two or three are gathered together in my name, there I am in the midst of them." (*Matthew* 18.20) This is the potency of the holy name.

This is all very much in line with the Vedic process of *bhakti-yoga* and *mantra-yoga*. In fact, that is all that has been explained in this segment, using only the evidence as presented in the form of biblical references. Obviously, it means that everyone should sing or chant the name of God, but the Bible does not clarify which name, so what name do we use?

THE NAMES OF GOD

God is called by many names, such as Jehovah, Allah, El Shaddai, Elohim, Adonai, Yahweh, Krishna, Govinda, Vishnu, and so on, according to particular traditions. Any bona fide name of God that one chants sincerely will help one attain spiritual emancipation, if for no other reason than it focuses one's mind on the Supreme to some degree. But some names of God are more direct in their descriptive power and in their relationship with the Supreme, while other names are nothing more than titles. For example, Allah simply means "Great One," Adonai means "Lord," Elohim means "The Almighty," and some say that Jehovah is not a name at all but merely refers to the name. The word "God," which can be traced back to the Sanskrit through the Old Teutonic language, simply means "to invoke" or "the object of worship." We all know God is great and is the supreme object of worship, but the above names really do not explain much about God.

Some people call upon the name of Jesus Christ in their prayers. This is also very effective because the name Christ comes from the Greek word *christos*, which means the anointed one or messiah, and *christos* is the Greek version of the name Krista or Krishna, which is a direct name of God, which means the one who is all-attractive and who gives the greatest pleasure. So no matter whether we call on "Christ," "Krista," or "Krishna," we are referring to the same Supreme Being. Also, the name Jesus is spelled Iesus in Latin, and Issa in Arabic, which is linguistically connected with Isha, the Sanskrit root for Ishvara, which is the name for God meaning the Supreme Controller.

Some names, however, like Krishna, Vishnu, Govinda, or Rama are more direct and potent in addressing God and His energies and in reawakening our spiritual awareness. These names address the various qualities and pastimes of God, which are eternal and transcendental to material nature. In other words, these names are spiritual vibrations which exist on the same spiritual platform as the Supreme. Thus, by always invoking the transcendental energy of God through the chanting of His holy names, one comes in contact with this eternal energy which works to spiritualize our consciousness. As our consciousness becomes more and more purified, we actually become more in tune with God and His spiritual energy. This continues to the point in which we actually reawaken our spiritual vision that allows us to understand exactly who and what we are. This is called self-realization. Thus, as it is instructed in the Bible, the Vedic literature, and other scripture, one should systematically chant and meditate on the spiritual names of God. This is explained more fully in Chapter Ten.

CHAPTER SEVEN

The Origins of Vedic Society: Source of the World's Spiritual Heritage

With only a small amount of research, a person can discover that each area of the world has its own ancient culture that includes its own gods and legends that explain the origins of various cosmological realities. But where did all these stories and gods come from? Did they all spread around the world from one particular source, only to change according to differences in language and customs? If not, then why are some of these gods and goddesses of various areas of the world so similar?

Unfortunately, information about prehistoric religion is usually gathered through whatever remnants of earlier cultures we can find, such as bones in tombs and caves, or ancient sculptures, engravings, wall paintings, and other relics. From these we are left to speculate about the rituals, ceremonies, and beliefs of the people and the purposes of the items found. Often we can only paint a crude picture of how simple and backwards these ancient people were while not thinking that more advanced civilizations may have left us next to nothing in terms of physical remains. They may have built houses out of wood or materials other than stone that have since faded with the seasons, or were simply replaced with other buildings over the years, rather than buried by the sands of time for archeologists to unearth. They also may have cremated their dead, as some societies did, leaving no bones to discover. Thus, without ancient museums or historical records from the past, there would be no way of really knowing what the prehistoric cultures were like.

If a few thousand years in the future people could uncover our own houses after being buried for so long and find television antennas on top of each house wired to a television inside, who knows what they would think. Without a recorded history of our times they might speculate that the antennas, being pointed toward the heavens, were used for us to commune with our gods who would appear, by mystic power, on the screen of the television box inside our homes. They might also think that we were very much devoted to our gods since some houses might have two, three, or more televisions, making it possible for us to never be without contact with our gods through the day. And since the television was usually found in a prominent area, with special couches and reclining chairs, this must surely be the prayer room where we would get the proper inspiration for living life. Or they might even think that the television was itself the god, the idol of our times. This, of course, would not be a very accurate picture, but it reflects the difficulty we have in understanding ancient religion by means of analyzing the remnants we find. However, when we begin comparing all the religions of the world, we can see how they are all interrelated and have a source from which most of them seem to have originated. And most of them can be traced to the East.

Most scholars agree that the earliest of religions seems to have arisen from the most ancient of organized cultures, which is either the Sumerians along the Euphrates, or the Aryans located in the region of the Indus Valley. However, these two cultures may have been related. C. L. Woolley, one of the world's foremost archeologists, establishes in his book, *The Sumerians*, that the facial characteristics of the Sumerian people can be traced to Afghanistan, Baluchistan, and on to the Indus region. The early Indus civilization, which was remarkably developed, has many similarities with Sumer over 1500 miles away, especially in regard to the rectangular seals that are identical in the subjects on them, the style of engraving, and the inscriptions. There are also similarities in the methods used in the ground plans and construction of buildings. Woolley suggests that, rather than concluding too quickly that the Sumerians and Indus civilization shared the same race or political culture, which may actually have been the case, or that such similarities were merely from trade connections, the evidence at least indicates that the two societies shared a common source.

The researcher and scholar L. A. Waddell offers more evidence to show the relation between the Aryans and the Sumerians. He states in his book, *The Indo Sumerian Seals Deciphered*, that the discovery and translation of the Sumerian seals along the Indus Valley give evidence that the Aryan society existed there from as long ago as 3100 B.C. Several Sumerian seals found along the Indus bore the names of famous Vedic Aryan seers and princes familiar in the Vedic hymns. Therefore, these Aryan personalities were not merely part of an elaborate myth, like some people seem to proclaim, but actually lived five thousand years ago as related in the Vedic epics and *Puranas*.

Waddell also says that the language and religion of the Indo-Aryans were radically similar to that of the Sumerians and Phoenicians, and that the early Aryan kings of the Indian *Vedas* are identical with well-known historical kings of the Sumerians. He believes that the decipherment of these seals from the Indus Valley confirms that the Sumerians were actually the early Aryans and authors of Indian civilization. He concludes that the Sumerians were Aryans in physique, culture, religion, language, and writing. He also feels that the early Sumerians on the Persian Gulf about 3100 B.C. were Phoenicians who were Aryans in race and speech and were the introducers of Aryan civilization in ancient India. Thus, he concludes that it was the Aryans who were the bearers of high civilization and who spread throughout the Mediterranian, Northwest Europe, and Britain, as well as India. However, he states that the early Aryan Sumero-Phoenicians did not become a part of the Aryan Invasion of India until the seventh century B.C. after their defeat by the Assyrian Sargon II in 718 B.C. at Carchemish in Upper Mesopotamia. Though the Sumerians may indeed have been Aryan people, some researchers feel that rather than being the originators of Vedic Aryan culture, or part of an invasion into India, they were an extension of the Vedic culture that originated in India and spread through Persia and into Europe.

THEORIES ON THE ARYAN ORIGINS

This brings us to the different theories that scholars have on the origins of the Aryan society. Though it seems evident that an Aryan society was in existence in the Indus Valley by 3100 B.C., not everyone agrees with the dates that Waddell has presented for the Aryan Invasion into India, and whether the Aryans were actually invaders is still questioned. Obviously, different views on the Aryanization of India are held by different historians. Some scholars say that it was about 1000 B.C. when Aryans entered Iran from the north and then occupied the Indus region by 800 B.C. In this scenario, the Aryans had to have entered India sometime after this. But others say that it was between 1500 and 1200 B.C. that the Aryans entered India and composed hymns that make up the *Rig-veda*. So some people calculate that the *Rig-veda* must have been composed around 1400 B.C.

Mr. Pargiter, another noted scholar, contends that Aryan influence in India was felt long before the composition of the Vedic hymns. He states that the Aryans entered India near 2000 B.C. over the Central Himalayas and later spread into the Punjab. Brunnhofer and others argue that the composition of the *Rig-veda* took place not in the Punjab, but in Afghanistan or Iran. This theory assumes that Aryan entrance into India was much later.

As we can see from the above examples, analyzing these theories can get rather confusing. In fact, so many theories on the location of the origins of the Aryans or Indo-Europeans have been presented by archeologists and researchers that for a time they felt the location could change from minute to minute, depending on the latest evidence that was presented. In many cases over the years, archeologists presumed they had located the home of the Sumerians or Aryans any time they found certain types of metal tools or painted pottery that resembled what had been found at the Sumerian or Indus Valley sites. Though such findings may have been of some significance, further study proved that they were of considerably less importance than had been originally thought, and, thus, the quest for locating the original Aryan home could not be concluded.

V. Gordon Childe states in his book, *The Aryans*, that though the idea of an Asiatic origin of the Aryans, who then migrated into India, is the most widely accepted idea, it is still the least well documented. And this idea is only one of the unfounded generalizations with which for over seventy years anthropology and archeology have been in conflict. In fact, today the northern Asiatic origin of the Aryans is a hypothesis which has been abandoned by most linguists and archeologists. So who were the real Vedic Aryans, and from where did they originate?

The presence of the Vedic Aryans in the Indus region is undeniable, but the evidence indicates they had been there long before any invaders or immigrating nomads ever arrived, and, thus, the Vedic literature must have been in existence there for quite some time as well. In fact, the Vedic literature establishes that they were written many years before the above mentioned date of 1400 B.C. The age of Kali is said to have begun in 3102 B.C. with the disappearance of Lord Krishna, which is the time when Srila Vyasadeva is said to have begun composing the Vedic knowledge into written form. Thus, the *Rig-veda* could not have been written or brought into the area by the so-called "invaders" or whoever these immigrants were because they are not supposed to have come through the area until 1600 years later.

In his commentary on *Srimad-Bhagavatam* (1.7.8), A. C. Bhaktivedanta Swami, one of the most distinguished Vedic scholars of modern times, discusses the estimated date of when the Vedic literature was written. He writes that there is some diversity amongst mundane scholars as to the date when *Srimad-Bhagavatam* was compiled. But from the text it is certain that it was compiled after Lord Krishna disappeared and before the disappearance of King Pariksit. We are presently in the five thousandth year of the age of Kali according to astrological calculation and evidence in the revealed scriptures. Therefore, he concludes, *Srimad-Bhagavatam* had to have been compiled at least five thousand years ago. The *Mahabharata* was compiled before *Srimad-Bhagavatam*, and the major *Puranas* were compiled before *Mahabharata*.

Furthermore, we all know that the *Upanishads* and the four primary *Vedas*, including the *Rig-veda*, were compiled years before *Mahabharata*. This would indicate that the Vedic literature was already existing before any so-called invasion, which is said to have happened around 1400 B.C. In fact, this indicates that the real Aryans were the Vedic kings and sages who were already prevalent in this region, as explained by L. A. Waddell, and not the other uncertain tribe of nomadic people that some historians inappropriately call "invading Aryans."

One of the major reasons why a consideration of the idea of an Aryan invasion into India is prevalent among some Western researchers is because of their misinterpretation of the *Vedas* that suggests that the Aryans were a nomadic people. One such misinterpretation is from the *Rig-veda*, which describes the battle between Sudas and the ten kings. These kings, though some are described as Aryans, were actually fallen Aryans, or rebellious and materialistic kings who had given up the spiritual path and were conquered by Sudas. Occasionally, there was a degeneration of the spiritual kingdom in areas of India, and wars had to be fought in order to reestablish the spiritual Aryan culture in these areas. Western scholars could and did easily misinterpret this to mean an invasion of nomadic people called Aryans rather than simply a war in which the superior Aryan kings reestablished the spiritual values and way of life.

Sir John Marshall, one of the chief excavators at Mohenjo-Daro, also offers evidence that India may have been following the Vedic religion long before any so-called "invaders" ever arrived. He points out that it is known that India possessed a highly advanced and organized urban civilization dating back to at least 2300 B.C., if not much earlier. In fact, some researchers suggest that evidence makes it clear that the Indus Valley civilization was quite developed by at least 3100 B.C. The known cities of this civilization cover an area along the Indus river and extend from the coast to Rajasthan and the Punjab over to the Yamuna and Upper Ganges. At its height, the Indus culture spread over an area larger than Western Europe. Cities that were a part of the Indus culture include Mohenjo-Daro, Kot Diji east of Mohenjo-Daro, Amri on the lower Indus, Lothal south of Ahmadabad, Malwan further south, Harappa 350 miles upstream from Mohenjo-Daro, Kalibangan and Alamgirpur further east, Rupar near the Himalayas, Sutkagen Dor to the west along the coast, Mehrgarh 150 miles north of Mohenjo-Daro, and Mundigak much further north. Evidence at Mehrgarh shows a civilization that dates back to the sixth millennium B.C. It had been connected with the Indus culture but was deserted for reasons unknown in the third millennium B.C. around the time the city of Mohenjo-Daro became prominent.

The arrangement of these cities and the knowledge of the residents was much superior to that of immigrating nomads, except for their military abilities at the time. A lack of weapons, except for thin spears, at these cities indicates they were not very well equipped militarily. Thus, one theory is that the invaders, whoever they may have been, rather than encouraging the advancement of Vedic society when they came into the Indus Valley region, may have helped stifle it or even caused its demise in certain areas. The Indus Valley locations may have been one area where the Vedic society disappeared after the arrival of these invaders. Many of these cities seemed to have been abandoned quickly, while others were not, although Mohenjo-Daro shows some evidence that the inhabitants may have been killed in a final massacre. This indicates that the immigrating nomads could have been superior in military capabilities. However, some geologists suggest that the cities were abandoned because of environmental changes. Evidence of floods in the plains is seen in the thick layers of silt which are now thirty-nine feet above the river in the upper strata of Mohenjo-Daro.

144 The Universal Path to Enlightenment

Others say that the ecological needs of the community forced the people to move on, since research shows there was a great reduction in rainfall from that period to the present.

The best known archeological sights of these Indus cities are Mohenjo-Daro and Harappa. Excavation work at Mohenjo-Daro was done from 1922 to 1931 and 1935 to 1936. Excavation at Harappa took place from 1920 to 1921 and 1933 to 1934. Evidence has shown that temples played an important part in the life of the residents of these cities. The citadel at Mohenjo Daro contains a 39-by-23 foot bath that seems to have been used for ceremonial purposes similar in the manner that many large temple complexes in India also have pools for bathing and rituals. Though deities have not been found in the ruins, no doubt because they were too important to abandon, images of a Mother goddess and a Male god similar to Lord Shiva sitting in a yoga posture have been found. Some of the Shiva seals show a man with three heads and an erect phallus, sitting in meditation and surrounded by animals. This would be Shiva as Pashupati, lord or friend of the animals. Representations of the *lingam* of Shiva and *yoni* of his spouse have also been easily located, as well as non-phallic stones such as the *shalagram-shila* stone of Lord Vishnu. Thus, the religions of Shiva and Vishnu, which are directly Vedic, had been very much a part of this society long ago and were not brought to the area by any invaders who may have arrived later.

More light is shed on the advanced civilization of the Indus Valley and how it influenced areas beyond its region when we consider the subject of Vedic mathematics. E. J. H. Mackay explains in his book, *Further Excavations at Mohenjo-Daro*, that the whole basis of Vedic mathematics is geometry and geometrical intruments have been found in the Indus Valley which date back to at least 2800 B.C. The Vedic form of mathematics was much more advanced than that found in early Greek and Egyptian societies. This can be seen in the *Shulba-Sutras*, supplements of the *Kalpasutras*, which also show the earliest forms of algebra which were used by the Vedic priests in their geometry for the construction of altars and arenas for religious purposes. In fact, the geometrical formula known as the Pythagorean theorem can be traced to the *Baudhayans*, which are the earliest forms of the *Shulba-Sutras* dated prior to the eighth century B.C.

It is Vedic mathematics that originated the decimal system of tens, hundreds, thousands, and so on, and in which the remainder of one column of numbers is carried over to the next column. The Indian number system was used in Arabia after 700 A.D. and was called Al-Arqan-Al-Hindu. This spread into Europe and became known as the Arabic numerals. This, of course, has developed into the number system we use today, which is significantly easier than the Egyptian, Roman, or Chinese symbols for numbers that made mathematics much more difficult. It was the Indians who devised the methods of dividing fractions and the use of equations and letters to signify unknown factors. They also made discoveries in calculus and other systems of math several hundred years before these same principles were understood in Europe. Thus, it becomes obvious that if the Europeans had not changed from the Roman numeral system to the form of mathematics that originated in India, many of the developments that took place in Europe would not have been possible. All evidence indicates that it was not any northern invaders into India who brought or originated this advanced form of mathematics, but it was from the Vedic Aryan civilization that had already been existing in India and the Indus Valley region. Thus, we can see that such intellectual influence did not descend from the north into India, but rather traveled from India up into Europe.

Further evidence that it was not any invaders who originated the highly advanced Vedic culture in the Indus Valley is the fact that various Sumerian seals, that Waddell dates back to 2800 B.C., have been found bearing the image of the water buffalo or Brahma bull. Modern zoologists believe that the water buffalo was known only to the Ganges and Brahmaputra valleys and did not exist in Western India or the Indus Valley. This would suggest a few possibilities. One is that the Sumerians had traveled to Central and Eastern India for reasons of trade and for finding precious stones since Harappa was a trading center connected by way of the Indus river with the gold and torquoise industry of Tibet. Thus, the Sumerians learned about the water buffalo and used images of them on their seals. The second and most likely possibility is that the Aryan civilization at the time extended from Eastern India to the Indus region and further west to Mesopotamia and beyond and included the Sumerians; so, trade naturally brought the image of the water buffalo to the Indus Valley region.

The *brahmana* priests and Indian scholars believe that it is the Ganges valley region that is the origin of Indian civilization and the Aryan race. This can be given some credence when we look at the cities in this region. North of Delhi is the town of Kuruksetra where the great battle of the *Mahabharata* took place when Sri Krishna was still on the planet over 5,000 years ago. There is the old Hastinapura that was once situated along the Ganges until the river changed its course and swept the city away in 800 B.C. This is the old capital of the Kuru dynasty in the *Mahabharata*. Pottery remains have been found near this location that are traced back to at least 1200 B.C. In New Delhi we find the Purana Qila site, which is known to have been part of the ancient city of Indraprastha. South of New Delhi are Vrindavan and Mathura along the Yamuna river. Both of these towns are known for the Vedic legends that go back thousands of years. Further south, located on the Yamuna, is the ancient city of Kaushambi. This city still has the remains of massive defense structures from the tenth century B.C. that are very similar to buildings in Harrappa in the Indus region that use baked brick for construction. The next city is Allahabad (Prayag) where we find the confluence of the Yamuna and Ganges. This location abounds with importance and Vedic legends that are so remote in antiquity that no one can say when they originated. Then there is Varanasi along the Ganges that is another city filled with ancient Vedic legends of importance. And, of course, there are the Himalayan mountains, particularly Mount Meru, that have many Vedic stories connected with them.

Though some archeologists claim they have discovered no evidence for the ancient existence of the Vedic Aryan culture in this region, even a casual tour through this area makes it obvious that these towns and holy sites did not gain importance overnight, nor simply by an immigration of people who are said to have brought the *Vedas* with them. These places could not have become incorporated into the Vedic legends so quickly if the Vedic culture came from another location. Therefore, the argument that the early Vedic literature was brought from another region or describes a geographical location other than India cannot so easily be accepted. Furthermore, the ancient *Rig-veda* (10.75.5; 6.45.31; 3.59.6) mentions the Ganges, sometimes called the Jahnavi, along with (*Rig-veda*, 10.75.1-9) the Yamuna, Sarasvati, and Sindhu (Indus) rivers. And the *Yajur-veda* (*Vajasaneyi Samhita* 23.18) mentions the town of Kampila, which is located about halfway between Hastinapur and Kaushambi. So the rivers and settlements in the Ganges region did have significance in the Vedic literature, which shows that the *Vedas* were written in India and not brought into the Ganges area after they had been written at some other location.

Furthermore, the *Manu-samhita* (2.21-22) describes Madhyadesa, the central region of India, as being where the Aryans were located between the Himavat and Vindhya mountains, east of Prayaga and west of Vinasana where the Sarasvati River disappears. The land that extends as far as the eastern and western oceans is called Aryavata (place of the Aryans) by the wise. This means that the center of Vedic civilization at the time was in near the Saravati River. Some people feel that the Sarasvati is simply a mythical river, but, through research and the use of aerial photography, they have rediscovered parts of what once was the river bed of the Sarasvati. As the *Vedas* describe, and as research has shown, it had once been a very prominent river. Many hundreds of years ago it flowed from the Himalayan mountains southwest to the ocean at the Rann of Kutch. However, it is known to have changed course several times, flowing in a more westerly direction, and then dried up sometime near 1800 B.C.

The point of this is that here is more evidence that the Vedic Aryans could not have invaded India or written the *Rig-veda* after 1800 B.C. and known about the Sarasvati River. In fact, for the river to have been as great as it is described in the *Vedas*, the Aryans had to have been existing in the area for many hundreds of years before the river began to dry up. And if the Aryans were not the first people in this area, then why are there no pre-Aryan names for these rivers? Or why has no one discovered the pre-Indus Valley language if it had been inhabited by a different people before the Aryans arrived? And why is there no record of an Aryan invasion?

THE VEDIC EXPLANATION OF THE ORIGINAL ARYANS

How the Aryan name was given to those who are said to have invaded the Indus region is regarded as uncertain, and whether there really was any invasion is still questioned. But the term *aryan* has been applied to those people who occupied the plains between the Caspian and Black Seas. The hypothesis is that they began to migrate around the beginning of the second millennium B.C. Some went north and northwest, some went westward settling in parts of the Middle East, while others traveled to India through the Indus Valley. Those that are said to have come into India were the "invading Aryans."

The *Vedas* establish a different scenario. They present evidence that ancient, pre-historical India covered a much broader area, and that the real Aryans were not invaders from the north into the Indus region, but were the original residents who were descendants of Vedic society that had spread over the world from the area of India. Thus, the name Aryan, as is generally accepted today, has been misapplied to a group of people who are said to have migrated from the north into India. Some call these people Sumerians, but L. A. Waddell, even though he uses the name, explains that the word *Sumerian* does not exist as an ethnic title and was fabricated by the modern Assyriologists and used to label the Aryan people. And Dr. Hall, in his book *Ancient History of the Near East,* says that there is an anthropological resemblance between the Dravidians of India and the Sumerians of Mesopotamia, which suggests that the group of people called the Sumerians actually came from India. With this information in mind, it is more than likely that the real Aryans were the Vedic followers who were already existing throughout India and to the north beyond the Indus region.

In the Vedic *sutras*, the word *aryan* is used to refer to those who are spiritually oriented and of noble character. The Sanskrit word *aryan* is linguistically related to the word *harijana* (pronounced hariyana), meaning one related to God. Therefore, the real meaning of the word *aryan* refers to those people related to the spiritual Vedic culture and has little to do with those immigrants that some researchers have speculated to be the so-called "invading Aryans." Aryan also refers to those who practice the Vedic teachings and does not mean a particular race of people. Therefore, anyone can be an Aryan by following the Vedic philosophy, and those who do not follow it are non-Aryan.

The name Harijana or Aryan evolved into Syriana or Syrians in Syria, and Hurrians in Hurri, and Arianna or Iranians in Iran. This is also similar to the name Parthians in Partha, another old country in Persia. Partha was the name of Krishna's friend Arjuna, a Vedic Aryan, and means the son of King Prithu. So the name Parthian indicates those who are the descendants of King Prithu. Parthians also had a good relationship with the early Jews since the Jews used to buy grains from the Parthians. The Greeks referred to the Jews as Judeos or Jah deos or Yadavas, meaning people of Ya or descendents of Yadu or Krishna. Although the Vedic tradition does not necessarily support the idea that the Jews and the Yadus are related, it is regarded that the basis of the *Kabbalah*, the book of Jewish mystical concepts, as described in *The Holy Kabbalah* by Arthur Edward Waite, is linked with Kapila Muni, the Indian sage and incarnation of Krishna who established the analytical *sankhya-yoga* philosophy. Therefore, a connection between the early Jews and ancient Vedic culture may be evident.

According to the Vedic literature, Yadu was the eldest of five sons of Yayati. Yayati was a great emperor of the world and one of the original forefathers of those of Aryan and Indo-European heritage. Yayati divided his kingdom amongst his sons, who then started their own dynasties. Yayati had two wives, Devayani and Sharmistha. Yayati had two sons from Devayani: Yadu, who was the originator of the Yadu dynasty called the Yadavas, and Turvasu, from whom the Yavana or Turk dynasty began. From Sharmistha, Yayati had three sons: Druhya, who started the Bhoja dynasty; Anu, who began the Mleccha or Greek dynasty; and Puru who started the Paurava dynasty, which is said to have settled along the Ravi river and later along the Sarasvati. These Aryan tribes, originating in India by King Yayati and mentioned in the *Rig-veda* and *Vishnu* and *Bhagavat Puranas*, spread all over the world.

The Yadava kingdom later became divided among the four sons of Bhima Satvata. From Vrishni, the youngest, descended Vasudeva, the father of Krishna and Balarama and their sister Pritha or Kunti. Kunti married the Yadava prince Pandu and became the mother of Yudhisthira, Bhima, and Arjuna (Partha), the three elder Pandavas. The younger Pandavas were Nakula and Sahadeva, born from Pandu's second wife Madri. Having been forced to the west coast of India because of the tyranny of King Kamsa who hated the Pandavas, they lived at Dwaraka under the protection of Lord Krishna. After Krishna's disappearance from earth, a fratricidal war broke out and killed most of the Pandavas, who had grown to become a huge clan. Those that survived may have gone on to the Indus Valley where they joined or started another part of the advanced Vedic society. Others may have continued further west into Europe, as previously explained.

This is further substantiated in the *Mahabharata* which mentions several provinces of southern Europe and Persia that were once connected with the Vedic culture. The *Adi-parva* (174.38) of the *Mahabharata* describes the province of Pulinda (Greece) as having been conquered by Bhimasena and Sahadeva, two of the Pandava brothers. Thus, the ancient Greeks were once a part of Bharata-varsa (India) and the Vedic civilization. But later the people gave up their affiliation with Vedic society and were, therefore, classified as *Mlecchas*. However, in the *Vana-parva* section of the *Mahabharata* it is predicted that this non-Vedic society would one day rule much of the world, including India. Alexander the Great conquered India for the Pulinda or Greek civilization in 326 B.C., fulfilling the prophecy.

The *Sabha-parva* and *Bhisma-parva* sections of the *Mahabharata* mentions the province of Abhira, situated near what once was the Sarasvati River in ancient Sind. The Abhiras are said to have been warriors who had left India out of fear of Lord Parashurama and hid themselves in the Caucasion hills between the Black and Caspian Seas. Later, for a period of time, they were ruled by Maharaja Yudhisthira. But the sage Markandaya predicted that these Abhiras, after they gave up their link with Vedic society, would one day rule India.

Another province mentioned in *Mahabharata* (*Adi-parva* 85.34) is that of the Yavanas (Turks) who were so named for being descendants of Maharaja Yavana, one of the sons of Maharaja Yayati, as previously explained. They also gave up Vedic culture and became *Mlecchas*. They fought in the battle of Kuruksetra against the Pandavas on behalf of Duryodhana and lost. However, it was predicted that they would one day return to conquer Bharata-varsa (India) and, indeed, this came to pass. Muhammad Ghori later attacked and conquered parts of India on behalf of Islam from the Abhira and Yavana or Turkish countries. Thus, we can see that these provinces in the area of Greece and Turkey (and the countries in between there and India) were once part of the Vedic civilization and had at one time not only political and cultural ties, but also ancestral connections. This is the Vedic version of the origin of Aryan civilization and how its influence spread in various degrees throughout the world.

LINKS BETWEEN THE VEDIC TRADITION
AND OTHER CULTURES

Further evidence on how Vedic influence spread throughout the world can be seen when analyzing other cultures. Numerous countries shared many of the same gods in various ways, although they called them by different names. They also had many similarities in the legends and stories which explained the creation of cosmological realities. Often these were variations or condensations of other neighboring traditions or previously established truths. By studying some of these connections and similarities we can see how many of these cultures are connected to each other and related to the earliest traditions that came out of the Vedic Aryan civilization. We can also recognize how the Vedic influence extended over a vast area and traveled west into Europe and other regions and affected these countries in greater or lesser degrees.

Ancient India no doubt covered a much larger area of land than it does today and spread much further to the north and west. At least there are historical indications showing that the Aryan influence was felt over long distances. The Vedic gods, for example, were known over a wide area. V. Gordon Childe, in his book *The Aryans*, states that evidence makes it clear that the Aryans had been established in centers on the Upper Euphrates in 1400 B.C. These centers were similar to the cities of the Indus Valley and later in Media and Persia. In fact, Hugo Winckler, in 1907, identified the names of four Vedic gods (Indra,

Varuna, Mitra, and the Nasatya twins) along with ten Babylonian and four Mitannian gods that were invoked as witnesses to a treaty signed in 1360 B.C. between the kings of Mitanni and the Hittites. There are also tablets at Tell-el-Amarna that mention Aryan princes in Syria and Palestine. But these Aryans were not necessarily permanent residents of the area but dynasts who ruled over the non-Aryan subjects of that region. This would explain why some scholars such as Jacobi, Pargiter, and Konow accept the deities of the Mitanni in the Upper Euphrates in Syria and Palestine as being Indian, introduced to the area through a Sanskrit speaking people who came from the Punjab. Furthermore, L. A. Waddell claims that the first Aryan kings can be traced back to at least 3380 B.C. They had a capital north of the Euphrates near the Black Sea in Cappadocia in 3378 B.C., and these Hittite kings of Cappadocia bore Aryan names. This means that the Aryans had to have been very well settled in the area during this time.

* * *

One widely held view about the Sumerians is that they arrived in Mesopotamia before 3000 B.C. when they acquired the prosperity of the inhabitants that were living there. But another view is that the Sumerians were actually the earliest cultivators in Mesopotamia. They had a philosophy which was especially influential on the succeeding Babylonians and Assyrians who assimilated much of their beliefs. The Sumerians believed the universe and all within it reflected the supreme mind and supernatural activity. They believed that the universe was created from the primeval sea along with all the planets, stars, sun, and moon, each of which had its own orbit. After the creation of the planets came superhuman and invisible beings, who then made human, animal, and plant life. This Sumerian theology, very similar to the Vedic version, can still be found in the detailed texts dating back to 1900 B.C.

Though the Mesopotamian cities shared a common pantheon, not all of the gods were worshiped in all of the cities, neither were they known by the same names. And when the Semites invaded the area, they changed the gods' names, characteristics, and relations. So presently it is not clear which were the Sumerian gods or which were carry-overs from the Vedic Aryans, to whom the Sumerians were closely related.

The Sumerians had many temples, such as the temple of Enki at Eridu, or of Marduk at Babylon. The images of the gods were worshiped by being given offerings of food and drink, fruit, incense, and new garments on festival days. This is the same system used in worshiping the Vedic deities in India. Anu was the god of heaven and was at first the ruler of the other gods, such as Enlil (lord of the winds and creator of the sun, moon, and vegetation), Ninki (lady of the earth), and Enki (lord of the underworld). Anu was especially worshipped at Uruk, around 300 B.C., but was replaced by Enlil when the city of Nippur defeated Uruk, the biblical city of Erech and modern Warka. However, the god Marduk, son of Enki, replaced Enlil in Babylonia when his city of Babylon ruled Mesopotamia by the influence of a powerful dynasty, and was also replaced by Ashur in Assyria near the middle of the second millennium. The consort of Enlil, Ninlil, became the Babylonian Ishtar, who represented many earlier female deities and was also known to Syrians as Anat, and to Arabs as Atar, to Greeks as Astarte, and to Egyptians as Isis. In Assyria, Adad was the god who controlled the rain, in Syria he was called Ramman the thunderer, among the Hittites he was Teshub, and the Vedic tradition called him Indra.

* * *

In Persia there are many similarities between the Indians and the Iranians. As V. Gordon Childe points out, there are linguistic resemblances found in the Sanskrit of the *Rig-veda* and the Iranian in the *Gathas* of Zoroaster and Darius the Great. Both Indians and Iranians had called themselves Aryas, and worshiped the same deities, such as Mitra, Aryaman, Indra, Varuna, Agni, and so on. They also once knew the same set of rivers, the Sarasvati and Hara 'uvatis, as well as shared the Soma ritual. Thus, one can conclude that they were once of the same background. Even the word *Iran* or *Ariana* means "Land of the Aryans" as pointed out by Hermann Kulke in his book, *A History of India*. And the Druze, an unorthodox sect of Islam, is known to have philosophical origins in the Vedic culture. They believe in reincarnation, *karma*, incarnations of God in the world when He appears in order to establish religious principles, and many other points that are found rooted in the Vedic culture. All this signifies that the early Iranians were a part of or at least affiliated with the Aryan civilization.

* * *

Many of the Vedic Aryan concepts of God were adopted by Zoroastrianism. In fact, its basic doctrines and conception of its god, Ahura Mazda, can be traced back to the *Purusha-sukta*, which is in the *Rig-veda*. And Zoroastrianism, as explained in a previous chapter, had a great influence on the Judeo-Christian religion. Waddell points out that the Adam of the Adam and Eve story of the Hebrew *Genesis* came about from the traditional history in late Babylonia that described the oldest kings known to the ancient world of the Aryan dynasties. The Hebrew rabbis who composed the book of *Genesis* (said to be a book of Moses) heard these histories of the great supermen Aryan kings. Not understanding them, they distorted the historical facts about the great king Adda (the Babylonian name of an early Aryan king who was also called Addamu), and simply changed the name Addamu into "Adam," the first created man said to have been formed by God in 3761 B.C. Thus, Waddell concludes that the story of the Hebrew genealogy of Adam, Cain, Enoch, Noah, and Japhet are variations of the names and distortions of the Babylonian history of the earliest recorded Aryan kings.

The Hebrew Adam was the Sumerian Adar or Addamu and the Aryan Iksvaku. The name Cain is the English equivalent of the Hebrew Qain, who was called in *Genesis* by the title of Aysh, similar to Ayus of the Vedic epics. Cain is said to have built a city and named it after his son Enoch, which is the English version of the Hebrew name Hanuk. Biblical authorities say this city is identical to the old Sumerian seaport of Unuk in Lower Mesopotamia that Chaldeans later called Erek. And the name Enoch or Hanuck equates with Janak of the Vedic epics. Thus, as pointed out to a small degree in the previous chapters, the religion of the Jews and Christians is naturally similar in many respects to the Vedic traditions, though they may have used distortions of neighboring histories to fabricate their own folklore. And they also adopted various customs as well. For example, the baptism ritual that is practiced throughout Christianity originated in India in the form of immersion in the Ganges River for spiritual rebirth and purification. More information is found in Chapter Six.

* * *

A look at the Egyptian culture may also shed light on the ancient existence of Vedic civilization. In some ways it is confusing to get a grasp of exactly what their theology was because it changed according to locality. Egyptian theology was also forced through a number of changes because of the demands of different pharaohs who preferred the worship of one god over all others and ordered the people to follow accordingly. In various cities, different gods were held to be supreme and the theory of creation was presented differently according to which Egyptian text was consulted.

The premise of Heliopolis, the Lebanese city of Baalbek, presented Atum as the first self-manifested creator who is characterized as the sun-god Ra. Atum emerged from the primeval waters and by masturbation created Tefenet (moisture) and Shu (air) who manifested Geb (earth) and Nut (sky), and through the procreation of Geb and Nut came Osiris, Isis, Seth, and Nephthys.

In Memphis, the creator-god was Ptah, who created by means of his intelligence and spoken word. In the temple of Edfu the texts explain how the earth emerges from a lotus flower which rises from the primeval waters, a story with similarities to the Vedic version of creation. Furthermore, the animal of Ptah is Apis the bull, similar to Lord Shiva whose carrier is Nandi the bull.

At Thebes, in southern Egypt, the chief god was Amun, god of life. Later the chief god was Amun-Ra, uniting Amun and Ra. Nearly everyone also worshiped Osiris, god of fertility, and his wife Isis, the great mother goddess of the moon and agriculture, and their son Horus, god of the day.

In the 14th century B.C. the ruler Amenhotep IV banished all other gods but Aton and claimed that he was the one god. Aton was the god of love, peace, and beauty. Amenhotep, who changed his name to Ikhnaton (spirit of Aton), wanted to spread peace and beauty throughout the world. But Ikhnaton reigned for only 15 years, after which the worship of other gods resumed.

The Egyptians worshiped their temple deities in a similar fashion as that found in India. The priests practiced cleanliness, shaved their heads, and wore white cloth. They would take a bath early in the morning to purify themselves and at dawn they would enter the temple. Opening the sanctuary where the deity was, the priest would prostrate before the image and then sit and chant prayers and burn incense. Then he would bathe the deity and dress it in fresh clothes and offer it food and drink, and then clean the altar and temple. They would sometimes take the deity of the Lord on a boat on the Nile and give it rides, something which is still practiced in India. In Egyptian paintings, Osiris is often depicted as black, similar to the dark color of Krishna. In some paintings, there are little snakes or *nagas* holding round disks or planets on their heads, similar to Lord Seshanaga supporting the planets as described in the Vedic literature.

The Egyptian philosophical teachings and rites for the initiates took place either in the secret parts of the temples or in the pyramids. It is now generally understood that the pyramids were not tombs but places where the secret and intense initiation rituals into the mysteries of Egyptian philosophy were performed. In the lower phases of initiation the candidates were taught the knowledge of the soul. They accepted the soul as eternal and that it would leave the body at death and reappear in another state of being, usually in higher realms. In the higher phases of initiation, direct realization of the soul and communion with the Divine was to be attained. This is practically identical with the knowledge provided in the *Vedas* and shows there must have been a strong connection between India and Egypt in the early part of Egyptian civilization.

Other similarities are in the names. The name of the Egyptian sun-god Ra is derived from Ravi, the Sanskrit name for the sun. The name Heru (Horus is the Greek pronunciation) or Nar Heru is derived from Hari, which is the Sanskrit name for the Supreme or Vishnu. Nar Heru is called Naar Ari in Hebrew, which is the Nara Hari in Sanskrit, another form of the name of Vishnu or Krishna.

One of the main Egyptian hieroglyphs representing Hari is the round disk, appearing either singularly or with other symbols such as the hawk. A disk with wings was often the representation of Hari. The hawk is the Egyptian hieroglyph for Hari and is also symbolized by a number of other birds like the peacock, swan, or parrot, which all play a prominent role in Egyptian hieroglyphics. The peacock was the symbol of Heliopolis, which was the capital for the worship of Ra or Re, or Hari, until 2100 B.C. when Thebes became the state capital. The peacock had been imported by Solomon and was the symbol for the house of David and sacred to Eli, the god of the Jews and Hebrews.

Egyptian civilization is said to have made rapid development, from primitive to advanced, around 3000 B.C. The first pyramid at Sakkara is said to have been built during this time, while the Great Pyramid of Cheops at Giza is said to have been built around 2900 or 2800 B.C. The way the Great Pyramid is made shows the characteristics of an advanced society. If the Egyptians changed from primitive to advanced in only a century or two, then how did they become so advanced in such a short time? Some say that people from Atlantis arrived and settled in the land of Egypt and began teaching their knowledge to the Egyptians. But we know that the idea of the lost continent of Atlantis came primarily from Plato who wrote about it in his *Dialogues* called "Critias" and "Tamaceus." Plato heard about a sunken land from a man named Critias, who heard about it from Critias the elder, who heard about it from Solon, an Athenian statesman, who is said to have heard a description of it from an Egyptian priest named Neith Sais.

Atlantis may have actually existed, as some people think, but no archeological evidence has been found. And since we are primarily focusing on historical, linguistic, or archeological evidence, which unfortunately only goes back to about 3000 B.C. or later in regard to any culture you are discussing, a review of any similarities between Atlantis and other cultures will have to wait.

Another explanation for the sudden rise in Egyptian civilization is found on a script of simple hieroglyphics located in a tomb, which was written during the time of the building of the first pyramids. The script tells of a sailor who survived a shipwreck and reached a land of abundant fruit trees and gardens of vegetables, and where many advanced and wise men resided. The land sank beneath the sea and the survivors fled in all directions. Some are said to have found a home in Egypt. The story writer suggests the land was near the coast of Africa. Where exactly, no one knows.

Whether this describes Atlantis or not, no one can be sure. But it would correspond to the coastal city of Dwaraka located in India across the Arabian Sea from Africa. Present day Dwaraka is situated on the mainland north of Bombay and some distance south of the Indus river. Ancient Dwaraka is described in the Vedic texts as an island city off the coast of India that was very advanced and organized for its time. The *Bhagavat Purana* relates that the outer wall of the huge fortress covered as much as 96 square miles. Within the city were paved roads, gardens, and palatial buildings made of gold with rooms decorated with the finest of gems on the walls and floors. It was the heavenly city where Lord Krishna lived part of the time while on earth. It was also the capital of the Yadu dynasty, said to have had a population of one billion people. It is also recorded that it did sink into the ocean after Krishna departed from the planet about the time of 3100 B.C. This is near the era when the pyramids were supposed to have been built and when Egyptian culture made great progress.

The remains of buildings and huge fort walls of the sunken city have been found off the coast of present day Dwaraka. Professor S. R. Rao of the National Institute of Oceanography has found under the sea such items as pottery, seals, inscribed jars, a coppersmith's mold, as well as copper and bronze articles, etc., proving that a sophisticated city did exist there. Other structures and walls have been found further beneath the sea, buried under sediment. On the island off the coast the remains of a massive wall some 550 metres in length, usually submerged, proves that it was a fortified structure. Excavations near the sea by the present city have revealed that a settlement had been established there from at least the 15th century B.C. where the people built great temples and buildings. And on the beaches at low tide, people can be seen panning for gold, and, indeed, finding it. People say it washes onto the beach from the ancient city.

It would be feasible then that survivors from the sunken city of Dwaraka could have sailed across the sea to northern Africa or may have gone north toward the Indus Valley where another advanced society was begun or already in progress. From there some could have crossed Mesopotamia over trade routes and gone on to Egypt to the Nile where they shared their knowledge with the local inhabitants and started the Egyptian culture with variations in the Vedic traditions, legends, and local names for the demigods. However, Waddell, in *The Makers of Civilization*, claims that it was indeed the early Aryan kings who became the predynastic Pharaohs of Egypt. If this is true, it would certainly place the beginning of Egyptian civilization at a very early date, at least five thousand years ago. It would also explain why there would be hardly any Egyptian records of how the culture began or who the earliest rulers were, since accurate Egyptian records were not kept until after the dynastic Pharaohs had been established. It would also explain why much of the spiritual aspect of Egyptian philosophy is so similar to that of the Vedic teachings.

L. A. Waddell establishes in his book, *Egyptian Civilization*, that Menes, the original founder of Egypt's first dynasty, was the predynastic Aryan Pharaoh that united Egypt. Menes is the Manasyu mentioned in the *Mahabharata* (specifically the Calcutta edition published in 1834, Volume One, Section 94, verses 3695-3697) to which Waddell referred. Manasyu is described as the son of Pravira or Pravireshvara, the son of Puru, and is in the line of the Prabhu of Gopta, or Pharaoh of Egypt.

Manasyu was known as Manis or Manas in Mesopotamia (the affix *yu* means the Uniter in Sanskrit), and some of the seals found in the Indus Valley region refer to Kings Puru and Manis as rulers of the area, including Egypt. Waddell and other Egyptologists contend that Manasyu or Menes took his military and naval forces and sailed from the Indus region across the Arabian and Red Seas and entered Egypt east of Koptos or Abydos. Koptos was a town known as an ancient center for trade and still has some of the oldest statues of Egyptian gods. There are also illustrations of ships on the ebony labels at Menes' tomb at Abydos which signifies the importance of his sea travel. The inscriptions about Menes at his tomb, found by Sir F. Petri, are the earliest of hieroglyphs which are in Sumerian script and language.

After Menes' arrival, he began organizing Egypt and establishing the Aryan culture, especially in regard to its metal industry, irrigation systems, its form of tombs, and system of writing. The Egyptian hieroglyphs are a modified form of the Sumerian-Aryan picture-writing which was used during the rule of Menes. Many of the important Egyptian words are of Sumerian-Aryan origin, though many were changed years later because of the influence of the Semitic speech. Menes also adopted the sun-hawk as his royal emblem in Egypt because he engaged in sun-worship as was common amongst Aryans at the time. All this indicates that the first rulers of Egypt were indeed the Aryan monarchs. Even the Egyptians accepted the idea that their culture originated from across the sea to the East. Where else would this be but India?

It is also suggested that Menes is the same King Minos of Crete of the Greek fables. The reasoning for this is that Sir A. Evans, the great explorer of ancient Cretan culture, places the beginning of Cretan civilization at the same time as the First Dynasty Period of Egypt. He further believes that Cretan civilization was of an independent origin appearing within Crete that brought the sudden rise of the Copper or Bronze Age to the area. Like Menes, Minos was a sea-emperor of the Mediterranean who established laws over the land. Menes and Minos both used writing on clay tablets, had ceramic ware and painted pottery of similar design. The drain-pipes in ancient Crete are also similar to those found in Sumerian Ur and the cities of the Indus Valley. This could not be possible without some connection between Crete and the Aryan culture.

Waddell, however, stands alone in respect to the dates he sets for Manasyu's or Menes' invasion into Egypt. He suggests that Menes traveled to Egypt around 2704 B.C. But other Egyptologists suggest dates ranging from 5869 B.C. to 4400 B.C., which seem to corroborate more closely to the descriptions in the Vedic literature. Furthermore, some researchers say Minos arrived in Crete near 4000 B.C. Besides, bronze and copper casting was well established in the Middle East by 3500 B.C., so if Minos was Menes who brought the Bronze Age to Crete, it must have been before 2700 B.C. So Waddell's dates for Menes' invasion may have to be placed much earlier than 2704 B.C. The next few paragraphs may shed more light on this.

Another interesting point is that the great early Vedic Aryan King Ikshvaku may have become known as the god Osiris in Egypt. Ikshvaku was referred to as Asaru in Sumerian, which is changed to Asar or Asir in Egyptian, and then to Osiris. Ikshvaku originally may simply have been honored as a great ancestor and king by the early Aryan rulers, which is very likely in the Aryan tradition, only to later become the deified Father-god whom became the basis of many stories and legends embellished from whatever was heard of him at the time. Osiris is also known for being a legendary ruler of predynastic Egypt and is said to have provided the people with knowledge of agriculture and civilization, things that were very important to the Aryans.

Ikshvaku's position is described in *Bhagavad-gita* (4.1). It is explained that the Supreme Being originally instructed the spiritual science of yoga to Vivasvan, the sun-god, who then instructed it in Treta-yuga to Manu, who is considered the father of mankind. Manu instructed this knowledge to Maharaja Ikshvaku who was the king of the earth planet many hundreds of years ago, and the forefather of the Raghu dynasty, which he started in Ayodhya. Many years later Lord Ramachandra appeared in this dynasty. This is further explained in *Mahabharata* (*Shanti-parva*, 348.51-52). Thus, the spiritual knowledge of the Vedic literature, whether in written form or not, has existed in human society from the time of the great Aryan King Ikshvaku.

This information also indicates that Vedic culture has been in existence many more years than most scholars think. According to the Vedic tradition, Treta-yuga lasts 1,200,000 years. After this is Dvapara-yuga which lasts 800,000 years. And we have now gone through 5,000 years of Kali-yuga. So if this spiritual knowledge was taught by Manu sometime in Treta-yuga, we can get some idea of how long it has been in existence on this earth. So this discourages us from believing in the time frame Waddell presents for the first time Egypt was ruled by the Vedic Aryans. In fact, there could have been many times when the area of Egypt and the Mediterranean had been influenced or colonized by Aryan emperors over many hundreds of years, each one developing the area to a higher degree of social progress.

One other account of how the Egyptian culture began goes back to the prehistoric times of Lord Parashurama in India. It is recorded in the Vedic literature that Parashurama killed all the ruling kings in India who were cruel, sinful, and against *brahminical* culture. It is explained in the *Mahabharata* that the earliest kings of Egypt were originally the miscreant kings and warriors who had fled India due to their fear of Lord Parashurama. Once they settled in Egypt, they started their own distorted version of the Vedic culture.

It is also interesting that some people believe that the Egyptian pyramids were built to help guide planes or spaceships to the area, and the Vedic literature has many references to flying vehicles. No Hindu today is unfamiliar with the idea that flying planes, called *vimanas*, existed 5000 years ago, although they were powered much differently than the planes of today. Did the early Vedic rulers use spaceships or planes to reach and colonize different areas of the planet? Were they possibly the same men and flying machines described in other tribal legends of men coming from the sky and helping the local inhabitants? No one can say for sure, but planes played a big part in the Vedic legends and many of the ancient battles that are described. So this would indicate that it is a possiblility. After all, the ancient *Bruhad Vimana Shastra* by the Vedic sage Bharadvaj describes the construction of these *vimanas*.

* * *

In looking at the Greek culture, Helios was the sun-god or Greek form of Ravi or Hari, and Helios contains the name of Eli, which is the name of the Jewish form of God the Father. The Sanskrit name Hari is linguistically related to the name Eli, and Elohim is the plural form of Eli which refers to the demigods or lesser representatives of the Supreme Deity. The popular Roman god Mithra can be traced to Mitra of the *Vedas*, who came to the Mediterranian through Asia Minor by the military forces who had been impressed with the philosophy. One of the most important of the Greek gods is Zeus, the god of the heavens and earth (the Vedic Indra). And Hades is god of the underworld (similar to Lord Shiva).

Poseidon, the Greek god of the sea, refers to *Pati dhana* in Sanskrit, which is a by-name of Seshanaga. *Dhana* means the support or the one who holds up the universe. And the Greek Prometheus comes from the word *Pramathes*, which is a name for Lord Shiva. The Greek name of *Patar Ouranos*, that is translated into "Heavenly Father" in the *New Testament*, refers to Pitar Varuna, the Vedic demigod Varuna.

It is also understood that the original name of Heracles comes from the Sanskrit words *Hare Krishna*. This is traced back to the way the early Greek writers who visited India said that the city they called Klessleboro (Mathura) was the capital of Krishna worship. The Greeks pronounced the name Krishna as klessle, and Hare as hera. Thus came the name of Heraklessle, or Heracles and Hercules, who is the muscular man who played prominent roles in the Greek myths. Interestingly, Krishna is also known for His mighty deeds, such as lifting Govardhana Hill with the little finger of His left hand while still a young boy.

Other linguistic similarities can be found. For example, the word *paradise* in English is related to *paradisio* in Greek, which is related to *pardes* in Hebrew (meaning the garden beyond), which is related to *paradesha* in Sanskrit, meaning the far away place of Para or Vishnu. And the Greek word *propheto* referred to the Egyptian high priest at the sacrifice. This was derived from the Sanskrit word *purohito*, which is the name of the high priest officiating at the fire sacrifice or Deity worship in the Vaishnava tradition. This word is the origin of the English word prophet. There is a linguistic similarity between the Christian word *Amen* and the Sanskrit word *Om*, and *Abraham* and the Sanskrit *brahmana*.

Furthermore, many of the Roman gods originated from Greek tradition and were characterized after the Vedic deities. For example, Zeus is Dyaus, Jupiter is Diupeter (or Dyaus Pitar, the Vedic Indra), Minerva is Pallas Athen, Diana is Artemia, Venus (the Vedic Lakshmi) became Aphrodite, Neptune is Poseidon, Vulcan is Hephaestus, Ceres is Demetri, Liber is Dionysus, Mercury became Hermes, and Hermes was formerly the Egyptian god Thoth. An interesting point concerning Hermes is described by Dr. Ginsburg in *Life of Levita*. It is mentioned that the way the god Hermes was worshiped was as a phallus, standing on a flat stone, which was anointed with oil, similar to the worship of the Shiva *linga*. But the Shiva *linga* is anointed with Ganges water, representing the way Shiva accepted the pounding force of the Ganges river on his head as it descended from the heavenly region to earth.

Rome also had been engaged in trade with India for many years. An example of how extensive trade was between Rome and India can be seen at Sisupalgarh. This was a fort located on the far eastern side of India, three miles south of Bhubaneshwar. It was built around the third century B.C. and abandoned in the fourth century A.D. Excavations revealed Roman and Indian coins that date back to the first and second centuries.

As Roman culture spread westward, it incorporated more gods and goddesses, such as those of the Celtics, like Sulis, the goddess at Bath, who was identified with Minerva. Maponus was identified with Apollo, and Mars (the Vedic Skanda) had many similarities with other gods. The name of the Roman god Janus was the latin word for the Vedic demigod Ganesh. A description of the worship of Janus is practically a duplicate of how Ganesh is worshiped.

As for the sculptures and images of the deities, their characteristics would change as they went from India to Egypt to Greece, etc., because the esthetic standards would change since the priests would emphasize certain aspects of the images according to regional and cultural preference. The early Greek sculptures seem to have been carved by the priests for the temples. In other words, they were the temple deities and were probably dressed rather than left naked, and then would be worshiped in the temples. Many of the early forms were almost always carved as a boy of 15 to 17 years of age with long hair like Krishna. Furthermore, Zeus, Jupiter, and Amon were all blue bodied, not because they were sky-gods like some say, but because they are related to the image of Krishna who is blue, which signifies His spiritual nature.

There is also archeological evidence that the Greeks were impressed with the Vedic culture as far back as 200 B.C. We can see this evidence in what is called the Heliodorus column which was erected by the Greek ambassador to India in 113 B.C. at Besnagar in central India. The inscription on the column, as published in the Journal of the Royal Asiatic Society, says:

This Garuda column of Vasudeva (Vishnu), the god of gods, was erected here by Heliodorus, a worshiper of Vishnu, the son of Dion, and an inhabitant of Taxila, who came as Greek ambassador from the Great King Antialkidas to King Kasiputra Bhagabhadra, the Savior, then reigning prosperously in the fourteenth year of his kingship. Three important precepts when practiced lead to heaven: self-restraint, charity, conscientiousness.

This shows that Heliodorus was a worshiper of Vishnu and well versed in the texts pertaining to this religion. How many other Greeks became converted to Vaishnavism if such a notable ambassador did can only be guessed.

The column also establishes archeological proof that knowledge of Krishna and the Vaishnava tradition antedated Christianity by at least 200 years, disproving claims of Christians and British that the stories of Krishna in the *Puranas* were modern and merely taken as adaptations from the stories of Jesus.

Considering the strong influence of Greek philosophy on western culture, we should also look briefly at the philosophers of Greek civilization. Many of them had ideas on life that were very similar to the Vedic view. Pythagoras (582-507 B.C.), one of the earliest Greek philosophers, taught that the soul wandered through many lives in this material creation, living even within the bodies of plants and animals. Thus, the goal of the soul, according to Pythagoras, was to attain freedom from the cycles of reincarnation through the performance of virtuous acts. These would attune the soul to God and bring deliverance. This philosophy is parallel to the Vedic knowledge of the soul and law of *karma*. Even the many mathematical theories that Pythagoras taught had already been known in the older Vedic times of India.

To help people purify themselves spiritually, Pythagoras set up communities that had laws similar to those of India and stressed vegetarianism and the wearing of simple clothes. He also taught that a person's life should be divided into four divisions, which were the same as the four *ashramas* in the Vedic plan of life. India no doubt had a great influence on Pythagoras. In fact, it has been said that in the travels of Pythagoras, India was one of the places he visited. And it was noted by his followers that he had been initiated into Vedic philosophy while studying in Ellora, India. It was no doubt while he was in India that he got many of his ideas on mathematics.

Socrates (469-400 B.C.) was the next great philosopher of Greece. From the *Memorabilia* written by Xenophon we get a picture of Socrates as a man wandering the streets of Athens talking to anyone about various aspects of life. There is every possibility that men from India had reached Athens by this time for purposes of trading spices and metals. Trade between India and the Tigris-Euphrates region goes back to ancient times. This was done by using land routes or by crossing the Indian Ocean and sailing up the Red Sea. Babylon was a center where those of the West and East would meet to trade their goods. It is here that Greeks and Indians may have discussed not only prices of goods, but also philosophies of life. And if there were any intellectual Indians in Athens, surely Socrates would have met them and engaged in lengthy discussions. In fact, Eusebius writes in his *Praeparatio Evangelica* (XI.3), written in 315 A.D., about an account told by Aristoxenus, one of Aristotle's pupils, of a meeting between Socrates and a group of Indian *brahmanas*. Such a meeting surely would have influenced Socrates' philosophical views.

Socrates' pupil, Plato (428-347 B.C.), had a philosophy of the soul that was also very similar to the Vedic conception. Plato believed in an immortal soul and a universal or supersoul as well as a God or Supreme Creator of the physical world. He believed that God was the perfect being and, therefore, changeless. The unfortunate thing is that the philosophers of this era had a habit of not acknowledging their sources of information, which may give a reason as to why Plato never mentions India in his writings. However, Plato must have been aware of India because Plato's pupil Aristotle did mention India in his writings, signifying he knew where it was.

Aristotle (384-322 B.C.) also had strong spiritual beliefs which were very similar to the teachings of the *Vedas*. Aristotle believed that God was the being who directed the world and that God's existence could be proven. His analysis was that every moment or "now" implied that there had to be a "before." In other words, everything that makes up the present was caused by what happened previous to that moment. Thus, time and motion, in respect to past, present, and future, must be eternal. Therefore, absolute reality is eternal without a creation. So if change is a constant factor, there must be an eternal cause of change which implies, according to Aristotle, that there is a prime mover who would be the cause (cause of all causes as the *Vedas* describe) that imparts motion or the affects of time without himself being moved or affected. This would be the absolutely perfect Supreme Being who moves the world through love.

Aristotle's conception of the soul was that the soul is divided into two parts. One part was the rational aspect or the intellect, while the other part is the irrational aspect where the desires are. This would correspond to the Vedic analysis of the difference between the rational intelligence and the irrational mind, which is the center of the senses and sensual desires. Aristotle concluded that the intellect could control the desires through developing reasoning and moral discipline. Such development leads a person to wisdom and understanding. Aristotle, by stressing this kind of progress, viewed self-realization as the purpose of life. This, of course, was also the ultimate goal of Vedic philosophy by which the Greek philosophers seemed to be strongly influenced.

Another point that shows Greek civilization was influenced by India is the use of animals in the Greek fables by Aesop. Such fables with animal characters are easily found in India in books like the *Panchatantra, Hitopadesa,* and *Jatakas.* The *Panchatantra* was written in the second century B.C., but the stories are much older, having appeared in earlier Sanskrit texts written many years before Aesop's time. Thus, some scholars, such as Max Muller, believed that renditions of these fables came to Greece from India. The reason for this opinion is that many of the characters in these fables are animals like the lion, jackal, elephant, peacock, tiger, monkey, and crocodile, which are found in India but not in Greece.

Furthermore, many of the fairy tales that are told in different countries and in different periods are so similar that they show they must have, at some distant time, originated with a common source, in one culture. But, as with spiritual knowledge, these stories must have undergone change as the people divided and moved and carried these tales to new localities. However, these legends of ancient heroes and stories that preserved and elaborated on spiritual truths that were clearly understood in the Aryan culture of India gradually became transformed into supernatural and unintelligible myths as they traveled through Persia, Greece, Italy, and then up through Germany and into Scandinavia. In other words, by comparison we can see how the original Aryan culture and its legends became more and more distorted as each region changed the stories as well as the names and activities of the characters within them and the traditions that were described.

* * *

There are other traces of the ancient Vedic influence throughout Europe as pointed out by Professor P. N. Oak. In language, the word *navy* comes from the Sanskrit *naa-vi*, which means "a collection of boats," and *navigability* is a Sanskrit compound meaning "that which has the capacity to allow ships maneuverability." Places like Solonica, Veronica, and Thessalonica refer to the presence of armies since the Sanskrit term *fonica* means an army. The same goes for Dorchester and Lancaster because the suffix *ster* is a Sanskrit term meaning "a place of arms." Places like Kilkenny and Kilpatric mean the place of forts because the Sanskrit prefix *kila* or *qila* means a fort even today in India. The name *Atlantic* is a Sanskrit word *a-tal-lantic* meaning "a sea of abyssmal depth." And *Mediterranean* in Sanskrit refers to a body of water in the middle of land since it divides Europe from Asia or Africa. *Ramsgate* in England is the same as the word *Ramsdvar*, meaning "door to the township of Rama," one of the incarnations of Lord Krishna. And *Rome*, which is spelled *Roma* in Italy, refers to Rama. Paintings from episodes of the *Ramayana* found in early Italian homes support this conclusion. The city of Ravenna in Italy, said to be founded after Ravan, Rama's adversary in the *Ramayana*, also corroborates this. Germany calls itself *Deutschland* and in Holland the people are called the *Dutch* because of their ancestral link with the Daityas, the descendants of Diti who were generally opposed to the Vedic demigods. Budapest is the ancient Buddhaprastha, the Hungarian city dedicated to Buddha. And the name *Hungary* has a linguistic connection with the Sanskrit term *shringary*, meaning "a beautiful hilly country." And *arya* is also connected to the word *eire* as found in the name Ireland, which is the land furthest west that is known to have been reached by the Aryans in ancient times. Other similarities exist in the Lithuanian language, which very closely resembles Sanskrit, along with Slavic. Thus, we can see how many references to Vedic influence throughout Europe remain to this day.

How the Vedic influence was felt in such far away places as England and Scandinavia is explained in *The Aryans* by V. Gordon Childe who mentions that in Britain, shortly after 2000 B.C., a people conquered the territory who were noted for their use of battle-axes. It was during this time that a period of rapid development began. It is now understood that these people were mixed with Aryans, who promoted what is now called the Western type of civilization that continued to develop.

L. A. Waddell also writes that the Trojans and their civilization were of Sumerian-Aryan origin. When the Trojan amulets were deciphered they were disclosed to be of the same religion with the same invocations and deity symbols as on the amulets of the Indo-Sumerian seals of the Indus Valley. These symbols were also the same as those on the ancient monuments in Britain. And Britain was first colonized by King Brutus the Trojan in about 1103 B.C.

Further Vedic influence in Britain was also brought by the Celts. Celts were Indo-Europeans who first emerged as a separate people near the source of the Danube about 1000 B.C. They swept over central Europe and arrived in Britain about 800 B.C. Ward Rutherford, in his book *Celtic Mythology*, points out many similarities between the Celtic and the early Hindu or Vedic traditions. He suggests that though the Celts and Vedic followers were separated by a large mass of land, they nonetheless must have originally come from the same source. Furthermore, Waddell, in *The Makers of Civilization*, provides some evidence that Saint George, Saint Andrew, Saint Michael, and the legend of King Arthur and the Holy Grail, as well as the Thor-Odin legend of the Britains and Scandinavians, were of Sumerian-Aryan origin.

Many forms of religion and philosophy can be found in the Vedic teachings, one of which is the respect for the sun as a representative of the Supreme. Sun worship was central to many European cultures from ancient to Roman times. Considering the many resemblances between the old pre-Christian and Vedic cultures in language, religions, their gods, goddesses, rituals, and legends, as well as the many similarities in modern Christianity, we can rightly conclude that *the Vedic culture is the real spiritual heritage of the European people.*

* * *

The *Mahabharata* and the *Puranas* describe many kings who had dominance over the whole world. Among some of the greatest colonizing Aryans were the sea-faring branches from the Gangetic region that had a great effect on the Indo-China area. T. de Lacouperie explains in his book, *The Western Origin of Chinese Civilization*, that on the China coast, in the Gulf of Kia-tchou, Hindu leaders established trading centers; one at Lang-ga to the south, and Tsih-miah or Tsih-moh to the north. These traders also established the system of coinage in China near 675 B.C., and made coins imprinted with their names and the names of various Chinese cities on them.

These Aryans controlled the Chinese sea-trade for many years and established many other centers and ports in Burma, Malaya, Siam, Cambodia, and islands such as Sumatra, Java, Borneo, and the Philippines. To this day in these areas most of the writing is in alphabetic letters derived from the Indo-Aryan version, and the popular religion is the old form of Buddhism that came from India. And anyone can recognize many similarities between the art, architecture, sculptures, and traditional dress of these areas and that of India.

There are many similarities between the Vedic literature and the Buddhist religion of the Far East. For example, the word *Ch'an* of the Ch'an school of Chinese Buddhism is Chinese for the Sanskrit word *dhyana*, which means meditation, as does the word *zen* in Japanese. Furthermore, the deity Amitayus is the origin of all other Lokesvara forms of Buddha and is considered the original spiritual master, just as Balarama in the Vedic literature is the source of all the Vishnu incarnations and is the original spiritual teacher. Also, the trinity doctrine of Mahayana Buddhism explains the three realms of manifestations of Buddha, which are the *dharmakaya* realm of Amitabha (the original two-armed form is Amitayus), the *sambhogakaya* realm of the spiritual manifestation (in which the undescended form of Lokesvara or Amitayus reigns), and the *rupakaya* realm, the material manifestation (which is where Lokesvara incarnates in so many different forms). This is a derivative of the Vedic philosophy. Thus, Lokesvara is actually a representation of Vishnu to the Mahayana Buddhists.

All the different incarnations of Vishnu appear as different forms of Lokesvara. For example, Makendanatha Lokesvara is Matsya, Badravaraha Lokesvara is Varaha, Hayagriva is the horse necked one as described in the *Vedas*, and so on. And the different forms of Lakshmi, Vishnu's spouse as the Goddess of Fortune, appear as the different forms of Tara in the White Tara, the Green Tara, etc. Even the fearful forms of Lokesvara are simply the fearful aspects of Lord Vishnu, as in the case of the threatening image of Yamantaka, who is simply the form of the Lord as death personified.

Many times you will also see Buddhist paintings depicting a threefold bending form of Bodhisattvas and Lokesvaras much the same way Krishna is depicted. This is because the Bodhisattvas were originally styled after a painting from India, which was a print of Krishna. Most images of Tara are also similar to paintings of Lakshmi in that one hand is held in bendiction. And Vajrayogini, the Buddha in female aspect, is certainly styled after goddess Kali or Durga. And Kuvera, the lord of wealth in the Vedic culture, is Kuvera Vaishravana in Buddhism. There are many other carry-overs from the Vedic tradition into Buddhism that can be recognized, such as the use of ghee lamps and *kusha* grass, and the offerings of barley and ghee in rituals that resemble Vedic ceremonies.

A more obvious form of Vedic influence in the Far East can also be seen. There were those who converted from the Far Eastern doctrines and directly engaged in the Vedic tradition. As far east as Kampuchea, we can find temples built by the kings of ancient Cambodia, such as Angkor Wat, a large and well known temple complex devoted to Lord Vishnu and the Vedic demigods.

The area of northwestern Cambodia was called Angkor, where the capital of the ancient Khmer Empire was located through the 9th to 15th centuries. The empire was one of the largest in the history of the area and had expanded to include all of Cambodia and most of Vietnam, Laos, and Thailand. It was Jayavarman II, the first great king of Angkor, who introduced the Indian Vedic system of philosophy to that area. Since his reign, it became a tradition that every king of the region would build a large temple which was dedicated to either Vishnu or Shiva. After the king's death, the structure would also serve in memory of the king who had built it. Over the years, more than 70 large and magnificently carved temples were built.

Hundreds of architects and thousands of laborers were required for years to build each of these temples. Angkor Wat ("temple of the capital"), the greatest and best known of these temples, was built by Suryavarman II in the early 12th century, taking thirty years to complete. The temple complex was designed to represent the Vedic descriptions of the cosmological arrangement of the universe. Thus, the Vedic knowledge had been known and respected in the orient for many years.

* * *

There are even similarities between Christian, Buddhist, and Vedic styles of meditation, such as with the use of prayer beads. The use of beads goes back to prehistoric times. The word *bead* comes from the word *bid*, to plead or petition, which is done to awaken the spirit of God, or to open the channel of communication between God and man. Thus, chanting the name of God is to invoke God Himself. The followers of the *Vedas*, the Vaishnavas, have 108 beads on their *japa mala* or rosary, while Buddhists have 108, Catholics have 54, and Muslims have 99 plus one head bead. Vaishnavas, Buddhists, and Muslims use beads to chant the names of God. Catholics chant prayers to God, and sometimes in the Eastern tradition they just chant the names. The names of Krishna, Rama, and Hare are the original names of the Supreme Deity before they were changed in their theosophical and linguistic forms through variations in location and cultural traits.

In other aspects of spiritual practices, many cultures provided a means of entering into the higher levels of knowledge, which was often kept secret from the uninitiated. The Persians, Egyptians, Syrians, Cretons, Greeks, Romans, Celts, Druids, as well as the Mayans and American Indians all had their rituals of initiation into the mysteries of the unknown after which, in many cultures, the initiates were called twice-born. This is identical to the practice of the Vedic *brahmanas* who are initiated into spiritual understanding and, thus, are called "twice-born" to signify their spiritual birth which is over and above the common animal birth that every ordinary creature undergoes when born from the womb.

* * *

Even in the Americas, there are similarities with Eastern cultures. In ancient Mexico the practice of sun worship was common, and the priests were represented with a serpent twined around their head. Ancient paintings were also found that showed heads of a rhinocerus, as well as paintings of a man with the head of an elephant, like Ganesh in India. And we all know that the rhinocerus and elephant are not animals found in the Americas. Plus, the architecture of the temples of ancient Mexico and Central America is very similar to the pyramids of Egypt and the temples of India. Some of the tribes of the American Indians of North America, especially the Hopi, also believed in the idea of four worlds, or four ages of the world, as well as the concepts of reincarnation, respect for nature and the nature spirits or demigods, etc., which are very similar to the concepts found in the Vedic philosophy. Studies have concluded that similarities in Mayan, Aztec, Incan, and North American Indian civilizations have a connection with India and the Southeast Asian countries. Such things as customs, art, sculptures of the native dress and solar symbolism and even elephants, along with architecture, gods, rituals of worship, time measurement, calenders, astronomy, and systems of government all have similarities to those of India and the Vedic Aryans.

These and other similarities in the philosophy of the ancient American people and that of the East show there must have been a link between the two areas. The speculation is that one geographic connection is the Bering Strait. The water of the Bering Sea is still comparably shallow. It is here that the Asiatic tribes may have traveled over to the Americas many years ago and planted their philosophy and religion, which was accepted in varying degrees by the people in different localities. Another possibility of how people of the East traveled to the Americas is by sailing by way of the Aleutian Islands, or the islands of the South Pacific, some of which had been colonized by the Aryans, as noted earlier. In any case, there are many things (only a very few that I have mentioned) that historians point to in regard to social, philosophical, as well as physical similarities that link the ancient people of the Americas to the people of the East.

* * *

Even though most of Africa may not have been influenced directly by Vedic culture, we can still recognize that the basic concepts regarding God and life on earth in the traditional African religions are in line with the essential principles of Vedic culture and the major world religions. Most all traditional African religions accept a Supreme Being, but His function differs according to region. They also accept lesser gods, respect the ancestors, and practice magical rituals.

The Mbuti Pygmies believe in a supreme Creator in the form of an old man as lord of the sky. They also have reverence for the moon. There is also a benevolent god of the forest to whom many pray and who exists in the trees. They also have ritual dancing and feasting at festivals for religious purposes, and at the puberty rites for the boys and girls. The Bushmen in Southern Africa believe in celestial spirits and have legends that explain their characteristics. The personifications of natural forces are also accepted, and these forces are invoked when the need arises, as in the case of rain.

From Kalahari and the Congo to Tanzania there is the belief in a omni-present supreme Creator who punishes and rewards people according to their works. But there are few organized religious societies and no big temples to regularly offer formal worship to the Supreme. However, the general belief is that anyone can pray to God in time of need, and He oversees all the functions of nature and the earth. Belief in life after death is found everywhere. Part of the funeral ceremony often contains rites to make sure the dead will remain at peace and not become a restless ghost.

The ancient African religions have faded as Islam (130 million followers) and Christianity (160 million followers and six thousand sects) continue to spread, but many of the old rituals and beliefs have simply merged with these new religions.

CONCLUSION

Although this chapter offers only bits and pieces of the whole picture of where the Vedic Aryans originated and how their influence can still be recognized in various ways throughout the world, the evidence makes it clear that it is to the East, especially the area of India, where the origins of advanced civilization and the essence of religion and spiritual philosophy can be traced. From there, the Aryan influence slowly spread to many other regions and cultures. Only a few open-minded people who look at the whole picture of this kind of religious development will understand the inherent unity the world and its history contains. Such unity is disturbed only by mankind's immature, dogmatic, and self-centered feelings for regional and cultural superiority. We have seen this in the propaganda that was effectively used by the Nazis and is presently used by neo-Nazis and white supremacist groups who now use the modern myth that the original location of the Aryan race was in northern Europe, and imply that members of this race are superior over all other races in physique, language, mental capabilities, and culture. This myth must be seen for what it is because there is no doubt that the real Aryan people originated and spread from the region of India and the Indus Valley, not Europe.

To help understand how the Aryan influence spread through the world, L. A. Waddell explains that the Aryans established the pre-historic trade routes over land and sea from at least the beginning of the third millennium B.C., if not much earlier. Wherever the Aryans went, whether in Egypt, France, England, or elsewhere, they imposed their authority and culture, much to the betterment of the previous culture of the area. They brought together scattered tribes and clans into national unity that became increasingly bright in their systems of social organization, trade, and art. In seeking new sources of metal, such as tin, copper, gold, and lead, the Aryans established ports and colonies among the local tribes that later developed into separate nations which took many of their traditions and cultural traits from the ruling Aryans. Of course, as trade with the

Aryans diminished, variations in the legends and cultures became prominent. But this accounts for the many similarities between the different ancient civilizations of the world, as well as those resemblances that still exist today.

The point of all this is that even if Muslims, Christians, Jews, Buddhists, Hindus, etc., all keep their own ideology, legends, and traditions, we should realize that all of these legends and conceptions of God and forms of worship ultimately refer to the same Supreme God and lesser demigods, although they may be called by different names according to present day variations in region and culture. In other words, all these doctrines and faiths are simply outgrowths of the original religion and worship of the one Supreme Deity that spread throughout the world many thousands of years ago from the same basic source, and which is now expressed through the many various cultural differences in the world. Therefore, no matter what religion we may consider ourselves, we are all a part of the same family, merely another branch of the same tree which can be traced to the original pre-historic roots of spiritual thought that are found in the Vedic culture, the oldest and most developed philosophical and spiritual tradition in the world.

CHAPTER EIGHT

The Real Purpose of Yoga and Religious Systems

Now that we have reviewed the basis of the most important religions and philosophies of the world, let us understand the real goal of yoga and religion. When we mention the word *yoga*, it conjures up different things in the minds of different people. Some people think of yoga as being various exercises a person does to lose weight or help stay in shape. Others may think of yoga as something one does for attaining peace of mind or for tolerating occupational stress and nervous problems. Others may think that it consists of breathing exercises for developing more energy or for enhancing one's sex life. Yoga may help one accomplish any of these things, but they are hardly the ultimate goal.

The word *yoga*, based on *yuj*, the root of the word, means to "link up" or "unite." Interestingly enough, the word *religion* is based on the Latin word *religio*, which means to "bring back" or "to bind." What is to unite with or to bind to is the individual's soul with the Supreme Soul. This involves uniting one's body, mind, will, emotions, and intellect to God while becoming detached or less attracted to the material world. Thus, the ultimate aim of yoga and religion is the same, which is to spiritualize our consciousness, transcend all forms of temporary material happiness and distress, and increase our understanding and realization of the Supreme. Yoga or religion, therefore, is a science which must be clearly understood in order to accomplish this. Otherwise, religion without philosophy is merely sentiment or fanaticism, while philosophy without religion is only mental speculation.

The reason why spiritual progress is considered so important is that the material body, which is subject to birth, death, old age, and disease, is the cause of all the living entity's suffering. In one's constitutional spiritual position, the living entity is eternal, full of bliss and knowledge. Foolish people forget this problem. They fail to realize that death is continuously approaching and may strike at any moment. At that time all their material assets will not help them.

169

Still they engage in so many temporary pursuits based on their body, home, family, society, country, etc. This is called illusion and will not actually help solve the real problem of repeated birth and death in this material existence. Therefore, through yoga one can learn to work for the ultimate goal and not simply for fleeting moments of pleasure. Only through regular yoga practice will one's mind be fixed at the time of death, allowing one to concentrate on the supreme goal and free oneself from future material entanglement.

One's progress on the spiritual path depends on one's sincerety. Sincerety is the essence of purity, and if one is sincere, all obstacles on the path will gradually be removed. However, this age of Kali-yuga is very dangerous for those interested in self-realization. In the age of Kali, society is filled with atheists and materialists who engage in sense gratification as if it is the only reason for living. They have forgotten the real aim of life and how brief is this lifetime. Out of madness they say there is no need for spiritual advancement, and so most educational institutions intentionally teach students nothing more than how to continue in materialistic existence. Practically, very few people ever have the chance to hear about the ultimate goal of life or learn how to make tangible spiritual progress. There may be some fundamental information in conventional religion about believing in God and going to heaven, but this is usually not very advanced. Real spiritual understanding goes much deeper than simple moralistic values or the hope of going to heaven.

Those who are interested in yoga or spiritual life often must come in contact with many others in their daily affairs who are not at all interested in self-realization. Some may actually criticize the process of spiritual advancement. The *Bhagavad-gita* (4.40) states that those who are ignorant and doubt the revealed scriptures do not attain happiness in this world nor the next, nor can they attain God consciousness. And (*Bg.*9.3) those who are devoid of faith on the path of devotional service do not attain the Supreme nor the spiritual strata, but must continue in the cycle of birth and death in this material world.

We must also understand that we cannot attain real spiritual knowledge simply by logic and argument. We may try to strain our brain in so many ways and come up with so many philosophical ideas, but we will still not know what is the Absolute Truth. The only way to understand spiritual truth is by engaging in the process which spiritualizes our consciousness. Otherwise, by remaining in material consciousness, it is not possible to comprehend the Absolute. As Sri Krishna explains in *Bhagavad-gita* (7.25), He does not reveal Himself to the foolish. He is covered by His *yogamaya* potency, so those who are deluded by the material energy cannot understand Him who is unborn and infallible. But we find in *Srimad-Bhagavatam* (10.14.29) that one who is slightly favored with the Lord's mercy can understand the greatness of God. But those who are absorbed in speculation are unable to know the Supreme's greatness, even though they study the *Vedas* or other scripture for many years.

It is said that the real way of attempting to understand the infinite nature of the Absolute is not by trying to see God with our limited capacity, but by acting in such a way that God sees us and reveals Himself to us. This is the beauty of *bhakti-yoga*, as revealed in the *Caitanya-caritamrta* (*Adi-lila*, 7.145) which states that the infinite Supreme Lord becomes submissive to the insignificant devotee because of the sincere devotional service rendered by the devotee. This is the exalted nature of devotional service. Through this devotional sentiment, the devotee experiences the spiritual bliss of reciprocation of the Supreme.

Even if one engages in devotional yoga and later falls down due to some shortcoming, or for one reason or another cannot complete the process, he still is not the loser. Whatever progress one makes is very beneficial. It is explained that when leaving his body at death, the unsuccessful yogi can enter the heavenly planets due to living in the mode of goodness from his yoga practice. In his next life he may be born in a wealthy family or a family of very pious people so that he may again have the opportunity of engaging in spiritual pursuits. This is further explained in *Bhagavad-gita* (6.41-44) which states that the unsuccessful yogi, after many years of living in the heavenly planets of the pious, is reborn in a family that is pure and prosperous. Or he may be born in a family of spiritually advanced people, which is a very rare birth to attain in this world. There he regains the divine knowledge of his previous life and is automatically attracted to spiritual life. Such a yogi, striving for perfection, can reach the Supreme Goal.

If a yogi who has not been quite successful receives such good results, we can well imagine how much greater the rewards are for one who perseveres to the end. The *Bhagavad-gita* (6.40) explains that one who engages in spiritual activities does not meet with destruction in this world or the next, and is never overcome by misfortune. And (*Bg*.6.45-46) when the yogi perseveres with sincerety, becoming cleansed of material contamination after many births of practice, he attains the Supreme Goal. Such a yogi is superior to the ascetics, the learned, and the fruitive workers. Therefore, one should be a yogi.

PURIFYING THE MIND

One of the most important purposes of any religion or yoga system is to purify the mind. The mind is the center of the senses and is where we harbor our material desires. The mind exists on the material platform of duality and is always feeling attraction and repulsion towards different objects or experiences. It is always hankering after that which gives comfort or pleasure to the body and disdains that which causes pain. On the spiritual platform there is no duality, since everything is absolute. Therefore, to progress spiritually, we must either rise above the influence of the mind or purify it so it no longer keeps us bound up in material desires. *Bhagavad-gita* (3.34) points out that everyone experiences attraction and aversion toward various sense objects, but this must be controlled or it will become an obstacle to one's spiritual progress.

The mind can be the cause of bondage if absorbed in sense objects, or it can be the cause of liberation if it is detached from sense objects. In this way, the mind can be our enemy or friend. As explained in *Bhagavad-gita* (6.5-9), a man must elevate and not degrade himself by his mind. Thus, the mind can be the friend or the enemy of the conditioned soul. The mind is the best of friends for one who has conquered it, but it can be the enemy if it is not controlled. Tranquility and the Supersoul can be reached for one who has conquered the mind. He then perceives pleasure and pain, heat and cold, honor and dishonor, as all the same. A person who is satisfied with spiritual knowledge, whose senses are controlled, and sees earth, stones, and gold as equal, is said to be a yogi. Further advanced in self-realization is one who regards well-wishers, friends, foes, the envious, the sinful, and the pious with an equal mind.

For one who has not been able to control the dictates of the mind, making spiritual progress becomes very difficult. In *Bhagavad-gita* (6.34-36) Arjuna says that the mind is restless, turbulent, strong, and unyielding, and as hard to control as the wind. But Sri Krishna explains that though this is true, by practice and detachment it can be controlled. Self-realization is difficult for the person with an uncontrolled mind, but one who has controlled the mind can achieve success.

Even though one's mind may act in various ways to the things around him, if he remains undisturbed and continues on the path of yoga, his mind will become steady. In *Bhagavad-gita* (2.56, 59-61) we are told that he who is not perturbed by adversity, who does not crave happiness, is free from attachment, fear, and anger, is a sage of steady mind. However, one may obstain from sense enjoyment, though the longing for it remains. *Only by experiencing a higher taste can one cease sensual gratification and remain fixed in higher consciousness.* The senses are so strong that they can even carry away the mind of a man of wisdom who is endeavoring to control them. But one who controls his senses and focuses his mind on Sri Krishna is a man of firm intelligence.

Here is the secret to making real progress in spirituality. By experiencing a spiritually higher taste, even those material engagements we thought we could not live without become less and less attractive. Materialists often wonder how mystics can live in such a simple manner. They may ask, how can a person live without cigarettes, without a car, without television, without eating meat, or especially without sex? But the point is that after one experiences a higher happiness, a more refined and sophisticated pleasure, then such gross levels of gratification are not only less desirable, but they even become disgusting. Thus, a yogi or mystic lives without interest in what materialists cannot live without.

Naturally in the beginning stages of spiritual practice, even though we may try to control our mind, it is so strong that there may be times when the mind carries our concentration a long distance away before we realize what happened. When this takes place we cannot become too discouraged, but simply must take advice from *Bhagavad-gita* (6.26) which tells us that due to the unsteady nature of the mind, it wanders in any direction. But from wherever the mind strays you must bring it back under the control of the Self.

When one gets a higher taste from spiritual engagement, the mind becomes fixed and is no longer such a disturbance. In any case, one may fall down at the beginning, but if he continues he will advance. However, one who gives up his practice altogether will achieve no benefit. As Krishna warns in *Bhagavad-gita* (3.31-32), men who practice this teaching of His with faith, free from envy, are released from the *karmic* bondage of fruitive activities. But those who disregard these teachings and act whimsically are considered bereft of knowledge, deluded, and doomed to continued material existence.

On the other hand, one who engages in the practice of yoga yet meditates on the activities of sense gratification is simply fooling himself. He will not make any substantial progress if all he does is go through the motions of religious activities while the mind is absorbed in thoughts of sensual delights. From *Bhagavad-gita* (3.6-7) we learn that the man who controls his actions but thinks in his mind of sensual delights is deluded and called a pretender. But the person who controls his actions by the mind and engages in devotional activities without attachment is superior.

The point to remember is that to begin purifying the mind we have to start by purifying or spiritualizing our activities. When our activities are purified, then the mind becomes pure. When the mind is pure, then our desires become pure or spiritualized. When our desires or consciousness become spiritualized, entrance into the spiritual world follows. Thus, yoga and all genuine religious processes are for regulating and spiritualizing our existence so that we can become free from materialistic activity and its reactions.

SPIRITUALIZING OUR EXISTENCE

Spiritualizing our existence is a matter of regulating our activities in accord with the rules of yoga or religion. This is a method which not only raises our consciousness and mode of living, but also helps us avoid obstacles that deter our spiritual progress. This may mean dedicating a few hours a day toward spiritual advancement, or even changing our whole lifestyle and outlook on life, depending on how committed we are to the path of spiritual realization. However, different processes require different commitments.

The importance of spiritual advancement is not for a few people, but is actually meant for everyone. Regardless of who one is or what his of her background may be, everyone can approach the ultimate goal of life through yoga and authentic religious practices. As Lord Krishna explains in *Bhagavad-gita* (9.32), those who take shelter of Him, even though they be of lower birth, can approach the supreme destination. He further says (*Bg.* 4.36) that even if one is considered to be the most sinful of sinners, he will be able to cross the ocean of miseries by becoming situated in the boat of transcendental knowledge. Therefore, everyone has the opportunity to attain the spiritual goal of life.

We should understand that suffering, which everyone undergoes, is caused by the polluted aim of life in society. When people do not actually know the purpose of life or what their real identity is, they do not know what is to be done and what is not to be done. Thus, everyone is affected by a misdirected aim of life. We may feel that we are just trying to live a peaceful life and avoid trouble; yet, when robbers burglarize our home, when the world leaders threaten each other with war, when a woman is raped, when our children take drugs, or when terrorists attack innocent people, these are all types of troubles that signify a misunderstanding of the goal of life. How can we expect to live peacefully in a society where so many people are willing to try to satisfy their desires at any price, even at the expense and pain of others? It will not be possible. In fact, such a society can hardly be considered civilized, what to speak of peaceful. It is more like a society of polished cats and dogs, always quarrelling and fighting, chasing after a higher standard of animal pleasure in the way of eating, sleeping, mating, and defending. Without changing this polluted aim of life, society will only become more and more degraded.

The root cause for material existence is the desire for sense gratification. Therefore, getting free of the demands of the senses and mind is essential for entering the spiritual platform of life. Yoga enables us to become free from the influence of the materialistic mind and senses. By attaining such freedom we not only become happy in life and attain a steady and peaceful mind, but at the end we can enter into the eternal kingdom of the Supreme. How this is accomplished is explained in *Bhagavad-gita* (4.19-23). There it states that one who is free from the desire for sense gratification in his activities, and has consumed his *karma* in the fire of knowledge, the sages call a wise man. Always content and independent, with no attachment to the fruits of his actions, he does nothing that accumulates more *karma* though he may be engaged in all kinds of undertakings. Giving up attachment for his possessions, performing activities with the body only, with the mind and intelligence perfectly controlled, he incurs no sinful reactions. Content with what is obtained without undue labor, free from envy and dualities, steady in success or failure, although acting, he is free from material entanglement. The work of such a person, unattached, performed for spiritual progress only, whose thought dwells in Transcendence, makes him free from all *karma* and he merges into Transcendence.

The kinds of activities the yogis engage in for advancement that do not produce *karmic* reactions are varied, as described in *Bhagavad-gita* (4.25-32). One does not renounce bodily activities thinking one should simply sit in trance for long hours, but one must learn how to use the body and senses in the proper way. It is explained in *Srimad-Bhagavatam* (1.2.9-10) that real religion means those occupational engagements that are meant for ultimate liberation from material existence within this universe, and not those activities done for gratifying the senses or for material gain. One should work enough to maintain oneself and stay healthy, and utilize the rest of his time for spiritual inquiry and advancement. From *Bhagavad-gita* (5.3, 11) we learn that he who neither hates nor desires the results of his activities is known as renounced. Free from all dualities, he is easily liberated from the bondage of material existence. Those yogis, giving up attachment, act with the body, mind, intelligence, and the senses, only for spiritual purification.

The art of spiritual purification exists in knowing how to engage ourselves in a way which will spiritualize our lives and consciousness. That is the essential principle of any bona fide religion or yoga system. But we must know which path will work for us regardless of whether we are living in the high mountains of the East, or in a modern city in the West.

THE SUPREME YOGA

As has been previously stated, perfection in life is attained by one who practices the supreme yoga. There are many systems of religion and types of yoga for advancing one's consciousness or elevating one to various levels of the spiritual platform, as we have been describing thoughout this volume. But how do we know what the supreme form of yoga is? Which religion delivers the real essence of the Absolute Truth? And what is the process for attaining the highest level of spiritual realization?

This question is answered by Sri Krishna in *Srimad-Bhagavatam* (3.25.13), where He says that the highest yoga system of all is that which is related to the Supreme Being and the individual soul, and is meant for the ultimate benefit of the conditioned soul, and which causes detachment from happiness and misery within this world. It is also stated: "That religion is best which causes it's followers to become ecstatic in love of God which is unmotivated and free from material impediments, for this only can completely satisfy the self." (*Bhag.*1.2.6)

From these verses it is clear that whatever yoga or religion we follow must be able to unite us with God and give us a higher spiritual taste through that unity, which is based on love. This is further elaborated as follows:

O yogis, unite the soul with God and enjoy happiness. Always expand the delight of salvation. Employ your acts of devotion, and arteries full of breath, in worship of God. Having thus purified the mind, sow the seed of knowledge in it through yoga. May we through God's grace obtain the mature fruit of pure joy. Yogic functions are like sickles in allaying sufferings. (*Atharva-veda* 3.17.2)

Also in *Bhagavad-gita* (6.27-28), we learn that the highest happiness comes to that yogi whose mind is calm, whose passions are stilled, freed from sin, and whose mind is fixed on Sri Krishna, the Supreme. Such a yogi, freed from material contamination, attains the ultimate happiness in touch with the Supreme Consciousness. And in *Srimad-Bhagavatam* (11.14.12-13) the explanation is given that those who give up material desires and fix their consciousness on the Supreme can experience a happiness that cannot be achieved by those engaged in sensual pleasure. Such a person who has given up material desires, is at peace with controlled senses, and is satisfied in thinking of the Supreme, is content and finds happiness wherever he goes.

From this information it is obvious that the more one unites or links their consciousness with the Supreme, the more aloof they become from the ups and downs of material life, and the more happiness one feels in spiritual consciousness. This is the true goal of yoga or religion, as confirmed in *Bhagavad-gita*: "And of all yogis, he who always abides in Me [Sri Krishna] with great faith, worshiping Me in transcendental loving service, is most intimately united with Me in yoga and is the highest of all." (*Bg*.6.47)

Whether one practices *jnana-yoga, karma-yoga, astanga-yoga*, or any other yoga, or is a Catholic, Protestant, Muslim, or whatever, the primary purpose is to detach one's senses from the material world. "The greatest common understanding for all yogis is complete detachment from matter, which can be achieved by different kinds of yoga." (*Bhag*.3.32.27) However, let us remember that the final results of the various yoga systems or religions are different and may not bring one to the ultimate position. For example, the *jnana* yogi tries to detach his senses from attraction to the material world simply by the cultivation of knowledge. He believes that matter is false and Brahman is truth, and he thus undergoes austerities with the aim of becoming one with the Brahman effulgence.

Through *astanga-yoga* one tries to release oneself from sensual engagement by the regulative process of meditation, concentration, sitting postures, etc. By this practice he tries to realize the impersonal Brahman. The goal of *sankhya-yoga* is to attain freedom from the material world by understanding the difference between the ephemeral material elements and the Absolute Truth. The yogis who follow the yoga system that is explained by Patanjali accept the personality of the Absolute Truth; yet, they want to merge into the body of the Absolute. Such yogis meditate on the Supersoul in the heart to merge into His body and do not engage in serving the Lord. In other words, even though meditating on the Supreme is a form of service, they have no service attitude. They believe that on the perfectional platform one does not remain a person, but loses one's individuality. So although they at first accept the Supreme Personality of God, they later give this up to become impersonalists. Therefore, due to the different methods practiced among the yoga processes, one gets varied levels of spiritual tastes and happiness. Because of the dry philosophy found in these impersonalistic yoga systems, the higher spiritual bliss is not so easily attained.

These days, especially in the Western countries, it is often seen that if people do not attain some immediate result or higher taste from yoga practice, or if the thrill fades away, they will soon give it up to go back to their materialistic activities. People in general are not very philosophically inclined, and such dry philosophy as found in these forms of impersonal yoga will not attract many people to continue the process. But because the Lord desired the living entities to return to the spiritual world, He explained the yoga systems. But, as indicated, some yoga systems are more effective and can provide a faster means of spiritual development than others.

In *Srimad-Bhagavatam* (11.20.6-11), the Supreme describes to Uddhava the three processes of yoga for one's advancement. Because Krishna desires that people achieve perfection in attaining liberation from material existence, He presents three paths for advancement. For those who are disgusted with material life and fruitive activities, the path of philosophical speculation, *jnana-yoga*, is recommended. For those who still prefer to fulfill their desires through material life, *karma-yoga* is recommended. For those who are neither very averse or attached to material existence, and have faith in hearing and chanting about the Supreme, it is advised that they take to *bhakti-yoga*, the path of engaging in loving devotional service to the Supreme, Sri Krishna. If one still hankers for fruitive activity and has not developed a taste for devotional service, one should follow the regulative principles of the *Vedas*. One who becomes cleansed of material contamination, free from engaging in sinful acts, and engages in the prescribed duties, will obtain spiritual knowledge and devotional service to Krishna in this very life.

This puts it all into focus. Depending on one's position in life, a person can take up a particular path, but should eventually be elevated to the stage of understanding transcendental knowledge and, thus, engage in devotional service (*bhakti-yoga*) to the Supreme. In this way, all the different kinds of yoga, such as *hatha-yoga, karma-yoga, raja-yoga*, etc., do not exist separately, but are meant to lead up to and include *bhakti-yoga*, the yoga of love and devotion to the Supreme. Similarly, any religion that leaves out or does not center its principles on *bhakti* or devotional service to God can never be considered complete. Through *bhakti* the Supreme Lord becomes satisfied and naturally reveals Himself to the aspiring devotee. Thus, *bhakti-yoga* is the supreme form of yoga and the highest principle of religion.

This is verified by Lord Krishna Himself in *Srimad-Bhagavatam* (11.14.20-22, 25-28). He explains that loving devotional service rendered by the devotees brings Him under their control. He cannot be so controlled by any other process, whether it be mystic yoga, Sankhya philosophy, pious work, Vedic study, austerity, or renunciation. Only by unalloyed devotion can one obtain the Supreme. By pure devotional service even dog-eaters can be purified from their low birth. Without loving devotional service, no amount of religious activities or austerities can completely purify one's consciousness. As when gold separates from its impurities and regains its brilliance when smelted with fire, so the soul throws off the *karmic* contamination and returns to its spiritual position with the Supreme when absorbed in the fire of *bhakti-yoga*. As a diseased eye gains acuity of vision when treated with medicine, so a person is cleansed of material contamination by the repeated hearing and chanting of the spiritual qualities of the Supreme, and reaches the stage of seeing the spiritual form of the Supreme. Thinking of material objects causes the mind to cling to such objects, while remembering Krishna causes the mind to become absorbed in Krishna. Therefore, one should cease thinking of sensual pleasures, which are like temporary dreams, and absorb the mind in Krishna, which purifies the consciousness.

From this information we can begin to understand the potency of engaging in *bhakti-yoga* and how we can easily and rapidly unite ourselves with the Supreme Personality. This also explains why the higher spiritual happiness that we are looking for is often lacking in other forms of religion or yoga that do not accept the Supreme to be a person, or that simply do not know the intricacies of His personality. This is because such impersonalistic forms of yoga or religion do not provide a means for reciprocation to develop between the individual souls and the Supreme Soul. Without this spiritual reciprocation, which is all that can completely satisfy the soul, one remains discontent and restless to various degrees, and will continue in his search to find happiness by some means. Therefore, the path of *bhakti* is recommended in order to reawaken the loving relationship between the soul and Supersoul.

By engaging in *bhakti-yoga* one automatically achieves everything attainable by any other process, as confirmed in *Bhagavad-gita* (8.28) where it explains that a person who knows and engages in devotional service also achieves the results of studying the *Vedas*, the performance of austerities and sacrifices, giving charity, and philosophical and fruitive activities. In fact, he transcends it all and reaches the supreme abode. This is confirmed in *Srimad-Bhagavatam* (11.20.31-33) where Sri Krishna says that for the yogi who loves Him and whose mind is always fixed on Him, neither knowledge nor renunciation is the means for achieving the supreme goal of life. What can be obtained by the performance of fruitive *karmic* activities, austerities, knowledge, detachment, yoga, charity, doing good or pious work, or by other virtuous deeds, may easily be achieved by the devotee from his devotional service to Krishna alone. If such a devotee wants existence in heaven, liberation from material existence altogether, or entry into the highest spiritual abode, all these are easily attained.

Herein is sufficient evidence to show that the highest form of yoga and religion is that in which the practitioner simply develops attachment to the Supreme Lord and detachment to the world. Through this process, everything else is accomplished and one becomes assured of reaching the highest happiness and purest state of spiritual perfection. As Lord Krishna says in *Bhagavad-gita* (11.54), only by undivided devotional service can a person understand Him as He is or see Him directly. By no other means can one enter into the mysteries of understanding the Supreme. Also (*Bg*.8.8), a person is sure to reach Him when one's mind is undeviated in remembering Him, and (*Bg*.8.14-15) for one who continually engages in such service, He is easy to obtain. After the great souls reach Him, the highest perfection, they never return to this miserable and temporary material existence. Therefore, (*Bg*.9.34) by absorbing one's thoughts and worship in Krishna, a devotee will surely reach Him.

In this way, the Vedic literature establishes that the topmost religious principle and spiritual path is that of *bhakti*, and any process that is based on something other than this is incomplete.

*   *   *

It may appear that in this chapter I did not use much information from other books, such as the Bible, *Koran*, etc., to explain the ultimate purpose of religion or yoga. Though the basic form of worship described in such books is to love and serve God with devotion, or *bhakti*, the intructions in these books that explain why and how to engage in such service on a practical level are either absent, unclear, or, in some cases, simply too elementary and inadequate. But the Vedic literature gives a much clearer explanation of the potency of *bhakti* and how to develop and engage in it for attaining the highest spiritual realizations. Therefore, those who study and follow the Vedic path of *bhakti* will find it more complete. This is why I primarily have used the Vedic texts as the basis for explaining this information. In the next chapter we will understand more about this path from the descriptions in the Vedic texts, and see why this process is so important in the present age.

CHAPTER NINE

The Spiritual Path For the Present Age

We all know that there are various spiritual paths and processes of self-realization, but we may not understand that different systems were recommended for different ages. To explain further, there are four ages or millenniums called *yugas*. These are Satya-yuga, Treta-yuga, Dvapara-yuga, and Kali-yuga. The aggregate number of years of these combined ages equals 4,320,000 years. The duration of Satya-yuga is 1,728,000 years. The duration of Treta-yuga is 1,296,000 years. The duration of Dvapara-yuga is 864,000 years. The duration of Kali-yuga, the present age, is 432,000 years, and began 5,000 years ago. These four *yugas* make one cycle, and one thousand cycles equal one day of Brahma, after which there is a partial annihilation of the universe during Brahma's night. Lord Brahma lives for 100 years, 365 days in each year.

In Satya-yuga there is virtue, wisdom, religion, and no ignorance or vice. People are strong, healthy, clear-minded, content, and are said to live up to 100,000 years. The process for self-realization in that age is prolonged meditation, as in the *raja-yoga* or *astanga-yoga* systems, which can take many years to perfect. In Treta-yuga vice appeares and people are less virtuous and religious. In that age, when the duration of life is not longer than 10,000 years, the process for self-realization is opulent rituals. In Dvapara-yuga there is a greater increase in vice, and virtue and religion continues to decline. The duration of life is reduced to no more than 1,000 years, and self-realization is attained by opulent worship of the Lord in the temple. In the present Kali-yuga, which lasts 432,000 years, vice, ignorance, strife, quarrel, and irreligion spreads everywhere. Virtue and religion practically fade to nil, and the average duration of life is less than 100 years and continues to decrease as Kali-yuga progresses. The recommended process for self-realization is *bhakti-yoga*, beginning with hearing and chanting the holy names, qualities, and pastimes of the Supreme.

In the present age of Kali, we hardly have the duration of life or the patience to be successful at engaging in prolonged meditation, as is recommended in Satya-yuga. Opulent ritualistic worship is also impossible to perform in Kali-yuga. Some of the essential items for performing these rituals, as listed in *Srimad-Bhagavatam* (2.6.25-27), include simple things, such as flowers, leaves, utensils, grains, ghee, honey, water, and so on. But other items, such as a gold sacrificial altar, and qualified *brahmana* priests who can correctly chant the *mantras* from the *Vedas* are not easily found. Therefore, it is advised that in Kali-yuga one take up the easy process of *bhakti-yoga* by which everything can be accomplished in this short life.

BHAKTI-YOGA

Bhakti-yoga is not a recently conceived path for Kali-yuga. It can be traced to many of the old Vedic hymns, although not often referred to in the *Upanishads*. But, as explained in the previous chapter, it is the final connecting link between all yoga systems and is necessary in order to attain the most elevated stage of self-realization. Therefore, we find that *bhakti* is considered the topmost yoga system in such books as *Bhagavad-gita* (6.47), in which Krishna says that the person who is always absorbed in Him with great faith and loving service is most intimately united with Him and is the topmost yogi.

Not only is *bhakti-yoga* considered the highest system of religion, but it is also the easiest and the most auspicious, as confirmed in *Srimad-Bhagavatam* (2.2.33-34) which says that for those who have fallen into the whirlpool of material existence there is no higher path than that which gives one devotion to Lord Krishna. Even the great personality Brahma concluded, after studying the *Vedas* three times, that devotion to Lord Krishna is the highest perfection of spiritual knowledge.

Ultimately, only by worshiping the Supreme can one attain *bhakti*, by which one can be graced with *mukti*, liberation from material existence and entrance into the spiritual atmosphere. The worship of the demigods or love of anything else other than the Supreme is not *bhakti*. Worship of the demigods, like Shiva, Brahma, Ganesh, Murugan, or the demigoddesses, such as Durga, Kali, Sarasvati, Lakshmi, etc., is *karma*. It is ritualistic service for the attainment of some temporary result, such as getting money, good position, heavenly existence, knowledge, intelligence, and so on. Offering respects to the demigods is rightly done, but real love of God, beyond material considerations, is attained only by worshiping the Supreme in His most excellent and transcendental form of Krishna or His incarnations, such as Vishnu, Rama, Narayana, etc., and by worshiping or respecting His devotees.

Essentially, the science of *bhakti-yoga* is a matter of learning how to dovetail all our activities for the service of the Supreme, the Soul of all souls. Such service can completely satisfy the self. This is verified in *Srimad-Bhagavatam*

(1.6.35), which explains that even though one who is smitten by lust and greed can attain some relief by practicing sense control through the yoga system, this still does not satisfy the soul which can only be satisfied through the performance of devotional service to Krishna. In this way, devotional service is the supreme occupation that one gets a chance to learn about and engage in only after many births. The *Srimad-Bhagavatam* (5.19.20) also explains that after many births of pious activities a person may earn the chance to associate with a pure devotee who can give them knowledge of devotional service to the Supreme Person. Such knowledge and devotional service cuts the knot of ignorance and bondage to material activities. Thus, *bhakti-yoga* is the path to spiritual liberation.

From this description we can begin to understand how rare it is for one to have the opportunity to learn about *bhakti-yoga*. But *bhakti* is not for a certain class of people, it is for anyone. It can revive everyone's spiritual life. As related in the *Bhagavatam* (7.7.54), by engaging in the practice of *bhakti-yoga* everyone can revive their eternal spiritual consciousness, no matter whether they are demoniac and sinful beings, lower animals, birds, or common laborers. Thus, anyone who wants to live forever or escape the repeated cycle of birth and death, as found everywhere in material existence, should simply practice *bhakti-yoga*. Otherwise, especially in this age of Kali, there is no sure way for escaping material life.

The *Srimad-Bhagavatam* has several other verses that emphasize this point. In the Eleventh Canto (11.11.48), Krishna explains that He is the ultimate shelter for all saintly liberated persons, and, if one avoids engaging in devotional service, there is no other effective means to gain release from material existence. Furthermore (11.19.9), without taking shelter of the Supreme who can end one's material suffering, there is no other shelter. Also (12.4.40), material existence, which is like a burning ocean, is very difficult to cross. For those who seek freedom from this ocean, the only means of rescue is to engage in hearing the pastimes of the Supreme Personality. And (4.31.11-12) without such devotional service, all other processes for attaining knowledge have no value, such as severe austerities, mystic yoga, analytical study, etc. Unless they culminate in understanding the Supreme Personality, Krishna, all such practice is useless.

From this we can understand that we might try to perform any process for spiritual upliftment; yet, if we still do not understand the Supreme, then we have simply wasted our time. But why is there so much emphasis on engaging in devotional service to Lord Krishna? To answer this we must remember that the Absolute Truth is realized in three stages. First we understand the all-pervading spiritual force or Brahman effulgence. Then we may understand the localized expansion of the Supreme, the Lord in the heart, Supersoul or Paramatma. But the Paramatma and Brahman effulgence are only partial manifestations of the Supreme. If we are fortunate, we will find out about the personal aspect of God, the Supreme Personality, Sri Krishna, who is described in the Vedic literature as the source from which everything else manifests, including all forms of material and spiritual energies, and all other incarnations of God. Therefore, the Absolute Truth is completely realized by engaging in devotional service to the Supreme Personality who is the Absolute Truth in full. In this way, it becomes obvious that without *bhakti* no process of self-realization is complete. In fact, as verified in the *Bhagavad-gita* (18.58), if one becomes conscious of Krishna, he can rise above material life by Krishna's grace. But if one avoids such spiritual consciousness and acts as his false ego dictates, he is lost.

Here it becomes plain that one can give up the process of mystic yoga, philosophical speculation, and even the search for liberation, but one cannot give up devotional service. As *Bhagavad-gita* (9.3) explains, attaining God is not possible without accepting the path of devotional service, and those who do not engage in *bhakti* remain in this world of birth and death. But those persons who do render devotional service to Krishna are in the very best situation because Krishna becomes pleased by their sincere service.

As stated in the *Bhagavatam* (7.7.50-52, and 11.14.20), whether one is a human being, a demon, a demigod, or anything in this universe, the best position in life is to engage in the service of Mukunda (another name of Krishna). The Lord cannot be pleased by one's learning, charity, sacrifice, austerity, vows, or by becoming a *brahmana* or saint, or by engaging in *astanga-yoga*. Only by unalloyed devotion is the Lord pleased. A few other verses (*Bhag.*7.9.9-10) state the same thing but continues to point out that even if one is wealthy, educated, beautiful, strong, intelligent, has mystic powers, or is even a great and powerful *brahmana*, if he is averse to the Lord he is lower than a devotee who is a dog-eater who has dedicated everything he has to the Supreme. Such a devotee can purify his whole family, but the averse *brahmana* cannot even purify himself. And the *Caitanya-caritamrta* (*Adi-lila*, 17.75) states that the paths of sense control, fruitive activity, philosophical knowledge, and mystic yoga cannot satisfy Krishna. Krishna is satisfied only with one's devotional love.

Even if some people do not take to devotional service to serve the Supreme directly, they are forced to serve the material energy of the Supreme. The material energy takes the shape of wife or husband, children, friends, society, government, banks, landlord, boss, etc. We must satisfy our wife or husband, take care of the children, take care of ourselves, pay taxes to the government, pay the landlord our rent, pay our utility bills, pay back the loans to the bank, pay the mechanics for maintaining our car, make sure we do everything our boss told us to do so we can keep our job and keep getting a paycheck in order to continue serving the material energy, and on and on. It is a never ending battle to get ahead and there is always something more that must be done. So we have to serve someone whether we like it or not. But it could all change if we simply redirect our service propensity by engaging in devotional service to the Supreme. Serving the material energy or the small parts and parcels of the Supreme is certainly not as rewarding as directly serving the Supreme. We may spend our whole life serving the material energy and maintaining our attachments; yet, we have little or nothing to show for it in the end. Even if we have amassed great fortunes, what can it do for us after death? Therefore, of what use is this life if we have made no spiritual progress?

As the *Bhagavatam* (2.3.17-20) points out, except for one engaged in hearing about the Supreme Being, the rising and setting of the sun decreases his span of life. Only those who are like dogs and asses adore those men who never discuss the spiritual attributes of the Supreme. Those who do not engage in hearing or talking about the spiritual qualities of the Supreme Personality are said to have ears like those of a snake and a tongue like a frog. From this description we can see how it is considered that we have lived our life uselessly if we have made no spiritual advancement. What else is there to attain that is not of a flickering and unsteady nature? Therefore, attaining *bhakti* is the topmost position of life.

As further substantiated in the *Caitanya-caritamrta* (*Madhya-lila*, 19.174), the practice of devotional service lifts one above the modes of nature to the platform of offering direct service to the Supreme Lord. Thus, *bhakti* is the ultimate goal of life. And in the *Bhagavatam* (7.7.53, 55) we find it said that all the revealed scriptures explain that to offer service to the Lord and see Him everywhere is the highest goal of life.

HOW BHAKTI-YOGA WORKS

Someone may question how *bhakti-yoga* works. What is it that makes it so effective? We first must understand that we all have various desires. We want to love and be loved, and feel happy and joyful. We all have these essential longings that need fulfillment. We cannot remain without desires, but when we direct these desires towards the Supreme Person rather than the fleeting objects and temptations of the world, then those feelings of love become a powerful force. When we are able to take our love of material objects and redirect that love towards the Supreme, we can begin to spiritualize that sentiment and attain the stage of *bhakti*.

> *Bhakti*, or devotional service, means engaging all our senses in the service of the Lord, the Supreme Personality of Godhead, the master of all senses. When the spirit soul renders service unto the Supreme, there are two side effects. One is freed from all material designations, and, simply by being employed in the service of the Lord, one's senses are purified. (*Narada-pancaratra* and *Bhakti-rasamrta-sindhu*, 1.1.12)

Through the process of *bhakti* one attains realization of their true spiritual identity and purifies the mind and senses from being attracted to material engagement. This is an important factor in any religious or yoga system, but is easily accomplished through *bhakti*. Krishna says in *Bhagavad-gita* (2.50-51), a man casts off from himself both good and bad actions when he engages in devotional yoga. Therefore, one should engage in yoga as the wise do, who free themselves from rebirth and reach the place beyond all suffering.

The first step in engaging in devotional service is to simply hear about the Supreme, especially from the pastimes described in the Vedic *Puranas*. This not only satisfies the Lord but also invokes the Lord's blessings on the person who sincerely listens to or reads such transcendental information. This is verified in *Srimad-Bhagavatam* (1.2.17) which states that for the devotees who like to hear about the Supreme, the Lord as Supersoul cleanses material desires from their hearts. And *(Bhag.*11.29.28) anyone who faithfully listens to this knowledge while engaged in *bhakti* will not accumulate *karma* from material work.

There are, however, those persons who would never think of trying to understand their spiritual nature or hear the pastimes of the Lord. These persons are of four kinds and are described in *Bhagavad-gita* (7.15): those who are very foolish, the lowest among men, those whose knowledge has been stolen by illusion, and those who act in demoniac ways. The Lord never reveals Himself to these four kinds of people. They have no real way of knowing about the immortality of the soul, nor of the qualities of the infallible Lord. They are simply absorbed in continuing to work hard for very little benefit, like beasts of burden toiling for long hours only to be rewarded with a little grass. Therefore, Krishna says that foolish men do not know His supreme and higher spiritual nature and think He has become an ordinary human while in this world. For them He is covered by His eternal potency *yoga-maya*, so those who are deluded never know Him who is unborn. *(Bg.*7.24-25)

Furthermore, there are four kinds of pious persons who do have a chance to hear about God and engage in devotional service. These are the distressed, those who desire wealth, the inquisitive, and the wise who are searching for spiritual knowledge of the Absolute. *(Bg.*7.16)

These four kinds of persons may not seek God due to pure motivations, but may have desires or needs they wish to fulfill in their approach towards God. In fact, most pious people fit into either one or all four of the above categories. But, as described in *Bhagavad-gita* (7.17), the wise person who is devoted to Krishna in pure devotion is topmost. He is dear to Krishna and Krishna is dear to him. Nonetheless, anyone who approaches God, even if for material reasons, is considered to be a great soul because so few living beings in the material world sincerely wish to understand anything about the Supreme. All such devotees are great souls, but the man of knowledge of Krishna dwells in Krishna consciousness. At the end of many lives such a devotee who is very rare surrenders to and attains Krishna, knowing Him to be all that is. *(Bg.*7.18-19)

Here we can begin to understand who is eligible to take up the path of *bhakti-yoga*. Those who are foolish, atheistic, duplicious, determinedly sinful, and always endeavoring for materialistic goals are likely to avoid and even blaspheme the process of devotional service. But those who are pious and sincere can easily begin to take to it. As stated in *Bhagavad-gita* (7.28), those who are free from sinful actions and duality, who have been pious for many lives, determinedly engage in devotional service to the Lord.

The way to engage in devotional service can be done through any of nine basic processes. Prahlada Maharaja says in *Srimad-Bhagavatam* (7.5.23-24) that hearing and chanting about the transcendental name, form, qualities, paraphernalia, and pastimes of Lord Vishnu, or remembering them, serving the Lord, offering respectful worship, offering prayers, becoming His servant, considering the Lord one's best friend, and surrendering everything unto Him are the accepted types of pure devotional service. Those engaged in any of these nine methods should be understood to have acquired complete knowledge.

Simply by reading about the pastimes and qualities of the Supreme in books such as *Srimad-Bhagavatam* or *Bhagavad-gita*, hearing and talking about them, or remembering and serving the Lord, can give one rapid advancement in *bhakti-yoga*. But learning how to engage in devotional service is not for the Lord's benefit. When something is offered to the Supreme, it is for the benefit of the devotee since the Supreme is always self-satisfied and never needs service from anyone, as related in the *Bhagavatam* (7.9.11).

Learning devotional service is simply regaining our natural constitutional position of being a servant of God. In the spiritual world everyone is eternally engaged in performing unlimited kinds of service to the Supreme. This may include cooking for the Lord, making flower garlands, singing, playing instruments, dancing, feasting on food offered to the Supreme, discussing with others about the Absolute, and so on, all for the pleasure of the Supreme Being. The devotees, being spiritual parts and parcels of the Supreme, are all filled with spiritual ecstasy from engaging in such service because it is centered around the source of the ever-increasing bliss for which we are always hankering.

In the spiritual world everyone is a pure devotee. No nondevotees or materialists can live there, so there is no question that everyone knows how to work harmoniously together. Everyone knows exactly what is to be done. However, in the material world such is not the case, and we may find those who invent their own form of worship. But it must be based on the authority of Vedanta, as explained by Srila Rupa Gosvami, who says, "Devotional service performed without reference to the *Vedas, Puranas, Pancaratras*, etc., must be considered sentimentalism, and it causes nothing but a disturbance to society." Therefore, if one wants to reach the highest standard of devotional service, he must follow the prescribed principles without changing them or mixing them with other less advanced processes. Otherwise it simply becomes a hodgepodge.

When people begin to lose respect for Vedic authority and begin to invent or add new ideas or concepts to the bona fide religious system, things gradually deteriorate and become diverted from the truthful and reliable process. This is a great danger because it can mislead people for many generations, or it may eventually form offshoots based on someone's speculations that may never be corrected or brought back to the bona fide path. Therefore, the *Srimad-Bhagavatam* (1.2.12) states that the serious student or sage realizes the Absolute Truth by engaging in *bhakti-yoga* according to intructions he has heard from the Vedic texts.

The point is that everything should be done for Krishna. Therefore, all we have to do is take instruction from Krishna and act accordingly. That will keep everything simple and only the crooked will find it difficult. And what Lord Krishna says about performing devotional service is found in such places as *Srimad-Bhagavatam* and *Bhagavad-gita*, where He states: all that you do, all that you eat, all that you offer and give away, and all austerities you perform, should be done as an offering unto Me. (*Bg*.9.27)

In this way, as one increasingly centers his or her activities around Krishna and becomes more absorbed in thinking of and remembering the Lord, one's life becomes more spiritually focused and sublime. When one's higher taste and *bhakti* for Sri Krishna increases, a person's desires for other short-lived pleasures decrease. Thus, a person's spiritual progress is assured. And when one wants Krishna only, He is easily obtained through continual devotional service and undeviated remembrance, as verified in *Bhagavad-gita* (8.14).

The difference between *bhakti-yoga* and any other form of religion is that engagement in devotional service frees our real spiritual senses within our physical senses. This is the secret of *bhakti-yoga*: by engaging in it we directly engage our spiritual body in spiritual activities although we are still covered by the material form. Right now, due to material contamination, we are engaged in activities that are controlled by the dictates of our mind and senses which hanker for material gratification. By engaging our mind and senses in *bhakti-yoga*, this contamination gradually disappears, the material mind dissolves, and the body becomes spiritually surcharged so that gradually there is no difference between the soul and body. In such a case, there is no interference between the material mind and the propensities of the soul and the actions of the body. As the *Bhagavatam* (3.25.33) explains, *bhakti* automatically dissolves our subtle body the same way the stomach digests what we eat. Thus, a person regains his spiritual position or eternal form while still inhabiting the material body.

A person can realize what an impediment the material body is by making a little advancement. This body and our attachment for it is the cause of all our problems. By recognizing this fact, one becomes disgusted with this bodily situation just as Devahuti did when she said that she was sick of the disturbance caused by the material senses because the disturbance caused her to fall into the abyss of ignorance (*Bhag*.3.25.7). However, by the process of *bhakti-yoga* one can rise above the bodily and mental problems, as mentioned in *Srimad-Bhagavatam* (7.7.33), and mitigate the influence of lust, anger, greed, illusion, madness, and jealousy, and then engage in loving service to the Supreme.

This is the power of devotional service. Whatever can be accomplished by other means, only after much practice and difficulty, can be immediately accomplished through *bhakti-yoga*. *Srimad-Bhagavatam* (11.2.12) emphasizes that whether hearing or talking about it, meditating on it, faithfully accepting it, or praising others who perform it, pure devotional service to the Supreme is so powerful that it can purify any living being, even those who hate the demigods. Furthermore, Krishna explains (*Bhag.*11.29.33) that people try to advance their lives through religiosity, economic development, sense gratification, knowledge, mundane work, business, politics, or yoga and rituals. But whatever can be accomplished in these endeavors a devotee can easily attain from Krishna.

This is God's promise to His devotee that in whatever situation one is in, just depend on Him. This is the essence of all other religious and yogic processes which manifests to its fullest within *bhakti-yoga*. Krishna says that one who follows the path of devotional service with complete faith, making Krishna the ultimate goal, is very dear to Him (*Bg.*12.20). Plus, one who gives up all work for fruitive results and offers himself entirely to Krishna and His service attains freedom from birth and death and shares Krishna's opulences (*Bhag.* 11.29.34). This is obviously a very high status to achieve and is the ultimate position of any spiritual process. As Krishna verifies in *Bhagavad-gita* (18.62), by utter surrender to Him, one attains the supreme peace and eternal abode.

Of course, there may be those who appreciate this philosophy and want to learn more about it, but do not feel they can drop everything and engage in the continuous practice of *bhakti-yoga*. But renouncing everything is not necessarily a part of *bhakti-yoga*. To give up that which can be used in Krishna's service is a characteristic of one who is not very advanced in spiritual understanding. The art of *bhakti-yoga* is knowing how to use your life and everything in it for service to the Supreme. One can use his intelligence, his speech, his strength, or the money he makes from his business in the service of the Supreme in many different ways. It is not that you have to give it up, but you simply learn how to use it properly. However, it has been recognized that determination for devotional service does not take place in those who are still too attached to sensual pleasure and opulence (*Bg.*2.44). Yet for those who may be materially attached but still want to advance spiritually, all hope is not lost. There are still other aspects of *bhakti-yoga* that one can follow that will still guarantee continued progress for the aspirant.

In this regard Krishna Himself explains in *Bhagavad-gita* (12.9-12) that if you cannot focus your mind on Him, then practice the principles of *bhakti-yoga*. If you cannot do that, then try to work for Krishna by offering the results to Him. If you cannot do that, then try to be self-satisfied and be unattached to the results of your work. If you are unable to do this, then cultivate spiritual knowledge, or better than this is meditation, and renunciation of the results of action is still better because by doing so gives peace of mind. Doing any of these will help one along the path to spiritual enlightenment.

From this description we can analyze our present situation and tendencies and understand what we need to do. Then we can begin those practices that would be most appropriate for us. The point is that devotional service is dormant in everyone's heart. We all have an eternal relationship with the Lord and we simply need to engage in the process that will most easily awaken it. This is called *sadhana-bhakti*, or regulated practice. Such practice has different aspects, which may include hearing and chanting about Krishna, reading scriptural texts, rising early to meditate, associating with other devotees, eating food that has been first offered to Krishna, taking initiation from a spiritual master, engaging in devotional service in a temple or under the guidance of a spiritual master, and so on. All of these help purify our consciousness and speed the way for clearing all obstacles from the devotional path. In this way, as the *Caitanya-caritamrta* (*Madhya-lila*, 19.177) explains, rendering devotional service increases one's attachment to the Supreme, which becomes love when intensified.

Even if a person fully takes to devotional service and accidently falls down, he is still considered saintly. Even if one is considered most abominable he is considered righteous if he is engaged in undivided devotional service, for he quickly becomes virtuous and attains everlasting peace (*Bg.*9.30-31).

We should note that when one is just beginning on the path of *bhakti*, they may still be conditioned by so many bad habits. It is not easy to suddenly give them up, and the illusory energy is very powerful on a weak mind. Therefore, if one accidently falls down his continued practice in *bhakti-yoga* will purify him, and Krishna is always ready to forgive any accidental offense of a sincere devotee. In many ways our actions may be so faulty that we make numerous mistakes without knowing it. In the beginning stage these may be overlooked to some degree, but as one advances such falldowns must be reduced. If, however, after years of practice one continues to fall down from the principles of *bhakti-yoga* time and time again without remorse or reconciliation, then he is not serious about making spiritual advancement.

If one sincerely gives up all material engagement to become completely absorbed in devotional activities, but returns to material activities due to an immature level of spiritual realization, his life is still changed. What little spiritual advancement he might have made will leave a lasting impression on his consciousness. One may be sincere, yet due to a lack of maturity may not be able to persevere. This is different than being a hypocrite who considers himself advanced but cannot follow the process. A person who is sincere will still gradually meet with success, if not in this life then in a future life because whatever spiritual progress one makes is eternal. This is described in *Srimad-Bhagavatam* (1.5.17, 19): even if a person gives up his material occupation to perform continual devotional service and later falls away from such engagement while in an immature stage, he still will be successful. But nothing spiritual is gained when a person performs no devotional service to the Supreme and is fully engaged in his occupational duties. Even though a devotee may fall away, he does not undergo material existence like common materialists. After once relishing the taste of spiritual engagement, a person remembers that ecstasy again and again.

This information certainly illustrates the effectiveness of the devotional process, which Lord Krishna explains in the *Bhagavatam* (11.29.19-22) as being the most practical method for spiritual advancement. Krishna says the process of using one's body and senses for realizing Him is the best way to attain spiritual enlightenment. Since the Lord Himself established this process of *bhakti-yoga*, it is completely spiritual and beyond all material contamination. Anyone who engages in this process, even though it may appear useless to some, never suffers the slightest loss because it is the actual process of religion. By practicing it one can use this temporary lifetime to attain the eternal reality.

It should be easy to understand by now that devotional service, *bhakti-yoga*, is no cheap thing. Not only is it rare to be able to learn the process of *bhakti-yoga*, but it is even more rare to ever meet a pure devotee. An example to show how uncommon it is for a living entity to meet a pure devotee in this material creation would be if a turtle on the bottom of the ocean swam up to the top and just happened to put his head through the knothole of a board that was floating somewhere on the surface. Therefore, though we may find many people who pose as elevated preachers who are close to God, a real devotee who is spiritually pure in consciousness is a very uncommon person in this world.

Further elaboration is found in the *Srimad-Bhagavatam* (6.14.3-5). It says that in this material world there are as many living beings as there are atoms, out of which only a few are humans, of which only a few are interested in religious practice, and out of these only a few are interested in attaining liberation from material existence. Out of thousands who strive for liberation, only one may detach himself from his identity with society, family, country, etc. Even among millions who have become free from bodily identification, only one may have actually realized the self and be solely devoted to Lord Krishna.

Obviously, if we come in contact with a devotee from whom we can learn the science of *bhakti-yoga*, we should take it very seriously. For out of all the innumerable living entities in this universe and all the activities that they are engaged in, only through *bhakti* can they achieve the Lord's favor and attain the ultimate goal of life, as stated in the *Bhagavatam* (8.6.12). Furthermore, by achieving the Lord's favor, God becomes pleased to reveal Himself. Otherwise, there is no other way of knowing God and all His potencies. "The Supreme Lord is not obtained by expert explanations, by vast intelligence, or even by much hearing. He is obtained only by one whom He Himself chooses. To such a person, He manifests His own form." (*Mundaka Upanishad* 3.2.3)

To one who is purified by intense service, the form of the Lord is easily visible. This is how one can experience the presence of God. As the *Bhagavatam* (1.3.38) points out, only those who offer sincere and continual devotion to Lord Krishna can fully know His spiritual characteristics and power.

In this way, for one who is sincere, it is not as difficult to realize the Absolute Truth as it may seem. Lord Krishna helps His devotee by removing the inauspicious obstacles that are on the path as well as by giving the knowledge that one needs for spiritual realization. It has been said that for every step we take towards Krishna, He takes ten steps toward us. Or as Krishna Himself says in *Bhagavad-gita* (10.10-11), He gives the knowledge by which those who are constantly devoted in love can reach Him. Out of His compassion He destroys the darkness of ignorance with the lamp of knowledge.

This is an example of the reciprocation between the Lord and His devotee. The devotees are ever satisfied by seeing the smiling face of the Lord, and the Lord, seeing how enlivened the devotees are, also becomes more satisfied. Therefore, no one is more dear to Krishna than His pure devotees, as Krishna describes in the *Bhagavatam* (9.4.68), the devotees are His heart and He is in their heart. They know no one but Him and He knows only them.

The *Caitanya-caritamrta* (*Adi-lila*, 6.100-104, 7.145) further elaborates that being a devotee can be considered higher than God because devotees are dearer to Krishna than Himself. But the sweetness of Krishna can only be tasted when one is in the mood of servitude, and not by thinking himself to be equal to Krishna. This is verified in all the revealed scriptures, but fools cannot fathom the meaning of such devotional emotions. The exalted nature of devotional service is that the Lord, who is infinite, reciprocates with the insignificant devotee by being submissive to the loving service offered by the sincere devotee.

The beauty of devotional service is made quite clear in this information. This is how the infinite Lord becomes submissive to the tiny living entity. When the devotee advances in devotional service and relishes the spiritual taste in the reciprocation between himself and the Lord through the process of hearing about Him from the revealed scripture, praying to Him, chanting His holy names in meditation, etc., he certainly attains the goal of *bhakti-yoga*. His attraction for God increases and, being absorbed in such meditation, he easily crosses over death and enters the spiritual world. Krishna says in *Bhagavad-gita* (7.30, 8.5) that those who know Him as the Supreme Being and maintainer of this world can understand and think of Him at the hour of death. And whoever gives up his body remembering Him alone at once attains His spiritual nature without doubt.

In this way, thinking of Lord Krishna at the time of death will assure one of returning to the spiritual world. This is the goal as verified in the *Bhagavatam* (7.1.30-32) where it says that many people have attained liberation from material existence by fixing their minds on Krishna through feelings of attachment, affection, devotion, or even hatred and fear, and by giving up sinful acts. Hence, in any way possible one should fix his mind on Krishna to return to the spiritual world.

Krishna also assists His devotees in remembering Him during the time of leaving the material body. At death the senses and mind become very disturbed unless one is extremely fixed in yoga. The mind naturally drifts toward past attachments and activities which then bind the soul to continued material existence. Therefore, Krishna is ready to help His devotee through any such danger. The *Bhagavatam* (1.9.23) relates that the Supreme Lord releases His devotee from the bondage of *karma*, or fruitive activities, when the devotee quits his body at death with a mind fixed on the Lord through devotion, meditation, or chanting His holy names.

Since the sincere devotee is always concentrating on the form of Krishna by some means or other, liberation follows the devotee just like a maidservant. In other words, a devotee does not have to make a separate endeavor for liberation as one does in other yoga systems. Simply by his devotional service he automatically achieves liberation from the material world. Since devotional service is the only activity one finds in the spiritual world, by one's engagement in pure devotional service here in the material creation one is practically already in the spiritual realm. As the *Bhagavatam* (4.21.32) explains, if a devotee has taken shelter of the lotus feet of the Supreme he becomes completely free from all mental impurities and doubts, which is accomplished only by *bhakti-yoga*. Then a devotee never comes back to this world of material existence which is full of misery in the struggle for survival.

THE ECSTASY OF DEVOTIONAL SERVICE

Even in this material world, as one advances in *bhakti*, one can begin feeling spiritual emotions that are like nothing felt in material or physical exchanges. The beginning of spiritual emotion is called *bhava*, or the stage prior to love of God. From the point of *bhava*, there is no end to the increase of spiritual feelings of love and ecstasy that one may develop. Such feelings are practically unimaginable for the average person, but we can begin to get a glimpse into the unlimited spiritual bliss available to the devotees by considering the following references in the Vedic literature:

If multiplied billions of times, the transcendental pleasure derived from impersonal Brahman realization still could not compare to even an atomic portion of the ocean of *bhakti*, or transcendental service. (*Bhakti-rasamrta-sindhu*, 1.1.38)

For those who take pleasure in the transcendental topics of the Supreme Personality of Godhead, the four progressive realizations of religiosity, economic development, sense gratification and liberation, all combined together, cannot compare, any more than a straw, to the happiness derived from hearing about the transcendental activities of the Lord. (*Bhavartha-dipika*)

My Lord, I do not worship You to be liberated from this material entanglement, nor do I wish to save myself from the hellish condition of material existence, nor do I ever pray for a beautiful wife to enjoy in a nice garden. I wish only that I may always be in full ecstasy with the pleasure of serving Your Lordship. (*Mukunda-mala stotra* 6)

The *Bhagavatam* (4.9.10) also says the bliss felt through meditating on Krishna and hearing narrations about Him is far above the pleasure of *brahmananda*, merging into the impersonal Brahman. How then can it compare to the temporary pleasure in the heavenly planets which comes to an end by the sword of time? And (*Bhag.*7.7.34-36) when the activities and qualities of the Supreme and His incarnations are heard by the pure devotee, the devotee sheds tears, his voice falters, and his hair stands on end in ecstasy. He may also loudly sing, dance, or laugh in his blissful realizations. Like one possessed by spirits, an ecstatic devotee sometimes laughs, cries, or sits in meditation, greets all living beings as devotees, or carelessly chants "Hare Krishna. O Lord of the universe." The devotee becomes free from all material desires because of his continual contemplation on the Lord's activities, and thus he becomes completely spiritually surcharged. Then he attains full shelter of the Supreme.

The *Caitanya-caritamrta* (*Adi-lila*, 6.44; 8.27; and *Madhya-lila*, 2.49) elaborates further that even one drop of love of Krishna, which is like an ocean of happiness, could drown the whole world. Even though one should not express such confidential emotions, a madman must speak about it though no one believes him. The bliss of merging into oneness with the Brahman, even if multiplied one thousand times, cannot compare with the joy that comes from serving Krishna. Bodily transformations like trembling, perspiration, unsteady heart, faltering voice, and tears are experienced by those who actually awaken their spiritual loving service to God.

From these verses we can obviously understand that the highest pleasure and ecstasy that one can experience comes from contact with the Supreme Lord, the Absolute Truth. This is eternal and is attained when one establishes themselves in their constitutional position through *bhakti-yoga*. This is the real goal of life. Thus, the superexcellent qualities and benefits as well as the most rare position of engaging in *bhakti-yoga*, the devotional service of the Supreme Personality, has been described.

In this regard, the *Srimad-Bhagavatam* (7.7.37) concludes that the real problem of life is getting free from the cycle of repeated birth and death. The wise know that the spiritual bliss realized by those engaged in devotional service to the Supreme is the means for the conditioned living beings to become liberated from material existence. Therefore, everyone should worship and think of the Lord who is the Supersoul in everyone's heart.

CHAPTER TEN

Mantra-Yoga:
A Necessity for this Age

Mantra-yoga is actually a mystical tradition found in almost every spiritual path in the world. It may involve the softly spoken repetition of a prayer or *mantra* for one's own meditation, or it may be the congregational singing of spiritually uplifting songs, prayers, or the sacred names of the Supreme Being. It all involves the same process, but in the Eastern tradition it is called *mantra-yoga* because it is the easy process of focusing our minds on the Supreme, which helps spiritualize our consciousness. *Man* means the mind, *tra* means deliverance. Therefore, a spiritual *mantra* is the pure sound vibration for delivering the mind from material to spiritual consciousness. This is the goal of any spiritual path. Although all spiritual traditions have their own prayers or *mantras*, the Vedic *mantras* are especially powerful and effective in uniting us with the spiritual realm. However, a complete yoga process is generally a blend of a few yoga systems. Therefore, *bhakti-yoga*, as described in the previous chapter, also includes *mantra-yoga*, or the process of concentrating on the sound vibration within a *mantra*. This is especially important in this age of Kali.

Many years ago the *brahmana* priests could accomplish many kinds of wondrous deeds simply by correctly chanting particular *mantras*. Many of these *mantras* still exist, but it is very difficult to find those who can chant them accurately. This is actually a safety measure because if the wish-fulfilling *mantras* were easily chanted, there would no doubt be many people who would misuse them. But other *mantras* that are available can easily help purify one's consciousness, give spiritual enlightenment, and put one in touch with the Supreme.

In *Bhagavad-gita* (10.25) Sri Krishna explains that He is the transcendental *om mantra* and that the chanting of *japa* (chanting a *mantra* quietly for one's own meditation) is the purest of His representations and sacrifices. It is understood that by chanting *japa* and hearing the holy sounds of the *mantra*, one can come to the platform of spiritual realization. This is the process of *mantra-*

yoga. Even though the *mantra* is powerful in itself, when the *mantra* is chanted by a great devotee, it becomes more powerful. This is the effect when a disciple is fortunate enough to take initiation from a spiritually powerful master who gives him a *mantra* for spiritual purposes. Then the disciple can make rapid progress by utilizing the *mantra*.

In this age of Kali-yuga the process of chanting *japa* or *mantra* meditation is much more effective than practicing other spiritual paths that include meditating on the void or Brahman effulgence, or trying to control the life air within the body as in *raja-yoga*. Only a very few can become perfect at moving the life air up to the top of the head or raising the *kundalini* force up through the various *chakras*. And meditating on the void becomes useless as soon as there is the slightest external distraction, which in this age of Kali is a continuous thing. Therefore, the most effective means of focusing the consciousness is to concentrate on the sound vibration of a *mantra*.

There are two *mantras* that are especially recommended in the Vedic literature. One is *omkara* or the *om mantra*, and the other is Hare Krishna, Hare Krishna, Krishna Krishna, Hare Hare/Hare Rama, Hare Rama, Rama Rama, Hare Hare, which is known as the *maha* or great *mantra*. It is explained that these two *mantras* can deliver one to the realm beyond material existence.

Omkara (pranava) is considered to be the sound incarnation of the Supreme Personality of God and is identical with the Supreme Lord. The *Narada-pancaratra* states: "When the transcendental sound vibration is practiced by a conditioned soul, the Supreme Lord is present on his tongue." The *Atharva-veda* and the *Mandukya Upanishad* both mention the importance of *omkara*. *Omkara* is said to be the beginning, middle, and end, and is eternal, beyond all material restrictions. *Omkara* is unlimited, transcendental, and indestructible. As such, it is not so easy for the average person to understand all the intricacies of *omkara* or to chant *om* properly.

Actually, the chanting of *omkara* is generally practiced by impersonalists and those engaged in the mystic yoga process. By chanting *om* and controlling the breathing perfectly, which is mostly a mechanical way of steadying the mind, one is eventually able to go into trance or *samadhi*. Through this system, one gradually changes the tendencies of the materially absorbed mind and makes it spiritualized. But this takes many years to perfect and such a slow process is not practical in this age. If one is not a *brahmana*, he will not understand *omkara* and will not be able to get the desired results from chanting it. Therefore, it is not advised that people chant *omkara* in this age of Kali-yuga because they are generally not qualified to chant it properly. The *mantra* that is meant to be chanted in this age is easy and is actually more directly connected with the Supreme than the impersonal sound vibration of *omkara* because it contains the holy names of the Lord. The *mantra* for Kali-yuga is the *maha-mantra*, or great *mantra* for deliverance, which is Hare Krishna, Hare Krishna, Krishna Krishna, Hare Hare/Hare Rama, Hare Rama, Rama Rama, Hare Hare.

CHANTING THE MAHA-MANTRA

There are many Vedic references which specifically recommend the chanting of the Hare Krishna *maha-mantra* as the most effective means of reaching spiritual realization and counteracting all the problems of this age. Some of these verses are the following:

These sixteen words--Hare Krishna, Hare Krishna, Krishna Krishna, Hare Hare/Hare Rama, Hare Rama, Rama Rama, Hare Hare--are especially meant for counteracting the ill effects of the present age of quarrel and anxiety. (*Kali-santarana Upanishad*)

All *mantras* and all processes for self-realization are compressed into the Hare Krishna *maha-mantra*. (*Narada-pancaratra*)

Chant the holy names, chant the holy names, chant the holy names. In this age of Kali [the age of quarrel and confusion] without a doubt there is no other way, there is no other way, there is no other way. (*Brihan-naradiya Purana* 38.126)

In this age there is no use in meditation, sacrifice and temple worship. Simply by chanting the holy name of Krishna--Hare Krishna, Hare Krishna, Krishna Krishna, Hare Hare/Hare Rama, Hare Rama, Rama Rama, Hare Hare--one can achieve perfect self-realization. (*Vishnu Purana* 6.2.17)

The self-realization which was achieved in the Satya millennium by meditation, in the Treta millennium by the performance of different sacrifices, and in the Dvapara millennium by worship of Lord Krishna [as the Deity in the temple], can be achieved in the age of Kali simply by chanting the holy names, Hare Krishna. (*Bhag.*12.3.52) (Verses similar to this are also found in the *Padma Purana, Uttara-khanda* 72.25, and the *Brihan-naradiya Purana* 38.97)

Living beings who are entangled in the complicated meshes of birth and death can be freed immediately by even unconsciously chanting the holy name of Krishna, which is feared by fear personified. (*Bhag.*1.1.14)

The reason that chanting the Lord's names is such an effective process is because the Lord and His names are identical: they are the same spiritual energy. By chanting Hare Krishna we are in immediate contact with God. If we chant someone else's name, we cannot enjoy their association because the name and the person are different. For example, by chanting "water, water, water," we do not quench our thirst because water and the name are two different things.

But in the spiritual world everything is absolute. Krishna is nondifferent from His names and, therefore, we can feel His presence simply by chanting His names. This is further elaborated in the *Caitanya-caritamrta (Madhya-lila*, 17.131-133), which explains that there is no difference between the Lord's name, form, or personality, and they are all transcendentally sweet. Krishna's name is the same as Krishna Himself, and is not material in any way. It gives spiritual benedictions and is full of pleasure. But in the material world everything is different. Furthermore, in *Caitanya-cartamrta (Adi-lila*, 17.22, and the *Padma Purana*), the Hare Krishna *maha-mantra* is said to be the sound incarnation of Krishna, and anyone who chants this *mantra* is in direct association with Krishna and is delivered from the clutches of the material energy.

Because chanting the names of God brings us in direct contact with God in proportion to the chanter's purity, this process of self-realization is the way of success for everyone. The *Bhagavatam* (2.1.11) discloses that the chanting of God's names in the manner of the great authorities is the doubtless way to spiritual success for everyone, no matter whether they are full of material desires or free of all desires or self-satisfied because of their spiritual knowledge.

Simply by relying on the chanting of the holy names of God, one need not depend upon other processes, rituals, paraphernalia, or persons. One does not even have to be initiated by a spiritual master to chant the *maha-mantra*. As the *Caitanya-caritamrta (Madhya-lila*, 15.108) says, one does not have to take initiation, but only has to chant the holy names. Thus, deliverance is available to even the lowest of people. Furthermore, Rupa Gosvami writes about the potency of the holy name in his *Padyavali*:

> The holy name of Lord Krishna is an attractive feature for many saintly, liberal people. It is the annihilator of all sinful reactions and is so powerful that save for the dumb who cannot chant it, it is readily available to everyone, including the lowest type of man, the *chandala*. The holy name of Krishna is the controller of the opulence of liberation, and it is identical with Krishna. Simply by touching the holy name with one's tongue, immediate effects are produced. Chanting the holy name does not depend on initiation, pious activities or the *purascarya* regulative principles generally observed before initiation. The holy name does not wait for all these activities. It is self-sufficient. (*Padyavali* 29)

Herein is evidence that the Hare Krishna *maha-mantra* is so powerful that one who sincerely takes shelter of it will attain all the desired results of connection with the Supreme. The *Skanda Purana* gives further evidence of how powerful is the *maha-mantra*:

> The name of the Lord need not be chanted with regard to place, time, circumstantial conditions, preliminary self-purification or any other factors.

Rather, it is completely independent of all other processes and rewards all the desires of those who eagerly chant it. (*Skanda Purana*)

Therefore, without a doubt, the Hare Krishna *mantra* is the most potent *mantra* one can utilize for spiritual upliftment. The *Caitanya-caritamrta* (*Madhya-lila*, 15.107) also points out that one is freed of all sinful reactions simply by chanting Krishna's names. And all the nine types of devotional service are completed by this process. Thus, in Kali-yuga only the chanting of the holy names is necessary for worshiping the Lord. However, if one is not able to chant purely or follow the regulations for chanting, it is recommended that one get further guidance from a bona fide spiritual master.

In Kali-yuga the chanting of the holy names is certainly the most practical and effective process for the conditioned souls. It is also the easiest process whether one finds himself in Kali-yuga, Satya-yuga, Treta-yuga, or Dvapara-yuga. Regardless of what age one may be living in, the process of chanting the holy names is always recommended for everyone. "The names of the Supreme Lord who has the disc as His weapon should be glorified always and everywhere." (*Vaisakha-mahatmya* section of the *Padma Purana*) But since the age of Kali is the most difficult, where men have short durations of life, it is also the most fortunate age. This is explained in *Srimad-Bhagavatam* (11.5.36-37, and 12.3.51) which states that those who are wise know the value of this age of Kali because, in spite of the fallen nature of this age, the spiritual perfection of life can be attained by the easy process of *sankirtana*, the congregational chanting of Krishna's holy names. No better position can be found to attain freedom from material existence and entrance into the spiritual kingdom than joining the Lord's *sankirtana* movement.

Even those living in other ages desire to take birth in Kali-yuga to take advantage of this special concession of a speedy delivery from the cycle of birth and death through the process of *sankirtana*. This is confirmed in *Srimad-Bhagavatam* (11.5.38) where we find it said that those who live during Satya-yuga and other ages wish to be born in Kali-yuga just to take advantage of associating with the devotees of Lord Narayana, who are especially found in South India.

The *Srimad-Bhagavatam* (11.5.32) explains that intelligent persons perform congregational singing of Krishna's names to worship the incarnation of Krishna who sings His own names, and who is accompanied by His associates and confidential companions. Therefore, as the *Caitanya-caritamrta* (*Adi-lila*, 7.74) specifically says, the essence of all scriptural teachings is that the only religious principle in the age of Kali is to chant the Lord's holy names, which are the basis of all Vedic hymns. "In this way the most perfect penance to be executed in this world is the chanting of the name of Lord Sri Hari. Especially in the age of Kali, one can satisfy the Supreme Lord Vishnu by performing *sankirtana*." (*Caturmasya-mahatmya* section of the *Skanda Purana*)

The fact of the matter, as explained in *Srimad-Bhagavatam* (3.33.6-7), is that regardless of what one's present situation is, if a person once speaks about the activities and chants the holy names of the Supreme, or hears about and remembers Him, he becomes eligible to engage in the Vedic rituals. And how much more glorious are those who regularly chant the holy names. Such people are indeed worshipable, for they must have performed all kinds of austerities, achieved the characteristics of the Aryans, studied the *Vedas*, bathed at all the holy places of pilgrimage, and done whatever else is required.

In this way, we can begin to understand how elevated the writer of the Vedic scripture considers those who have adopted the process of chanting Krishna's holy names. However, for those who do not like the chanting of the holy names and blaspheme the process and criticize or try to restrain those who do chant, we can understand that their sentiment is due to their sinful and offensive activities. Such people are said to have no intelligence and work for no useful purpose and simply contribute to the chaos and confusion within society. The *Bhagavatam* (3.9.7) confirms that those who do not engage in the blessed chanting and hearing about the activities of the Supreme are bereft of intelligence and good fortune. They perform sinful activities to enjoy sensual pleasure which lasts only for a short time.

THE POWER OF THE MAHA-MANTRA: HOW IT WORKS

It may be somewhat surprising for the average Westerner to hear about the power within the vibrations of words or *mantras*, but the potency is real. For example, any numerologist will tell you that each letter has a particular value and a group of letters pronounced as a word invokes the power of those letters. Therefore, someone's name contains the subtle formula for signifying to varying degrees one's characteristics, qualities, and future. By associating with particular sound vibrations one becomes influenced by them.

A good example of this is when one country tries to take over another in war, or one political party tries to defeat another. The first thing they try to do is take over the lines of communication and the media, such as radio, television, and newspapers. By sending out its propaganda through sound, a government can influence people's minds and stay in power, or a political party can remove the leaders of the opposition. In the latter case, a new government may become established.

According to the predominant types of sound vibration people associate with through T.V. and radio, or in reading articles in magazines and newspapers, they become attracted to certain things or drawn towards certain viewpoints. When television shows, songs on the radio, stories in magazines, and advertising everywhere propagates the concern for temporary sense gratification, then people lose their interest in the real goal of life. They simply become absorbed in the thoughts of whatever type of sound vibration enters their consciousness. When nonsensical sound vibrations enter and contaminate the ether, the air, water, and the very molecular structure of each and every person, place, and thing, then we cannot expect anything else but continued and worsening turmoil and perplexities in the world.

Let us try to understand how this happens. First of all, energy pervades the atmosphere of this creation in the form of vibrations, as in sound waves, light waves, radio waves, and so on. The mind can especially be affected by the kind of energy or vibration it picks up or tunes into. The function of the mind is twofold: it joins thoughts and concepts into theories and goals or desires, and it simplifies or interprets experiences that are gathered through the senses. This is controlled by sound vibration or thought waves. For example, when you hear the following words, an image will form in your mind: dog, cat, insect, man, woman, politician, automobile, and sunset. We can take the experiment a little further as follows: snarling dog, sleeping cat, biting insect, ugly old man, beautiful voluptuous woman, conniving politician, sleek automobile, and tranquil red sunset.

The second set of words may have brought images to your mind that were completely different than the first set. This is all due to sound which triggers the mind to react and form thoughts or images related to the words by interpreting past experiences. Such thoughts and images may also form into goals or desires of what we want to attain or wish to avoid. When throughout our life we are bombarded by different kinds of sound waves, whether from schoolbooks in our early years, or to present day radio, television, and movies, our consciousness is led through particular changes and different levels of development. This might be controlled by others so that we act in a certain way according to someone else's design, whether we know it or not. If you start listening to the radio all the time and all they play are songs about making love under the apple tree, you will not have to tell anyone what you will be thinking about. It is not difficult to figure out. This is how we are controlled by sound.

Another example is that sometime we may be feeling peaceful and decide to spend a nice, quiet evening watching television. After several hours of being exposed to all kinds of sound vibration in the form of game shows, cop shows, comedy, soap opera, news, and a multitude of advertising, we may wake up the next morning unrested, agitated, and disturbed without knowing why. In this way, the kind of sound vibration we associate with can make a big difference on our consciousness.

There are, however, many kinds of beneficial sound vibrations that we can utilize. A friend of mine once cut his finger down to the bone while he was in India. It was a serious cut and he was not able to do much to stop the bleeding. He told one of the Indian men nearby who took him into his house. The man put some mustard seed oil on the cut and stroked it with his finger while chanting a certain *mantra*. At that point the bleeding stopped. He did it again and the cut closed. The man did it a third time and, to my friend's amazement, the cut on his finger was healed. Some farmers also use *mantras* to produce better crops. Plants are very sensitive to vibrations and different sounds can assist plants in their growth.

In the Vedic literature there are, of course, many stories which describe the use of *mantras*. The *brahmana* priests produced many kinds of magical results by using them. They could even curse others or, if necessary, kill someone with the use of *mantras*. The warriors or kings could also attach a *brahmastra* weapon to the arrows they shot. A *brahmastra* is a weapon equivalent to the atomic bombs of today, but were produced by perfectly chanting particular *mantras*. However, the *brahmastra* could also be called back by using a different *mantra* and the extent of damage could also be controlled. They were not like the bombs of today that, when released, are completely uncontrollable and kill and hurt everyone and anyone.

There are many other kinds of sound vibrations, *mantras*, or prayers that can be used for gaining money, maintaining health, defeating enemies, getting good luck, subduing evil spirits, counteracting snake bite, and so on. There are countless *mantras* or prayers for temporary results, not only in the Vedic culture but in other cultures as well. The most powerful *mantras* are those that can completely free one from this material world and the cycle of birth and death and allow one to enter the spiritual realm. As already established, there is no *mantra* more powerful for this purpose than the Hare Krishna *maha-mantra*.

The way the *maha-mantra* works is a science. One thing we must first understand is that there are channels by which the Infinite descends into this world. One channel is through transcendental sound. The *maha-mantra* is a purely spiritual vibration. It cannot be chanted with a material tongue nor heard with a material ear. In this way, the holy name reserves the right of not being exposed to organic senses or understood by someone in materialistic consciousness. However, the Infinite has the power of making Himself known to the finite mind. When He reveals Himself to His devotee, the devotee experiences the perception of God. This is called self-realization and transcendental revelation. This can be attained through the process of purely chanting the *maha-mantra*.

The holy names are not revealed simply through Vedic writings, but they are revealed to the world through the spiritual tongues of the pure devotees. Such pure devotees are the real spiritual masters of everyone in the universe. But if the guru is not genuine, then the sound or *mantra*, though seeming to sound the same, will not produce the real effect.

The audience of the pure devotee hears the name of Krishna but may not fully recognize or comprehend it. Yet the name enters the ear and vibrates the eardrum which touches our mind. There is still not genuine spiritual realization at this point because the soul remains untouched. Yet the name begins to affect our mind by cleansing the dust within. This dust is the materialistic consciousness which causes forgetfulness of our real spiritual identity. This forgetfulness manifests in forms of bodily attachment, lust, greed, envy, anger, etc. Therefore, by chanting the *maha-mantra* we wash our mind and enable it to get free of the contaminating dust. Then the mind and intelligence become very clear and sharp.

The mind is the connecting link between the body and the spirit soul within. The soul, which does not actively engage in any material activities, remains in a state of suspended animation while covered by illusion, as in the case of a materially conditioned person who engages in material activities. Through the vehicle of the mind, the senses act and we perceive things around us and form theories. If the mind is unclear or dusty due to the influence of the material energy, we then become confused about the goal of life and may engage in so many material pursuits. When the mind is cleansed or purified by associating with the Infinite in the form of the *maha-mantra*, all our material concoctions are forced out. By inundating our mind with the transcendental sound of the holy names, all of our misconceptions, which is the cause of our material suffering, are completely conquered, leaving no more enemies within the mind. Then the mind reflects the quality and nature of the soul.

The holy sound of Hare Krishna, as uttered by the pure devotee, moves our intellect and we begin to consider the Vedic philosophy. When the intelligence is thus energized by spiritual knowledge, the transcendental sound vibration, after cutting through the senses, mind, and intelligence, makes contact with the soul. Thus, we are able to hear the holy name with our real spiritual ear, and actual spiritual revelation and self-realization is open to us. Then the soul, having made contact with the Supreme in the form of transcendental sound, recapitulates, sending the vibration back through our intelligence, mind, and senses. At that time, when we chant Hare Krishna, the Supreme Infinite Lord is there and our whole being experiences a deluge of unlimited spiritual ecstasy.

From this level of spiritual realization, we can enter into the understanding of the very cause of everything that exists. The mind, body, and soul, and even material nature itself can be changed into transcendental energy by one pure exclamation of Hare Krishna. This is very important to understand because when everything becomes saturated with this transcendental sound, the result is total transformation of energy. Thus, what is material can be changed into something spiritual. If this can be done on a grand scale, then the material world can be transformed into the spiritual world.

Another example of how the holy names of Krishna work, and how powerful they are, can be cited from the *Srimad-Bhagavatam*, Sixth Canto, in the story of Ajamila. Ajamila was born of good parents who trained him in knowledge of the *Vedas* to become a perfect *brahmana*. Yet one time, while walking along the road, he happened to see a man and a prostitute in a state of intoxication, frolicking in the grass. The woman was not covered properly and was uninhibitedly engaging in amorous pastimes with the man. Upon seeing this,

Ajamila became very agitated and later sought the company of the prostitute. He left his young beautiful wife and lived with the prostitute, giving up all regulative principles. He begot ten sons in the womb of the prostitute and named the youngest son Narayana, a name of one of the expansions of Krishna.

To maintain himself and his family, Ajamila cheated others in gambling or by robbing them. While he spent his time in abominable, sinful activities, eighty-eight years of his life passed by. Since his youngest son was born while Ajamila was very old, Narayana was very dear to him. Because of the child's awkward manners and speech, Ajamila delighted in the child's activities. When Ajamila ate or drank, he always did so with his son, Narayana. Ajamila, however, could not understand that the length of his life was decreasing and death was approaching. When the time of death arrived for Ajamila, he began to think only of his son.

At the moment of death, Ajamila became extremely frightened when he saw three persons with deformed bodies, fierce, twisted faces, and their hair standing erect. With a noose in their hands, they had come to take him to Yamaraja, the lord of death. Because of attachment to his son, Ajamila fearfully began to call him loudly by his name, Narayana.

Just then the Vishnudutas, soldiers of Lord Vishnu, arrived when they heard the holy name of their master from the mouth of the dying Ajamila. Ajamila had certainly chanted the name of Narayana without offense because he had chanted in complete anxiety. The Yamadutas, soldiers of Yamaraja, were snatching the soul from the heart of Ajamila, but the messengers of Lord Vishnu forcefully stopped them from doing so. The Yamadutas inquired why they were being stopped from taking Ajamila. The Vishnudutas then asked the Yamadutas that if they were really servants of Lord Yamaraja, then explain the meaning of religious and irreligious principles.

The Yamadutas replied that from their master, Yamaraja, they had heard that which is prescribed in the *Vedas* constitutes religious principles, and the opposite is irreligion. They continued to explain that Lord Narayana is situated in His own abode in the spiritual world, but controls the entire cosmic creation.

The sun, fire, sky, air, demigods, moon, evening, day, night, directions, water, land, and Supersoul Himself all witness the activities of the living entities. Those that deserve punishment are those who are confirmed by these witnesses as having engaged in unrighteous activities. Everyone engaged in fruitive activities deserves punishment in proportion to their sinful acts. In this way, they must enjoy or suffer the corresponding reactions of their *karma* in the next life.

The Yamadutas continued to explain the laws of *karma* and the position of the living entity, pointing out that in considering the sinful life of Ajamila, they had the right to take him to hell in order to rectify his sinful behavior.

The Vishnudutas, however, stated that Ajamila had already atoned for all of his sinful actions, not only for this one life but for those performed in millions of lives, simply by chanting the holy name of Narayana in a helpless condition.

Even though he had not chanted purely, he chanted without offense, and, therefore, was now pure and eligible for liberation. Throughout Ajamila's life, he called the name Narayana. Although calling his son, by chanting the name Narayana, he sufficiently atoned for the sinful actions of millions of lives. At the time of death, Ajamila had helplessly and very loudly chanted the holy name of the Lord. That chanting alone had already freed him from the reactions of all sinful life. Therefore, the soldiers of Lord Vishnu forbade the servants of Yamaraja to take Ajamila for punishment in hell. Anyone who takes shelter of the Supreme through His holy names can similarly be saved from the dark future of sinful reactions after death.

Although *Srimad-Bhagavatam* relates the full story of Ajamila and how he witnessed the discussion between the Yamadutas and Vishnudutas and then went on to achieve ultimate spiritual perfection by taking to the process of *bhakti-yoga*, our short summary here is to show the potency of the holy names. Ajamila is not much different than most people in this age of Kali who are attracted to sinful activities. Therefore, we should seriously try to understand and take advantage of the chanting of the holy names, for by doing so even the greatest sins we may have committed can be atoned, as the following verses explain:

Simply by chanting one holy name of Hari, a sinful man can counteract the reactions to more sins than he is able to commit. (*Brihad-vishnu Purana*)

As when all small animals flee in fear when a lion roars, similarly all one's sinful reactions leave when a person chants the Lord's holy names while in a helpless condition or even if he has no desire to do so. (*Garuda Purana*)

The path to liberation is guaranteed when a person once chants the holy name of Lord Hari. (*Skanda Purana*)

The *Srimad-Bhagavatam* (6.3.31) explains that chanting the holy names can negate the reactions of the most serious of sins, and, therefore, everyone should take this seriously and join the *sankirtana* movement, which is the most auspicious activity in the universe. And the *Caitanya-caritamrta* (*Madhya-lila*, 15.109) discloses that beyond dissolving one's entanglement in material existence, by chanting Krishna's names one develops attraction and awakens his love for Krishna.

From these verses we can understand that there is no impediment for everyone to readily utilize the holy names to purify themselves of even the worst sins, providing they are sincere and chant purely. Even those who cannot speak properly can repeat the *maha-mantra* within their minds. From those who are the most saintly to those who are in the most abominable position, all have the opportunity of chanting the holy names to begin the escape from *karmic* reactions and to free themselves from material entanglement.

As described in *Srimad-Bhagavatam* (6.2.9-10), the chanting of the names of the Supreme is the best atonement for one who is a thief, a drunkard, a killer of *brahmanas*, or one who kills women or kings or cows or his own parents, or for any other kind of sins. Simply by chanting the holy names one attracts the attention of the Supreme who gives that person special protection.

Herein we can discern that attracting the attention of the Supreme by chanting His holy names is the best means of protecting ourselves from our past impurities. When the Supreme is pleased with someone, what can they not accomplish? Anything can be done by one who becomes spiritually powerful. Therefore, out of all the various processes of atonement that are prescribed by different scripture, engaging in the chanting of the holy names is best because it actually uproots the material desires in the heart. As the *Bhagavatam* (6.2.12) confirms, the various processes of atonement are not complete if one's mind still runs back to unwanted material habits. Therefore, those who want freedom from their *karmic* reactions, chanting of the names and pastimes of the Supreme is the best because it completely purifies the mind. Furthermore, the *Bhagavatam* (6.2.15) relates that chanting the holy names of the Lord before dying by some misfortune is enough to deliver a person from having to enter hell to suffer for his bad *karmic* reactions.

Not only is the name of the Lord so powerfully effective on one who seriously chants it, despite the fact that he may have been sinful in his past, the name also acts on one who chants it in a very casual manner. The *Bhagavatam* (6.2.14, 19) points out that even if one chants the holy names neglectfully, jokingly, or simply for entertainment, the holy names are nonetheless effective enough to free the person from unlimited sins, just as a powerful medicine is effective whether a patient who takes it understands it or not.

Pondering all these points, Lord Yamaraja, in *Srimad-Bhagavatam* (6.3.26), concludes that all intelligent men take to devotional service by chanting the holy names of the Supreme because even if they accidentally perform some sinful act, they are protected since the chanting of the Hare Krishna *mantra* obliterates all sinful reactions.

ATTAINING LIBERATION THROUGH CHANTING

In the previous segment it is mentioned that there are certain channels through which the Infinite descends. Similarly, there are certain channels that the living beings can use to escape material existence and return to the spiritual realm. Of course, the final goal of any religious process or yoga system is to get free from material entanglement and enter directly into spiritual existence. This happens easily for one who learns how to purely chant the holy names, as verified in the *Caitanya-caritamrta* (*Adi-lila*, 8.26, 28) which states that the chanting of the Hare Krishna *mantra* vanquishes all sins and makes way for the performance of devotional service to begin. The chanting of this *maha-mantra* gives so much spiritual advancement that one easily ends his material existence and attains love of God.

From everything that has been described so far about the glories of the holy name, such as its potency to purify the mind, to relieve us of material activities and the reactions to sinful acts, as well as to put us in direct contact with the Supreme and reawaken our attraction for Him, it is obvious, especially for this age of Kali-yuga, that the most worshipable object is the Lord's holy name as found in the Hare Krishna *maha-mantra*. The *Bhagavatam* (6.3.22) also confirms this by stating that the topmost religious principle for the entire human race is to engage in devotional service beginning with the chanting of the Lord's holy names. Therefore, those who chant the holy names have reached the ultimate position in civilized life and, if they continue on the path, will attain further realizations in spiritual life up to reaching the platform of pure, unadulterated devotional service. All such transcendental opulences, as stated in the above verses, are attained simply by chanting the Hare Krishna *maha-mantra* without offenses. In this way, one attains the supreme spiritual bliss. The *Caitanya-caritamrta* (*Antya-lila*, 20.14) explains that by chanting the spiritual names of Krishna one tastes spiritual ecstasy when his love for Krishna awakens. Then one attains Krishna's direct association and feels like he is in an ocean of love.

The name "Krishna" literally means "the greatest pleasure." All living entities are looking for pleasure and happiness. God is the storehouse of all pleasure and whatever happiness we feel in this material world is simply due to contact with His energy. However, by chanting His holy names, we can transcend whatever temporary pleasure is found on the material platform and experience actual spiritual happiness by coming in direct contact with the Supreme, the source of all pleasure. The *Caitanya-caritamrta* (*Adi-lila*, 7.73) verifies that simply by chanting the Hare Krishna *mantra* a person is freed from material life and will be able to see the Lord.

The mystery behind these names of God is further explained in the *Sri Caitanya Upanishad*, texts 12-14. It explains that the names of the Supreme that are used in the Hare Krishna *mantra* have specific meanings. *Hari* refers to "He who unties the knot of a person's material desires." Krishna is divided into *Krish*, which means "He who is attractive to everyone," and *Na*, which means "the greatest spiritual pleasure." And *Rama* means "He who is full of spiritual bliss and attracts all others." The Hare Krishna *mantra* consists of the repetition of these names of the Supreme (Hare Krishna, Hare Krishna, Krishna Krishna, Hare Hare/Hare Rama, Hare Rama, Rama Rama, Hare Hare) and is the best of all *mantras* and most confidential of secrets. Those who are serious about making spiritual progress continually chant these holy names and cross over material existence.

For one who takes shelter of the *maha-mantra*, he is sure to reach the Supreme because such mystic meditation engages the mind and intelligence in

Krishna. By such continued remembrance of Krishna, even though one may seem to be engaged in so many duties, one regains his spiritual consciousness which is the prerequisite for entering back into the spiritual world. As Sri Krishna explains in *Bhagavad-gita* (8.7-8), a person should think of Him as Krishna and carry out one's duty with the mind and intelligence fixed on Him. Thinking and meditating on Krishna in this undeviated way, one can be sure to reach the divine Supreme Spirit.

From this information we can understand that if we can continue setting some time aside everyday for chanting the *maha-mantra* and spiritualizing our consciousness, we will be prepared for entering the spiritual realm after death. This is the most important aspect of any yoga or religious system--being free from material consciousness and remembering the Supreme at the time we give up our body. This requirement is easily fulfilled simply by remembering the Lord through chanting His holy names. This is confirmed in the *Srimad-Bhagavatam* (3.9.15) which declares that one who takes shelter of Krishna by invoking His spiritual names at the time of leaving the body is cleansed of many lifetimes of sin and attains Krishna without fail.

The most practical example of this is Ajamila, as previously discussed. The *Bhagavatam* (6.2.49) describes that at the time of death Ajamila chanted the Lord's name and returned to the spiritual world, although he was calling for his son, Narayana. So where is the doubt that if one seriously chants the Lord's holy name he will return to the spiritual world? Therefore, as the *Bhagavatam* (6.2.46) elaborates, for one who is serious about attaining freedom from material existence, there is nothing more effective than chanting the holy names of the Supreme and discussing His pastimes and qualities. Other processes are not as complete and leave one's mind tainted with passion and ignorance. Furthermore (*Bhag*.6.3.24), all of one's sinful *karmic* reactions are wiped out simply by chanting the Lord's names and glorifying His qualities and activities. Even if one cannot properly pronounce the holy name, a person will achieve liberation if he chants without offense.

GOD INAUGURATES CHANTING THE HOLY NAMES

We should not think that *sankirtana*, the chanting of the Lord's holy names, is simply part of the system of *mantra-yoga*, or is merely a formula that has been passed down through the ages like other yoga systems. Nor is it a ritual, ceremony, or activity meant for producing good *karma* or positive fruitive results. Neither is it merely a way to focus the mind and achieve peace and tranquility. It is more than any of these.

As previously explained, there is a system of self-realization especially recommended for each age. In the age of Kali, people are not attracted to spiritual pursuits and are often rebellious against anything that seems to restrict or stifle their freedom to do anything they want. Since in this age we are so easily distracted by so many things and our mind is always in a whirl, we need an easy path. Therefore, the Vedic *shastra* explains that God has given us an easy way to return to Him in this age. It is almost as if He has said, "Since you are My worst son, I give you the easiest process." The *Caitanya-caritamrta* (*Adi-lila*, 3.40) confirms this and says that the Supreme Being descends as Sri Caitanya, with a golden complexion, to simply spread the glories of chanting the holy names, which is the only religious principle in this age of Kali. In this way, God Himself has given the method of chanting His holy names as the most effective means to reach His spiritual abode.

The Lord always descends to establish the codes of religion. This is confirmed in *Bhagavad-gita* (4.6-8) where Lord Krishna explains that although He is unborn and the Lord of all living beings, He still descends in His spiritual form in order to re-establish the proper religious principles and annihilate the miscreants whenever there is a decline of religion and a rise in irreligious activity.

Though there are many incarnations of God, all incarnations are known and predicted in the Vedic literature. Each incarnation performs many wonderful pastimes. But in Kali-yuga the Lord descends as His own devotee in the form of Sri Caitanya in order to show the perfect example of how devotional service should be performed, and to stress the chanting of the Hare Krishna *mantra* for this age by inaugurating the process of *sankirtana* movement.

Predictions of the appearance of Lord Caitanya can be found in many Vedic texts. One of them is from the *Svetasvatara Upanishad* (3.12): "The Supreme Personality of God [Purusha] is Mahaprabhu [great master], the propagator of transcendental enlightenment." Another is from the *Vayu Purana*: "In the age of Kali I shall descend as the son of Sacidevi to inaugurate the *sankirtana* movement." The *Bhagavatam* (11.5.32) also describes how intelligent men sing the holy names to worship the incarnation of God who is accompanied by His associates and always sings the names of Krishna. And in the *Caitanya-caritamrta* (*Adi-lila*, 3.19-20) the Supreme Lord Himself describes how He will appear as His own devotee to perform and teach devotional service by inaugurating the *sankirtana* movement, which is the religion for this age.

The *Sri Caitanya Upanishad* (texts 5-11) of the *Atharva-veda* contains the most detailed prediction of Lord Caitanya's appearance and activities. When Pippalada asked his father, Lord Brahma, how the sinful living entities will be delivered in Kali-yuga and who should be the object of their worship and what *mantra* should they chant to be delivered, Brahma told him to listen carefully and he would describe what will take place in the age of Kali. Brahma said that the Supreme Lord Govinda, Krishna, will appear again in Kali-yuga as His own devotee in a two-armed form with a golden complexion in the area of Navadvipa along the Ganges. He will spread the system of devotional service and the chanting of the names of Krishna, especially in the form of the Hare Krishna *maha-mantra*; Hare Krishna, Hare Krishna, Krishna Krishna, Hare Hare/Hare Rama, Hare Rama, Rama Rama, Hare Hare.

These and other predictions confirm the fact that Sri Caitanya Mahaprabhu would appear to specifically propagate the chanting of the holy names. Of course, now, five hundred years after Lord Caitanya's appearance, we have complete descriptions and elaborations on His life, activities, and philosophy, as written by His close associates. This verifies the fact that the chanting of the *maha-mantra* is the rare and special opportunity given by God for all to be relieved from the problems of the age of Kali and of material life in general. As confirmed in the *Caitanya-caritamrta* (*Adi-lila*, 3.77-78), it is Sri Krishna Caitanya who inaugurates the congregational chanting of the holy names, which is the most sublime of all spiritual sacrifices. Intelligent people will worship Him through this means, while other foolish people will continue in the cycle of repeated birth and death in this material world.

In another place in the *Caitanya-caritamrta* (*Antya-lila*, 20.8-9), Sri Caitanya specifically tells Svarupa Damodara and Ramananda Raya that chanting the holy names is the most practical way to attain salvation from material existence in this age, and anyone who is intelligent and takes up this process of worshiping Krishna will attain the direct shelter of Krishna.

HOW TO CHANT THE MAHA-MANTRA

There are no hard and fast rules for chanting the Hare Krishna *maha-mantra*. One can chant anywhere, anytime, in any situation. In fact, the *Caitanya-caritamrta* (*Antya-lila*, 20.18) describes that chanting the holy name at any time or place, even during sleep or while eating, brings one all perfection. However, there are different stages of chanting. The first stage of chanting is the offensive stage, the second stage is offenseless chanting, and then is the third or pure stage of chanting, which is when the chanting becomes extremely powerful.

The proper way to chant is to give up all of our internal thoughts. As mentioned before, it is almost impossible to meditate on the void and empty our mind of all thinking. Our mind is always being pulled here and there by something. But the chanting process is easy because we simply concentrate on the *mantra*. However, our meditation on the *mantra* will be most effective if we can avoid the internal dialogue we always have within our mind. We should not be chanting while we make plans for the day, or while focusing our attention on other things. The *maha-mantra* is the Supreme in the incarnation of sound. Therefore, we must chant with complete respect and veneration. We must give the *mantra* our full attention, otherwise it is offensive. The process is to simply chant and hear. That is all. If we can do that, then we will make rapid progress and quickly attain the second stage of chanting, which is the offenseless stage.

As one progresses through the second stage and enters the third or pure stage of chanting, one gains direct perception of their spiritual identity and is immediately liberated while still in the material body. The Lord reveals Himself to such a sincere devotee and the devotee relishes the taste of transcendental life. As Srila Rupa Gosvami states in his *Sri Upadesamrita* (text 7), everything about Krishna is spiritually sweet, such as His names, qualities, and activities. But one who suffers from the disease of ignorance cannot taste this sweetness. Yet by chanting the names everyday, a person can destroy this disease and relish the natural sweetness of Krishna's names.

The essential state of mind that one should have while chanting the *maha-mantra* is described by Sri Caitanya Mahaprabhu Himself in the third verse of His *Siksastaka* prayers:

One should chant the holy name of the Lord in a humble state of mind, thinking oneself lower than the straw in the street; one should be more tolerant than a tree, devoid of all sense of false prestige and should be ready to offer all respect to others. In such a state of mind one can chant the holy name of the Lord constantly.

The names of God come directly from the spiritual world, Vaikuntha, which means the place of no anxiety. Therefore, the more we are absorbed in *kuntha*, or anxiety caused by material pursuits, the longer it will take for us to reach the Vaikuntha platform. But the more we associate with the Vaikuntha vibration of the *maha-mantra*, the sooner we will progress to the stage of experiencing the ecstasy that comes from awakening our transcendental love for the Supreme. The *Caitanya-caritamrta* (*Adi-lila*, 8.27) confirms that bodily transformations of spiritual ecstasy, such as trembling, perspiration, a faltering voice, and tears, may manifest when one's spiritual love for the Lord is actually awakened.

*　*　*

To begin progressing on the path of chanting the *maha-mantra*, it is prescribed that the practitioner chant on beads called *japa-mala*, similar to a rosary, that consists of 108 beads with one extra head bead, which is larger than the others. This represents the 108 *Upanishads*, or, as described elsewhere, Krishna in the form of the head bead surrounded by 108 of His most advanced devotees. One chants the Hare Krishna *mantra* once on each bead from the head bead all the way around the 108 beads. This is one round, or one *mala*. Then without chanting on the Krishna bead, turn the beads around in your hand and go in the opposite direction and chant another round. One should try to set a certain amount of time aside each day, preferably in the morning, to peacefully sit down or walk and chant the particular number of rounds you have set for yourself. One may chant two rounds, four rounds, or whatever one can do.

For those who are serious, it is prescribed that they chant a total of at least sixteen rounds everyday. With a little practice, this normally takes about two hours. Two rounds will take about fifteen minutes. But one should set a fixed number of rounds to chant everyday. Then one can also spend some time reading *Bhagavad-gita* or *Srimad-Bhagavatam* to enhance his spiritual development. A daily program of chanting and reading will produce definite results very quickly.

You may be able to purchase a set of *japa* beads at certain import shops. If you cannot find them anywhere, you can also make them. Simply go to a crafts shop and purchase 108 beads of the same size and one larger bead of your choice for the Krishna bead. Also get a length of durable nylon cord. String the 108 beads with a knot in between each one and bring the two ends of the cord through one hole of the Krishna bead and out the other side where you tie the two ends of the cord together in a firm knot. Then cut the remaining lengths of the cord so you have a small tassle. Now you have got your own set of beads for *japa* meditation.

CONCLUSION

This chapter contains descriptions of the glories and effectiveness of chanting the *maha-mantra*. Those who are intelligent will certainly add this spiritual practice to their lives. By taking it seriously, they will soon notice a change in their disposition. They may feel more peaceful, content, happy, etc. One trait that is always noticeable in a person who seriously takes to *bhakti-yoga* and the chanting of the *maha-mantra* is a decrease in such feelings as anxiety and distress, up to the point of complete fearlessness. Once someone is no longer afraid of death, then what is there to be afraid of in this material world? One loses such fear when he or she is spiritually self-realized and knows he or she is not this body and, therefore, not actually subject to death, but merely undergoes a transformation of giving up the body. And by taking shelter of the protection of the holy names of Krishna, one will remain spiritually safe in any condition of life.

It is unfortunate that many people in the world are either not aware of this transcendental knowledge or have no taste for it. For such people, extensive material engagements and plan-making are their only occupations. But this kind of activity is like working hard for nothing because in the end one is awarded only with death, in which all material assets are lost. As stated in *Srimad-Bhagavatam* (3.9.10), nondevotees engage in very troublesome work and cannot sleep well at night because they are absorbed in worldly plans. By providence their ambitions are frustrated and they continue in the cycle of repeated birth and death in material existence.

The only way, therefore, to get release from such material problems and be free from the contamination of the age of Kali is to take up the practice of *bhakti-yoga* and regularly chant the Hare Krishna *maha-mantra* while observing the regulations as best as one can. By chanting the *maha-mantra* with faith, a person will eventually purify his or her consciousness and reach success. As more people begin to chant the holy names, the troubles and upheavals found everywhere will diminish, and this age of Kali-yuga can become like the peaceful and bountiful Satya-yuga--the golden age. This is actually the prediction made by Lord Sri Caitanya Mahaprabhu, who said (in *Caitanya-caritamrta, Adi-lila*, 7.26) that love of God will one day inundate the world and drown everyone, regardless of who or what they are. Then many beneficial changes in this world will be seen. Therefore, the best thing any of us can do is to take it seriously.

Let there be all victory for the chanting of the holy name of Lord Krishna, which can cleanse the mirror of the heart and stop the miseries of the blazing fire of material existence. That chanting is the waxing moon that spreads the white lotus of good fortune for all living entities. It is the life and soul of all education. The chanting of the holy name of Krishna expands the blissful ocean of transcendental life. It gives a cooling effect to everyone and enables one to taste full nectar at every step. (*Siksastaka* 1, written by Sri Caitanya Mahaprabhu)

CHAPTER ELEVEN

Qualifications of a Spiritual Leader

Taking to a spiritual path and learning spiritual knowledge means accepting information as given by someone else, whether it is from a personal teacher or from someone's book. Of course, this is the case in any field of study. So how do we find a qualified spiritual teacher? And do we need one?

When we talk about what a spiritual master is and whether we need one, there is often a tendency to think that there is no reason for us to have a personal spiritual guide advising us what we should or should not do. "After all," we may tell ourselves, "I've gotten this far on my own, why should I let anyone else cramp my style or tell me how to live? I'm getting along alright." Thus, due to pride and a large ego, we may dismiss the idea of trying to understand what a qualified spiritual master is and whether there is a need for us to have one.

We may also have a stereotyped idea of what is a guru. Practically speaking, a spiritual master is any spiritual leader, whether a rabbi, ayatollah, pope, bodhisattva, a minister, the preacher on your television, etc., who is meant to guide people by disseminating spiritual knowledge. But, unfortunately, many times in novels, movies, or television shows, a guru is presented as someone talking in an Eastern accent, barely able to speak English, comically unfamiliar with Western habits, or speaking flowery words about some vague philosophy that may seem far out yet remains completely impractical or useless for our daily life. This is hardly anything like a real spiritual master.

We may also hear of different *svamis* who have come to the West and started controversial *ashramas* or cults where they engage in questionable activities or are looking for ways to gain political power. Such cults may also be plagued with various power struggles from within. And let us not forget about all the televangelists who have gotten caught with their pants down. Of course, this makes for good stories on the nightly news, but it still does nothing to provide society with any understanding of what is a real spiritual master or how

213

civilization can benefit from authentic spiritual knowledge. In fact, it usually makes people more skeptical about accepting anyone as a spiritual authority.

Accepting a spiritual master is by no means a fad that we follow because our neighbors did it. Neither do we take a guru in order to get his blessings for any foolish thing we want to do by paying him money so he can keep himself fat and living comfortably. And neither do we accept just anyone who calls himself a spiritual teacher. There are so-called spiritual teachers who encourage everyone to engage in as much sex as they like as a means to enlightenment. This is certainly a way to gain many followers very quickly and may sound very interesting at first to those who are gullible and inexperienced in spiritual matters. But, actually, such activities in the name of spiritual progress are a waste of time and produce results in the mode of ignorance, such as getting sexually transmitted diseases. Similarly, a gospel preacher may be on a stage ranting and raving about how you are going to hell if you do not accept Jesus as your personal savior, when actually his main interest is getting your dollars into his pocket. These sort of things are not the purpose of a real guru, minister, or spiritual teacher. Any so-called gurus or ministers who teach in this way are only rascals who cheat people out of attaining anything substantial. All sincere seekers of higher truths must be warned to steer clear of such bogus teachers. When we understand what the qualifications are for a real spiritual teacher, we will see how few are really qualified.

The way to know who is an authorized spiritual master or teacher is to be informed about the character, qualities, and knowledge that one must have in order to be a qualified spiritual authority. Not just anyone can call themselves a spiritual teacher or guru.

WHAT IS A SPIRITUAL MASTER

The first qualification one must have to be a bona fide spiritual master or qualified teacher is a complete understanding of the science of God. Regardless of one's social position or birth, if one is a pure devotee of the Lord, then he can teach others. This is verified in the *Caitanya-caritamrta* (*Madhya-lila*, 8.128) which explains that regardless of whether one is a *brahmana* (priest), *sannyasi* (renounced mendicant), or a *sudra* (laborer), if he knows the science of Krishna he can be a spiritual master.

The *Padma Purana*, however, mentions that even if one is a highly elevated *brahmana*, familiar with all the rituals of the scripture, if he is not purified, he cannot be a spiritual master.

The characteristics of one who is purified are stated by Sri Rupa Gosvami in his *Upadesamrta* (Text 1), in which he writes that a person is qualified to make disciples all over the world if he can control his mind, anger, tongue, belly, genitals, and the urge to speak. This means that such a spiritual master can control his senses, mind, anger, belly, and genitals because he is purified by transcendental knowledge and spiritual realizations. He is not just faking it by going through the motions and offering some lip service to maintain his honor and prestige. He actually knows he is not the body and, therefore, being completely self-realized, he is not bothered by bodily demands. If a spiritual leader cannot control his mind, his words, anger, belly, or genitals, then he obviously is not yet purified and not qualified to lead others. He still identifies with his body and, therefore, caters to bodily urges. For one to be a *svami* or master, he must be a master of his senses: a *gosvami*. If he cannot yet control his senses, then he is not yet ready to be a bona fide spiritual guide who can teach throughout the world. Instead, he must continue to accept instruction for his own purification from those who are more advanced. In other words, he cannot set others free as long as he is still tied up.

A few more of the characteristics of a qualified spiritual master are mentioned in the following verses:

If one is seen to be unlimitedly merciful, perfectly complete, distinguished by all good qualities, fixed in activities for the benefit of all living entities, free from lust, possessing all types of perfections, all-knowing [in spiritual knowledge], and capable of slashing all doubts of the disciple while always remaining alert to be engaged in the service of the Lord, then such a person may be known as a guru. (*Hari-bhakti-vilasa* 1.45,46, *Vishnu-smriti vacana*)

When one has fully assimilated all the conclusions of the revealed scriptures and thereby establishes the codes of perfect behavior for others, himself also acting strictly according to those codes, such a knower of the Absolute Truth of perfect character is glorified by the title of *acarya*. (*Vayu Purana*)

A real spiritual master teaches in accord with the previous saints and sages as well as the standard scriptural texts. For assuring ourselves of continued spiritual progress, these three guides of guru, *shastra* (scripture) and *sadhu* (saintly persons) must be consulted. If we find that, for example, a spiritual teacher diverts in behavior or differs in the philosophical teachings that are set by the standard Vedic references or previous *acaryas*, then his authority should be questioned and he should be avoided, unless it is otherwise shown that his purpose is justified. As stated in the *Hari-bhakti-vilasa* (1.101): "One who [assuming the position of an *acarya*] delivers irregular speeches contradictory to the standard Vaishnava scriptures, as well as one [as a disciple] who hears such unauthorized speeches, are both destined for hell." Thus, comparing the three above mentioned sources of knowledge (guru, *sadhu*, and *shastra*) as a system of checks and balances will enable us to be sure we remain on the right path.

The consciousness of the qualified spiritual master exists in the spiritual atmosphere, and he transmits from his lotus mouth the transcendental sound vibration of the spiritual planets in Vaikuntha. This is similar to a radio which transmits sounds from places many miles away. But to transmit the energy of the spiritual world, the master's consciousness must be completely purified. If one cannot control his senses, it shows that his consciousness is still on the material platform, at least to an extent. Therefore, he cannot deliver pure spiritual sound to his followers. Since the disciples or followers of a guru or spiritual leader cannot advance beyond the level of the teacher, such followers must be certain their teacher is qualified, or they should not accept him. "O Devi, there are many so-called gurus who amass wealth from their disciples, but the bona fide spiritual master who can destroy all the miseries of his disciples is rare." (*Purana-vakya*) Furthermore, "A person who by keeping disciples becomes desirous of receiving personal service and fame is certainly unfit to be considered on the platform of guru." (*Vishnu smriti*)

Also, one should not pose as a spiritual master if he cannot deliver those who depend on him. The *Srimad-Bhagavatam* (5.5.18) explains that a person should not become a spiritual master, nor a father, husband, mother, or a demigod if he cannot deliver those who depend on him from the cycle of repeated birth and death in the material worlds.

The original spiritual master is actually God Himself. The Lord appears as both the *acarya*, the spiritual master, and as the Supersoul to deliver the living beings. As stated in *Srimad-Bhagavatam* (11.29.6), the Lord appears externally as the spiritual master and internally as the Supersoul in order to help guide the living being back to the Lord's spiritual abode.

Naturally, the Lord as Supersoul in the heart instructs and guides us from within, as confirmed in *Caitanya-caritamrta* (*Madhya-lila*, 8.265). So why not simply take quidance from the Supersoul? The problem is, as explained in *Srimad-Bhagavatam* (8.24.52), that although the Supersoul is always ready to instruct us, and is the dearmost friend and well-wisher of everyone, because we are filled with lusty desires for bodily pleasure, we cannot hear or understand the Lord. So to cure us of such misguided lusty desires which bind us to repeated birth and death in this material world, and causes us to forget the real goal of life, the Supreme manifests Himself externally in the form of the spiritual master and Vedic texts and instructs those of us who will listen. This is how the Lord is always ready to help us from within and from without. Thus, the pure devotee spiritual master, who can receive the message of the Supersoul within and deliver that pure sound vibration to his students in an untainted and unchanged form, is practically identical with God, as confirmed in *Caitanya-caritamrita* (*Adi-lila*, 1.61).

This is how God delivers the living entities from the material world through the bona fide spiritual master. Therefore, a real spiritual leader should not be considered an ordinary person. As explained in *Caitanya-caritamrta* (*Adi-lila*, 1.45, 47), the spiritual master and Krishna are nondifferent in that the Lord instructs the devotees through the pure representative. Furthermore, in *Srimad-*

Bhagavatam (11.17.27) we find that no one should disrespect the spiritual master in any way, thinking him to be ordinary, because he is the representative of the Supreme and all the demigods. The *Padma Purana* also warns that any person who considers the authentic spiritual master to be an ordinary human is to be taken as a resident of hell.

If the pure spiritual leader is practically identical with God in his ability to enable the living entities in the material creation to become enlightened and provide them with proper instructions for getting free from material suffering, then it is especially important for us to make sure we are not cheated by a bogus teacher. If someone poses as a great spiritual leader but is not qualified, he actually becomes a great disturbance to society. Not only are his instructions ineffective because they lack potency, but he cannot deliver the true, untainted message of God because he is not in tune with God. He will not be able to deliver himself, what to speak of those who depend on him for guidance. Therefore, the sign of a pure devotee is that he is one hundred percent always engaged in the service of the Supreme and has no other motive. The spiritual master never claims to be God, but is a servant of God. If he claims to be God, then you can know he is a number one fool. He simply wants to imitate God, which no one can do. No one should allow themselves to be exploited by such a fool.

> It is enjoined that one must abandon a guru who is guru only in name, and who is polluted by sense enjoyment, a fool devoid of intelligence to discriminate between duty and non-duty, and who follows any path other than pure devotional service to the Lord. (*Mahabharata, Udyoga-parva*, 179.25)

> One must abandon a professional, materialistic or ancestral imitationist guru and thus accept the shelter of a bona fide spiritual master who is a genuine guru. (*Bhakti-sandarbha sankhya* 210)

Unfortunately, many people unknowingly put faith in so-called spiritual authorities who are actually not of much help. In many cases people do not know what to look for in a spiritual leader. This is actually very dangerous, as pointed out in *Srimad-Bhagavatam* (7.5.31): those entrapped in the delusion of trying to enjoy material life and have accepted other blind men as their leader or guru cannot understand that the real goal of life is to engage in devotional service to the Lord and return to the spiritual realm. As one blind man follows another blind man into the ditch, one materialist follows another into the strong bonds of fruitive labor to suffer the miseries of materialistic life.

For example, a materially attached political leader may seem attractive to people because of the promises he makes or the jokes he relates in his speeches. Or a so-called guru may perform some magic tricks or speak some flowery philosophy to impress other foolish men. But such leaders actually keep people bound up in the clutches of material existence. They may offer the people some hope that things will get better, but generally there is no substantial variation in the usual course of events. Therefore, people gradually become frustrated and want to elect a new leader. But if one simply accepts the Supreme and the bona fide representative of God as their authority and guide, they will know what to do. They will not have to worry anymore about being cheated in their search for answers. As stated in *Srimad-Bhagavatam* (8.24.50-51), people who are ignorant of the goal of life accept other foolish men as their leader. A materialistic guru only teaches economic development and sense gratification, causing his followers to continue in materialistic life. But intelligent men seek guidance from the Supreme Personality who sees everything and who gives spiritual knowledge by which one can quickly regain his original spiritual position.

The bona fide spiritual master can deliver the message of the Supreme to his disciple in several ways. One is that, as mentioned, he delivers the same spiritual sound vibration as that in Vaikuntha. Another is that he delivers the same instructions and guidance as the Lord does in such texts as *Bhagavad-gita*, *Srimad-Bhagavatam*, and others. He delivers the same process of enlightenment and awakens devotional service in the heart of the disciple. And the spiritual master also awakens the disciple's awareness of God as the Supersoul within every living entity. But to do this the spiritual master must be empowered by God. In other words, he must be completely pure and self-realized to the point of knowing what his relationship is with the Supreme. Only then can he reawaken the relationship that others have with the Supreme.

A spiritual master who can actually instruct others so they can attain the spiritual strata is considered the most respected and venerable of all persons. This is elaborated upon in the *Manu-samhita*:

> Of him who gives natural birth and him who gives the knowledge of the *Veda*, the giver of the *Veda* is the more venerable father; for the birth for the sake of the *Veda* ensures eternal rewards both in this life and after death. Let him consider that he received a mere animal existence when his parents begat him through mutual affection, and when he was born from the womb of his mother. But that birth which a teacher acquainted with the whole *Veda*, in accordance with the law, procures for him through *Savitri* [initiation into chanting the *mantra*, specifically the *gayatri*], is real, exempt from age and death. The pupil must know that that man also who benefits him by instruction in the *Veda*, be it little or much, is called in these institutes his guru, in consequence of that benefit conferred by instruction in the *Veda*. That *brahmana* who is the giver of the birth for the sake of the *Veda* and the teacher of the prescribed duties becomes by law the father of an aged man, even though he himself be a child. (*Manu*.2.146-150). . . For a man destitute of sacred knowledge is indeed a child, and he who teaches him the *Veda* is

his father; for the sages have always said 'child' to an ignorant man, and 'father' to a teacher of the *Veda*. (*Manu.*2.153). . . A man is not therefore considered venerable because his head is grey; him who, though young, has learned the *Veda*, the gods consider to be venerable. (*Manu.*2.156)

Many persons cannot even hear about the soul, and even after hearing about him, many cannot have any realization of him; this is because an instructor who is a genuine seer of the truth is rarely found, and realization can only be obtained by becoming very expert. And since to receive instruction from such an expert spiritual master is rare, only a selected few can know the soul in truth. (*Katha Upanishad* 1.2.7)

Herewith, the significance of the true spiritual master has been explained. The gift of spiritual knowledge as given by the *acarya* is priceless. It is difficult to find authentic spiritual knowledge, and once found it can be hard to understand, what to speak of knowing how to utilize it in our daily lives. But by the grace of the spiritual master, we not only are able to understand such knowledge, but we also learn how to practically apply it in our lives to solve all the problems of material existence.

The authorized spiritual master does not make up anything new or change the message or alter Vedic knowledge. He simply repeats the same instructions given by the previous authorities. This is the authorized process as given through the disciplic succession. The spiritual master finds new ways to preach the same message so that it can be practically applied in the present times.

The way the disciplic succession or *parampara* system works is that the bona fide guru is he who received the mercy of his guru. This goes on like this from generation to generation, extending back through time to Lord Krishna Himself. In other words, Krishna originally taught this knowledge to Lord Brahma, who taught Narada, who taught Vyasadeva, and so on. Therefore, this knowledge is carefully handed down from person to person in the present form we have today. These persons in the disciplic succession are not ordinary, but are perfectly self-realized and are the transparent medium by which this knowledge descends. In this way, we can directly hear Lord Krishna speak, although it appears as if we are simply getting instruction from the present spiritual master. This is the mystery of the disciplic succession. By coming in contact with this *parampara* network, we can directly hear the unadulterated message of the Supreme. If one avoids the disciplic succession, then one's spiritual knowledge remains imperfect.

In the Vedic tradition, there are four recognized *parampara* systems called *sampradayas*. One *sampradaya* comes from Lord Brahma, one from Sri (the goddess of fortune), another one comes from the four Kumara brothers headed by Sanat-Kumara, and another *sampradaya* comes from Lord Shiva.

An example of an authorized and complete disciplic succession is the one we belong to, the Brahma-*sampradaya*. The list of personalities in it are as follows: (1) Lord Krishna, (2) Brahma, (3) Narada, (4) Vyasa, (5) Madhva, (6) Padmanabha, (7) Nrihari, (8) Madhava, (9) Aksobhya, (10) Jayatirtha, (11) Jnanasindhu, (12) Dayanidhi, (13) Vidyanidhi, (14) Rajendra, (15) Jayadharma, (16) Purusottama, (17) Brahmanyatirtha, (18) Vyasatirtha, (19) Laksmipati, (20) Madhavendra Puri, (21) Isvara Puri, (22) Lord Caitanya Mahaprabhu, (23) Rupa Gosvami (along with Svarupa and Sanatana), (24) Raghunatha and Jiva Gosvami, (25) Krishnadasa Kaviraja, (26) Narottama, (27) Visvanatha, (28) [Baladeva] Jagannatha, (29) Bhaktivinode, (30) Gaurakisora, (31) Bhaktisiddhanta, (32) and our own spiritual master, His Divine Grace A. C. Bhaktivedanta Swami.

So if one is considering a particular spiritual master or teacher, first find out what disciplic succession to which he belongs. If he is not a part of any authorized disciplic succession, then his teachings and whatever *mantras* he offers will lack potency and you will not get full benefit. Therefore, if one feels perplexed about how to find a bona fide spiritual master, all one needs to do is first accept the Supreme as the original spiritual master and then seek out His pure representative. Simply understand what Krishna says in the revealed scripture, as presented in this chapter, and you will know what qualifications to look for in an authentic spiritual leader from whom you can take instruction and guidance. By coming in contact with a proper spiritual master, you will be able to understand transcendental knowledge which will answer all your questions and relieve you of your uncertainties. As stated in *Bhagavad-gita* (4.36, 39): even if a person is the worst of sinners, he can cross the ocean of material miseries by boarding the boat of spiritual knowledge. Such a man who is faithful and in control of his senses, quickly attains the supreme spiritual peace.

IS IT NECESSARY TO HAVE A SPIRITUAL MASTER?

Whether it is necessary or not to accept a spiritual master or recognize a spiritual authority from whom to take guidance is something that is often times unclear to people. But from the *Bhagavatam* (11.22.10) we learn that since a person cannot attain self-realization alone by his own effort, and since he has been covered by ignorance from the beginning of time, there must be another person who knows the spiritual truth and can impart this knowledge to him. In other words, though a person may be born with an intuitive awareness of God or have a natural tendency for searching out spiritual knowledge, one must approach an external source for enlightenment in order to fully awaken such spiritual consciousness. Furthermore, it has been understood by transcendental scholars that without the assistance of a bona fide spiritual guide, one will not be able to fathom the depths of spiritual knowledge. Therefore, even in such ancient writings as the *Atharva-veda*, it is recommended that we should take guidance from the learned masters:

O man, pass with devotion, ever fleeting day and night, born of Dawn, pervading all the four directions, bright and dark in appearance! Go near the learned gurus, who remain in pleasure in the company of God. Few learned persons attain to prosperity, few realize the real essence of things. There are others who speedily imbibe the knowledge of God. O man, approach all these learned persons and derive knowledge from them. (*Atharva-veda*, 18.2.11, 14)

If one is too rebellious to accept guidance and instruction from without, he will never become qualified to receive instruction from within, from the Supersoul, and will be forced to accept nothing more than his own foolishness. Therefore, Sri Krishna explains in *Bhagavad-gita* (4.34) that a person must approach a genuine spiritual master, inquire submissively and render service to him who can give you spiritual knowledge since he is relf-realized. The *Mundaka Upanishad* (1.2.12) also states: "To understand that transcendental science, one must approach a bona fide spiritual master."

For understanding transcendental knowledge there is no question that one must accept a bona fide spiritual master who can, with his mature spiritual realizations, aid people in general. This is further confirmed in *Srimad-Bhagavatam* (3.7.39) which emphasizes that a person cannot get the confidential knowledge of devotional service unless he is helped by the pure devotees. As also described in the *Bhagavatam* (11.3.21), a person must find and take shelter of a genuine spiritual master by initiation if he expects to find real happiness. A genuine spiritual master is one who knows the conclusions of spiritual knowledge and can teach them to others.

In the *Svetasvatara Upanishad* (6.23) it is explained that all the conclusions of the Vedic literature are revealed to those great souls who engage in exclusive devotional service to the Supreme Lord, and also similarly serve the spiritual master in such pure devotion. And the *Chandogya Upanishad* (6.18.2) states that a person who accepts initiation from the *acarya* and serves him with devotion knows the Supreme Absolute Truth.

The point to remember is that this life we are currently undergoing is nothing more than a moment on our great path towards spiritual realization. We have experienced the full range of problems that occur in material existence lifetime after lifetime. Now we find that we are not only still looking for happiness, but also searching for answers to our questions, solutions to our problems, an easier way to live, etc., etc. How many more lifetimes we continue with this process is up to us. But now that we are in the human form of life, we have particular advantages we can utilize. Some of these advantages are explained in *Srimad-Bhagavatam* (11.20.17). The human body, awarded by nature, is a rare achievement amongst the many species of life. The human form is like a strong boat, the spiritual master is the captain of the boat, and the instructions of the Supreme Being, as found in the Vedic literature, are compared to favorable winds that propel the boat on the proper course. A person who does not take advantage of such an opportunity to cross the ocean of material existence is comparable to one who kills his own soul.

This is the process for utilizing the human form of life properly in order to become free from fruitive activities which cause continued birth and death in the material world. Within this material creation, under the influence of the modes of nature and our accumulated *karma*, we are going up and down through various good or bad situations. But once we come in contact with a bona fide spiritual master, everything can change. Only the most fortunate, however, intelligently avail themselves of the association offered by the pure devotee spiritual master. This is further explained in the *Caitanya-caritamrta* (*Madhya-lila*, 19.151-164). Throughout the universe living beings are wandering amongst the lower and upper planetary systems because of their *karma*. Out of innumerable living entities, one is greatly fortunate if he meets a genuine spiritual master. Only by the mercy of such a master, and the mercy of the Supreme, does one get knowledge of *bhakti* (devotional service) to the Supreme. When he is given the seed of *bhakti*, he should plant it in his heart and care for it by watering it with hearing and chanting about Sri Krishna so the seed will sprout. If the creeper continues to grow with the practice of devotional service, it will grow beyond the boundaries of the universe and reach the spiritual world. There it grows more and enters the supreme spiritual planet Goloka Vrindavan and finally reaches the shelter of Krishna's lotus feet. There the creeper produces the fruit of love of God. When the fruit of love ripens, it falls and the gardener tastes the sweetness of this love with great happiness. This is the highest perfection of life and makes all other material perfections seem insignificant.

This is the perfection one can attain by the grace of the spiritual master. Therefore, by receiving the blessings of the guru, one can become very powerful, both materially and spiritually. If, however, one does not take a spiritual master, he remains like a ship without a rudder with no possibility of reaching the proper destination. Thus, throughout the Vedic literature, it is always emphasized that one should accept a bona fide spiritual master in order to keep advancing in one's spiritual development. "Unless one is initiated by a bona fide spiritual master, all his devotional activities are useless. A person who is not properly initiated can descend again into the animal species." (*Hari-bhakti-vilasa*, 2.6 from *Vishnu-yamala*)

> *Diksa* [accepting initiation from a bona fide spiritual master] is the process by which one can awaken his transcendental knowledge and vanquish all reactions caused by sinful activity. A person expert in the study of the revealed scriptures knows this process as *diksa*. (*Bhakti-sandarbha*, 283)

The above verse points out that by initiation one can be freed from sinful reactions. This is because when the spiritual master accepts one as a disciple in the Vedic tradition, he takes the disciple's *karmic* reactions. *Karmic* reactions always affect us in various ways, but they also take the shape of continuous material desires which bind us to further material activities and their reactions. When the spiritual master takes our *karmic* reactions at the time of initiation, he paves the way for us to make spiritual progress without any hindrances. In this way, we are protected by the spiritual master. If, however, one takes a spiritual master and gets initiated and then goes off to engage again in the same materialistic activities as before, ignoring the guru's instructions, then this is extremely offensive on the part of the disciple and leaves him with no chance of making any advancement. The offenses and sinful activities of the disciple can become an added burden for the spiritual master. Therefore, the disciple must take the process of initiation seriously.

Initiation essentially means to receive the pure knowledge of spiritual consciousness. At that time the disciple is usually taught how to chant the sacred *mantra* to awaken his spiritual vision. By the potency of the initiating process, one can immediately attain the level of a qualified *brahmana*. This is verified in the following verse: "By chemical manipulation, bell metal is turned into gold when touched by mercury; similarly, when a person is properly initiated, he can acquire the qualities of a *brahmana*." (*Bhakti-sandarbha*, 298, from the *Tattvasgara*) The disciple is then considered to be twice-born. Initiation by the bona fide guru is the second birth, above and beyond one's ordinary birth from the womb of a mother.

Becoming twice-born is also mentioned in the Bible: "Jesus answered and said unto him, Verily, verily, I say unto thee, except a man be born again, he cannot see the kingdom of God." (*John* 3.3) This refers to one's spiritual birth, as in taking initiation from a bona fide representative of God. In modern Christianity, this usually means accepting Jesus as one's personal saviour, taking vows or going through catechism, being baptized, and becoming a member of the Church. Of course, Christianity does not have an established *parampara* system as found in the Vedic culture, which has left the Bible open for many opinions of what it means. In fact, there are now so many different Christian sects, with more cropping up all the time, that it may be hard to decide which interpretation of Christian theology one wants to follow. This is a sensitive issue. This does not mean that there are not many interpretations of the *Vedas*, but we can at least see the qualifications of the commentator or interpreter by finding out what *parampara* he belongs to. If he does not belong to a *parampara*, or belongs to a bogus one, then his opinions need not be taken very seriously. Christianity does not have such a system of checks and balances. But, nonetheless, the Bible does stress the need for a second or spiritual birth. "Being born again, not of corruptible seed [from the womb], but of incorruptible, by the word of God [the spiritual *mantra* or scripture], which liveth and abideth forever." (*I Peter* 1:23)

Once initiated by a proper spiritual authority, one is connected through the *parampara* system to the Lord Himself, just as a light bulb is connected through the electrical line to the power house that charges it. If one adheres to the guidance of a bona fide spiritual master, nothing will prevent him from attaining complete spiritual perfection in this very life. One will not have to wait for his next birth, but can achieve everything in this present life in order to experience the Absolute Truth. Thus, by the grace of the Lord one gets a proper spiritual master, and by the grace of the spiritual master one gets the Lord.

The safest way, therefore, to become purified and remain on the proper path is to approach a pure devotee of the Lord for guidance. One will then be sure to be connected with the Supreme and receive good instruction for executing spiritual practices. As confirmed in the *Bhagavatam* (6.1.16-17), a sinful person can become completely purified simply by serving the pure devotee of the Lord and learning the art of devotional service. Austerity, penance, celibacy, or other methods cannot completely purify a person. The most auspicious path to follow is that of the pure devotees.

HOW THE SPIRITUAL MASTER TEACHES

Because a saintly person is always interested in seeing everyone in society advance, he is always ready to teach transcendental knowledge. He also teaches by setting the proper example that everyone should follow. As stated in *Bhagavad-gita* (3.21): whatever is done by a great man, and whatever standard he sets by his actions, common men follow. Therefore, a guru must be ready to teach in many ways. Because the spiritual master is the authority on transcendental topics, he sets the correct standard in everything he does. However, if a guru cannot follow the appropriate standard or maintain the exemplary criterion in order to show others how spiritual life is meant to be performed, then we can understand that he is not a guru.

When we have found a true saintly person, we should approach them with respect and be ready to hear their advice with open ears. The student receives knowledge from the spiritual master through aural reception, which also includes reading his books. In this way, the initiate learns how to proceed on the spiritual path while living in the material world.

A true spiritual leader is always concerned about the well-being of his followers and the people in general. He does not take the post of spiritual authority for his own benefit. This is one reason why he must maintain his purity. His duty is to train the disciple in a way that will enable the disciple to remain free from the influence of the illusory energy. The spiritual master recognizes the natural propensities of the student and instructs him how to use those propensities to make spiritual progress. Thus, the student becomes free from the modes of nature and can ultimately be released from the grip of material existence by acting according to his nature while under the guidance of his guru. This is how the bona fide spiritual master explains the scriptures so we can apply them in our lives in a practical way. For example, if one is an intellectual, one learns from the guru how to use that ability for spiritual progress. Or if one simply likes to work hard, the spiritual master can teach the disciple how to work so he does not unnecessarily waste his energy in useless endeavors and can make spiritual progress at the same time.

Some people have the idea that to receive enlightenment, the guru touches the disciple on the forehead and suddenly, in a flash of light, all the energy and knowledge of the guru is then transferred to the desciple. This is not exactly how it works, although coming in direct contact with a potent spiritual master can give the disciple special realizations and experiences. But in all cases, what is necessary is that the spiritual master be satisfied with the disciple. Only then is knowledge automatically manifest to the student of spiritual science. The point is that the spiritual teacher and student must both be bona fide. The spiritual master must observe the potential disciple for some time to find out whether he is sincere and will be a qualified disciple. Then the spiritual master explains everything to the disciple on the authority of Vedic wisdom. This is the process as practiced for thousands of years. Furthermore, the disciple receives spiritual knowledge through the process of submissive inquiries and a good service attitude. This makes the relationship between spiritual master and disciple very strong, whereas knowledge given from the guru to disciple in exchange for money lacks potency and is not so effective.

When the spiritual master teaches, he must continue to give instructions even if the disciple is sometimes unable to follow them. There is no benefit in compromising the authorized Vedic process in order to allow the disciple to justify continued engagement in faulty *karmic* activities. As questioned by Lord Rishabhadeva in *Srimad-Bhagavatam* (5.5.17), how can a person learned in spiritual knowledge engage someone in activities that will further entangle him in material existence? How can a gentleman allow a blind man to walk towards danger? No kind person will allow this. Therefore, the bona fide spiritual teacher must always explain the authorized and effective process for advancement regardless of whether everyone can perfectly follow it or not.

The spiritual master must also not become overly impatient with the disciple, otherwise the disciple may become too discouraged and give up or leave altogether. This, of course, is counterproductive. Everyone must be encouraged and taught properly. This is further explained in the *Manu-samhita* (2.159-161):

Created beings must be instructed in what concerns their welfare without giving them pain, and sweet and gentle speech must be used by a teacher who desires to abide by the sacred law. He, forsooth, whose speech and thoughts are pure and ever perfectly guarded, gains the whole reward which is conferred by the Vedanta. Let him not, even though in pain, speak words cutting others to the quick; let him not injure others in thought or deed; let him not utter speeches which make others afraid of him, since that will prevent him from gaining heaven.

We should understand, however, that even if the spiritual master does seem forceful in the way he teaches, this should be considered his mercy on us to make us serious and determined. This side of the spiritual master's personality is usually shown only to the more advanced disciples who can follow all the orders of the guru. But it is only the spiritual master who reminds us that in spite of all we have or hope to accomplish, the clock keeps ticking away and with every tick our life decreases in its duration. Similarly, we may have worked hard to build a nice big house, and now we enjoy having our friends over and hearing their compliments about how beautiful our house is and so on. But the spiritual master can see that actually the house is on fire and will soon be destroyed. He may firmly tell us to get out quickly because if we do not we will be destroyed along with the house. If we argue with him and say, "Why should I leave this house? It's a nice house and I like it here," then we are simply securing our doom. Everything in this material world is continually approaching its end, and for this we must prepare ourselves, of which the spiritual master always reminds us. In this way, he is actually our best friend.

In *Srimad-Bhagavatam* (5.5.16), Lord Rishabhadeva says the materialistic person is ignorant of the real goal of life. He is simply interested in fulfilling his lusty desires. The foolish person does not realize that his selfish interest for sense gratification causes him to dive deep into the ocean of suffering. Therefore, we need to take guidance from a bona fide spiritual master who can remove our ignorance by instructing us about the real goal of life and how to achieve it.

DUTY OF A DISCIPLE

The primary duty of a disciple is to follow the orders of the spiritual master. For one who does becomes very powerful. An example of this is King Citraketu, as described in the *Bhagavatam* (6.16.28-29). Citraketu attained the ruling position of the planet of the Vidyadharas because of his spiritual advancement after only one week of chanting the *mantra* that was given to him by his spiritual master. Within a short time he became more spiritually enlightened and attained the shelter of Lord Anantadeva.

We, of course, should not expect such rapid results in our own spiritual practice, but it is not impossible. The main point is that the disciple learns how to please the Lord and attain His shelter. This is verified in *Srimad-Bhagavatam* (11.3.22), which explains that the disciple should learn how to perform devotional service from the spiritual master. Since the Supreme Being reveals Himself to the pure devotee, if the disciple learns from the pure devotee how to favorably serve the Supreme, then the Lord will also reveal Himself to the disciple.

Another way we get the shelter of the Supreme is simply by accepting a bona fide guru who is connected with the proper *parampara* system, as explained earlier. The way this works is that whatever worship, love, and devotion the disciple offers to the spiritual master goes through the complete chain of spiritual masters in the disciplic succession and is received by the Lord Himself. Thus, when the spiritual master is pleased with the disciple, we can know that the Lord is also pleased. The disciple may not so easily develop love for God, nor may he be so qualified to render direct service to the Supreme. But by rendering personal service to the spiritual master who guides and encourages us, and by developing love for him, everything becomes easy.

If, however, we accept a genuine spiritual master and then reject him, this is a great offense and all our spiritual advancement becomes null and void. As the *Brahma-vaivarta Purana* states: "One pollutes his own intelligence and exhibits severe weakness of character when he rejects his own spiritual master. Indeed, such a person has already rejected the Supreme Lord Hari."

On the other hand, if, in our neophyte stage, we are initiated by a spiritual master who we later find is not authorized nor linked up to a bona fide disciplic succession, we should definitely reject him and take initiation from someone who is properly situated. This is confirmed in the *Narada-pancaratra* verse *avaisnavopadistena*, (also found in *Hari-bhakti-vilasa*, 4.366) which states: "One who is initiated into a *mantra* by a non-Vaishnava must go to hell. Therefore he should again be initiated properly, according to the prescribed method, by a Vaishnava guru." Once we have been initiated by an authorized spiritual master who is qualified and who represents a bona fide disciplic succession, and if we are sincere and ready to take advice from him, then all our problems will be solved. Of course, the disciple should also observe the spiritual teacher for some time to make sure he is qualified before taking initiation from him. If we find the teacher is not so qualified, then it is best simply to wait and approach someone later on who is a genuine spiritual guide.

Achieving the shelter of the Supreme is actually the ultimate goal of spiritual life and the reason for accepting a spiritual master. This success, however, depends on faith in both the Lord and the spiritual master. As it states in the Vedic verse, *yasya deve para bhaktir*: "Only unto those great souls who have implicit faith in both the Lord and the spiritual master are all the imports of Vedic knowledge automatically revealed." Therefore, the spiritual master must never be disrespected since he is, essentially, the door to such spiritual success. In fact, it is the genuine and authorized spiritual master who delivers us from the conditioned life of ignorance to the other side beyond birth and death, or life of freedom, by opening our eyes with spiritual knowledge. Therefore, if one is serious about making spiritual advancement, he or she should carefully consider whether to accept a spiritual master, and the qualities a master should possess.

CHAPTER TWELVE

The One World Religion

In observing any culture or religion, what we first notice are the superficialities, such as the dress, the outward formalities, the customs, rituals, festivals, etc. But deeper than this we find the basis of the culture's origin, the history of its development, the explanation of its philosophy, and the meaning and purpose of its rituals and customs. And deeper than this is the essence and goal of the religion. And, as already pointed out, that essence is usually based on the principle that the follower should learn and engage in the process of serving, glorifying, and loving the Supreme Being. So, on the essential platform, there is really not much that differentiates the ultimate goals of the world's major religions. The only difference in the authentic religions is the time in history in which they appeared, the place where they existed, and the people involved. But, due to these factors, there may be lesser or greater differences in doctrines, beliefs, and rituals. And depending on the intellectual ability of the people who were taught, there may be more or less spiritual knowledge that is provided. Thus, there are different levels of scripture. Some are more direct and complete than others in the same way an unabridged dictionary is more complete than one that is abridged; though they both essentially contain the same sort of information.

The most important difference, however, is the depth of philosophical understanding and spiritual knowledge each particular religious process has to offer, and the level of spiritual realization the aspirant can attain by following the process. Because of these differences, a person should be interested in finding and comprehending the process that offers the most complete spiritual knowledge. Such knowledge, however, is beyond the grasp of fundamental and materially motivated religions that are based on national or cultural traditions and feelings of superiority because of race or geographical region. Such religions fail in their attempts to promote universal or spiritual brotherhood because they lack the spiritual knowledge and potency necessary to do so. Furthermore, because

228

of this deficiency, they cannot give their followers the process that will enable them to become fully spiritually realized. So the members of such religions remain biased against others because they cannot rise above the materialistic vision that causes them to focus on superficial differences, such as race, creed, cultural background, sex, or dress, rituals, etc.

So how do we solve this problem that keeps people of different religions or cultures from accepting each other and working together? It is both easy and difficult. The easy part is to understand that the people merely have to be willing to share their spiritual knowledge with each other. They can all keep their own traditions, holidays, festivals, and rituals, but the essential knowledge and science of the individual souls, the Supreme Soul, and the relationship between them is what is important and what can be easily shared. This spiritual science is not explained more thoroughly than in the Vedic literature (as has been summarized in *The Secret Teachings of the Vedas*). In fact, comprehending this knowledge of the Absolute Truth is necessary for everyone's spiritual advancement, regardless of which spiritual process one is inclined to accept. Actually, there must be this kind of open and respectful exchange across global and cultural boundaries in order for peace and unity between all societies to exist. The hard part is to get people to agree to do this. But in some cases you have to look at other cultures and their philosophical systems to get answers that are not provided elsewhere.

For example, when we begin asking ourselves who we are and why we are here and cannot get satisfactory answers from one scripture or religion, it should not be surprising that we can find additional or more complete answers in other spiritual texts. As in the case of Jesus, he was not able to teach all he had to offer because of the crudeness of the people of that time and area. At one point he said: "I have yet many things to say unto you, but you cannot bear them now." (*John* 16.12) Even what he did say caused such a reaction that it was arranged that he be killed. So it is obvious that only so much knowledge can be given to certain people at certain times, according to their ability to understand. As Jesus also stated: "If you do not believe when I tell you of material things, how will you believe when I tell you of spiritual things?" (*John* 3.12) This is actually what Jesus and all teachers of the law of God have to deal with: a lack of faith and understanding amongst the people in general. Therefore, Jesus often spoke in parables whereby those who were ignorant of the law would hear only a simple, moralistic story, while the advanced initiates would understand the deeper meaning within. But Jesus also said: "These things have I spoken to you in proverbs; but the time cometh when I shall show you of the Father." (*John* 16.25) This meant that there was more knowledge to come and such knowledge would clearly describe the Absolute.

As anyone can see by reading the Bible, very little information is offered that directly describes God. At best, God is described as almighty, great, angry, greatly to be feared, the ever-lasting Father, the alpha and omega, etc. In the

Old Testament, God is described as appearing as a dove, a pillar of fire by night, a cloud by day, a burning bush, and so on. But this says nothing of His bodily features, His opulences, His abode, His activities, or exactly how He creates and manifests the material and spiritual worlds. Therefore, Jesus said there would be more knowledge to receive.

Researching the Vedic literature gives all the knowledge that easily fills the gaps left by such scriptures as the Bible, *Koran*, and so on. It is like the final piece of the puzzle that connects all spiritual paths and religions. In fact, the Bible agrees with the idea of researching other scripture for answers, because in *II Timothy* (3.16-17) we find the following quote: "All scripture is given by inspiration of God, and is profitable for doctrine, for reproof, for correction, for instruction in righteousness, that the man of God may be perfect, thoroughly furnished in all good works." Therefore, it is without a doubt that all scripture everywhere is meant to uplift our consciousness. Such being the case, it is not contradictory to see similarities in various scriptures and spiritual cultures, and it actually adds to and proves the glory of God amongst all nations. One quote that nicely elaborates on this point is the following:

> Know ye not that there are more nations than one? Know ye not that I, the Lord your God, have created all men, and that I remember those who are upon the isles of the sea; and that I rule in the heavens above and in the earth beneath; and I bring forth My word unto the children of men, yea, even upon all the nations of the earth? . . . Wherefore, because that ye have a Bible ye need not suppose that it contains all My words; neither need ye suppose that I have not caused more to be written. For I command all men, both in the east and in the west, and in the north and in the south, and in the islands of the sea, that they shall write the words which I speak unto them; for out of the books which shall be written I will judge the world, every man according to their works, according to that which is written. (*Book of Mormon, 2 Nephi*, 29.7, 10-11)

The above quote is not unlike the Bible verse in *Romans* (10.12-13): "For there is no difference between the Jew and the Greek: for the same Lord over all is rich unto all that call upon him. For whosoever shall call upon the name of the Lord shall be saved."

We herewith have the reasoning why all our petty quarrels, whether between Catholics and Protestants, Hindus and Muslims, nation and nation, are nothing more than a sign of our ignorance and animalistic tendencies which actually disqualify us from making any spiritual advancement. We may think we are a chosen people, but if we have no spiritual vision to see the unity between all people, then the "promised land" is a lot farther away than we think. For God remembers all of us and, indeed, supplies all nations the knowledge by which they can advance, depending on their ability to understand and use it. After all, those who are sincerely trying to advance are all sons of God, as verified in *Romans* (8.14): "For as many as are led by the spirit of God, they are the sons of God." A similar statement is in *John* (1.12): "But as many as received him, to them gave he the power to become the sons of God, even to them that believe on his name." Thus, we are all God's children, as also confirmed by Lord Krishna in *Bhagavad-gita* (9.17-18) in which He says that He is the father of the universe, the mother, the grandfather, the object of knowledge, the purifier, the sacred *om*, and the *Rig, Sama,* and *Yajur Vedas.* He is the goal, the support, the master, the witness, the abode, and the most dear friend. Krishna also says (*Bg.*7.6) that He is the origin and dissolution of the entire universe, and (*Bg.*4.35) by knowing the truth you will see that all beings are a part of Him and belong to Him. Thus, by understanding how we are all spiritually related, all sincere souls will find no difficulty in harmoniously working together and helping one another to understand the laws of the Supreme and advance accordingly, whether we are brother and brother, or nation and nation.

So if we are all spiritually related and can find similarities in the basic law of all religions, then what is the essential principle we are all meant to follow? The essence of the law, as found in the Vedic, the Judaic, the Christian, the Islamic, and other cultures, instructs us to surrender to God. For example, when the Pharisees asked Jesus which was the great commandment in the law, he told them: "Thou shalt love the Lord thy God with all thy heart and with all thy soul, and with all thy mind. This is the first and great commandment." (*Matthew* 22.37-38) Lord Krishna taught the same thing in *Bhagavad-gita*: "Always think of Me and become My devotee. Worship Me and offer your homage unto Me. Thus you will come to Me without fail. Abandon all varieties of religion and just surrender unto Me. I shall protect you from all sinful reaction. Do not fear." (*Bg.*18.65-66)

In the *Koran* (9.112) we find it said that those who turn to God in repentance and serve and praise Him, and engage in devotion to God, who bow down and pray, who do good and avoid evil, will rejoice. So proclaim these glad tidings to the believers. We also find it said (19.65) that everyone should worship the Lord of the heavens and the earth and be patient in constant worship. For who is worthy of the same name as God?

In Zoroastrianism it is believed that a person must live according to the religious tenets if one hopes to joyfully go before the Creator in the next world. The best of all practices is the worship of God, for all are servants of God. So one must lead a righteous life since it is one's thoughts, words, and deeds that determine one's next life after death. Similarly, in Sikhism we find the precept that a true follower serves the Supreme Soul alone.

All of this information makes it clear that regardless of what rituals or practices are employed in a religious system, which depends on the culture and background of the people, the first principle of any bona fide religion or spiritual path is to worship and develop love (*bhakti*) for God. The topmost expression of this love is in reawakening one's personal loving relationship with God. In the perfectional stage, this can take on many intimate characteristics between the living entity and the Supreme Being. The topmost qualities of such loving exchanges between the Supreme and the living beings are described no where else but in the highest levels of Vedic literature.

The path of *bhakti*, devotional service, is the easiest and most recommended way to attain this stage of spiritual realization. And once having reached it, a person sees everything in relation to the Supreme. All the universe becomes a reminder of His greatness, a display of His energies, and one recognizes all people and all living entities as spiritual parts of the Supreme. In this way, the topmost characteristic of any spiritual path is that it is a religion of the heart by which our reawakened love for the Divine is reflected in our mutual respect for each other. This is due to perceiving that we are all parts of the Divine, and that the Divinity is also in each of us.

Unfortunately, before we reach this advanced stage we are in the lower levels of *bhakti*. This immature level of love can take on the characteristics of a blind and fanatical allegiance to a particular process of religious expression rather than attachment to real love for God. In this situation, one may proudly and unnecessarily feel that he is on the highest path, and then will denounce every other process and culture without the proper spiritual understanding of himself or others. This is actually nothing more than sentimentality and fanaticism. Real love of God, which also displays love for all other living beings, will not be able to develop within a person if he or she harbors such a divisive mentality. The sort of people who show their love for their own religion by hating all others will spiritually stagnate and cause disharmony and quarrels between those of their religion and those of different religions. Someone may be a kind, generous, and devout person amongst those of his own culture, while ready to howl, insult, hate, and do injury to those of another. This is love of the lowest level, similar to the way a dog may love its master but will snarl at anyone else. Only those individuals and dry forms of religion that are bereft of real *bhakti* look at all others with hate and suspicion.

Only when *bhakti* becomes mature within an individual does this form of fanaticism or immature enthusiasm subside. Then real love and respect for all will naturally emanate from that person. As one becomes closer to the all-loving Supreme Being by the development of his own love for God, no longer can he be an instrument of hatred or prejudice because he sees everyone equally with spiritual vision. Thus, he walks away from the animalistic quarrels and wars that others take so seriously due to their ignorance of spiritual reality.

So how do we work together to attain this loving mood for the Supreme? Simply by looking through the major religious texts of the world the answer becomes obvious. They all say that one should praise and chant the names of the Supreme. For example, some of the oldest instructions in this regard are found in such ancient writings as the *Atharva-veda*:

O worshiper of God, sing His glory day and night, sing loudly, contemplate upon the Refulgent God. Praise the All-creating God! Yea, praise Him Whose home is in the inmost recesses of the heart, Who is the preacher of truth, Whose word is guileless, Who is a gracious friend. The same All-creating God grants us various means of acquiring salvation. Both morning and evening eulogies are meant to sing His glory. (*Atharva-veda*, 6.1.1-3)

In *Srimad-Bhagavatam* (2.1.11) we read that the doubtless and fearless way for spiritual success is to constantly chant the holy names of the Lord in the same manner as the great spiritual authorities. This is recommended for those who are filled with desires for material enjoyment, as well as those who are free from all desires or are satisfied by their spiritual knowledge. (Many other related verses from the Vedic literature are included in Chapter Ten.)

Similar to the Vedic teachings, Sikhism proclaims that those engrossed in sinful life will be taken by the angels of death to suffer punishments. Only by loving and serving God, and chanting God's names, does one get liberation from death. By chanting the Lord's names one attains divine knowledge. By hearing God's names a mortal being becomes perfect. By hearing God's names one procures meditation on the Lord, the blind find their way, and the mortal becomes a spiritual guide for others. The Sikh scripture further relates that when the hands, feet, and other parts of the body are dirty, they are cleansed with soap and water. When the clothes are polluted, they are washed. So when the mind is defiled by sin, it is cleansed by the love of the Name.

Zoroastrian scripture also proclaims that the names of God should be recited day and night with a loud voice:

Worship Me, O Zarathustra, by day and night with offerings of libations well accepted. I will come to thee for help and joy. . . If thou wantest, O Zarathustra, to destroy the malice of Daevas and men, of the oppressors, of the blind and the deaf, of the two-legged ruffians, of the two-legged heretics, of the four-legged wolves; and of the hordes with the wide front, with many spears, bearing the spear of havoc; then recite thou My names every day and night. (*Yasts and Sirozahs* 1, 9-11)

Even Buddhism instructs that those who call upon the name of Amida Buddha will meet him after death and go to paradise. But in order to accomplish this, one should repeat the name throughout the day in all situations with all one's heart. Furthermore, as we reflect on the passing of time we must make haste to invoke the sacred name, for our end is drawing near. To ignore this opportunity leaves us with nothing but future remorse.

Similar instructions are found in the *Koran* (17.110): "Call upon God or upon the Merciful. By whatever name ye call upon Him. For His are the most excellent names. Be neither strident nor speechless. Set your heart on the due path of prayer." Also (87.1) we find it stated: "Happy shall be the man who purifies himself, who remembers the name of his Lord and prays to Him." Another example is (76.25): "Remember the name of your Lord morning and evening; in the night time worship Him: praise Him all night long." The fact is that the word *koran* (or *quran*) means to recite, and throughout the *Koran*, at the beginning of each Surah (except Surah 9), there is the invocation, "In the name of Allah, the compassionate, the merciful." Thus, by reciting the *Koran* one also chants the name of God.

In the Christian tradition it is also understood that only by the chanting of the holy names does one become purified. This is verified in *Hebrews* (10.4, 6; 13.15): "For it is not possible that the blood of bulls and of goats should take away sins. . . In burnt offerings and sacrifices for sin thou hast had no pleasure. . . By him therefore let us offer the sacrifice of praise to God continually, that is, the fruit of our lips giving thanks to his name." Also in the Latin Mass before the gospel is read there is the prayer spoken by the priest, *Dominus sit in corde meo et in labiis meis*: "May the Lord be in my heart and on my lips." The Lord is on one's lips by chanting His names. (Many similar verses that emphasize this process in the Judaic and Christian traditions are included in Chapter Six.)

In this way, throughout many cultures and scriptures from around the world, it is emphasized that one should engage in the devotional activities of chanting or singing God's names. Therefore, this is the essence of all religious processes. For as it is said in the Bible: "For whosoever shall call upon the name of the Lord shall be saved. That ye may with one mind and one mouth glorify God, even the Father of our Lord Jesus Christ. And again, Praise the Lord, all ye Gentiles; and laud him, all ye people." (*Romans* 10.13; 15.6,11)

As the Vedic, Zoroastrian, Sikh, Christian, Islamic, Judaic, and other philosophies maintain, all creatures can join in the universal acclaimation of the one Supreme Being. Thus, chanting the names of God is not only a privilege, it is also the duty of everyone who expects to enter the spiritual strata and conquer over the adversity of this world. In fact, according to the *Revelation of St. John* (15.4), this is what is expected from people of all nations: "Who shall not fear Thee, O Lord, and glorify Thy name? for Thou only art holy: for all nations shall come and worship before Thee; for Thy judgements are made manifest." This, therefore, is the process that can unite all people, as Christ also explained in his prayer to God the night before his crucifixion: "Holy Father, keep through Thine own name those whom Thou hast given me, that they may be one, as we are. While I was with them in the world, I kept them in Thy name: those that Thou gavest me I have kept, and none of them is lost, but the son of perdition; that the scripture might be fulfilled." (*John* 17.6, 11-12) In this way, by accepting this process, it is surely possible that all people everywhere can live together in peace with a common cause, and also live in harmony with the universe and with God. This is one of the main goals of all spiritual paths.

We have to remember that we are in this world but not of it. We are all spiritual beings who are temporarily residing in the material creation. It is futile to try and make a permanent home here, or attempt to be fully content and happy by being absorbed in material pleasures. This world does not and never will offer that kind of accomodation. A spiritual being in the material world, which is what we all are, is like a fish out of water: it is an incompatible situation. So we must understand the reality of our circumstance, that we are all transients evolving in a temporary situation on our way from one point of existence to another. So what is this life? It is nothing more than a moment on our great path towards full spiritual realization. But if we forget that, then we get caught in the illusion that this world is the cause and basis of our happiness, and our temporary body is the basis of our identity. Nothing can be further from the truth, and anyone with some common sense or spiritual understanding will see this. (This is especially explained in Chapter Four of *The Secret Teachings of the Vedas*.)

Basically, you cannot look for security in a world that offers only insecurity. Insecurity in this world is a constant factor because the material world, by its very nature, is impermanent and full of continuous change. The remedy for this insecurity, which is essentially the fear of change and the future, is to advance in spiritual consciousness. Then one will realize his or her spiritual identity and know that the spiritual realm pervades everything within as well as outside this material creation. Therefore, one who has become spiritually evolved and detached from the material focus of life knows that he is a spiritual being and a part of the spiritual strata. In this sense, wherever he goes, he is already home. A person who lives in this consciousness knows that the only things which are eternal are (1) the Supreme Being, (2) all the individual spiritual entities, and (3) the relationship between them, which is based on spiritual love. This love is all that has to be reawakened. This is the real goal of life.

If somehow or other the people of the world could give up their superficial differences and join together in singing or praising the holy names of the Supreme, the consciousness of society in general could change to such a degree that this very planet could become spiritually surcharged. It is not that we have to work for a specific change to bring about solutions to the world's problems, but when the consciousness of the people becomes purified, or spiritualized, the solutions to the problems will become obvious and the necessary changes will automatically begin to manifest. The process starts from within, as the Bible states: "And when he (Jesus) was demanded of the Pharisees, when the kingdom of God should come, he answered them and said, The kingdom of God cometh not with observation: Neither shall they say, Lo here! or, Lo there! for, behold, the kingdom of God is within you." (*Luke* 17.20-21) Therefore, entering the spiritual realm, or changing the world in which we presently live, is simply a matter of reawakening our dormant spiritual consciousness. It is not a matter of outward observation, but it is an inward process of transformation and development.

If the people of the world would be more inclined to recognize that spiritual advancement is a process of inner transformation and participate in this process, and share with each other the different levels of spiritual knowledge from other cultures, rather than merely accepting one particular religious dogma and rejecting all other forms of spiritual growth, then it becomes possible for all of humanity to be a united people. After all, a true religion respects whatever level of universal spiritual truth is found in any other culture and religion. Everyone could band together with a common cause of helping each other become spiritually advanced: a universal religion based on hearing about and glorifying the Supreme. The only difference then would be whether people were theists or atheists, and atheists are simply those who have no spiritual experience or cannot fathom the depths of spiritual knowledge.

This does not mean that all religions should become merged into some impersonalistic and ineffective hodgepodge, but it means that each process should include the knowledge and system by which all followers can completely understand the science of the soul, their true spiritual identity, and attain their own realizations of the topmost levels of spiritual reality and the real nature of the Supreme Being. If a religion or spiritual path does not provide these things, then it is not complete. In such a case, a person should seek out the highest available level of spiritual science that does provide the above mentioned factors and gives the connecting link between the fundamental principles of all religions. Otherwise, a world full of isolated religious cultures and doctrines is a world full of scattered and incomplete portions of the universal path to the Absolute. Thus, we must seek to unite these paths by finding the common source from which these portions have sprung, as we have tried to point out in this volume. When you find that source, you will find the doorway that leads to full realization of the Absolute Truth. The next step is to simply use the knowledge to walk through the door.

Herewith, in this chapter, we have given evidence that throughout the world and within the essential teachings of all scriptures thereof, those who shall realize their true spiritual identity and be released from material entanglement and enter the spiritual strata are those who have taken shelter of the Supreme through *bhakti*, devotion, and the process of *sravana* and *kirtana*, hearing about, glorifying, and chanting the holy names of the Supreme. On this path, which has been recommended the world over, other than one's own immature prejudice, there are no superficial differences, such as race, creed, nationality, tradition, sex, age, etc., that can stop the people of the world from being united and engaging in this process together, for this is the one world religion.

SEEING SPIRITUAL INDIA (PART 2)

The Major Holy Places in East and Central India

In the last volume we had just finished our tour of the temples and holy sites of South India. In this volume we will travel through eastern and central India, which has some of the most important holy places of many religions.

As we begin our travels, we should bear in mind that India, at its present place in time, may be materially less advanced than the West but is far more developed spiritually. The average person in the streets of India knows more about spiritual science than most educated Westerners. Though someone from the West may know about religion, they still may know very little about real spirituality, which includes the knowledge of the soul, what happens at death, reincarnation, *karma*, etc. Try to have a conversation with a Westerner on these topics and it usually will not last long. But take any person from the East and the talk can last for hours. Thus, there is a big difference in cultures from the spiritual point of view.

To truly understand spiritual topics requires a change of consciousness, not simply a change of intellectual disposition or viewpoint, as many academicians tend to think. It requires one to rise above the bodily concept of life. Thus, even a poor man who superficially might appear to be uneducated may still attain great levels of spiritual realization. But some people may not agree with or understand spiritual knowledge because they, quite simply, might be incapable of changing their consciousness or of rising above the material conception of life. The ability to do this is a qualification that is far removed from simply acquiring a material education. Thus, regardless of one's position in life, everyone can try to understand spiritual knowledge. And one of the best ways, aside from studying spiritual texts, is to travel and experience the special nature of the sacred places that exist in India.

By entering deeply into the mysteries of spiritual India a person may experience a culture shock. Not a culture shock merely in the sense of having to deal with strange new situations and customs that you find in a different country, but also in the sense of taking a new look at yourself and the world and what your position really is in this world. When you are traveling in the East,

237

you are occasionally forced to be somewhat defenseless to new ideas, values, and perceptions. You may not have the easy access to Western forms of escapism. In India, life and death as it is stares you in the face, and you can either come to terms with it or simply try to avoid thinking about it. But by understanding the transitory nature of life through the spiritual knowledge that India is known for is something that can give you levels of realization you never had before. These may be simple realizations that you might reflect on from time to time, or they might be the kind that makes you change your way of seeing yourself, the world, and the way you want to live. So in spite of customs or traditions that you may not be used to or able to fully accept, you may still attain a new understanding of your real identity, or even of the infinite realm of divine consciousness. What you find within yourself depends on you and how open you are to new perceptions. So let us begin our journey and see what happens. (I must clarify that when I say *we*, I mean *I* the traveler and *you* the reader. Together on this tour in the following pages *we* see these places.)

We begin in Madras by rising early for the morning train. On our way out of our hotel we see that several blocks of the city streets just north of the train station have been turned into a large fruit and vegetable market where farmers sell their produce to local merchants. Though it is still dark and street lights provide the only illumination, there are many trucks, horse carts, old men, women, and even young girls and boys everywhere selling and buying a wide variety of produce as we pass through it. By noon they will all be gone, but will somehow be back early the next morning to start again.

At the station the train we want is the Coromandel Express. The trains leaving Madras are usually crowded with travelers, many of whom will be taking the three day train ride all the way up the coast to Calcutta. We won't be going that far. Our destination is Jagannatha Puri, a major pilgrimage center. Even to Puri we may be on the train for two nights, so whether traveling first or second-class, make sure you've made your reservations. Some people, however, may like to break the long ride to stop at a few places at some towns which might be interesting to see. This is what we will do. From Madras we take the train to Vijayawada where we arrive in mid-afternoon. We get off here and make reservations for the next morning's train before leaving the station.

Luckily, Hotel Vikram (not the greatest, but not the worst) is located a few blocks away, so the *ricksha* ride is a short one. I book a room and, the way I travel, I barely lock my things inside and I'm back on the streets looking for a motor *ricksha* to take me to a few temples.

The first temple we want to see is an ancient cave temple in Undavalil, a suburb south of Vijayawada. It is hardly used anymore and not maintained very well, and is visited only by a few local people. It does not attract tourists and some *ricksha* drivers don't even know how to locate it. But we find a driver who not only knows where it is but also speaks English. So we head through Vijayawada and take the road south over the Krishna river. After a few minutes we turn off the highway and take a bumpy road that sees little use. After passing the homes of many villagers who look at us with wonder, we finally arrive at the deserted looking temple. The temple is not very large but is nonetheless an interesting place. It is a cave temple carved out of the solid rock hillside. It dates back to the sixth century A.D. and is dedicated to Lord Vishnu. It is four storeys tall and each level has many pillars that help support it. Scattered around inside are wall carvings of deities and scenes from the Puranic legends. The place still smells of the smoke that has passed through the halls over the years from ghee lamps, wood fires, or incense.

On the highest level of this simple but massive stone structure we reach an area that is secured by a wooden fence and with a locked gate. Fortunately, an old guard has followed us and unlocks the door to let us inside. Here we find the main Deity of this temple, and it is quite a Deity. Carved out of the stone is the largest Deity we have ever seen in our travels so far. The Deity is a 29 foot long Lord Vishnu reclining on a Seshanaga. Carved on the walls nearby are demigods and other personalities that are offering prayers and obeisances. The Deity is still well preserved and instills a feeling of reverence and wonder in us as we look on and think of how much worship and attention this Deity must have been given by the local people many centuries ago. We spend a few minutes here because, though we knew the temple might be interesting though out of the way, we had no idea that such an awesome Deity of Lord Vishnu existed here.

Farther south of Undavalil in the hills known as Mangalagiri, about 7 miles from Vijayawada, is the Pana-narasimha Temple. It is a temple at the top of a flight of 600 steps. Climbing the steps causes some fatigue, but after reaching the top we feel rewarded by entering the temple to see the Deity of Lord Narasimha, the form of God who displays His lion-like anger to protect His devotees.

Before entering the sanctum we purchase some tickets for the cost of performing the *pana* (water) ritual. As we wait, we can hear the sounds of bells ringing and *mantras* being chanted as the Narasimha Deity is being worshiped by the people ahead of us. After a few more minutes it is our turn to enter the sanctum. In the dim light of a ghee lamp the Deity of Lord Narasimha can be seen. The Deity is a brass image about a foot or two in height, set on the side of the rock wall on a little altar, and is shaped more like a cat than a lion. The mouth of the Deity is large and open. The priest guides us through the water ritual in which he offers prayers, flowers, incense, ghee lamp, and lots of water to the Deity. In front of the Deity is a bucket of sweetened water. The priest takes a conchshell and fills it with the water from the bucket and pours some of it into a bowl and the rest of it directly into the mouth of the Deity. Try as I might, I can't hear any sound of water hitting anything after the priest pours more and more water into the Deity's mouth. It's as if there is no limit.

When the ritual is over, we step out of the temple and an assistant gives us a cup of the water that was poured into the bowl. This is considered part of the offering to the Deity and we drink the whole cup of refreshingly sweetened water. In the temple there is also a conchshell said to have been used by Krishna Himself, which was given to the temple by the late King of Tanjore. And in 1512 Sri Caitanya visited this temple where He ecstatically offered many prayers to the Deity of Narasimha.

After our privileged visit is over, we ride back to town where our *ricksha* driver takes us to see the famous Durga temple on the hilltop that overlooks the town of Vijayawada. This is an interesting temple only if you've got the extra time to see it. And for those who wish to continue to explore the area, further upstream at Amaravathi are the excavated rock temples along the banks of the Krishna River. This used to be an important Buddhist center 2000 years ago with over 1000 monks and a large decorated marble *stupa*. But now ruins are all that's left. Anyone interested in ancient Buddhist relics will find this place interesting. And if you like this, much further upstream is the Nagarjunakonda site. This was one of the biggest of the Buddhist centers in southern India for about 500 years, starting in the 2nd century B.C. Excavations have uncovered the ruins of *stupas*, temples, *chaityas*, etc., which have been moved to a museum for preservation before the Nagarjunasagar Dam causes the area to be submerged under water.

In the morning we are up before dawn and get a short *ricksha* ride from our hotel to the train station. This is one of the advantages of getting a hotel near the station, even if the hotel is not that great. The train is half an hour late, not unusual in India, which forces us to be patient during our travels in this country. But once the train arrives and we get settled in our seats, everything is all right as we begin heading north.

We arrive at our next stop at Visakhapatnam where we will visit the Jiyada Narasimha (Simhachalam) temple located about ten miles north of the city near Waltair. After leaving the train station, we book a room at Prince Hotel and arrange that a taxi will pick us up at nine the next morning. The drive to the temple takes almost an hour, and going up the hill on which the temple is located provides some good views. Buses take pilgrims up from the foot of the hill to the temple for two rupees. Along the streets in front of the temple are rows of shops offering all kinds of devotional paraphernalia. Other little shops offer snacks and drinks. We leave our shoes at the shoe stall and make our way into the temple compound through a side door. We climb a stairway and pass through columned halls, walls with delicately carved figures, and gateways that lead to the main temple. Before entering the main hall we pass by an altar with beautiful Deities of Radha and Krishna. In the main sanctum is a silver throne with the Deity of Narasimha, but He is covered with dried sandalwood paste. In fact, you cannot see any of the Deity's features at all. There is simply a three foot mound of sandalwood. Lord Narasimha is known to get very hot from anger when He sees the activities of the demons and materialists, and the sandalwood helps keep Him cool. I have heard that there is a festival once a year in which all the sandalwood is removed and many pilgrims come to see the Deity. But by evening the priests again begin covering the Deity with sandalwood paste.

This Simhachalam temple is a very affluent temple with fine architecture. It has many residences for visiting pilgrims. The priests are generally members of the Ramanuja-*sampradaya*. This temple was visited by Sri Caitanya Mahaprabhu on His South Indian tour and is considered an important place of pilgrimage by many Hindus of the area. Visakhapatnam also has the Sri Venkatesvara Konda Temple that you may want to visit.

From Visakhapatnam we take a short train ride to Sri Kakulam to visit Kurmaksetra. The temple at Kurmaksetra is noteworthy because it is the only temple dedicated to Krishna's incarnation as Kurma, and many visitors come through to see it. Kurmaksetra is 22 miles south of Sri Kakulam and takes an hour to reach by bus. It is best to get a hotel at Sri Kakulam because there is not much to choose from at Kurmaksetra. Kurmaksetra is a small town and the temple is easy to find near a small lake called Kurma Lake. Anyone there can point the way. The temple is in the middle of a courtyard surrounded by a large wall and topped by a silver dome over the sanctum. There are as many as 500 carved and ornate columns and many other figures on the walls. Through a narrow and dimly lit corridor we enter the sanctum where the Deity of Kurma is located. The temple is lit by torches and has paintings of Lord Vishnu's ten incarnations on the walls and ceiling. On the main altar is the Deity where the *brahmana* priests are engaged in chanting hymns and making offerings. Another altar is for Lakshmi Devi and Bhu Devi, the consorts of Vishnu. The priests are very friendly and glad to see Western pilgrims and will give you a few drops of *caranamrita* and flowers and fruits that have been offered to the Deity, so it is fitting to give a nice donation. Just south of the temple on a small hill is a little shrine built by Srila Bhaktisiddhanta Sarasvati Thakur in 1930. Inside are the footprints he installed of Sri Caitanya Mahaprabhu to commemorate Lord Caitanya's visit here in 1512 A.D. When we are finished visiting Kurmaksetra we return to Sri Kakulam, which has a few more Krishna temples we can search out while we have time. Otherwise, we are soon back on the train heading north past Chilka Lake and on up to Bhubaneswar where we get a connecting train or take a bus to Jagannatha Puri.

Jagannatha Puri, a town of 75,000, is one of the most important pilgrimage centers and one of the four holiest cities in India. These four cities are Badrinatha in the north, Dvaraka in the west, Ramesvaram in the south, and Puri in the east. Badrinarayan in Badrinatha was especially worshiped in Satya-yuga, Rama in Ramesvaram in Treta-yuga, Dvarakanatha in Dvaraka was especially worshiped in Dvapara-yuga, but Lord Jagannatha in Puri can be worshiped by everyone in Kali-yuga. In fact, the importance of Jagannatha Puri, sometimes called Purushottama-Ksetra, is explained in chapters 52 through 57 of the *Uttarabhaga* section of the *Narada Purana*. There we find it stated that simply by visiting Puri, which is rarely achieved except for those who have performed many pious acts, and by seeing the Deity of Jagannatha (Krishna), one can easily attain freedom from future births and reach the spiritual abode.

In the middle of this city is the large temple dedicated to Lord Krishna as Jagannatha, meaning "Lord of the Universe." It is in a huge complex where buildings house as many as 5,000 priests and assistants. The whole compound is surrounded by a thick stone wall 20 feet tall that encloses an area 665 feet by 640 feet. The wall has four large gates, one on each side. The main temple building, called Sri Mandir, was built in the 12th century by King Chodaganga Deva, though the site is said to go back at least 2000 years, if not much further. The additional smaller buildings were added after the 16th century. The main temple, which reaches 215 feet in height, is where we find the five foot tall Deities of Jagannatha, Balarama, and Subhadra. They stand on a five foot high throne facing the pilgrims as they enter the temple room. Outside the main temple hall are over 100 smaller shrines dedicated to the various demigods. There is an arati ceremony six times a day from 4 AM to 9 PM when devotees come in for *darshan*, in which they sing, chant, or worship the Deities in ecstasy. As many as 50,000 people come to the Jagannatha temple in a day. Unfortunately, foreigners are not allowed into the temple grounds, but you can get a look at the temple from the roof of the Raghunandan Library across the street for a donation.

The temple compound also has a huge kitchen, employing over 650 cooks and helpers who make hundreds of vegetarian preparations for the 54 separate offerings that are given to the Deities every day. After the food is given to the Deities it becomes *prasada*, or the Lord's mercy. By taking such spiritually powerful food it is said that one becomes more and more spiritually surcharged and free from past *karma*. Much of the prasada is sold or given to people who depend on the temple. When I had my *ricksha* driver buy some for me, I got a basket with several clay pots filled with a variety of rice, vegetable, dahl, and sweet preparations. It was absolutely delicious and was enough for breakfast, lunch, and dinner. Taking this *prasada* at Puri is to partake in a tradition that goes back thousands of years and is considered especially purifying. It is said that only by Krishna's grace does one get the opportunity to receive the remnants of food offered to Him.

The significance of Jagannatha Puri and the story of how the Deities first appeared goes back many hundreds of years to the time of King Indradyumna, who was a great devotee of Lord Vishnu. One time in his court the King heard from a devotee about an incarnation of Lord Vishnu, named Nila-madhava. (Nila-madhava is the Deity form of Lord Vishnu.) The King very much wanted to see this form of the Supreme and sent many *brahmanas* to search for Nila-madhava. All came back unsuccessful except for Vidyapati, who did not come back at all. He had wandered to a distant town which was populated by a tribe of people known as Shabaras of non-Aryan heritage. He had stayed in the house of Visvasu, and later, at Visvasu's request, married his daughter, Lalita.

After some time Vidyapati noticed that Visvasu would leave the house every night and return at noon the next day. Vidyapati asked his wife about this. Though her father had ordered her not to tell anyone, she told Vidyapati that Visvasu would go in secret to worship Nila-madhava. After repeated requests, Vidyapati finally got permission to go see Nila-madhava, only if he went blindfolded. But Vidyapati's wife had bound some mustard seeds in his cloth so that a trail could be left to follow later. When they reached the shrine, Vidyapati saw the Deity Nila-madhava after the Shabara took off the blindfold, and he felt great ecstasy.

The story continues to relate that while Visvasu was out collecting items for worship, Vidyapati saw a bird fall into the nearby lake and drown. The soul of the bird suddenly took a spiritual form and ascended back to the spiritual world. Vidyapati wanted to do the same and climbed the tree to jump in the lake. Then a voice from the sky declared that before he jumped he should tell Indradyumna that he had found Nila-madhava.

When Visvasu returned to worship the Deity, Nila-madhava spoke and said that He had accepted the simple worship from him for so many days, but now He wanted to accept the opulent worship that would be offered by King Indradyumna. When Vidyapati went back to tell the King, Indradyumna immediately went to find Nila-madhava but could not locate Him. So the King arrested Visvasu, but a voice told him to release the Shabara and that he should build a temple on top of Nila Hill where the King would see the Lord as Daru-brahman, the wooden manifestation of the Absolute.

After great endeavor, King Indradyumna built the temple at Sri Kshetra, now known as Jagannatha Puri, and later prayed to Lord Brahma to consecrate it. However, Lord Brahma said that it was not within his power to consecrate the temple since Sri Kshetra is manifested by the Supreme's own internal potency and is where the Lord manifests Himself. So Brahma simply put a flag on top of the temple and blessed it, saying that anyone who from a distance saw the flag and offered obeisances would easily be liberated from the material world. Nontheless, after much waiting the King became anxious since Nila-madhava had not manifested Himself. Thinking his life was useless, the King decided he should end his life by fasting. But in a dream the Lord said that He would appear floating in from the sea in His form as Daru-brahman.

The King went to the shore and found a huge piece of wood that had the markings of a conch, disc, club, and lotus. This was Daru-brahman. But try as they might, the men could not budge the wood. In a dream the Lord spoke to the King and instructed him to get Visvasu and put a golden chariot in front of Daru-brahman. After doing this and forming a *kirtana* party to chant the holy names, and praying for Daru-brahman to mount the chariot, Daru-brahman was easily moved. Lord Brahma performed a sacrifice where the present temple now stands and installed a Deity of Lord Narasimhadeva, the Deity that is now on the western side of the temple.

From the wooden Daru-brahman, the King requested many expert carvers to carve the form of the Deity, but none could do so for their chisels immediately broke when they touched the wood. Finally the architect of the demigods, Visvakarma, (some say the Lord Himself) arrived as an old artist, Ananta Maharana, and promised that he would carve the Deity form of the Lord inside the temple in three weeks if the King would allow him to work behind closed doors. But after 14 days the King became very anxious because he could no longer hear the sounds of the carving. Finally he could stand it no more. On the advice of the queen he personally opened the doors of the temple to see what was happening. Then he saw the forms of Lord Jagannatha, Lord Balarama, and Lady Subhadra. But because the King had opened the doors sooner than he was supposed to, the Deities were not completed; Their feet and hands had not yet been carved. Thus, the Supreme manifested Himself in this form.

The King felt he had committed a great offense for having opened the doors before the alotted three weeks had passed, so he decided to end his life. But in a dream Lord Jagannatha told the King that though he had broken his promise, this was just a part of the Supreme's pastimes to display this particular form. Occasionally the King could decorate the Deity with golden hands and feet. Yet those devotees filled with love would always see the form of Lord Jagannatha as the threefold bending form of Syamasundara, Krishna, holding a flute. Thus, the Supreme appeared in this form so that people could approach and see Him, especially as He rides on the huge carts during the Ratha-Yatra festival.

In fact, during the Ratha-Yatra festival is the most popular time to go to Jagannatha Puri. This is usually in July when it is very hot. But thousands upon thousands of pilgrims flock to Puri to take part in this auspicious event, which is said to have been celebrated for thousands of years, making it one of the oldest and one of the biggest religious festivals in the world. This is the time when the Deities come out of the temple for all to see. It is also the time when as many as a million people gather in this small city with one purpose: to show their faith and devotion to God in the form of Lord Jagannatha.

As big as this festival is, it can be quite expensive. The only festival in the world that is bigger than this is the Kumbha Mela festival that draws many millions of people. The Ratha-Yatra festival is financed primarily by the Orissan government with an annual budget of $50,000, which is a very large sum for India. But with the number of pilgrims that come to Puri each year, the temple and surrounding businesses also are benefited with the extra financial income.

The construction of the carts or chariots begin several weeks before the festival. In the main road in front of the temple huge stacks of wood are used to assemble the three chariots which will reach up to three storeys tall and will roll on 16 wheels, each eight feet high. The chariots are painted with bright colors and the tops are covered with red, black, yellow, or green canopies. The colors signify which chariot is for which Deity.

About two weeks before the festival the Deities of Jagannatha, Balarama, and Subhadra are given a ritual bath, after which They play the pastime of getting a cold. They are then taken to a designated area and given special treatments and offerings. They may also be repainted at this time. About every 12 or 19 years the Deities are replaced with new ones carved from a ritualistically selected Daru-Brahman in the form of a *nima* tree.

As the festival draws near, thousands of pilgrims come to Jagannatha Puri, but as many as a million people may be in town on the day of the festival. Some are top officials in the Indian government. Many people begin arriving in front of the temple near the carts on the morning of the festival. At first it is very interesting to wander about looking at the nicely decorated carts and all the pilgrims who have attended. But then the police begin cordoning off the area around the carts. Then there are only certain areas where people can get betweeen the carts and the buildings. This creates bottlenecks which can be very dangerous when too many people are pushing on each other trying to get through. I saw people begin to panic at times because of the pressure on them, and worried mothers had to hold their babies above the crowd to make sure they did not get crushed.

The Ratha-Yatra festival can be both spiritually ecstatic and physically exhausting. Though July is in the monsoon season, if the rains have not arrived yet, it gets very hot. When it is hot, you will be soaked with sweat a few hours after the sun comes up. In fact, from where I was, I saw dozens of Indian people who had collapsed from the heat and had to be carried away from the crowd on stretchers. The heat can take a lot out of you, especially when in a crowd of thousands. So it is best to have a source of water with you, like a canteen.

A good place to be during the festival, if you do not want to be on the street amongst the people, is on a rooftop. But you have to make reservations and pay for your seats several days in advance. Even then there may not be any guarantee that you will get the seats you want.

Around eleven in the morning the temple priests come out to sanctify the carts. They walk up the gangplanks to the platform on the cart and sprinkle holy water around while circumambulating it three times and chanting specific *mantras* for purification. Then, after much waiting, the priests bring out the small Deities that will also ride on the cart. Later, around two o'clock, the King of Puri arrives in a procession, walks up the planks to the platform and sweeps the cart with a gold handled broom. He circumambulates the platform three times and is assisted by the priests. He does this to each of the carts. Only after this are the carts ready for the big Deities.

It should be pointed out here that the way the King sweeps the carts is an example of how the festival has changed over the years. If you read accounts of the Ratha-Yatra festival as described in the *Caitanya-caritamrta*, there are some major differences in the festival we find today compared to 500 years ago. The King used to sweep the street in front of the carts as they paraded down through the town. The reason he no longer does this is related in a story I was told. It seems that at one time years ago a King of Puri was to marry a princess who was the daughter of a king from a local district. When the Ratha-Yatra festival was to take place, the father of the princess was invited. When he attended, the King of Puri performed the devotional tradition of sweeping the road in front of the carts. The visiting King, however, rather than being impressed with the devotion of the King for Lord Jagannatha, objected to the idea of his daughter marrying the King of Puri since he was merely a street sweeper. From then on the King of Puri discontinued sweeping the streets and now sweeps the carts.

The festival parade also used to start in the morning and stop at noon near the Jagannatha Vallabha Garden where the Deities would get offerings of food, worship, etc., from the many devotees. Now this does not take place. There would also be many groups of people singing devotional songs, and though you will still see some people in *kirtana* groups, there are very few. Now, once the carts get going, you mostly hear people simply shout out, "Jayo, Jai Jagannatha," and raise their hands in the air and watch the cart go by. And when it's gone, that's it: back to business. So in this way the festival has lost much of its devotional atmosphere. However, the Calcutta Ratha-Yatra festival put on by ISKCON is said to be as popular as the Puri festival and is sweeter and more devotional in the way it is carried out. There are many more *kirtana* groups, huge *prasada* distribution for feasting, large beautiful carts that parade through the city, and seven days of plays and programs before the Deities return to the temple. So many people are prefering to go to the Calcutta festival instead of the one in Puri.

In any case, after the King of Puri sweeps the carts, they are ready for the big Deities of Lord Jagannatha, Balarama, and Subhadra. Suddenly excitement fills the air when many men blow conchshells and bang on drums and cymbals to announce the arrival of the Deities at the main gate of the temple complex. Then the smiling face of Lord Balarama appears through the doorway and the crowd shouts and chants, "Jai Balarama. Baladeva ki jai!" Generally, however, unless you are situated on a tall building, you cannot see the faces of the Deities because there are so many assistants that help move Them. But you can easily see the huge headdress They wear. Once the Deity is on the cart, the headdress is torn off and distributed amongst the people as *prasada*.

Daityas, strongly built men who lift the Deity, carry Lord Balarama from one large cotton pillow to another. Lord Balarama is five feet and five inches tall and has an arm span of 12 feet. When carried, there are five men on each arm, with up to 50 men pulling in front and 20 offering support in the back. All of these carriers are members of the Dayitapati family. Gradually, after about an hour, Lord Balarama moves to the chariot and is placed on it so everyone in the crowd can see Him. Then Subhadra, who is less than five feet tall, is also taken from the temple to Her chariot. And finally Lord Jagannatha is brought out. He is five feet and seven inches tall with an arm span of 12 feet, and also needs many assistants to be moved.

There are special names for the chariots. Jagannatha rides on the 14-wheeled Nandigosha, which means tumultuous and blissful sound. Balarama rides on the 16-wheeled Taladhvaja, meaning the sound of significantly powerful rythm. And Subhadra rides on the 12-wheeled Darpadalana, which means destroyer of pride. The chariots are also painted with certain colors to signify which chariot is meant for which Deity. The Deities are also painted with particular colors that mean something. Jagannatha's blackish color represents faultless qualities; Balarama's white color signifies enlightenment; and Subhadra's yellow color signifies goodness.

When the Deities are on the chariots, many thousands of devotees surround them and the people in the front take up the long, thick ropes to pull the chariots down the main road to the Gundicha temple, where the Deities stay for a week. When everything is ready, a whistle is blown by the chariot driver and a hundred people on each rope begin to pull the chariots. Many police have to guard the chariot wheels to make sure no one gets too close and is crushed under them. It was after five o'clock when Lord Balarama's cart got started and loudly rumbled down the road and soon reached the Gundicha temple. Subhadra's cart began to move a while later. Lord Jagannatha's cart did not get started until after six o'clock, but did not make it to the Gundicha temple until the next day. The people pulled it about two-thirds of the way before it almost ran into some shops on the side of the road. So the following morning the people redirected the cart and finished pulling it to the temple. The parade is a fascinating event in which to participate and see. But when the chariots get rolling, the crowd gets very intense. You either have to get out of the way to let them by, or struggle to move with the crowd as it goes with the cart. Many people try to pull the ropes and it is not easy, and can be dangerous, to get a place near them.

Sometimes the chariots mysteriously stop, though everyone is pulling hard. In fact, it is not unusual, as in the case of this festival, that a chariot may stop completely and stay there overnight and then continue the next day. Sometimes if there is difficulty, the local government minister will pray to Lord Jagannatha for forgiveness from whatever offenses the residents of the town may have committed. Then the chariots begin to move again as if they move only by the will of Jagannatha. The chariots continue to the Gundicha temple about two miles down the road from the main temple where the Deities stay for a week before returning to the temple in a similar parade.

The Deities may spend the first two nights on the carts outside the Gundicha temple. During this time, pilgrims can climb up on the carts and see the Deities very closely and even embrace Them. But the priests are quick to charge everyone a certain number of rupees for this opportunity, which makes for a very good business. When I climbed a cart and was about to give a "donation," as many as five of the attendants grabbed the money at once before I let go of it. And when I did not let go of it right away, they started to get very angry. This was after I had been assured that I could climb the cart to see the Deity of

Lady Subhadra and there would be no charge, and I would also be allowed to take a photograph. I indeed was allowed to see Lady Subhadra and even embrace Her, which is a rare event for any pilgrim, what to speak of a Westerner. But after I had given my donation, I took out my camera to take a photograph and a guard immediately came over and objected and ordered me to get down off the cart. So that brought an abrupt end to the episode. Nonetheless, if one can overcome this businesslike atmosphere, it can still be a very devotional and memorable event. Some people simply stay on the ground and offer prayers and small ghee lamps from a distance. Others climb all three carts to get the personal *darshan* of all three Deities, though the carts of Lord Jagannatha and Lord Balarama are very crowded.

The Deities stay on the carts for a night or two and are then taken inside the Gundicha temple for special treatment. After the Deities' stay at the Gundicha temple, They return a week later to the main temple in a similar parade that is attended by far fewer people. This can be a time when you can get much closer to the carts and walk more easily with the parade, providing you have time to stay in Puri until the next week.

The meaning of the Ratha-Yatra parade is steeped in religious sentiment. The form that Lord Krishna takes as Jagannatha is the manifestation of His ecstasy that He feels when He leaves the opulance of His palaces in Dwaraka, represented by the Puri temple, to return to the town of Vrindavan and the simple and pure spontaneous love the residents there have for Him. Thus, there is no difference between Lord Krishna and Lord Jagannatha. So in the mood of separation from His loving devotees, Jagannatha mounts His chariot and returns to Vrindavan, which is symbolically represented by the Gundicha temple. In this way, the esoteric meaning of the Ratha-Yatra parade is that we pull the Lord back into our hearts and rekindle the loving relationship we have with Him. Many great poems and songs, such as *Jagannatha-astakam*, have been composed describing the event and the highly ecstatic devotional mood one can enter into. Many verses are also written in the *Caitanya-caritamrta* that describe the pastimes Sri Caitanya Mahaprabhu had during these Ratha-Yatra festivals 500 years ago.

It is also explained that by participating in this festival, chanting and dancing, or helping pull the ropes of the chariots, one becomes free of many lifetimes of *karma*. One can even become liberated due to the spiritual potency of Lord Jagannatha's presence. How this happens is explained as follows: at the very end of one's life when the memories of his activities pass through the mind, when he remembers the amazing Ratha-Yatra festival his mind stops and focuses on that event. Thus, he dies thinking of Lord Jagannatha and is liberated from material existence and returns to the spiritual world, just like a yogi is transferred to the spiritual strata when his mind is fixed on the Supersoul at the time of death. This is why thousands of pilgrims come to Jagannatha Puri every year for Ratha-Yatra.

While in Jagannatha Puri, there are many other places of interest that pilgrims come to see, so I will describe a few of these. About a quarter mile from the Jagannatha temple, walking toward the beach, is Siddha Bakula. This is where, 500 years ago, the great saint Haridas Thakur used to live and chant the Hare Krishna *mantra* 300,000 times a day and where Sri Caitanya would visit him. Haridas attained such an elevated position of ecstasy from chanting the Hare Krishna *mantra* that even though a beautiful prostitute came to tempt him with sex, he was not interested. Thus, he is called the *namacarya*: the master of chanting the holy names. Presently, a small shrine is found here, along with the old and bent tree under which Haridas would chant. The tomb of Haridas Thakur is located next to Purusottama Gaudiya Math where you'll also see beautiful Radha Krishna Deities as well as an image of Haridas. This is an important place of pilgrimage.

A 15 minute walk from here is the temple of Tota-Gopinatha. The Radha Krishna Deities here are very beautiful and it is accepted that Sri Caitanya ended his life by entering into the Deity of Tota-Gopinatha. Also near this area is the old house of Kashi Mishra. It is now used as part of a temple and has nice diorama exhibits of Sri Caitanya's life. It is here we find the Gambhira room, which is where Sri Caitanya lived for 12 years. Through a small window you can see Caitanya's original wooden sandals, water pot, and bed.

A short walk to the east of the Jagannatha temple is the Jagannatha Vallabha Garden, which is almost across from the Balagandhi temple which used to be where Lord Jagannatha would stop during His Ratha-Yatra parade to accept food offerings from all the devotees. At this garden, Sri Caitanya had many pastimes and is where He saw Lord Krishna manifest Himself. A little ways away from the garden is Narendra Sarovara, a small lake where many festivals have taken place with Sri Caitanya and his associates. Even now many pilgrims will visit and take a holy bath in this lake. The Govinda Deity from the Jagannatha temple is brought here for festivals. There is also a little temple with Lord Jagannatha Deities located here. So if foreigners want to see Lord Jagannatha they can come here for *darshan*.

Further down the main road of town near the Gundicha Mandir is the very old temple dedicated to Lord Narasimha, which we can enter to view the Deity of Narasimha. This is also where Sri Caitanya engaged in many *kirtanas* with his close associates. Not far away is Indradyumna Lake where Sri Caitanya once manifested His Mahavishnu form showing His associates His supernatural qualities as an incarnation of God.

About 14 miles from Jagannatha Puri is the Alalanatha temple at Brahmagiri. This is a temple with Jagannatha Deities where there is a large stone slab with the imprint of Sri Caitanya's body. Once when He fell onto the stone in an ecstatic trance and the stone melted leaving the imprint of Sri Caitanya's body as we find it today.

Nineteen miles north of Jagannatha Puri is Konarka, a most interesting temple to Surya, the sun-god. Although it is very old and no longer used for worship, many people come here every day. A Surya temple was here as long ago as the 9th century, but the present temple was built in the 13th century to resemble a huge chariot and has 24 gigantic stone wheels all around it. There are also carvings of seven strong horses who pull the chariot, and the temple is covered with many panels of stone figures depicting many aspects of life, such as scenes with hunters, soldiers, ascetics, maidens, birds, and elephants, etc. There are also three green chlorite deities of Surya in niches on the outside of the temple, reached by ascending flights of stairs. The interior has been filled in and blocked up to help support it. Outside the temple grounds are many shops who sell food or the usual gamut of nick-nacks.

About six miles from Puri is the Saksi-gopala temple, located between the Jagannatha Puri and Khurda Road Junction railway stations. A new station called Saksi-gopala is there where people get off to visit the temple. The Saksi-gopala Deity is the Gopala Deity who walked from Vrindavan to Vidyanagara, a town located 20 to 25 miles from Rajahmundry on the banks of the Godavari River. How this happened was that two *brahmanas* were traveling and visiting the holy places. One was poor and young and was serving the older and richer *brahmana*. The older one was so satisfied with the charitable service of the younger *brahmana* that he vowed in front of the Gopala Deity that he would give his daughter to the younger *brahmana* to be his wife. Later, when they returned home, the older *brahmana* hesitated to fulfill his promise due to pressure from his family. There was some controversy about this between the two *brahmanas* and in a meeting with the people of the town it was agreed that if the Deity Gopala would come to testify as a witness, the older *brahmana* would give his daughter as promised.

The younger *brahmana* went back to Vrindavan and related the situation to Gopala who finally agreed to walk. He told the *brahmana* that He would follow him and that the sound of His ankle bells would indicate He was there, but if the *brahmana* turned around to look, He would walk no farther. So for 100 days they walked toward Vidyanagara, then the sound of the Deity's ankle bells ceased to sound. The *brahmana* looked back and the Deity was standing there smiling. The *brahmana* went to gather the people of the town who were amazed to see the Deity. Then the older *brahmana* agreed to give his daughter in marriage as promised and a temple was built for the Deity. Later the King of Orissa, Purusottama, was insulted by the King of Kataka (Cuttack). So Purusottama fought and defeated the King of Kataka and took charge of the city. He then brought the Gopalaji Deity from Vidyanagara to Kataka and built a temple there. The Deity also stayed in the Jagannatha Temple for some time, but then was moved to a village about six miles from Puri, called Satyavadi. Some time after that a new temple was constructed where we find the Saksi-gopala Deity today. Though the temple does not allow foreigners inside, many people visit this temple with the understanding that whether the Supreme is in the spiritual realm or expands Himself in the material realm in the form of a stone Deity, He can change what is spiritual into material and vice versa whenever He wants. This is why a stone Deity can do what is considered miraculous things, like walk, talk, etc. Thus, it is accepted that the bona fide Deity of the Supreme is nondifferent from the Supreme Himself.

Once our visit to Puri is finished we travel a short ways to our next stop. Bhubaneswar, 60 kilometres from Jagannatha Puri, is a busy town of 125,000, and has been the capital of Orissa since 1956. There are many government buildings and a variety of people who have governmant positions in this city. But as the city name implies, it is a city of Lord Shiva and is especially known for its numerous Shiva temples. Many years ago there used to be over 1000 temples. Most of them that still exist in varying degrees of preservation or decay can be found by walking or taking a *ricksha* around the area of the Bindusagar lake. I'll mention several of these that can be easily found and are noteworthy for their Orissan architecture and the ornate carvings that cover the temple exteriors. Some of these temples are no longer used for worship and are locked up, so the interior is not possible to see. In most cases, the interior is not nearly so ornate as the exterior, so we would not be missing much.

First of all, Bindusagar is the water tank that is said to contain water from the Ganges, Yamuna, Sarasvati, and every other holy river and lake in India. Therefore, many pilgrims come to bathe in the spiritually purifying water. Once a year there is a festival when the deity from the Lingaraja temple is brought to the pavilion in the lake to be bathed.

The Lingaraja temple, just to the south of the Bindusagar lake, is the most important in Bhubaneswar and is known all over India. It is dedicated to the demigod Shiva as Bhubaneswar, or Tribhuvaneswar, "Lord of the Three Worlds," and dates back to 1090 A.D. The temple tower reaches 40 metres high and houses the Shiva *linga* which is bathed daily in milk, water, and *bhang*. The outside of the stone temple is covered with intricate Orissan designs. Non-Hindus are not allowed in the temple complex, but on the north side is a viewing platform near the wall that lets you see the temple and the numerous smaller shrines dedicated to other demigods in the courtyard. The only problem is that when you use the platform, you will be approached by men asking for a donation for either some local cause or helping maintain the platform, which gets little if any upkeep. Everybody knows that these guys are frauds, so we don't give them any money. A few men dressed as *brahmanas* approached me and gave me the hard sell when I was there. They said they had a food distribution program to feed many of the local poor people, but the smell of cigarettes was on their breath, and strict *brahmanas* don't smoke *bidis*. So that was enough to turn me off from giving them anything. But when it was time to leave I had to move quickly to get away from them.

North of the Bindusagar is a group of temples noted for their fine architecture and carved stonework. The small Muktesvara temple, reaching 11 metres high, the Kedareshvara temple across the path, the Siddeswar temple, and the well preserved Parashurameswar temple, built in the 7th century and one of the oldest. All are worth visiting and allow foreigners inside. The exteriors of these temples are exceptional for all the delicate carvings and sculpture work. There are images of important demigods, such as Ganesh, Kartikeya, Durga, Shiva, and figures of animals, birds, etc., or scenes from the *Puranas*.

There is also the Raj Rani temple about 100 metres down the road in a field. It has many carved stone figures decorating the exterior, but the door to the interior is locked. It is one of the finest examples of the Orissan style of temple architecture, and is profusely covered with many ornately carved images. Farther down the road is the Brahmeshwar temple, with four smaller shrines at each corner of the courtyard. This temple dates to the ninth century. Some of the carvings on the outside include the deities of the nine planets, demigods like Ganesh and Brahma, and different aspects of Shiva and Durga. We can also go inside to view the Shiva *lingam* which is worshiped in the morning. Not far away are the Bhaskareswar and Megheswar temples, though less interesting.

On the other side of Bindusagar is the Vaital Deul Shiva temple, built in the 8th century A.D., which has an image of a fearsome form of Durga as an eight-armed Chamundi or Kapalini. She is the goddess who killed the buffalo-headed demon Mahishasura. A scene of this is carved on the northern wall of the temple. Near the Vaital is the Sisiresvara temple, which is worth seeing while you're here, but is not in as good of condition. The Markandesvara and Jambesvara temples are also in the area, but are not in the best of shape. The Rameshvar temple, some distance away from most of the others, is also an interesting and still functioning Shiva temple. Many other temples of less importance can also be found scattered throughout Bhubaneswar.

If you've seen enough Shiva temples, one of the few Vishnu temples in the area is the Ananta Vasudeva temple on the southeast side of the lake. This is an active temple that, unlike others in the area, allows everyone in to see the Deities of Vishnu (Jagannatha), Balarama, and Subhadra. They also have a free food distribution program in which they take food that has been offered to the Deities out to the poor in the nearby villages.

Located on the other side of town on Highway Number 5 is the beautiful ISKCON temple, with lovely Deities of Krishna-Balarama, Sri Caitanya and Nityananda, and Jagannatha, Balarama, and Lady Subhadra. This temple is open to everyone.

If you see Bhubaneswar on a bus tour you'll see a few of the nicest temples, but you may not have as much time to look them over as you'd like. But by taking a morning to walk or take a *ricksha* to these temples you will have enough time to easily wander around and look at each one. Remember that most of the active temples close between noon and four PM.

If you've had enough of temple hunting, you can spend the afternoon visiting a museum or two. There is the nearby Orissa State Museum, which has displays of Hindu, Buddhist, and Jain sculptures. There is also the Tribal Research Bureau, and the Handicrafts Museum that has displays of local folk art.

Five kilometres outside of Bhubaneswar are the Udayagiri and Khandagiri hills. These hills have small caves or cells that were once occupied by Jain monks, the oldest of which date back to the second century B.C. Some of these have some nice stone carvings of Jain *Thirtankaras* or Vedic images, but most of them are quite simple. At the top of the Khandagiri hill is an 18th century Jain temple where you can get some fine views over the area with the city of Bhubaneswar in the distance. Lots of people come here for picnics or short excursions, but unless you're on a tour bus that stops here and you just want to check it out, this place may not be interesting enough for you to make a special trip to see. The small caves are not really that significant.

Heading back towards Puri, eight km south of Bhubaneswar is Dhaulagiri. It is here that King Ashoka is believed to have been converted to Buddhism. Here we find a large new Peace Pagoda built on top of the hill by the Japanese Buddhists Biswa Buddha Nipon Sangha. It has four lifesize images of Buddha facing each of the four directions. Behind the pagoda is a Shiva temple. At the base of the hill are the edicts of King Ashoka carved into the side of a rock that is five by three metres in dimension. The edicts describe the King's reasons for converting to Buddhism.

After we've seen as much as we want to see in Bhubaneswar, we'll take the morning northbound train to Balasore. Some pilgrims will want to get off here in order to take an hour long bus or *ricksha* ride to Remuna. In Remuna is the temple of Ksira-cora-gopinatha, which is an important place of pilgrimage. This was the Deity who hid a pot of sweetrice for His devotee Madhavendra Puri. The story is that once Madhavendra Puri, while visiting Vrindavan, was told in a dream by Krishna that the Gopala Deity had been placed in a thick bush by a temple priest to keep Him hidden from the Muslim invaders. Gopala wanted Madhavendra Puri to find Him and establish a temple. So Madhavendra Puri gathered the local residents, found the Deity in the woods and built a temple. But in another dream the Deity told Madhavendra that He was still very hot from so many years of living outside and needed some sandalwood paste to help cool Him. So Madhavendra Puri traveled to Jagannatha Puri to get some nice sandalwood to bring back to Vrindavan.

On his way, he stopped at the Remuna Gopinatha temple and was attracted to the idea of learning how to make sweetrice the way the cooks prepare it there so he could make similar sweetrice for his Gopala Deity. But thinking that he was offensive for wanting to taste the preparation that was to be offered to the Deity, he decided not to taste any at all. But that night the Deity told the temple priest in a dream to wake up and find a pot of sweetrice that the Deity had hidden behind His dress and to give it to Madhavendra Puri. When the priest awoke and looked behind the Deity's dress, there was the pot of sweetrice. Then the priest went out, found Madhavendra Puri and gave him the sweetrice. From that time the Gopinatha Deity at Remuna has been known as Ksira-cora-gopinatha, the Deity who stole the pot of condensed milk for His devotee.

Furthermore, after Madhavendra Puri had secured a large amount of sandalwood and was on his way back to Vrindavan, he again stopped at Remuna. Then the Gopala Deity in Vrindavan spoke to Madhavendra Puri in a dream telling him that he should simply turn the sandalwood into paste and offer it to the Gopinatha Deity at Remuna. Since Krishna as Gopinatha in Remuna or as Gopala in Vrindavan or wherever He might be are equally the same, offering the paste to Gopinatha would also cool Gopala in Vrindavan. Thus, Gopala relieved His devotee Madhavendra Puri from the task of bringing the heavy load such a great distance back to Vrindavan. In this way, we can see that the Krishna Deities of this region, such as Jagannatha, Saksi-gopala, and Ksira-cora-gopinatha, are very active Deities and display Their supernatural qualities in a way that attracts many pilgrims to the temples of this area.

The Ksira-cora-gopinatha temple is in good condition, and to the left of the entrance are footprints of Sri Caitanya that were installed by Srila Bhaktisiddhanta years ago. When I visited the temple I was able to sit in the temple room watching the priest dress the beautiful Deity of Gopinatha. The main Deity is flanked by two other three foot tall Deities of Krishna. After taking *darshan* I purchased a clay pot of *ksira* (sweetrice) *prasada*, the kind Madhavendra Puri had tasted. It has a thick consistency and is very sweet, the likes of which I've tasted no where else. It is especially auspicious to take this *prasada* while thinking of the pastime of Gopinatha and Madhavendra Puri.

After our visit we ride three minutes farther down the road to visit Madhavendra Puri's *samadhi* tomb. Inside the room is also a display case that shows Madhavendra's shoes. Seeing Deities like Gopinatha and visiting the shrines of such powerful saints like Madhavendra Puri is not only spiritually enlivening, but also very purifying. It is because of saints like Madhavendra Puri that the mysteries of the Supreme become revealed to us. After this most auspicious visit we ride back to Balasore.

In this region of India there is also the Kutopokhari temple, which contains a two metre high granite image of Durga with 18 arms. Some distance away at Sajanagarh the Bhudhara Chandi contains a three-faced, eight-armed image of Shakti standing on seven boars. And on Devagiri Hill stands the Panchlingeswar temple that has five stone Shiva *lingas*.

When our visit to the Balasore area is finished, we can take the morning train to Calcutta which arrives at the Howrah station around two PM. Coming into Calcutta by train can be somewhat intimidating. Calcutta is not the beautiful city it once was. Now it has many areas that are slums, and much of it is dirty, smelly, and hopelessly congested. Arriving at the Howrah station, which is a big and busy place, we make our way through the crowds and out onto the streets where we find a taxi to take us downtown to the Sudder Street area. Staying at a hotel in this area of town allows a person to walk to many of the tourist attractions one may find in Calcutta, such as the Victoria Memorial, the Indian Museum (probably the best in India, though I still prefer the one in Madras), the Birla Planetarium, the Maidan Park, and the downtown shops and bazaars. There's also decent restaurants in the area, and South Indian style vegetarian *thalis* are available at the Hindustan restaurant nearby.

Many young tourists like this area of Calcutta because it is a good meeting place and a lively area. But over the past few years that I've been coming through this city, I've noticed a great deterioration. The city seems like it just keeps getting more run down and filthier with each visit. Though there are many people who seem to take it in stride, I personally no longer look forward to coming through this city.

Calcutta, like any big city, has many things a tourist may want to see. But for the pilgrim there a few places of particular interest. One important temple in this city is the Kali temple, also called Kalighat from which the name Calcutta originates. The temple is said to be about 200 years old and many local people visit it every day. It is surrounded by shops that create a dark narrow lane that a person walks through in order to enter the temple. Many people continually surround the altar to see and offer respects to the deity, which is a large form of Kali. The Ganges used to flow not far from the temple where it would carry away the bodies from the cremation ground. But now the stream is only a small canal of stagnating water. It is said that human sacrifices used to take place here many years ago in the worship of Kali. But now only a buffalo is occasionally sacrificed, and a goat is offered to Kali every morning in a sacrifice that is sponsored by a family who then take the offered meat home to eat as Kali *prasada*. This form of worship, however, is said to be in the mode of darkness. The *Bhagavat Purana* explains that goddess Kali does not actually accept offerings of meat, but that she allows her demoniac associates to accept such offerings. Thus, these animal offerings do not become Kali *prasada*, but are only remnants of lower beings in the mode of darkness. Therefore, one does not often see worshipers of Krishna or Vishnu visiting this temple. Other temples to Shiva, Vishnu, and Radha-Krishna are along Alipore Chetla and Tollygunge roads. And the ISKCON Radha-Govinda temple is at 3C Albert Road.

There is also the Dakshineshwar Kali temple ten km north of town. This is another important temple, built in 1847. The temple complex has a central temple with a deity of Kali, plus two shrines dedicated to Radha-Krishna, and a smaller one for Ganesh. Across the courtyard are 12 smaller Shiva temples with a *linga* in each one. The Indian mystic Ramakrishna was a priest here, and there is a room commemorating his stay. The headquarters of the Ramakrishna mission is downstream across the river at Belur Math, which is a building made to look like a combination of a church, mosque, and a temple to represent the unity of all religions.

Durga is the a goddess of both terror and placidity and is known by many names. Her terrible aspect is in the form of Chandrika or Chamunda and Kali.

Mahishasuramardini is her most terrible form, said to personify the collective strength of the demigods who prayed for her to destroy the demons, such as Mahishasura. Durga is also called Gauri, Uma, Parvati (daughter of the Himalayas), and Ambika (the embodiment of feminine beauty and motherly affection).

If you are in Calcutta in late summer or early fall, you may want to see the festivals of Durga, Kali, and Lakshmi *puja*. Durga and Kali are both forms of the wife of Lord Shiva, and Lakshmi is the wife of Lord Vishnu. During the festivals the temples dedicated to these goddesses become very crowded with pilgrims. There is a grand celebration all over Calcutta, but especially near Babu, Outram, and Princep *ghats* where they take the deities of Durga to the river and celebrate. Durga *puja* begins on the seventh day of the bright half of the month of Aswin (Sept.-Oct.) and ends on the tenth day when processions take the images to the *ghats* and immerse them in the Ganges or other local lakes or rivers.

For the Muslims, Calcutta has the Nakhoda mosque, said to be able to accomodate up to 10,000 worshipers. For Christians, there is the beautiful St. Paul's Cathedral, completed in 1847, but redesigned after 1934. It is one of the most important churches in India. For Jains, there is the Sitambara temple, which is in a complex of four beautiful Jain temples, each built by one of four rich brothers. The main temple is extremely ornate with the interior walls covered with mirrors, colored stones, and mosaics. In fact, the deity, Sheetalnathji, the 10th of the 24 Jain *tirthankaras*, has a 10 carat diamond on its forehead. There is a garden in the middle of the temple grounds which is very pleasant and clean. All the temples are very richly decorated with lots of gold and silver.

When we are finished seeing Calcutta, Sagar Island or Sagardvipa is where some touring pilgrims may want to go. Sagardvipa, south of Calcutta, is the last town along this branch of the Ganges, called the Hugli River. This is where the Ganges completes its journey across India and flows into the ocean. It is said that this place is so spiritually powerful that dying here brings salvation. So this can be an important place for some people, especially in mid-January when the Gangasagar Mela festival is held. At that time a half-million or more pilgrims gather to bathe at the confluence of the Ganges and the ocean to cleanse themselves of all sins. After this, people go to the small temple that is dedicated to Kapila Muni, the philosopher and incarnation of Sri Vishnu who performed austerities and died on the island, and also taught the *sankhya-yoga* system.

Sagar Island is a little out of the way and most tourists avoid the trouble of going. The best way to get there is to take a train from Sealdah station to Diamond Harbor, where the Ganges makes its last turn and heads to the ocean. Taking one of the completely overcrowded buses out of Calcutta is not worth the trouble. After arriving at Diamond Harbor you still must take a bus (one and a half hours) to the ferry (30 minutes), and then another bus to the town at the southern tip of the island (one and a half hours). Then another six hours of bus, ferry, bus, and train to get back to Calcutta after visiting the temple. But the temple is one of the only ones you'll find dedicated to Kapila Muni.

North of Calcutta by about 90 miles or 125 kilometres is one of the holiest places in West Bengal. This place is known as Nabadvipa or Nadia and covers nine islands on the Ganga. In the central island of Antardvipa is Mayapur, the birthplace of Sri Caitanya Mahaprabhu. By understanding a little about Sri Caitanya Mahaprabhu we can better appreciate the importance of Mayapur.

Sri Caitanya was born on the 18th of February in 1486. His father, Jagannatha Misra, and mother, Saci-devi, were both in the family line of Vedic *brahmanas*. He was called Nimai for having been born under a *nima* tree, and the local ladies called Him Gaurahari because of His golden complexion. As He grew up He performed many extraordinary pastimes that indicated exceptional qualities and character. In fact, it became understood that He was an incarnation of Krishna in the guise of His own devotee.

During Sri Caitanya's tenth year He became a scholar in grammar, logic, and Vedic scripture. By the time He was 15 He was considered one of the best scholars of the area, and He defeated many of the most prominent pandits of the region. Scholars from other schools of thought were afraid to meet Him, fearing that they too might be defeated in their philosophy.

When He was 16 or 17 He went to Gaya where He was initiated by the great Vaishnava spiritual master Ishvara Puri, disciple of the renowned Madhavendra Puri. Thereafter, when Caitanya returned to Mayapur, His disposition changed from that of an argumentative scholar to a religious Vaishnava preacher who was steeped in love for Krishna. It was at this time when He began the *sankirtana* movement, gathering friends and associates and engaging in congregational chanting of Krishna's holy names for long hours through the night. He also showed many miracles of ecstasy, and all those who came in contact with Him were also infected with spiritual ecstasy.

When He was 24 years old He took *sannyasa* initiation from Keshava Bharati and renounced family life. He then went to live in Jagannatha Puri, where He did much preaching and performed many wondrous pastimes. He also went on a tour of South India which lasted 2 years. During His travels He talked with many Buddhists, Jains, and Mayavadi impersonalists, converting all of them to Vaishnavism. He also went to Vrindavan and began the rediscovery of many of the holy sights with the assistance of some of His renown followers, such as Rupa and Sanatana Gosvami. Sri Caitanya then traveled down to Prayag (Allahabad) where He used the *Koran* as the basis of His arguments to convert many Muslims to Vaishnavism. From there He went to Benares where He gave spiritual instruction and turned many of the people and most learned scholars of the area into Vaishnavas.

From His 31st year, Sri Caitanya lived in Puri where He was surrounded by His close associates and followers, and where the depths of His spiritual ecstasy increased without bounds. Thus, His life continued until His forty-eighth year when He left this world. Though this short description is most inadequate to understand Sri Caitanya Mahaprabhu, His biographers have left us many details of His life to study.

Mayapur is considered one of the special holy places, no different in its spiritual nature than Vrindavan or Jagannatha Puri. Visiting Mayapur is considered exceptionally purifying and beneficial for one's spiritual progress. Staying in Mayapur for only a few days can give one liberation from the material world through Krishna *bhakti*.

The ISKCON (Hare Krishna) center in Calcutta organizes bus trips to Mayapur a few times a week. But the best time to visit is during the celebration of the birth of Sri Caitanya (Gour Purnima festival), which is on the full moon night of the month of Phalgun (February-March). Every year some 500,000 pilgrims come to visit Nadia from all parts of India. There are many simple guest houses for pilgrims, but the best place to stay is at the ISKCON center in Mayapur, Sri Mayapur Chandrodaya Mandir. You'll find many guest quarters there (which may fill rather quickly during the festival), a temple with beautiful Deities of Radha-Krishna and the eight principal *gopis*, along with stores, a restaurant, gorgeous flower gardens, exhibits, and excellent food for all who want to participate in the festival. And the sacred Ganges is right across the road. Everything you need for staying at a holy place can be found here, plus nice saintly association with other pilgrims from all over the world.

There are many sacred places to see while visiting Mayapur and the Navadvipa area. Many pilgrims go on a *parikrama* or foot journey to see all the significant places and temples of the area that are connected with the pastimes of Sri Caitanya. In some cases this includes a route of up to 50 kilometres. To do this independently would take several days with the help of a dependable guide. But the best way to see the most important places where spiritual events took place is to arrive in Mayapur a few weeks before the Gour Purnima festival. As of this writing, the devotees of ISKCON organize a week long *parikrama* for all interested persons to go around in a large group and visit these places. If one cannot do this, there are other *parikramas* to places much closer to the Mayapur temple. Actually, a complete guidebook could and should be written describing all these places and their importance, and directions on how to get to each one. I can't do that here, but I will try to describe a few of them.

The area of Navadvipa-*dhama* (including Navadvipa city, which has a population of 150,000) covers nine islands which manifests in the form of an eight-petalled lotus flower, with the *dvipa* or island of Antardvipa being the whorl. Antardvipa has a perimeter of 10 miles. In the center of Antardvipa is Mayapur, where Lord Caitanya was born in the small house of Jagannatha Misra under the *nima* tree. This most important spot, called Yogapitha, is only a short walk or *ricksha* ride from the ISKCON temple. The *nima* tree which is there now is a cutting of the original tree under which Sri Caitanya was born.

Farther down the road is Srivasa Angan, the place that marks the spot where the house of Srivasa used to be. This is where Sri Caitanya would perform ecstatic *sankirtana* with His close associates. This is where the *sankirtana* movement originated.

Farther into the small village is the *samadhi* tomb of Chand Kazi, who was a Muslim magistrate of Nadia during the time of Sri Caitanya. The Kazi tried to stop the *sankirtana* movement, but Sri Caitanya organized a large *sankirtana* party with many people to demonstrate in front of the Kazi's house. Caitanya also defeated the Kazi in arguments based on scripture. Thus, the Kazi surrendered to Sri Caitanya and promised never to interfere with the chanting of Krishna's holy name again. Actually, the Kazi was an incarnation of Krishna's wicked uncle King Kamsa, who was deservedly killed by Krishna. But this time Krishna, in the form of Sri Caitanya, dealt with His uncle, the Kazi, in a much different way. At this *samadhi* where the body of the Kazi is buried, a *nima* tree, representing Sri Caitanya, and a Champa flower tree, which sprouted as soon as the Kazi had been buried, grew intertwined showing the eternal relationship between the Kazi and Sri Caitanya.

Not far from here by *ricksha* we can arrive at the Jagannatha Mandir. The Deities here are very special and the story about Them must be told. At the time of Lord Caitanya, 500 years ago, there lived in Navadvipa a great Vaishnava named Jagadisha Ganguli. He would walk 600 miles to Puri each year to participate in the Ratha-Yatra festival. But he was an old man and was affected with a disease that left him blind. Thereafter, his friends advised him not to attempt the long trip to Puri since it would be too dangerous.

Feeling despondent he thought of committing suicide. But Lord Jagannatha spoke to him in a dream one night and told him that while bathing in the Ganges the next day a log floating down the river would bump his head at which time his sight would be restored. Then he should take the log to a particular devotee carpenter and ask him to carve the Deity of Lord Jagannatha. When all this had happened, he took the log to the person to carve the Deities, but the carver was very hesitant to take up the task since he was a leper. Not only did he feel unqualified to do it, but it would also be extremely painful since his hands were diseased. Jagadish insisted, however, explaining that Lord Jagannatha Himself had ordered this. So the carver began the work. To his surprise as he worked he became cured of his leprosy.

Jagadish brought the Jagannatha Deities to where They are now located and established Their worship. But after the disappearance of Jagadish, the worship of the Deities decreased until They were forgotten. Over the years They became completely covered under a termite mound. Centuries later the local villagers noticed a beautiful flower growing on the mound. When they went near it they could hear a voice saying, "Please bring me water, I'm thirsty." Thus, some 50 years ago, the villagers cleared away the dirt and found the Deities unharmed, even though They had been neglected for many years. In spite of the fact that the Deities were carved from wood and covered by a terminte mound, They were still intact. The villagers then established a simple temple for Lord Jagannatha, Lord Balarama, and Subhadra to resume worshiping Them.

Since that time the Deities had been worshiped by Phatik Chaterjee. But in 1979 the aging priest realized he would soon die. After much consideration he decided to make sure the Deities would continue being properly worshipped by giving Them to the care of the devotees of ISKCON. Phatik died shortly thereafter. Now the Deities have a nice, new temple and are visited by many pilgrims from around the world. Many come here to try the *maha-prasada* (food preparations offered to the Deities) and relish its spiritual taste. The scriptures state that Sri Ksetra, or Jagannatha Puri, is eternally manifest in this area of Mayapur. Thus, one gets the same benefits of visiting Jagannatha Puri by visiting this Jagannatha Mandir in Mayapur.

There are many other places in Navadvipa-*dhama* that should be visited. Across the Jalangi river from the large ISKCON temple is the house and *bhajan kutir* of Bhaktivinoda Thakur. He was the father of Bhaktisiddhanta Sarasvati who was the spiritual master of A. C. Bhaktivedanta Swami Prabhupada who, under the orders of Bhaktisiddhanta, came to America almost penniless and started the ISKCON movement. Here at this house Bhaktivinoda spent much time chanting, reading, and writing. It was also from here where he could see by transcendental vision that in the future many people from all over the world would come to engage in *sankirtana*, which is now taking place.

Narasimha Polli (22 kilometres from Vidyanagar) is where Lord Narasimha came to rest and dig out a small lake to wash Himself after He had killed the demoniac Hiranyakasipu. It was at this spot that all the demigods and Prahlada Maharaja worshiped Lord Narasimha to try and calm His anger.

Shantipur is where Sri Caitanya distributed and took Krishna *prasada* with many of His associates on the disappearance day of Madhavendra Puri. He proclaimed that anyone who partakes in this yearly festival in Shantipur achieves devotion to Krishna. There is also a reconstruction of the house of Sri Advaita (a very important associate of Lord Caitanya) and a temple commemorating the site where he resided.

Simantadvipa, on the edge of Navadvipa on the south bank of the Ganges, is where Parvati, wife of Lord Shiva, meditated on Sri Caitanya. When she saw Him she took the dust from His foot and placed it on her head. This showed how even the wife of Lord Shiva recognized the superior position of Sri Caitanya. To the west of the Alakananda river is Kashi, called Mahakashi, where Lord Shiva resides and chants Gauranga, another name of Caitanya. Liberation is said to easily be achieved simply by chanting Gauranga at this spot.

Beside the Gomati river is the forest of Naimisa where Saunaka *rishi* and many other great sages, including Lord Shiva, held the sacrifice of listening to the *Srimad-Bhagavatam* at the beginning of Kali-yuga.

These are only a few of the many places in the area that lend spiritual merit when you visit them. It is also said that whoever fasts and worships Sri Caitanya Mahaprabhu on Gour Purnima, the full moon and appearance day of Sri Caitanya in the month of Phalgun (February-March), and bathes in the Ganges, crosses over material existence along with 1000 of his ancestors and attains the spiritual abode of Goloka-Vrindavan after death. Thus, the importance of Mayapur can not be overlooked by any sincere pilgrim.

After visiting Mayapur and acquiring our new spiritual assets, we take a taxi or temple bus back to Calcutta. Other places important to various pilgrims in the area of West Bengal include the temple of Tarakeshwar Babu, 57 km west of Calcutta. The main deity here is a black stone Shiva *lingam*. The architecture is nothing outstanding but many pilgrims visit this temple, especially for the Shivaratri or Kasta-mela festival when they may carry pots of water all the way from the Ganges river (22 miles away) to pour on the *lingam*. Karmarpukur is further west where the philosopher Ramakrishna was born. There is a temple with a marble statue of him that marks the spot where he took birth. Further on is Vishnupur (200 km from Calcutta) which has about 30 Hindu temples, the oldest of which dates back to the 17th century. The most impressive of these temples are the Madan Mohan, Madan Gopal, Kalachand Sri Mandir, the Shyama Raya, and the Shridhara temples. These temples have very interesting architecture with terra cotta panels that illustrate the pastimes of Krishna.

North of Nadia, some 130 km from Calcutta, is Shantineketan. This place is where the poet Rabindranath Tagore established a university from what began as an *ashram* that his father started in 1861. Nearby is Kendubilwa where the great poet and Vaishnava philosopher Jaidev was born. Each year in mid-January many come here for a few days to perform non-stop recitations of Jaidev's poems. Fifty-eight km north is Bakreshwar, and about 20 km further is Tarapith, both small towns that are sacred to Shiva and Kali worshipers.

From Calcutta some people go to Darjeeling. This town sits on a narrow mountain ridge and was once the summer headquarters of the Bengal government. The best way to go is to fly to Bagdogra and then continue by bus or train. The miniature railway or "Toy Train" is a famous experience that many tourists like when going up to this mountain resort. But it takes longer and some people have said that the seven hours of continual winding through the hills gets repetitious. At Darjeeling you can get a great view of some of the Himalayan mountains. From Observatory Hill, or a better view from Tiger Hill 10 km south of Darjeeling, one can easily see Mount Kanchenjunga flanked by Kabru and Pandim. To the right you can also see Mount Everest, Makalu, and Lhotse if the weather is good. The view of the mountains is actually the main attraction of Darjeeling, aside from being an escape from the heat of the plains. The general tourist may like the atmosphere and feeling of this town with all its little shops and a variety of local people from the Himalayan region. And some come here to go on treks into the mountains. But if touring is your main interest, then a better place that is more easily reached is Kathmandu, which I'll describe later.

There are some Hindu temples in Darjeeling like the Dhirdham temple, and Buddhist monasteries such as the Ghoom and the Aloobari monasteries, and some Christian churches. And on Observatory Hill, where there is now a Shiva temple, there used to be a monastery of the Red Hat sect before it was destroyed in the 19th century by the Nepalis. The monastery was called Dorjeling (the place of the thunderbolt) from which Darjeeling got its name. But other than this, Darjeeling has no spiritual significance. However, some pilgrims come through this area on their way farther east to places like Sikhim, Assam, or Arunachal Pradesh.

Most of the far eastern states of India are restricted areas and foreigners are given entrance only with the proper permits. So plan accordingly if you want to go. The eastern part of the state of Sikhim is closed to tourists, but you can still visit the capital, Gangtok, which is easily reached by road from Darjeeling. Sikhim is a Buddhist state and has many monasteries, which some pilgrims may want to visit. But many are reached only by trekking to them. To the west of Gangtok is the town of Rumtek, which has the Dharma Chakra Center, a monastery in the lower valleys of Sikkim that is the headquarters of the Mahayana Kagyupa sect of Tibetan Buddhism. Farther west is Pemayangtse, located on a long ridge with good views of the Kanchenjunga mountain range. It is said to be the oldest monastery in Sikkim and is the headquarters of the Mahayana Nyingmapa sect of Tibetan Buddhism.

Assam has a few places that the serious pilgrim may want to see. In Guahati, the capital of Assam, there is the temple of nine planets, the Navagraha Mandir, on Chitrachala Hill and a Shiva temple on Peacock Island in the Brahmaputra river. Not far from Guahati on a hill at Hajo is the finely decorated Hayagriva Madadeva Mahdap temple where the Bhotias believe Buddha left this world and attained *nirvana*. Twelve km south of Gauhati is the Vasistha Ashram where the great sage Vasistha once lived. And taking a pilgrimage to the Pao Mecca mosque near Hajo is believed to equal one-fourth of a pilgrimage to Mecca.

On top of Nichala Hill, 10 km from Guahati, is the Kamakshya Mandir which attracts pilgrims from all over India. Nichala Hill is said to be a form of Lord Shiva's *lingam*. This temple is one of the main centers of the Shakti and Tantric philosophy in India and enshrines a *yoni* of Devi, Shiva's wife. It is said that many years ago this temple had as many as 5,000 dancers affiliated with it, which can give you some idea of how big and important it once was. The original structure, the ruins of which can still be seen, was destroyed in 1553 by a *brahmana*, Kalapahar, who had been rejected from his *brahmana* status for marrying a Muslim princess.

North of Assam is Arunachal Pradesh, which has India's largest Buddhist monastery at Tawang, located at an altitude of 10,000 feet. This is where the sixth Dalai Lama was born and where his footprint is still honored. There are more than 250 *lamas* of the Tibetan Gelugpa sect that reside here. The monastery shrine has bronze images of the Mahayana Buddhist pantheon and a

26 feet tall gilded deity of a seated Buddha. Many pilgrims attend the New Year's festival to watch the masked dancers. Another place of pilgrimage is the Brahmakund lake near the border of China and Burma. This is formed by the Brahmaputra river. Bathing here is said to wash away one's bad *karma*, which thousands of Hindus do, especially during the Makar Sakranti festival in mid-January. These are some of the noteworthy places of spiritual importance in the easternmost parts of India.

Back in Calcutta we arrange to leave by train from the Sealdah station to travel to another holy town called Gaya. The train ride is a long one, leaving at 11.30 in the morning and arriving at 9.30 at night. The problem with getting into Gaya at this time is that, being a small town with few good hotels, the better hotels are usually already filled. So we may have to look around and spend a night at wherever we can get a room, which may be at a place with a much lower standard than we'd prefer. Nontheless, Gaya is a very important holy place and many Hindus come here.

The significance of Gaya is described in chapters 43 through 50 of the *Vayu Purana*. In a conversation between Narada Muni and Sanat Kumara it is related that many, many years ago the demon Gaya performed a severe penance at Brahmajuni Hill. The penance caused such a disturbance throughout the universe that the demigods went to Lord Vishnu for advice. After conferring with Him, Lord Brahma went to Gaya and asked him to give his body in sacrifice, which he agreed to do. Then Gaya lay on the ground at Kolahala (Brahmajuni) Hill and Dharma placed a stone slab on the head of Gaya on which Brahma would perform the sacrifice. The stone, however, kept moving and many demigods who came to participate in the sacrifice put their feet on the stone to help steady it. Still it could not be kept steady, so Lord Vishnu also appeared and placed His foot on the stone to steady it. Thus, the slab of rock, that was once Dharmavrata, wife of Marici, was touched by Vishnu and all the demigods, such as Brahma, Shiva, Dharma, etc. Then Brahma performed the sacrifice at the beginning of the Sveta Varaha Kalpa.

Because Vishnu and the demigods were pleased with Gaya, they asked him if he wanted a boon. He asked them that the city be named after him and that Lord Vishnu and the demigods continue to reside in the town of Gaya forever in manifest and unmanifest forms. He also asked that those on whose behalf the *sraddha* ceremony is performed go to Brahmaloka, and that the sins of all those who visit Gaya perish. Lord Vishnu replied that all he had asked for would be granted. Thus, as stated in the *Vayu Purana* (45.55), "It is certain that a man who performs *sraddha*, etc., uplifts thousands of *Pitris* (ancestors) of his family, including himself, and leads them to Vishnuloka, the region of Vishnu." In this way, by performing the *sraddha* ceremony in the city of Gaya in which *pinda*, balls of rice *prasada*, mystically is offered to one's forefathers, they are relieved of any hellish existence. The person to whom the *pinda* is offered can then be liberated from material life. Furthermore, it is stated that if a son stays in Gaya for three fortnights, or fifteen days, or at least three nights, he sanctifies seven generations of his family. The opportunity to go to Gaya is considered very rare to achieve, and dying here confers salvation, even to Brahma. It is also stated that each step one takes on his journey to Gaya equals a flight of steps toward Svargaloka, the heavenly region, for ones ancestors.

For those who want to perform the *sraddha* ceremony, shops around the Vishnupada temple in the old part of town sell articles for the ritual and priests are ready to help the pilgrims perform it properly. Actually, some pilgrims may have started the ritual as far away as Varanasi where they might have cremated a relative. Then they come to Gaya to perform the *sraddha* ceremony in front of the Vishnupada temple on the banks of the Phalgu river. Sometimes cremations also take place here. The river flows during the monsoon season but completely dries up in winter. The *sraddha* ceremony also includes visiting several temples and sites of this town for spiritual purification. Before commencing the ritual, one crosses the river to the small Sitaji temple to offer garlands and respects to the Deities of Mother Sita, Lord Rama, and His brothers Laxman and Satrughna. Then they go back to the Vishnupada temple to continue. Thus, with the help of a priest, a person or family will be assisted in performing the ritual, and chanting the *mantras*, and making the beneficial offerings to help relieve their deceased ancestors of any suffering they may be enduring.

The Vishnupada temple is the main temple in Gaya. It was built in 1787 by the Maharani of Indore and houses the stone that has a 40 cm impression of Lord Vishnu's footprint. It is generally not open to westerners, but I visited it while wearing a *dhoti* and *kurta* and was allowed inside. I was also guided through the process of offering sweets to the footprint of Lord Vishnu. During a previous visit I was also guided through the *sraddha* ceremony, which I've briefly described. This is a tradition that goes back hundreds and thousands of years and is very rare for a Westerner to be able to participate in such traditions.

Just north of the Vishnupada temple is a temple to Surya the sun god. A kilometre southwest of Gaya is the Brahmajuni Hill. We can walk the steep 1000 steps to the top of the hill where there are a few small shrines to Narada, Buddha, and Mother Durga. From the top we get a good view over the area.

If we are interested we can visit Barabar Hill where there are seven cave temples, locally known as Satgharas, that were described in E. M. Foster's "A Passage to India." These are located 20 km north of Gaya and date back to 200 B.C. Two of them have inscriptions by Ashoka. They also served as retreats for Jain monks, and the inside walls are known for their polished surfaces. The interiors consist of vaulted roofs and sloping sides. The most noteworthy of these caves are the Sudama and Lomasa Rishi Caves. The latter has an oval chamber and a dome roof and the most elaborate doorway of all the caves. The interior stone is cut to resemble a hut with sloping timber supports and curved eaves carved in relief.

The town of Bodhgaya is 13 km from Gaya and is reached by taking a ride a bus or minibus. Bodhgaya is one of the most sacred places of Buddhism for it was here that Buddha became enlightened and where Buddhism really began. Many Buddhists as well as Hindus come here from all over the world. The most important place in this very small town is the Mahabodhi temple which has a pyramidal tower rising 180 feet high, situated next to the Bo tree. The present Bo tree is a direct descendent of the original tree that Buddha sat under in meditation when he became enlightened. On the north side of the temple is a platform marking where Buddha walked in meditation. In the tall spired temple, which is supposed to be similar to the original one that was built by Ashoka in the third century B.C., there is a large gilded image of the Buddha on the altar. Behind the temple is a lotus pond that the Buddha was supposed to have bathed in. It is pleasant to take some time here and sit under the Bo tree or near the lotus pond and meditate on the significance of this place. By the shoe stall are men who sell guidebooks that contain information on Buddha's life, which is worth some study.

There are several monasteries and temples in this town, most of which are interesting to see, such as the Tibetan monastery with a large wheel of law; the Thai monastery built like a typical *wats* with a beautiful altar inside; and the Japanese monastery with a beautiful deity of Buddha from Japan.

From Gaya we take a bus to Rajgir, which is another small but holy place with much history for Buddhists and Jains. The Buddha spent five rainy seasons here and did much teaching. After the Buddha's death, the First Buddhist Council was held here at Saptaparini cave. The Jain Mahavira also taught here for 14 rainy seasons, and the 20th *Tirthankara*, Muni Suvrata, was born here. This was also the place where Mahavira's earliest disciples died.

Across from the small square in town is Venuvana, the bamboo park where King Bimbisara built a monastery for the Buddha and his disciples. In the park is Karanda Tank where the Buddha used to bathe. Just south of the park are 22 hot springs with Jain and Hindu temples around them. A path leads to some natural caves on Vaibhara Hill where the first Buddhist Council took place. On top of the hill are several modern Jain temples. Gridhrakuta Hill has two natural caves where Buddha lived and is where he did much of his preaching. And on Ratna Giri hill is the World Peace Stupa built by the Japanese which can be seen from miles around. There are other things you can see here, including the Thai, Japanese, Burmese, and Jain temples. There are a number of things to see in Rajgir, and the best thing to do is stop at the Tourist Office and buy a guidebook to all the places of importance.

From Rajgir we continue six miles north to Nalanda, 90 km from Patna. Nalanda isn't really a holy place like the other towns I've mentioned, but it does have some importance for Buddhists and Jains. Buddha and Mahavira, the last Jain *Tirthankara*, visited and taught at this place often, and the Nalanda University became famous because of its exceptional professors and high standard of teaching. At one point, when Hieun Tsang visited in the seventh century, the students numbered over 10,000 and there were 2,000 teachers. The local princes supported the college, thus enabling it to accomodate the students' room, board, and education without charge. And many of the Gupta Kings built monasteries for the resident monks. The university started to decline during the eighth century because of political changes in India. But when the Mohammadan invaders arrived, they killed many of the monks and ransacked and burned the university. The library is said to have had over two million volumes and burned for six months.

Presently, the ruins of the university, the main point of interest in this town, can still be seen, and from a distance it looks like a huge fortress. You can go through what is left of some of the monasteries and temples and see how big they were, with rooms for students, lecture halls, kitchens, libraries, bathrooms, and wells. West of here is the Sariputra *stupa*, which was built by Ashoka in honor of Ananda, the first disciple of Buddha. Nalanda also has Jain, Japanese, and Burmese rest houses, as well as Thai and Chinese temples. There is also a research center on Buddhism and Pali literature set up by the Bihar government.

Another sacred place for Jains is the small town of Pawapuri. This is 25 km from Nalanda and 13 km south of Bihar city. Lord Mahavira attained salvation and was cremated here. A white marble temple in the center of a lotus pond marks the place. Five more Jain temples are located nearby.

Now we move on by bus to Patna, the capital of Bihar, what used to be the ancient Pataliputra. It is a busy city along the Ganges river with over half a million residents. It is not really a great tourist town, but it does have a few interesting things. The Patna Museum near High Court has many Hindu and Buddhist sculptures in stone, terra cotta, and bronze. Not far from the Maidan Park is the Golghar, a beehive-shaped building that was construced in 1786 by Captain John Garstin after a famine. It was to be used as a granary holding up to 150,000 tons of wheat. It was hardly ever used, but now people come to climb the steps up the 25 metre tall building to get good views of the city and Ganges river.

In the old section of the city is one of the most sacred places for Sikhs, the Har Mandir, where Gobind Singh was born in 1660. He was the 10th and last Sikh guru and made their scripture, the *Granth*, the spiritual authority in place of personal gurus. The Har Mandir is a pleasant temple and has a little museum as well. Anyone can go in as long as you leave your shoes outside and put a cover on your head. The easiest way to get to Har Mandir is to hire a motor *ricksha* from the east side of Maidan park. We'll go through the very narrow streets of the old town, which are hopelessly crowded with people, bicycle *rickshas*, ox carts, cars, motor bikes, etc., all trying to get through. And the exhaust fumes from other vehicles are horrendous. Also in the old town area is the Khudabaksh library, started in 1900, that houses rare Arabic and Islamic manuscripts, Moghul paintings, and other things.

One of the important reasons for our visit to Patna is that this is where we prepare for our trip to Kathmandu. The easiest way to get there from Patna is to simply fly. Once we're on the plane it's only about a 45 minute flight. And we can get seven day visas when we arrive at the Kathmandu airport. But going to Kathmandu by land is a different matter. We can use a tour company to arrange for our bus ride and overnight hotel stay at the border town. And we will want to get some small passport photos of ourselves for our visa applications at the Nepal border. Done locally, the photos may be of poor quality, but they'll work. After this there's nothing left to do but make sure we're on the bus on time. If we've booked our trip through a travel company, they may even escort us to our bus.

Some Jain pilgrims may want to divert their trip to see Vaishali, a town 40 kilometres north of Patna where the Jain saint Mahavira was born. The Second Buddhist Council was also held there in 383 B.C. However, there is really not much to see, except for an Ashok pillar and the ruins of some Buddhist *stupas*. Otherwise, if our bus leaves Patna by noon, after a long and boring ride, the bus will arrive at the border town of Rexaul around 7.30 PM. By that time it may be quite dark, and the town does not have an abundance of street lights. But there will be plenty of cycle *ricksha* drivers who will be able to take us where we need to go to get across the border. But be careful! Make sure you agree on the price of the *ricksha* ride BEFORE you go anywhere. This should cost no more than 20 to 50 rupees. If the driver doesn't agree to that, then walk along and find another driver even if you are tired from your long ride, unless you just don't care. And don't agree to let him exchange Indian rupees for Nepali rupees for you. He'll take a chunk of the change and say there was a charge or tax. He may also say he needs 75 rupees for the tax that's charged on *rickshas* crossing the border. There is no *ricksha* tax. And although not all drivers may try these tricks, some of them will tell you anything in an attempt to get your money if you look like you don't know the procedure for crossing the border. Don't listen to any of this and just give him the agreed price for the ride or find someone else or complain about it to someone.

In any case, crossing the Nepal border takes about 45 minutes from the time we get off the bus. Our first stop will be at the Indian immigration office to check out of the country and get our passports stamped. The misquitoes are so thick as we and the clerks fill out the forms in these offices that we practically have to dance to keep them from biting. Stop moving for a second and they've got us. When we leave this office we ride through the night along the dark, quiet, and deserted road and cross into Nepal. The next stop is to get our Nepal visa, if we don't already have one, which costs 282 Nepali rupees (in 1990). (It was 180 Nepali rupees for every 100 Indian rupees.) After this we continue our ride to the next stop at the Nepal immigration office to check into the country. Then it's on to Birganj, the Nepal bordertown, and our hotel, the standards of which depends on the travel company with which we booked. It could end up being very basic accomodations at a rinky dink house where we spend the night fighting misquitoes instead of sleeping. By the time morning comes we'll be relieved just for the chance to get the heck out of town and on our way to Kathmandu.

The buses leave Birganj between 6.00 and 9.00 AM. If we get the faster Japanese-made bus and leave around 7.30, we can expect to arrive in Kathmandu about 4.30. The ride is long and the bus is always filled with too many people. But we will notice a difference between the Indian and Nepali cultures right away. And the further we get into Nepal, the bigger the differences we'll find. At first the landscape is nothing special as we ride through the plains. But later we'll ride past steep hills with terraced slopes and little cabins precariously built on them that look as if they could tip over and roll down at any minute. We'll also ride next to rivers, some of which have swift rapids, flowing through the mountainous hills. Sometimes we'll go over a hill that allows us to see some snow capped peaks in the distance. A few times we'll stop at small Nepal towns and get out to stretch and buy some fruit, or have a noon stop for a vegetarian lunch at a little village restaurant where we can converse with the local people and our fellow travelers. Invariably there will be other Westerners on the bus, and it can be fun to talk and share stories of our journey.

Gradually, as we get closer to Kathmandu, the hills get quite big and the landscape is very beautiful; breathtaking in some parts. This is why we decided to come by land instead of plane. But for many people, taking this trip once is enough. Flying to Kathmandu and avoiding the two days of travel is just easier, unless you're on a low budget. As we creep up the last and biggest hill on the winding and narrow road that has a steep drop on one side, we hope the driver knows what he's doing. One wrong move and we're all finished. The roads here have no guardrails. Nonetheless, as the bus turns this way and that, it gives us a chance to look out over the picturesque landscape of Nepal. But soon we're over the top of the hill and we slowly start down the other side, riding past houses and little businesses or shops on the outskirts of Kathmandu valley. After about another 45 minutes or so, we make the last few turns into the city and here we are, on the other side of the world, in the foothills of the Himalayas, in that strange and exotic city of Kathmandu.

When we arrive, whether by bus or by air, many agents from hotels will be there to greet us and offer their rates and services. Some may even provide a free ride just for us to come and see the hotel. If it sounds good, check it out. It could be worthwhile. When I go to Kathmandu, rather than staying in the Thamel area where the newer hotels are located, I like to stay near Durbar Square in the old section of town. There we readily find much more of the old culture, which is the real Kathmandu as far as I'm concerned.

Kathmandu, a city of about 300,000, has many things of interest for any tourist. For those who wanted to get away from the heat of the plains of India and cool off near the Himalayan mountains, Kathmandu is far more interesting than Darjeeling. In fact, Kathmandu has so many things to see while we're in town that the best thing to do is get a good guide book that tells us all about the area so we can decide what to see and do. One of the things Kathmandu is known for is the treks that people can take up into the foothills of the Himalayas. There are many small travel agencies in the city that can make arrangements for you to trek solo or with a guide or with groups. And there are many routes one can take. I talked with one man who had just returned from the Everest trek and said that the views were fantastic. This is one of the better known treks of the area, but can be fairly rough, takes three weeks, and goes up to the base camp of Mt. Everest. So you should be in good physical shape if you want to go on this one.

Kathmandu has a wide variety of people from ethnic groups that include Tibetans, Indians, Sherpas, Rais, Limbus, Gurungs, Magars, Chetris, and the Newars, Kathmandu's original inhabitants. We'll also see tourists from all over the world, some of whom may live close to our own home. Near the Freak Street area there are still plenty of hippies wandering about who look like they're right out of the '60s era and haven't changed in 30 years. There are also local guys who come up to you and discreetly ask if you're interested in any grass, hash, opium, or in changing money. Kathmandu is a mixture of people and things the likes of which we'll see no where else.

Buddhism and Hinduism are the two main religions here, and they sometimes blend together so closely that it's difficult to tell where one leaves off and the other begins. Unfortunately, many of the Hindu temples are strictly off-limits to foreigners, although Buddhist temples are open to all and usually allow photography inside. In this way, the Buddhists, who are some of the friendliest people you'll ever meet, do far more to promote inter-cultural understanding than the Hindus. Therefore, Buddhism will continue to grow as they allow foreigners to enter their temples and look or participate in the activities and learn more about them, whereas the exclusiveness of the Hindu temples does nothing to increase cultural exchange. Nonetheless, whether we're allowed in all the temples or not, we'll see and appreciate the unique architecture of the many temples and older buildings.

There are many colorful shops in the area and vendors sell all sorts of items that include food, jewelry, Buddhist masks and deities, Tibetan carpets, caps, jackets, bags, lots of *thanka* paintings, and many other things, much of which is geared toward the tourist trade. There are a few designated streets that block all motor traffic in the morning to allow people to come in from the countryside and set up stalls to sell their fruit and vegetables. Such a marketplace always provides an interesting blend of local people to see. By noon they all go their way and the streets open up to traffic again.

There are also a number of vegetarian restaurants or cafes, some of which will remind us of the little cafes that were in San Francisco back in the '60s. Tourists from all over will come in and out of these cafes talking in all sorts of languages, but especially English, and will have a meal or tea and a desert to the background music of Western rock & roll. The hotel I stayed in, The Eden, has a rooftop restaurant where we can eat outside while hearing the sounds of the town below and viewing the sunset over the city skyline with the mountains all around us.

On the nearby corner of New Road and Surkha Path is the Super Market, which is like a small mall with a variety of stores where we can get some of the more practical things we might need, from flashlights, alarm clocks, locks, luggage, trekking clothes, or whatever. I mention this because by this time in our travels things that have become broken or lost, as things sometimes do when traveling, can easily be replaced here. Some of these itmes are not so readily found while traveling in India. And if you're interested in having custom jewelry made or embroidery work done on your jacket or jeans or something, there are shops that will offer this service in the Indrachowk area, north of the Teleju temple. These people can do it fast and for a very reasonable price.

As we walk through the streets of Kathmandu toward Durbar Square, we pass Basantapur Square, which is like an open flea market. It is used by the local people who set up dozens of tables to sell every sort of nick-nack from old Nepali or Tibetan jewelry, coins, deities, prayer wheels, beads, lots of *khukris* or decorated Nepali knives, metal pots, and anything else they think a tourist might like. Many of these tables are run by family members as an additional or only source of income. It's a great place to shop for souvenirs or little presents for friends back home, but we have to bargain. And if we ask about a price on something and then tell them it's too much and walk away, they'll follow us and keep asking how much we'll offer. As long as they think they might make a sale, they won't give up. This can become a real nuisance. But sometimes we can say a ridiculously low price and they'll accept.

Tourists, however, must be careful in buying certain items if they want something genuine. For example, the Buddhist *thanka* paintings are of two kinds: the Nepali paintings which may be detailed and interesting, but often have little philosophical basis; and the Tibetan *thankas* which are usually simpler in design but are painted by an authoritative artist or Tibetan monk. The Tibetan artist may gather herbs and semi-precious stones to grind into dust for making his own paints rather than using synthetic colors. The Tibetan style of painting is a science, and each painting may take the artist up to three months or longer to do, depending on the size, and is philosophically genuine. What this means is that every detail of the painting has a specific purpose and significance, whether it be the color of the deity, the hand gesture, the sitting posture, etc. Everything can be interpreted according to Buddhist philosophy, whereas the Nepali paintings, though more readily available and sometimes less expensive, often have no real esoteric meaning. Therefore, they are not genuine Buddhist *thankas*, but merely a conglomeration of designs and figures. Of course, if you see something you like and want to buy it, it's your decision.

Authentic Tibetan paintings are valued in three ways. Aside from the condition and size of the painting, it is also valued according to who painted it. There are paintings by monks who occasionally make a painting to sell. Then there are monks who paint only because they love to and do not sell the paintings but only give them to special friends, which make such paintings more valuable. The most valuable paintings are those painted by monks because of their love of the paintings and who keep them, which means the paintings go into circulation only after the death of the monk. Such paintings are the most rare.

Anyway, this has been some general information for any tourist. But getting back to the purpose of our journey, which is to see the spiritual side of this area, we'll now continue through Kathmandu valley by visiting some of the temples. This area has quite a number of temples, and you may not want to visit all of them, but I will describe some of the most interesting and you can take it from there.

Next to the flea market of Basantapur Square is the Kumari Chowk temple. This is the temple that houses a living goddess, Kumari Devi, considered to be an incarnation of Durga. She is a girl chosen from a Newar family, and is installed on the throne in a grand ceremony when the spirit of the goddess Kumari is said to enter the girl's body. The girl resides as a goddess in the temple until she reaches puberty when it is considered that she again becomes human. Then a new girl is chosen. Once a year during the Indra festival she is taken on a chariot around the city for all to see.

Beyond this temple is Durbar Square where there are many temples of various sizes. Some of them are very small, which allows you to easily see the deity just inside the doorway. Other temples are larger, but entrance may not be allowed for foreigners except in the Buddhist temples. Durbar Square is continually filled with the bustle of Nepalese life, whether it be men or women selling fruits, vegetables, spices, etc., from small shops or curbside stands, or children going off to school, devotees visiting temples, or the many tourists roaming through the streets. As we enter Durbar Square we face the Trailokya Mohan Vishnu temple, behind which is an image of Vishnu's bird carrier, Garuda. Behind this is a temple to Lakshmi-Narayan, and small Ganesh and Shiva temples. To our right is the three-roofed Maju Deval, and further right is the Shiva-Parvati temple where the images of Shiva-Parvati are looking out the window over the square.

Around the corner is the entrance to the old palace. At the gate is an image of Hanuman covered with red vermilion. To our left as we enter the courtyard is a beautiful Deity of Lord Narasimha in the act of killing the demon Hiranyakasipu. Across the courtyard is the Basantapur Tower covered with very ornate wood carvings. We can climb the stairways up inside the nine-storey tower to get a view over Basantapur Square, Freak Street, and the city skyline. When we leave the old palace we face an area with many temples that are dedicated to Vishnu, Krishna, Sarasvati, Jagannatha, Sweta Bhairab, Khaila

Bhairab, and others. The beautiful three-storey Taleju temple is one of the oldest, built in the 16th century, dedicated to Taleju, the Nepalese form of Bhairab. Past the Taleju temple on the left is a temple similar to the Pashupatinath (Shiva) temple, which we will visit later. On the left at Indrachowk is the temple of Akash (sky) Bhairab. The Deity here is a large, five foot tall mask of Bhairab. Bhairab, or Bhairav, is the fearful form of Shiva who protects his devotees. I actually entered this temple, not sure if I could or not, and though the people inside looked at me oddly, they said nothing, so I kept going. I got right up to the Deity before someone said I had to leave. Oh, well, sometimes you have to take a chance. But you can see the Deity through the second floor window from across the street when the sun shines on it in the morning.

Another block up the road is Kel Tole where the Machendranatha temple is located on the left. This temple has a shrine dedicated to Avalokiteshvara and is one of the most sacred Buddhist temples in the area. Many of the devout visit this temple every day early in the morning between six and seven. After this is Asan Tole, a square that has six roads intersecting it and is a major market place, especially in the morning. There are two pagoda style temples here; the three-storied one is to the goddess Annapurna, and the two-storied temple is to Ganesh. These are interesting and busy little temples, and are fascinating to watch as people continually go in and out. They are especially mystical after it has become dark and the temple lights go on, which also allows you to see inside from the street.

Walking through Durbar Square can be a most fascinating experience. It's like taking a trip back through time and seeing a city the way it was hundreds of years ago, except for the occasional motor vehicle and the Western tourists. The customs and ways of the people really haven't changed that much, which makes it like a living museum. Although modern amenities are now available in the form of cars, buses, planes, phones, electricity, etc., it's a place where age old customs that still exist meet the 20th century. This is the unique thing about Kathmandu. Although Nepal is still a developing country with much poverty, and over 16 million people with an average lifespan of only 45 years, and an illiteracy rate of about 70% among males and higher among women, it still has a high regard for its old ways and spiritual customs.

Outside of Kathmandu city are many temples in the surrounding towns and villages. To the west is one of the oldest (2500 years) and most famous of the Buddhist *stupas*, Svayambunatha, with the painted eyes which can be seen from anywhere in the city. It is located on a hilltop that may have been an island when Kathmandu was a lake many years ago. It's about 20 minutes away from Durbar Square by taxi or *ricksha*. As we go we pass by the Nepal Museum that you may find interesting. Arriving at the hill, we see the steep stairs leading up to Svayambunatha that takes us past statues and small *stupa* shrines. Getting to the top provides a great view of the valley, especially at dusk. In front of the *stupa* is a huge *dorje* or thunderbolt, and around the sides are many prayer wheels that are turned by the visiting devotees. Nearby there is a large image of the Buddha and in a pagoda style temple on the northwest side is an image of the goddess of smallpox, Hariti. Many people continually line up to enter this temple while a priest performs rituals in front. It is said that Hariti used to consume children until the Buddha stopped her and kept her at his side.

There are many smaller *stupas* here, and further back are many shops that sell all kinds of Buddhist paraphernalia and souvenirs. There is also a room where many monks who live here gather to chant *sutras*. When I was here a group of people were preparing vegetables for a large feast, and I passed by a room where two men were cutting up a dead animal for meat, while three dogs were outside looking in and waiting for scraps. Many Buddhists are vegetarian, but some still eat meat and hire others to do the butchering since they don't want to partake of the animal killing. Unfortunately, as the *Vedas* point out, anyone connected with killing, distributing, or eating animal flesh also partakes of the bad *karma* that comes from killing the innocent animals.

Another place we want to see to the north of Kathmandu by 11 kilometres is Budhanilkantha at the foot of Shivapuri hill. Here we find the large Deity of sleeping Vishnu, carved out of solid rock in the 11th century. One legend relates that the Deity was found when a farmer was tilling his field and saw blood oozing up from the ground after his plough struck something. The people dug into the ground and found the Deity. Many pilgrims come here, but not so many tourists. We reach it by getting a bus near the National Theatre, a pleasant ride, but the bus stops often to pick up passengers. When the bus makes its final stop, the Deity is only a few minutes away. Anyone is allowed in the courtyard and can see the Deity, but the central pool, where the Deity is reclining on Seshanaga, is for Hindus only, which means those who are born Hindu. At the feet of Lord Vishnu the devout chant their prayers and make offerings of rice, where the pigeons wait to eat it up. It is considered that the Deity sleeps continuously for four months in the rainy season, and in November there is a festival when thousands of devotees come to participate when the Deity wakes up. A two minute walk further west is the Hare Krishna temple that we can visit that has beautiful Jagannatha Deities. At the very end of the road they have purchased some land where they are slowly building a nice temple. Getting a bus back to town is easy, but the smaller commuter buses that serve the valley get extremely crowded.

East of Kathmandu, reached by bus, is one of the most important Shiva temples in Nepal, the Pashupatinatha temple. As we approach the temple from the front we pass by many stalls that sell items like *rudraksha* beads, incense, and supplies for worship, like flower garlands that pilgrims buy to offer the Deity inside the temple. The main Deity of Pashipatinatha (Shiva as Lord of the animals) has four heads and is said to be over 600 years old, installed after the Muslims destroyed the original Deity in the 14th century. There are also Deities of Vishnu, Narasimha, and others of Shiva, some dating back to the fifth century. Although foreigners are not allowed inside, you can cross the Bagmati river to get a good view of the temple and the many people who visit. On the hillside is a row of many small shrines with Shiva *lingams*. Along the walkway by the river are other small shrines, and sometimes there are cremations taking place on platforms near the river behind the temple. All in all it's a very mystical place. Across the road from the temple is a care facility that gives free medical assistance for the elderly and sickly and meals to those who need it.

Farther east by bus is the Bodnatha *Stupa*, the largest in the world. This *stupa*, dating back about five centuries, is said to house the bones of Kashyapa, a Buddha who preceded Gautama. This is where Tibetan culture is centered in the valley, and the people who live nearby and run the shops that surround the *stupa* are primarily Tibetan. People who want to study Tibetan Buddhism come here for extended stays. There are nearby monasteries, such as the Jamchen lhakhang that has a huge (about 30 to 40 feet tall) Deity of Maitreya, the coming Buddha, that is very beautiful to see. Many Westerners come to study Buddhist meditation at the Kappan monastery, located a little ways north of Bodnath.

South of Kathmandu is Patan, easily reached by bus, tempo, or bicycle if you're renting one. We first see the beautiful Hiranya Varna Mahabihar Buddhist monastery, which has a very ornate three-storied temple with a Deity of Buddha. Not far away is the Kumbeshwar Shiva temple, and south of that is Patan's Durbar Square. Here we find interesting architecture in the forms of several temples dedicated to such Deities as Ganesh, Shiva, Krishna, Narasimha, etc. Most of these were built in the 17th century. South of Durbar Square is the temple of Rato Machendranatha that has a beautiful image of Avalokiteshvar. About ten minutes walk southeast of Durbar Square is the Mahaboudha temple. This is a small monastery with an Indian style temple building resembling the Mahabodhi temple in Bodhgaya. Inside is an image of Buddha's mother, Maya Devi. Patan is also known for its bronze and brass work. You can get some fantastically detailed and beautiful images of the Buddhist pantheon here. But these higher quality images are not cheap, although very interesting to look at.

A distance further east is Bhaktapur, a city that has probably changed the least in the valley. The Durbar Square of Bhaktapur is an open area with various sizes of temples of Krishna, Shiva, Pashupatinatha, Vatsala, etc. There is also an art gallery with some old and rare Nepali manuscripts and paintings depicting types of Hindu and Buddhist Tantrism. Next to this is the golden gate, a most interesting piece of art that is the entrance into the pathway leading to a Hindu temple, all part of the "55 windowed palace." Through an alley past the Pashupatinatha temple we find the Nyatapola temple, a good example of Nepalese architecture that is often seen on postcards or in travel brochures about Nepal. This five-storied temple was built in the 18th century by King Bhupatindra and is the tallest in the valley. The Bhairabnath temple across from the Nyatpola is where they still occasionally sacrifice animals, such as goats or buffalo, to the Deity on special days. Ten minutes walk to the other side of town is another square where we find a Dattatreya temple, an image of whom can be seen looking out of the upper storey window. And the Pujahari Math is nearby, which is known mostly for its finely carved peacock window located in the small alley beside the monastery.

Past Bhaktapur is Nagarkot (20 km out of Kathmandu), reached by taxi or a special tour bus by following the winding road up into the hills located on a ridge. This is where many people go for the best view of the Himalayan mountains. Most people come at dawn or sunset. Unfortunately, when we leave Kathmandu for Nagarkot we can't be sure of how the weather will be in the mountains. If it's cloudy, we won't be able to see much. If it's clear, we'll get a fantastic view from Dhaulagiri to our west all the way to Kanchenjunga and Everest to the east, although they are very far away. It can be cool and windy at Nagarkot, so we must dress warm. Plans for building some big hotels there are now in the making.

There are other noteworthy temples in the area, such as the ornate pagoda style temple of Vishnu at Changunarayan, reached by foot two hours north of Bhaktapur. And one of the most important temples of Goddess Kali is at Dakshinkali in the southern part of the valley. This is reached by car or taxi. On Saturdays and Tuesdays many local people who eat meat take their goats or chickens there to be sacrificed to the deity of the Goddess under the direction of the priests. It's a bloody scene, after which they finish butchering the animals outside and take them home to eat later. This is, according to *shastra*, actually the way animal killing is supposed to be done for those who have to have meat to eat. It was never meant that animals were to be raised on factory farms and then conveniently killed in mass quantities at the slaughter house. The *shastra* explains that animals are supposed to be raised by their owners who then make their own arrangements to offer the animals in sacrifice, but only to Goddess Kali, since other Deities do not accept animal sacrifices. Afterwards the people can take the offered carcass home, while understanding that by the dictates of the law of *karma* the offered animal may get the opportunity to kill them in their next life. That is the meaning of the Sanskrit word for flesh, *mamsah* (me he). During the ritual the person who is offering the animal in sacrifice is supposed to say in the animal's ear, "*Mamsah*, me he will kill in my next life." Thus, the habit of thoughtlessly eating meat does not go without its consequences.

When our visit to Kathmandu is over, there are a few different directions we can take. Some people take a plane back to Varanasi, Patna, or wherever. Others fly or take a bus up to Pokhara. Flying to Pokhara offers excellent views of the mountains, while taking bus lets a person see the wide variety of landscapes in Nepal. Pokhara does not really have anything important to offer pilgrims, other than a few temples or monasteries. But it is an interesting place for the general tourist. It is especially known for its great views of the Annapurna mountain range and the treks that start from Pokhara. The best trek of all Nepal is the one that goes to the Muktinatha temple. It takes about two weeks, is relatively safe, not too rough, and provides a good adventure. A friend of mine went on this trek and liked it enough that he hopes to go back to Nepal sometime to do some more trekking.

When we leave Nepal, we take a bus to the town of Bhairawa because we want to see the holy place of Lumbini, the birthplace of Gautama Buddha. No matter whether we leave from Pokhara or Kathmandu, if we take a morning bus we will get to Bhairawa in late afternoon or early evening where we'll find a hotel to spend the night. The next morning we get a bus to Lumbini, 22 km away. There is not much to see in Lumbini, but since we are in the vicinity we can take the time. And, of course, this stop is essential for any Buddhist pilgrim. One of the main points of interest here is the Ashoka pillar, built in 244 B.C. by Emperor Ashoka near the site where Buddha was born. Not far away is a small temple that has a slab of rock with the scene of Buddha's birth carved on it. It shows Maya Devi holding onto a tree while Buddha is emerging from her side. Modern excavations have discovered the foundations of an old monastery, and there is the place where Maya Devi was supposed to have bathed before Buddha's birth and where ablutions were performed after his birth. There is also a Tibetan and a Buddhist monastery that you can visit if you're interested.

After Lumbini we go back to Bhairawa and on to the town of Sunauli where we cross the border. At the Indian bordertown of Nautanwa we get a bus for the four hour ride to Gorakhpur. Gorakhpur has the temple of Gorakhnath and is also the home of Gita Press, which publishes many books on Hindu or Vedic philosophy. The Buddhist pilgrims will take an eastbound bus from Gorakhpur to Kasia (Kushinagar) 55 km away. This is the town where Buddha was supposed to have died, thus entering Mahaparinirvana. There is a rather deteriorated temple which has an image of Buddha reclining in the position he was supposed to have taken when he passed from this world. The image is carved out of one piece of *chunar* stone and measures 20 feet in length. There is also the Mahaparinirvana *Stupa* which marks the place where the Buddha left his body. It was this spot that Buddha selected as the place of his passing after having announced his approaching disappearance three months in advance to Ananda. There is also an excavated area where the foundations of a few old monasteries have been found. There is also the Angara Chaitya, a *stupa* that is located about three-quarters of a mile away that is said to mark the spot where the Buddha's body was cremated. Years ago vandals bore into the *stupa* to steal whatever valuables they could find. Through this passage the bottom of the *stupa* can now be reached where one can still see the scorched earth, thus confirming that this was where the Buddha was cremated.

Back at Gorakhpur we board a bus bound for another important city, Ayodhya, where Lord Ramacandra was born and lived for many years. Lord Rama is the incarnation of Lord Vishnu and Krishna who appears as the most pious and authoritative king. Lord Ramacandra is worshiped by every Hindu, and a pilgrimage to this city is considered most auspicious. By visiting the temples in this town we rid ourselves of many lifetimes of *karma*. This place is a small and simple town that does not cater much to foreign tourists, but it is a very spiritual place with more temples than you can mention. And the nice thing about it is that Western pilgrims can enter almost every temple in town and see the Deities and watch the ceremonies, so you don't get that feeling of being excluded from the spiritual activities that go on here. Some people say that in Ayodhya every house is a temple, which means there are more than 8000 temples. And there are temples where you least expect to find them. You can be walking down the street at night passing by a plain looking building and be surprised when you look inside and see the flames of ghee lamps being swung in the air for the *arati* ceremony in front of the Deity of Lord Rama, while the sound of ringing bells and singing voices accompany it. Everywhere you go Lord Ramacandra is the central point of the lives of the people who live here. But it is also said that Buddha stayed in Ayodhya for some time, which became an important place for Buddhism for a while. Plus, Ayodhya is the birthplace of the first and fourth Jain *Thirtankaras*.

The town is located on the Gogra River, where there are some nice temples at the *ghats* of Rama ki Pauri. This is a very pleasant place to walk and visit the various temples, among which are the Sri Nagyshwarnath temple, which has a Shiva *lingam* that is said to have a connection with Lord Rama. Around the corner is the Sri Kaleram Mandir that has nice Sita-Rama Deities. Elsewhere in Ayodhya is the Sri Valmiki Ramayan Bhavan that has the complete Ramayan written on the inside walls. At this temple they hold regular discourses on the Ramayan in Hindi, and the temple fills up with many devotees, young and old alike, who will sit for hours to listen. Nearby is the Sri Charoo Dham Mandir that houses older male devotees and *brahmanas*. The Kanak Bhavan or Golden Temple is one of the older and more important temples in town. Many people gather here to perform *bhajans* and *kirtanas* in front of the most beautiful Deities of Sita-Rama, Lakshmana, Satrughna, and Hanuman. This temple even has bedrooms for the Deities.

The Vasistha Mandir is a recently remodeled temple that marks the place where Rama and His brother Lakshmana studied in their youth under the great sage Vasistha. This temple has paintings and dioramas that tell the story. Plus, there is a well (Vasistha *kund*) in the middle of the courtyard that is supposed to be the well where Rama and Lakshmana got water for bathing and drinking.

One of the most important Hanuman temples in all of India is also found in Ayodhya, the temple of Hanuman Ghri. Hanuman was the dear monkey servant of Lord Rama. The temple is up a flight of stairs in a small fortress on a hilltop. Many pilgrims, some pushing their way through the crowds up to the altar, come to see the Deity of Hanuman, which is so decorated with flower garlands and jewelry that you can only see his vermilion covered face. Around the small courtyard are other altars for Deities of Durga, Shiva, Ganesh and Sita-Rama.

In the evening some of the older people attend the discourses that are held in one of the rooms in the courtyard.

There is so much significance to this town that there could and should be a guidebook on Ayodhya that explains the historical background of the many temples and sites. However, as of this writing, I know of no such book, not in English anyway. But other fascinating temples you can visit include the Sri Tulsi Smarak Bhawan, Sri Raj Sadan, Dasaratha Mahal, and places like the Sarooj Kund, Sri Tulsi Park, Sri Janki Bhag, along with other temples you will find as you wander through the town. There is also a Jain temple here, though it is not so impressive, and the Birla family, the industrialists who are noted for building very nice temples in many major towns and cities, also have a nice temple here dedicated to Sita-Rama. The people are very friendly and, though they may stare at you out of curiosity, if you simply greet them by exclaiming "Jaya Rama. Sita-Rama ki jaya!" they will easily smile and similarly respond.

There is, however, some political trouble here, and it evolves around the place called Sri Ram Janma Bhoomi, or the location where Lord Rama is said to have appeared in this world during Treta-yuga, many years prior to the appearance of Lord Krishna. The problem stems from the fact that there is a 500 year old mosque (Babri Masjid) at the spot. I was told that there used to be a Rama temple there but it was torn down by the Muslims who then built a mosque in its place. This is not the only town where the Muslims have done this. They have also torn down the famous Visvantha (Shiva) temple in Varanasi, and the Sri Krishna Janma Bhoomi temple in Mathura and built mosques at the sites. They also cut five storeys off the seven-storey tall Govinda temple in Vrindavan. Incidents of Muslims destroying Hindu and Buddhist temples are known to have happened all over north and central India.

Anyway, the Hindus have always resented what the Muslims did in Ayodhya and now want to replace the mosque with a Rama temple as it had been years ago. But the Muslims don't want this, so there is trouble until some arrangement is made. In fact, there were big demonstrations here in which people were killed shortly after I had visited Ayodhya in early 1990. And this sparked off bitter demonstrations in other parts of India as well. So this explains why I saw so many police patroling the streets and important temples. In fact, in order to see Ram Janma Bhoomi, we are not allowed to bring in any cameras or shoulder bags into the mosque, and you have to pass through metal detectors. The mosque itself is highly fortified with barricades and barbed wire fencing, and police are all over the place. But once you get inside it doesn't seem like a mosque at all. Two of the three rooms are used as a Sita-Rama temple and have altars with small Sita-Rama Deities, which were installed in 1986, along with many pictures of Lord Rama. They still have the *arati* ceremonies several times a day, and many devotees visit from all over India. Only the third room has a few pictures of Muslim saints on the walls. So it certainly isn't used very much as a mosque and hasn't been in years, so why not let the Hindus build a nice temple to Lord

Rama? (As of this writing, preparations are being made to build a nice Sita-Rama temple very near this site.)

Six kilometres away from Ayodhya is Faizabad, a much bigger town of 120,000, where at Gupta Ghat is the very plain looking temple which honors the place from where Lord Ramacandra left this world. Inside it is an altar which has several sets of Sita-Rama Deities, along with *shalagram-shilas*, and Hanuman Deities. Not many people visit this temple, so the priest is glad to see any visitors. There is a special room which houses a little shrine marking the place from where Lord Rama ended His appearance in the material world.

When our visit to Ayodhya is finished it is easy to get a train since our hotel, the Prithek Niwas Saket, is only a few blocks away from the Ayodhya train station. Once we get our train, it is a pleasant ride to one of the most important holy towns and pilgrimage sites in India, Varanasi (Banaras). Varanasi is a city of many legends and numerous temples. Books have been written exclusively on the life, legends, and significance of the city. Many tourists from around the world come here to see the culture, the living religion which has gone on for thousands of years, as well as the *ghats* along the Ganges River. Varanasi is known for its silver, copper, brassware, and art work, as well as the excellent textiles, such as carpets, saris, and especially silks that are made here. There is an interesting museum showing some of the best examples of these kinds of craftsmanship at the Banaras University, the Bharat Kala Bhawan, and at the old palace in the Ramnagar Fort. Varanasi has been a centre for learning and spiritual pilgrimages for over 2500 years, and attracts many students and scholars on religion, philosophy, and music, and has some of the world's best astrologers. If you're interested in having your horoscope read, this is a good place to have it done. Tulsi das, who wrote the Hindi version of the Ramayan (the Ram Charit Manas), also lived here years ago. Many noted Indian musicians also have homes here. Especially important for the pilgrim are the many temples. But many of the temples, unfortunately, will not let foreigners inside. Nonetheless, there are still many important temples we will be able to enter for *darshan*.

For the general tourist from the West, Varanasi, out of many Indian cities, is a town that is probably least understood. The traditions of this town go back well over 2000 years, and most foreigners, when seeing these practices for the first time, can hardly comprehend what exactly is happening or the intent of it. But everything has its purpose and meaning. To understand the importance of Varanasi, you must familiarize yourself to some degree with its legends. For example, Varanasi is often referred to as the city of Shiva, but it wasn't always Shiva's city. The *Kashi Khanda*, a text that explains some of the glories of Varanasi (or Kashi, "the city of light"), explains that at one time many, many years ago, all the gods lived here. However, the rule of the city was given over to King Divodasa who made all the demigods leave. After a while Lord Shiva wanted to come back, but everything he tried in order to return failed. Finally he asked Lord Vishnu to help him. So Lord Vishnu went to Varanasi and first arrived at the confluence of the Varana and Ganges Rivers where He bathed. Now there is the Adi Keshava ("original Keshava" or Vishnu) temple at that location to commemorate the incident, which is now an important *tirtha* or holy place. Sri Vishnu then made His way into the city and again bathed at the Panchaganga Ghat. Then by His trickery He caused the departure of King Divodasa and gave Varanasi back to Lord Shiva, and Lord Vishnu and Shiva, along with other demigods and goddesses, have manifested themselves here in many ways ever since. Therefore, Varanasi (the city between the Varana and Asi Rivers) has always been a centre for pilgrimage. More legends of Varanasi could be explained, but there are so many that they easily could fill a separate volume. So I will only relate a few as we tour some of the many temples.

You can find temples dedicated to any personality of the Hindu pantheon in this city. Thus they say that all the gods reside here. And it is said that all of the holy places of India can be found in certain portions of the town. Mathura is found in one part of the town, Ayodhya in another, as well as Badrinatha, Dvaraka, and so on. In fact, some of the ancient texts say that Varanasi is not of this earth, but is a holy place and part of the spiritual realm. Therefore, dying in this city brings salvation from future material existence. So there is a strong atmosphere of devotion here as many pilgrims come from all over to spend their last days living in this city, bathing in the sacred Ganges, visiting temples, and having *darshan* of the Deities, all for spiritual purification.

Probably the best way to get to know Varanasi is to take a little tour of the important temples and river *ghats*. Many of the temples are not very important to the general tourist, and not all of them are so interesting or necessary to see, unless you are a serious pilgrim who wants to spend some time here. So I'll simply explain where many of the temples are and you can decide if you want to find them. The easiest way to locate them is to have your *ricksha* driver take you. But some of the temples in the old section of town can only be reached by foot because the lanes are too narrow even for cycle *rickshas*. Yet drivers can park their *rickshas* somewhere and lead you the rest of the way. The real adventure of finding these temples is not only seeing what they are like, but simply wandering around the town to experience the place and observe how the people live.

We can start our tour by taking a motor *ricksha* to the New Visvanatha temple in the Banaras Hindu University at the southern end of the city. This very nice temple was established by the Birla family, thus anyone is welcome. This is the temple that all Western tourists should visit if they want to see an authentic Shiva temple. It is well kept, clean, and surrounded by fountains, pools, and nice grounds. It was made in the architectural style of the original Visvanatha temple that was in the heart of the old section of town before the Muslims invaded and tore it down. This new temple has a large central room for a Shiva *lingam* that is attended by a priest. There are also two shrines in separate rooms, one for Parvati and Ganesh, the other for a five-faced Shiva *lingam*, Mahadeva. It is a very interesting temple and is easily reached without having to find your way through dark and dirty alleys that can be crowded with people, children, and wandering cows, which is the case in much of the old section of town. And the Banaras Hindu University is like a spacious park that is pleasant to walk or drive through.

From here we take a *ricksha* to Sankat Mochan, one of the most important Hanuman temples in the city. The architecture of this temple is not very elaborate, but it is a lively place and many people visit and offer respects to the Deities of Sita-Rama, Hanuman, Ganesh, etc. This is not far from Durga Kund Road where we can walk to the Tulsi Manas Mandir; a large temple that has beautiful Sita-Rama Deities and the complete Hindi Ramayan by Tulsi Das written on the inside walls. This temple marks the place where Tulsi Das lived while he wrote it. This is another temple that welcomes anyone, and Western tourists should also visit this clean and well kept temple to view the beautiful Sita-Rama Deities.

About a block or two further down the road is the Durga temple beside the Durga Kund. Many pilgrims go to this temple, which is commonly called the Monkey Temple because of the many monkeys of which you have to be careful. Anyone can go in and see the temple that is in the middle of the courtyard and houses a small deity of goddess Durga. This temple is completely filled with pilgrims during the Durga-*puja* festival. From here we take the road that leads toward the Ganges until we find Asi Ghat, where the small Asi River joins the Ganges. The best time to see the *ghats* is in the morning when you'll find the most activity, and also before it gets very hot from the sun. The Asi Ghat is busy in the morning with bathers, women collecting water for worship and washing, and others worshiping the Hanuman Deity and the Shiva *lingams* under the nearby *pipal* tree. Some men will be practicing yoga, sitting in meditation, eyes closed, facing the morning sun. Others sit near the river chanting the Hare Krishna *mantra* on beads, or will be doing other morning rituals. In fact, one old renunciant, seeing my own bead bag hanging from my neck, came up in a most friendly manner to tell me the glories of chanting the holy names. In essence, he stated that to always be chanting the names of God means that one is liberated from material life. But mostly he was expressing his happiness to see a Westerner taking to the process since he had obviously attained his own experiences of enlightenment through the chanting process.

The next *ghat* along the river as we head north is Tulsi Ghat, above which is Lolarka Kund and the house and temple of Tulsi Das. It is also advised to visit the temple of Ganesh that overlooks the Ganges here for your good fortune since Ganesh is believed to take away obstacles. Next is Shivala Ghat where we find the 17th century palace of Maharaja Chet Singh. After that is Hanuman Ghat which is where the great philosopher and Vaishnava Vallabhacarya was born. There is also a Ruru Bhairav temple above it. Beyond this is Harischandra

Ghat which is sometimes used for cremations. After that is Kedara Ghat where pilgrims bathe in the Ganges before climbing the steps to the Kedareshvara temple, with the red and white stripes on the outside of the building, which is one of the most important Shiva temples in Varanasi. The *Kashi Khanda* states that just deciding to come here destroys the sins accumulated in this lifetime, while seeing the temple destroys the sins of seven lifetimes. Bathing in the Ganges and then worshiping the Kedareshvara *lingam* is said to destroy the sins of 10 million lifetimes. The temple also has Deities of Durga, Ganesh, Shiva, etc., and Westerners are allowed inside.

Farther along we come to Chauki Ghat with a huge tree at the top of the stairs sheltering many stone *nagas*. Then there is a quiet section at Manasarovara Ghat and Chaumsathi Ghat, above which is the Chaumsathi temple dedicated to the 64 yoginis along with images of Kali and Durga.

Next we enter the busy Dashashvamedha Ghat where the bather gets the results of ten *ashvamedha* sacrifices. It was here that Lord Brahma performed ten *ashvamedhas* many, many years ago in order to attain the purity to see Lord Shiva at Varanasi. At this *ghat* people gather from all over the world, from all walks of life. Here they take their holy bath, or perform rituals to the Ganges, or consult with local priests found sitting under the rattan umbrellas and discuss their lives, horoscopes, and their spiritual progress. It is by far the busiest *ghat* in Varanasi and the most easily reached. Many foreign tourists come here as well, and in the morning you can see group tours or individuals climbing into the boats to float past the *ghats* and to watch the activities of the local people who use the *ghats* each morning along the riverside. A boat ride down the Ganges at Varanasi can be a very relaxing and interesting experience that should not be missed.

In the evening many people come to Dashashvamedha Ghat to sit on the steps, socialize, watch other people, and enjoy the cool breeze. Some people also come to worship in the nearby temples. Popular temples along the *ghat* include one to Shitala and the Dashashvamedheshvara Shiva *lingam*, another of Shulatankeshvara, and one of Brahmeshvara, which is a Shiva *lingam* said to have been installed by Brahma himself during his stay here.

Above the *ghat* along the steps near the temples you'll see lines of beggars sitting in the shade. Some of them are deformed from leprosy and nearly invalid. They will try to get your attention by reaching out with their begging bowls to you in hopes of receiving a donation. For many of them, handouts are their only source of income, especially for those who can do nothing else, like the lepers who have cloth rags covering their hands which have been eaten away by the disease. In other areas of Varanasi you may also find renunciants or poor widows spending their last days here who live only by begging. It can be shocking to the Western tourist, but such sights are common most anywhere you go in India. But begging isn't always the last resort of those who can do nothing else. In India, begging is also accepted by those who have renounced most of their earthly connections and now live by this most humble of means, which is to depend merely on the mercy of others, which in a sense is the mercy of God.

Farther above Dashashvamedha Ghat along the street are many stalls that sell souvenirs, beads, incense, brass pots to carry Ganges water, etc. There is also the scent of incense and perfumed oils in the air, and *ricksha* drivers that ask you where you want to go. Farther up the road are many more shops, restaurants, and stalls that sell snacks and create the strong aroma of fried foods. From here one gets into the business area of Varanasi, which is much more congested with pedestrian as well as motor traffic, and seems to leave the spiritual life behind.

Back along the Ganges, the next *ghat* is Man Mandir, above which we find the small but unique observatory of Jai Singh. Jai Singh was known for being a great king, musician, and astronomer. He built more elaborate observatories in New Delhi, Jaipur, and two smaller ones in Mathura and Ujjain. Not far from this observatory above Man Mandir Ghat is the *linga* temple of Someshvara, said to have been established by Soma. Above Mir Ghat is the well known Vishalakshi temple, one of the forms of Parvati. Not far away are the Shiva temples of Dharmesha (where it's said that Yamaraja received his authority over the dead), Divodaseshvara (the *linga* said to have been established by King Divodasa before he left Kashi), and the Dharma Kupa or Well of Dharma.

These temples are in the Godaulia area or the old part of the city which is a maze of narrow and crowded alleyways through decaying buildings that lead past many little shops, temples, guest houses or hotels, and homes of the local people. In the residential areas children often find just enough room to play in the dirt of these alleys, but if a stray cow comes walking through, it can sometimes take up the whole lane. The dust and smells in this area can be overwhelming, especially in the heat of summer. But, nonetheless, there are new discoveries and experiences to have amongst these alleys if one is open to them. You're never quite sure what you'll find next. You may see astrologers consulting clients, guides offering you their services (in hopes of getting you to their shop where they can sell you something), flower peddlers, a funeral procession, or people simply sitting together sharing tea and conversation.

In the middle of this area is the Temple of Visvanatha, Shiva as Lord of the Universe. This is a temple all pilgrims visit, although foreigners are not allowed inside. The present temple was built in 1776 by Ahalya Bai of Indore after the original temple was torn down by the fanatic Muslim Aurangzeb who built the mosque in its place. The mosque on the other side of the courtyard is separated from the temple by the Jnana Vapi well (Well of Wisdom) where the original Shiva *linga* was hid in order to keep the invaders from harming it. Some people say the original *linga* was never recovered from the well and is still at the bottom. Needless to say, with the temple and mosque so close, police patrol the mosque continually to prevent disturbances. The courtyard and temple are situated behind a large wall making it difficult to see from the outside, and the south entrance into the courtyard is for Hindus only, while the Muslims enter from the north entrance. But the towers of the temple that are plated with three-quarters of a ton of gold can be seen from a rooftop across the street. For Westerners it's the best view of the temple you're going to get.

Inside the temple is the Visvanatha *linga*, a smooth black stone sitting on a silver altar on the floor. Many other *lingas* are clustered around it. There are several other shrines around the temple, including one of Vishnu that must be worshiped as one enters the temple. The temple interior is not very ornate, but it can be quite crowded and filled with an intense mood of devotion. On the street just outside the courtyard entrance are many shops selling all kinds of religious paraphernalia, such as beads, flowers, incense, pictures of Shiva, etc. The street, Visvanatha Lane, has seen millions of pilgrims from all walks of life. And when they leave Visvanatha they stop at the small temple of Annapurna (Goddess of Plenty) across the street. She is considered the Queen of Varanasi, another aspect of the wife of Lord Shiva.

Making our way back through the alleys and down to the river, we find Lalita Ghat where there is the Ganga Keshava Vishnu shrine, and a Bhagirathi Devi or Ganges shrine. There is also an ornate Nepali temple with an image of Pashupateshvara, like the one in Kathmandu. Next is the Jalasai cremation *ghat*, which is often referred to as part of Manikarnika Ghat. You can see piles of logs stacked on the steps ready for cremations, and sometimes there can be as many as five or six cremations taking place at once. The fires can easily be seen at night from a long distance away, and the smoke can fill the air of the *ghat* by day. Anyone can watch, but this is no place for photography which you'll soon find out if you try taking photos. The fact that death is ever-present is obvious in India. Disease and death are not hidden away like in America, but are a fact of life that is dealt with on a daily basis; a reminder of the reasons why people are more spiritually inclined in India.

The cremations seem to be a morbid tourist attraction for foreigners, many of whom seem to think this is one of the most unusual sights in India. But there is a reason for the cremations at this location. The deceased are brought to the cremation ground by family members, and the eldest son shaves his head and dresses in a white cloth and, when everything is ready, lights the funeral pyre. The family stays until the body of the deceased has burned, and then the son throws the part of the body that does not burn into the Ganges, and douses the last embers with a pot of Ganges water, thus purifying whatever is left of their relative. Then they turn and leave. An excessive display of sorrow by family members at this time is said to be inauspicious for the dead, who is entering a new realm of existence. The Doams, who are the low caste people who manage the cremation grounds and collect fees for tending the fires and supplying the wood, gather the ashes of the deceased to be put into the Ganges. By cremating the body of the deceased, it is believed that the disembodied spirit will be more likely to go on to the next realm of existence. If the person had been very attached to life in the material body, the spirit may want to cling to the body in some way. If the body is cremated, then the spirit will be forced to move on. Furthermore, by pouring Ganges water on the body and the ashes, it is believed to help spiritually purify the deceased from past *karma*. It is said in *shastra*, such as the *Kashi Khanda*, that people who leave their bodies here will attain liberation and will receive spiritual existence. This is why it is the desire of many people to die and be cremated in Varanasi. It is also said that Lord Shiva whispers the *mantra* of liberation into the ear of those who die here, thus assuring them of a higher existence in their next life.

The next *ghat* is the Manikarnika, the most auspicious of all the *ghats*. On this *ghat* Lord Vishnu's footprints are set in a circular marble slab in a little shrine, the holiest spot in Varanasi. It is said that here is where the process of universal creation and annihilation begins. The little 20 foot square spring-fed pond or *kund* that is also found here above the *ghat*, which used to be a lake many years ago, is said to have been dug out by Lord Vishnu with His disc near the beginning of creation and was filled with the water of His perspiration. Inside on the north steps is a small shrine with little Deities of Vishnu. It was also here that Lord Shiva's jeweled-earring (Manikarnika) fell into the pool. But the *Shiva Purana* explains that it was Vishnu's earring that fell into the pool when the water expanded, upon which Lord Vishnu floated while bringing forth the cosmic egg or universe and the process of universal creation. It is also said that all the gods and goddesses come here to bathe in their subtle forms on a daily basis. Also on the *ghat* is the Tarakeshvara *linga* temple, which represents Shiva who whispers the *mantra* of liberation into the ears of those who die here. On the northern side of Manikarnika Ghat is a Shiva temple that has tilted and is no longer used. The foundation seemed to have given way during the construction of the Sindhia Ghat next to it. During the monsoon season the water level of the Ganges can rise quite high and flood the entrance to this temple.

Above Sindhia Ghat, the pilgrim walks through the narrow streets to visit some important temples. These temples are not easy to find but are well known to the locals, so only the more serious of the touring pilgrims will try to find them. These are temples dedicated to Vireshvara, Agnishvara, Nirriti, Upashanteshvara, and the goddess Sankata Devi above Sankata Ghat. Then there are temples of Katyayani Devi, Siddheshvari Devi, and the Lakshmanabala temple and Mangala Gauri temple above Lakshmanabala Ghat, just north of Rama Ghat.

The next important *ghat* is Panchaganga Ghat, a most holy confluence of the five (*pancha*) rivers, which include the Ganges, Yamuna, Sarasvati (which joined in Allahabad), and the Dhutpapa and Kirana, which are but trickling streams. Here we find many little niches on the steps housing various Deities on the steps, one with a reclining Vishnu. It was here that the famous poet Kabir was initiated by Ramananda. Above the steep and narrow steps leading through the buildings is the Bindu Madhava temple, one of the most significant Krishna temples in Varanasi. On the altar is a beautiful Krishna Deity which stands about two feet tall, and smaller Sita-Rama and Lakshmi-Narayana Deities. The present Bindu Madhava temple is in a quaint building but still visited by many pilgrims. It is known to have been rebuilt several times from the 12th to 16th centuries, and used to be a marvelous structure and a very rich temple in which the Deity, that had been quite large at that time, was dressed in a wide array of jewels. But the Muslim ruler Aurangzeb tore it down and built a mosque in its place. The huge mosque dominates the skyline, but is now unused and locked up. You can, however, get the guard from the nearby house to unlock the door to the mosque for you for a small donation. After climbing the steep stairs inside, you reach the rooftop for a good view of the Ganges as it flows past the city. In the back of the mosque you can see remnants of the old Bindu Madhava temple that the Muslims used for building the mosque.

The Bindu Madhava temple, along with the Adi Keshava temple, was where Sri Caitanya Mahaprabhu stayed and preached to the residents by chanting and dancing during His visit to Varanasi. When He first arrived He bathed at the Manikarnika Ghat and visited and preached at the Visvanatha temple where people lined up to see Him. He also held huge *kirtanas* at *ghats* such as the Panchaganga.

From the Bindu Madhava temple we go farther into the city in the Chaukhamba district where some other Krishna temples are located. There is a Gopala temple and another Radha-Krishna temple. Both have small Deities but are well known amongst devotees in this part of town. But in order to reach them you must find your way through many narrow alleys that make giving directions useless. It is best to use a guide or someone who will take you there.

Back at the river we next come to Brahma Ghat, then Durga Ghat, and further on is Gaya Ghat with nearby temples of goddesses Nageshvari Devi and Mukhanirmalika Devi. Next is Trilochana Ghat with the Trilochana temple in the alleyways above it, which contains a very old and famous *linga* in Varanasi, and also has a Deity of Varanasi Devi. Nearby is the Mahadeva temple.

After this lies nothing but a long walk to the Adi Keshava temple. Several hundred years ago this area had many important temples before the Muslims invaded. The Adi Keshava temple, next to the confluence of the Varana and Ganges Rivers, has a very ancient significance. As mentioned earlier, Lord Vishnu first appeared here when He came to get the city back from King Divodasa for Lord Shiva. Unfortunately, because of its distance from the other temples, and due to people forgetting its importance, few pilgrims from outside Varanasi visit, so they are glad to see anyone. The Sangameshvara *linga* in a shrine next to Adi Keshava is said to have been installed by Lord Brahma, as was the four-faced Brahmaeshvara Deity next to it. The *Linga Purana* states that those who bathe in the confluence of the rivers here and then worship Sangameshvara need never fear taking rebirth. After having *darshan* and offering our respects to the Deities, we take the long walk back to Manikarnika Ghat.

Many other temples and holy sites exist in this city, such as the Kapalamochana *tirtha* which is in the north part of town and is very auspicious to visit. This is where Shiva bathed and was purified from his sin of decapitating Lord Brahma's fifth head. He had carried this sin in the form of a skull, and after bathing at Kapalamochana the skull fell, meaning he had become purified. Other temples of Varanasi could be described, but for most people I think this is enough.

The pilgrims who take the route to the five main holy *tirthas* along the river start at Asi Ghat, then stop at Dashashvamedha Ghat, then go to the Adi Keshava temple, then back to Panchaganga Ghat, and at last the Manikarnika Ghat. Then they go to pay respects to Visvanatha at the Golden Temple. After touring the many *ghats* and temples along the river and elsewhere, and after seeing the Visvanatha temple, our pilgrim's tour of Varanasi is complete.

Though Varanasi is a special town, it is losing its spiritual atmosphere. When I was there, I talked with a few wandering mendicants who were disillusioned with the city. One was an old man who told me that things were changing too fast, prices had gone way up in the past several years for things like food and basic necessities. Why? Because of the growing number of tourists who have less respect for the spiritual culture that Varanasi has always been known for, and who are willing to pay more for everything, which makes it more expensive for the local people to live as they had. He also said the local priests were primarily concerned about business and family, though they may take some time for spiritual activities. He said that real *sadhus* in Varanasi and places that accomodate them are decreasing.

Then I talked with another monk who was standing nearby and who was from the south, Ramesvaram, where the standard of Vedic or *brahminical* culture is very high. He said that a few years ago a monk could sleep at night on the steps of the *ghats* along the river and not be disturbed. He had done that the previous night and awoke to find his belongings had been stolen. He was also upset that many priests in Varanasi had now given up their strict *brahminical* diet and were eating forbidden things, like eggs, fish, or even chicken and goat, and were also smoking *bidis* (Indian cigarettes). He told me that all he wanted to do now was collect enough money to leave Varanasi as soon as possible. So if you want to visit this city to see the spiritual side of it, you might want to go soon before it continues to lose more than it already has. But then I met another old *sadhu* who had just retired from being a teacher and moved to Varanasi and loved the place. He was staying at a local temple and had taken up some asceticism by eating only unspiced rice and dahl, nothing else. And he loved swimming in the Ganges. He had just moved here from Dacca, Bengladesh, where he said the Muslims were creating so much political trouble and terrorism that he no longer wanted to stay there. So compared to that, I suppose Varanasi was a big improvement, especially now that he wanted to utilize his final years to concentrate on spiritual life.

From Varanasi we catch a bus or a motor *ricksha* for a 10 kilometre ride to Sarnath, a holy place for Buddhists and one of the four main towns in regard to the life of Buddha. This is the place where Buddha, after having attained enlightenment in Bodhgaya, gave his first sermon about reaching *nirvana* through the middle way. Lord Buddha stayed for one rainy season here, but never made a permanent residence at Sarnath. Yet Sarnath became an important Buddhist center by the end of the fourth century B.C. when Ashoka ruled the area. It greatly flourished between the third and seventh centuries and was said to have as many as 1500 priests. During the 10th century the place declined and by the time the Muslims invaded in the 11th and again the 12th centuries, it was practically destroyed.

As we approach Sarnath, we first see the Chaukhandi Stupa on the left which is the remains of an ancient *stupa* from the second or third century A.D. On our right is the Archeological Museum that has a nice collection of ancient relics from the area. Across the road from the museum is a Jain temple built in 1824 which contains images of Shreanshnath, the 11th *Tirthankara* of the Jains. Behind the Jain temple are the excavations of the old temples and monasteries. This includes the main shrine, Kumara Devi's temple, and other things like the Ashoka Pillar, built around 250 B.C., which may mark the site of Buddha's first sermon. Beyond the ruins is a pleasant garden area called the Deer Park.

Near the Jain temple is the massive Dhamekh Stupa, built in the fifth century A.D. and stands 98 feet high. East of this *stupa* is the Mulgandha Kuti-Vihar, a modern replica of the Mahabodhi temple in Bodhgaya built by the Mahabodhi Society in 1932. Inside are very colorful murals of Buddha's life, and a beautiful image of Buddha on the altar. Next to the temple is a lifesize diorama exhibit of Buddha giving his first sermon to his first disciples under a Bo tree. This tree is a transplant of the tree in Sri Lanka which is a descendent of the original Bo tree that Buddha sat under when he became enlightened. Not far from here is the Chinese temple which contains a beautiful white marble Buddha. There is also a Tibetan Monastery at Sarnath. Everything at Sarnath can be seen in a few hours. So after our visit we are ready to head back to Varanasi and take a 135 kilometre train ride west to Allahabad.

Allahabad, though more spread out and less congested than Varanasi, has little that the general tourist would be interested in. There's the huge fort, which foreigners aren't allowed to enter, that has an Ashoka Pillar inside. But through a side door you can see the undying banyan tree that is over 1000 years old and still looks in very good condition. Also in the city is the Anand Bhawan, a two-storey mansion with a collection of personal items of the Nehru family. There is also the Allahabad Museum, but there are other cities far more interesting to see if your time is limited.

The name Allahabad, which was given to the city by Emperor Akbar in 1584, means the city of Allah. But prior to this the name was Prayaga or Prayaga Raja, which meant the place where the sacred rivers meet and where great sacrifices are performed. So for the pilgrim it is an important site since this is the confluence (*sangam*) of the sacred Ganges, Yamuna, and the mystical Sarasvati Rivers. The *Mahabharata* relates how Lord Brahma performed a sacrifice here thousands of years ago. Lord Ramacandra, His wife Sita and brother Lakshmana visited this place in Treta-yuga. They stayed at the *ashram* of the great sage Bharadvaja, which is now the location of the Allahabad University. The five Pandava brothers also visited the *sangam*, as described in *Mahabharata*. And 500 years ago Sri Caitanya also stayed for 10 days at the *sangam* and visited the Bindu Madhava temple, one of the important Krishna temples in Allahabad located several kilometres upstream. Sri Caitanya's footprints can also be found nearby at a place called Dashashvamedha Ghat, which is where He imparted His teachings to Srila Rupa Gosvami for several days. And across the river from the *sangam* is another temple on a small hill that Sri Caitanya visited, and about two miles downstream is the house of the saint Vallabhacarya, where Sri Caitanya had lunch with the saint.

Hundreds of people come to the *sangam* every day to bathe in the spiritually purifying water. But thousands of people come to the *sangam* area when there is the annual festival known as the Magh (January-February) Mela. And every 12 years the Magh Mela becomes the Kumba Mela which lasts for 41 days in which millions of pilgrims join together to bathe at the *sangam* and to perform other types of spiritual activities. In fact, during the last Kumba Mela festival in 1989 nearly 30 million people attended. It is by far the largest festival, what to speak of religious festival, in the world. The Kumba Mela alternates every three years between Allahabad, Nasik, Ujjain, and Hardwar. The next Kumba Mela in Allahabad will be in 2001.

During the Magh and Kumba Melas the 3600 acres called the Kumba Mela grounds that surround the *sangam* become its own city with roads, street lights, markets, medical facilities, and areas for food distribution, etc. Hundreds of large tents are erected as far as you can see to accomodate the thousands or millions of people. And it is not uncommon to see whole families, including babies, children, parents, and grandparents, come to the festival from any part of India. Some come by bus, train, plane, or even by foot.

Not only do ordinary pilgrims attend, but many of India's most elevated mystics, sages, and yogis also attend. Some of these sages are hundreds of years old, live in the pure atmosphere of the Himalayas, and are never seen except at such festivals. In fact, one of the most important aspects of the festival is to allow ordinary pilgrims the opportunity to associate with saintly persons for instruction in attaining spiritual realization. During the festivals some of the large tents also become the temporary dwellings for various *ashrams* or spiritual groups. You can often walk by the entrance and hear over the loudspeaker the lecture that's being given inside. This may attract people who then go in and sit and listen to the lecture and ask questions. At other times there may be a play on the Puranic pastimes being performed on the stage. At other times there might be devotional music being performed that people can listen to or join in singing. Wherever you go during the festivals there is something spiritual to watch, listen to, or engage in. With all the uplifting activities, such as lectures, plays, *bhajans*, worship, rituals, the presence of highly learned and experienced sages and yogis, and the holy *sangam*, the *mela* festivals are a highly energized and spiritual event for one to attend. However, many of these lectures and songs are not in English. But regardless of whether you are a serious pilgrim, businessman, teacher, student, housewife, or curious Western tourist, it is an event you'll never forget.

The significance of the *sangam* is related in the *Puranas*. It is told that many millions of years ago there was a battle between the demigods (*devas*) and the demons (*asuras*). Due to an offense to the powerful sage Durvasa Muni, the demigods had lost all of their power. So the demigods sought advice from Lord Vishnu who told them to make an agreement with the *asuras* to churn the ocean of milk together in order to get the nectar of immortality. After everyone agreed to it, they churned the ocean of milk and from it came various items and personalities. Finally, Lord Dhanvantari appeared carrying the *amrita-kumbha*, the jug filled with the nectar. The demons grabbed the jug and fighting immediately broke out between the *devas* and *asuras*. Over a period of twelve days of fighting some of the nectar was spilled from the jug onto four places: Nasik, Ujjain, Hardwar, and the *sangam* at Allahabad. In the end the demigods got possession of the nectar, but the nectar, which can spiritually purify all who come in contact with it, is said to become manifest in those four cities during certain auspicious times that are astrologically calculated. Thus, many people come to these cities for the Kumbha Mela festivals that signify the presence of the immortal nectar. To bathe in the *sangam* on the peak days, usually the mornings of the new moon, purifies one's existence and relieves one from the continued cycle of birth and death in the material world after this life. Thus, the importance and good fortune for those who can do this is taken very seriously.

Before anyone else bathes in the *sangam* the saints go first. Down the road through the middle of the crowd the saints parade past the people and enter the water once the astrologically auspicious moment has arrived. The first group of mystics given the opportunity is called the *naga babas*. These men wear no clothes and live in the mountains, but no one sees them traveling to the festival or going back to the mountains afterwards. It's as if they simply appear by mystic power. When they are done bathing, the other sects each have their chance to come down to the river. First there are the Vairagis, the Shaivites, Shankarites, Ramanujas, Madhvas, Nimbarkas, and the Gaudiya Vaishnavas. After all the prominent saints bathe in the sangam, everyone else rushes in to do the same. Then the *sangam* becomes a river of bodies, a roar of voices, all clamoring to get to the water while reciting or even shouting invocations to the Deities and to the Ganges and Yamuna Rivers. Each person blends in with everyone else regardless of race, caste, or sect, all with the intent of spiritual purification. But as you can imagine, when so many people gather in a relatively small area like this, safety can be a major concern. There have been instances in the past when hundreds of people have died when there is a rush to the river. Of course, newer arrangements have been made to help prevent this. But it is considered that to leave one's body during the Kumbha Mela or while in the *sangam* is especially auspicious and denotes liberation from material existence.

Where the Ganges and Yumana meet can be seen in the difference of the color of the rivers. The Ganges is shallower, muddier, and yellowish in color, while the Yamuna is deeper and greener. Many pilgrims enter the water from the shore in between the two rivers, while others take boats out to where the rivers actually mix. There is a small wooden platform for people to get out of the boats and dip into the water. Then they change into dry clothes on the boats. Some people also bring big jugs to fill so they can take the holy *sangam* water back with them to their homes. If you want to take a boat out, find one that is very close to the *sangam* where you can get the cheaper prices. In the annual Magh Mela season, the boatmen might want to charge a Westerner as much as 200 rupees or more to take you out to the *sangam*. But if you get closer on the shore, you can find boatmen looking for customers who will charge only 10 or 20 rupees. And if you don't mind taking a boat filled with other pilgrims, it may only cost you three to five rupees. Of course, you'll have to wait until everyone else is ready to come back to shore. In any case, be careful about prices.

After the grand festival is over and it's time to leave Allahabad, we take a train to Satna, and then a bus to Khajuraho. Along the way the bus makes many short stops at little towns that are so small they're not even on the map. And at most towns, vendors will pull their carts along the side of the bus to sell fruits, sweets, or other snacks. Sometimes little children will come up to the windows asking for rupees, or older children will walk through the bus with a tray of grapes or something else to sell. And, of course, there's always the tea vendor carrying a pot of tea and some cups, yelling in the most abrasive voice, "Chai, chai." Sometimes they keep walking through the bus until you're almost ready to tell them, "Alright, already, nobody wants any so get out of here." But soon the bus is rolling again and you can settle back to watch the scenery.

When we get to Khajuraho, we are again greeted by many men who want you to see their hotel. There was even one little boy who asked me if I wanted to stay in his father's house. He assured me it was very clean and for a very low price I could stay and his father would cook my meals, too. I opted for a hotel closer to the center of town.

Khajuraho is a very small village but is world famous for its wonderful temples. Lots of tourists come through this town even though it's out of the way and reached only by bus, plane, or taxi. Yes, it does have an airport because of the number of tourists. One evening I watched the skies and counted five airplanes that landed and took off from the airport, all within a half-hour. And as you wander around the town and temples, you'll see not only Indian but also

Western tourists from such places as Britain, France, Germany, Italy, America, and everywhere. I also saw a group tour of Japanese who were totally fascinated by the temples. So why do so many people come to this very small village just to see the ancient temples? Because these temples are in such good condition and have some of the most outstanding carved stonework you'll find anywhere.

Khajuraho is a good distance from the main lines of travel, which is one of the reasons why the temples were not destroyed or defaced by Islamic invaders like many of the other ancient temples in northern or central India. Here we get a good look at the Indo-Aryan architecture and the exceptional stonework that covers the exterior. The carved stone shows many scenes of what life was like 1000 years ago, and includes carvings of musicians, gods, goddesses, warriors, animals, beautiful ladies, and erotics. They have captured the interest of the world through magazine articles, travel brochures, and tours. Now many people include this town in their travels through India. And only a couple of these temples are still used for worship, so we can look at them to our heart's content without restriction.

The present 22 temples were a part of the 85 that were built during the rule of the Chandela kings. Most of them were constructed between 950 and 1050 A.D. from blocks of sandstone and built so the entrances face east. On the East side of town there are three Jain temples dedicated to Parsvanatha, Adinatha, and Shantinatha. Although not as big, these temples are just as ornately embellished as the other temples of Khajuraho. On them are carvings of scenes and gods from the Jain scripture as well as images of Vayu, Bhairav, Shiva, Vishnu, Brahma, and others from the Hindu *shastras*. The Parsvanatha temple has a black stone image of Parsvanatha, the 23rd *Tirthankara*, which was installed in 1860. This is the largest of the Jain temples. As you go inside, the interior, as with many of the temples at Khajuraho, is also richly carved. The interior doorway has figures of elephants, lions, goddesses, and guardians. The Shantinatha temple presents many good examples of Jain sculptures and has 12 altars in it, including one with a highly polished image of Lord Adinatha that is 14 feet tall. This temple was constructed about 100 years ago using the remains of other ruined Jain temples. A museum is also nearby with a larger collection of ancient images and stonework.

From here we turn south. A kilometre down the road is the Duladeo temple, which stands alone and is still used for worship by some of the local people. Inside is a unique Shiva *lingam* with 999 *lingams* carved on its sides. This way when a worshiper circumambulates it once, it equates with going around it 1000 times. Farther south beyond the river in the village of Jatkari is the Chaturbhuja temple. Above the doorway are the images of Vishnu, Brahma, and Shiva. The temple is ruined but still has an exquisitely carved Deity of Vishnu that stands three metres tall.

Closer to the village is the Jain Ghantai temple which is interesting, but not in very good condition. On the other side of the village near the Khajur Sagar lake is a small Brahma temple with a four-faced *linga* inside. It is actually a Vishnu temple and one of the oldest structures in town. Farther up the road is the Vamana temple, which was under repair when I visited. It is an interesting temple with a single tower above the sanctum. Inside the temple is an image of Lord Vamanadeva, plus images of Narasimha and Varaha. A little ways south of the Vamana temple, in the field, is the small Javari temple, dedicated to Vishnu and dating back to 1100 A.D.

As we make our way back through the village, some of the people who are very friendly may ask you if you'd like to see their house. So if you want, you can visit, take some photos, and leave some *baksheesh*, rupees. On the road heading toward the most impressive group of temples is a very small shrine to Hanuman. This shrine dates back to 922 A.D. and has an 8 foot tall Deity of Hanuman which is covered in vermillion.

The western group of temples are the most fascinating and exceptional showpieces of temple architecture in Khajuraho and Central India. Except for a few temples, they are all found within a fenced enclosure. The park-like enclosure is well maintained with watered and trimmed lawns. The temples are of various sizes and are covered with the usual carved figures. Starting in the front right corner of the enclosure is the Visvanatha temple, built around 1002 A.D., dedicated to Shiva with a stone *linga* inside. The north stairway leading to the entrance is flanked by two stone lions, and the south stairway has two stone elephants. The temple exterior and its tower is covered with rich carvings of a variety of subjects and designs. Across from the entrance is a temple for a huge Nandi, Shiva's bull carrier. Nandi is six feet high and seven feet long. You can sit in this little temple and easily look out over the rest of the park. Across from the Visvanatha temple is the smaller Parvati temple which now has an image of Parvati as Gauri. It is believed this was originally a Vishnu temple.

In the front left corner of the park is the Lakshmana temple, which dates back to 930 to 950 A.D. This temple is dedicated to Vishnu and is in the best condition of any of the temples. Above the entrance are images of Lakshmi, the goddess of fortune and Lord Vishnu's wife, and Brahma and Shiva on either side of her. On the doorway are carved stone illustrations of Puranic pastimes. There are four smaller shrines at each corner of the temple's terrace. One is for Lakshmi, wife of Lord Vishnu, and another is for Varaha, an incarnation of Vishnu. These five temples are exceptionally rich with elegant sculptures both inside and out. The sanctum has niches with other Vaishnava Deities in them amongst the many carvings that fill the interior. The main Deity in the sanctum is a four-armed three-faced Vishnu. The central face is Vishnu, while the other faces are of Narasimha and Varaha. The Deity was obtained from Devpal, the Pratihar king of Kanauj, and originally came from Tibet.

In the very back of the park starting on the left is the Kandariya Mahadev temple, the grandest of all the temples. It represents the culmination of temple art in Central India. The central tower reaches a height of over 100 feet, and the temple has as many as 646 sculptures on the exterior and 226 inside, most of which are two and three feet in height. The panels of sculptures depict the usual assortment of figures, including gods, goddesses, maidens, warriors, hunters, dancers, and erotics, for which these temples seem to be especially known. The main focus of worship is a Shiva *linga,* and Deities of Vishnu and Brahma on either side. The temple is made to look like a mountain and the word *kandariya* means a cave, which symbolically represents Shiva's cave abode in the Kailash mountain. At one time it had four smaller shrines at the corners of the terrace, but they have since perished.

On the same raised terrace as the Kandariya temple is the Devi Jagadambi temple and smaller Mahadeva temple. The Mahadeva temple, between the larger ones, still stands though its sanctum is ruined. It now houses a *sardula,* or a sculpture of a man or woman holding a lion. The Jagadambi temple was originally dedicated to Vishnu, but now has an image of a black painted Parvati in the sanctum who is generally called Kali, but in this case is called Jagadambi. Across from this temple is the large Chitragupta temple which is the only local temple dedicated to Surya the sun god and has a Surya Deity inside that is five feet tall. On the exterior's south wall in the central niche is a fine carving of an eleven-headed Vishnu. The central head is Vishnu and the others represent His ten incarnations.

If you prefer to see these temples with few people around, the best time is at 6.30 AM when the ticket booth opens. No one is there at that time and you have the whole enclosure to yourself. It is quite fascinating to walk around or be in one of these temples in the quiet and coolness of the morning while the sun is coming up. The place takes on a special mystical atmosphere that is quite unlike the way it feels when all the tourists show up a few hours later. By nine or ten o'clock all the group tours start arriving and some of the temples can get rather crowded as people shuffle in and out.

Outside the park enclosure and right next to the Lakshmana temple is the Mantangeshvara temple, dedicated to Shiva, and is still used for worship. It dates back to about 900 A.D. and is much simpler in design than the other temples and is not covered by the usual stone carvings. This temple is very busy with devotees coming and going. In front of the temple to the left is a Deity of Ganesh that many of the women worship by offering incense and flowers. Then climbing the steps you enter the cave-like temple and make your way to the back of the huge circular (20 feet) and raised *Gauri-patta* upon which is a polished Shiva *linga* over a metre in diameter and 2.5 metres (about eight feet) tall. People go up the stairs onto the *Gauri-patta* and splash pots of water onto the Shiva *linga* and then continue down another stairway that leads out a side door. The water is brought from the nearby Shivsagar Lake. You can see people continually repeat the process of getting water from the lake, go through the temple to worship the *linga* by pouring water on it, exit out the side door, and then go back to the lake for more water.

In front of the Mantangeshvara temple is the Varaha temple. This is built merely as a *mandap* hall about 20 feet by 16 feet, but has a huge Deity of Varaha, the boar incarnation of Lord Vishnu. The body of the Deity is carved with rows of small figures, as many as 764, that consist of various members of the Hindu pantheon.

Another temple is located past the Shivsagar lake and across the field. It is the ruined Chausath temple, dedicated to Kali and the 64 yoginis who tend to the goddess. It is built on a terrace 18 feet high, but has no ceiling or tower over it. You can see the 65 little cells where the small images used to be kept, but there is really little else to see. Another 600 yards to the west is the small, ruined shrine to Shiva, the Lalguan Mahadeva temple next to the Lalguan Sagar lake. This is another ruined temple with little to see.

Across from the Shivsagar lake is the Archeological Museum. It offers an interesting assortment of ancient sculptures from the area and is worth checking out. Entrance is free with your ticket to the western group of temples. Around the corner from the museum is the main street with a number of shops that sell the usual variety of nick-nacks from which you might find some souvenirs if you're so inclined. This area gets pretty busy in the evening, mostly with Indian shoppers and tourists. It's an interesting place to hang out and watch the people for a while.

After our visit to Khajuraho is complete, we take an early morning bus to Jhansi. From Jhansi most people take the train north toward Gwalior or Agra. But in our case we are going to take a short excursion south to Vidisha and Sanchi near Bhopal. Most trains stop at Vidisha, but not all of them stop at smaller Sanchi, so we have to check where we need to get off. In our case, the train stops at Sanchi so we'll get off there and stay at the Ashok Travelers Lodge, which is one of the better hotels in the area. But *rickshas* are hard to find in this town, so we have to walk several blocks from the train station to the hotel. It's a good thing we have traveled with little luggage. If we have left Khajuraho in the morning and reached Jhansi around noon, the afternoon train to Sanchi will arrive in the evening. By then we'll be ready for a small meal and a good night's rest, both of which are available at the lodge. We can tour the area the next day.

Sanchi is a very small and simple town. The significance of it is that on the hilltop that overlooks the town is a Buddhist place of pilgrimage. Buddha never spent any time here, but it had been an important center while Buddhism flourished. Gradually Buddhism declined and the site became neglected and forgotten until it was rediscovered in 1818 by a British officer. It has a wide variety of high quality sculptures and monuments. The hilltop is surrounded by a stone wall, and in the center of the site is a huge *stupa* that was constructed by Ashoka, said to cover some relics of Lord Buddha. It is 120 feet in diameter and encases an earlier *stupa* of the 3rd century B.C. It has four finely carved gateways, built in the first century B.C. The panels are in very good condition and illustrate pastimes from Buddha's life, the worship of the Bodhi tree, as well as scenes of sports, animals, and designs. *Stupa* three, though somewhat inferior in quality, contains relics of two of Buddha's foremost disciples, Shariputra and Maudgalyayana. Around the site are many other ancient and interesting Buddhist structures that have been restored and are well preserved. Some of the oldest of these antiquities date back to the third century B.C. and belong to the Maurya and Gupta periods. You'll find *stupas*, columns, gateways, etc., most of which have excellent carvings with many designs and scenes of Buddha's life. There are also the remains and foundations of temples, monasteries, and other ancient ruins. The best way to see Sanchi is to buy a guidebook, pay your admission fee, and simply wander around the site for a few hours. More artifacts are found in the Archeological Museum a short distance from the base of the hill.

After our visit to the Buddhist site, we walk back down the hill and are fortunate to find a motor *ricksha*. So we take a 45 minute ride on the very bumpy road to Vidisha or Besnagar where we find the Heliodorus column, locally known as the Khamb Baba pillar. This was erected by the Greek ambassador Heliodorus who writes on the stone pillar the time it was erected and the fact that he had converted to Vaishnavism, or the worship of Vishnu. This was the archeological discovery that proved to the disappointed British that knowledge of Krishna predated Christianity by at least 200 years. It also signified that the Indians did not adopt legends of Christ to put in their *Puranas* to be used for the stories of Krishna as the British had hypothesized. One point to consider is that if a Greek official was so impressed with the philosophy of Vaishnavism that he converted to it in 200 B.C., then it means that Vaishnavism had to have been developed several hundred years if not several thousand years earlier.

Seven more very bumpy kilometres north of Vidisha is Udayagiri, which is known for the sandstone ridge that has 20 cave temples that date back from 320 to 600 A.D. Two of the caves are Jain and the others are Hindu. Half of these are merely little niches and of the others only a few are worth mentioning. Cave five has a sculpture of Lord Varaha rescuing the earth, represented as goddess Bhudevi. Brahma and Agni are also in the illustration, along with musicians and sages. A few caves, such as caves four and nineteen, have Shiva *lingas*, and others have images of Varaha and Durga, or Puranic legends on the walls or doorways, but most of these are well worn.

Personally, I could easily find only four of the caves and some of the others after exploring the ridge. Though they were a little interesting, I thought they weren't worth the endeavor. So after looking around for a while, we take another very bumpy hour long ride back to our hotel in Sanchi. Once we're back at the hotel we make arrangements with our *ricksha* driver to pick us up at five the next morning to get the early train at Vidisha since it doesn't stop at Sanchi. If he picks us up, then we'll pay him for both today and tomorrow. If he sleeps in, then our ride today is free. This is the way to be sure he'll show up on time.

And now we can spend the rest of the day relaxing, catching up on our writing, or whatever, while sitting in the garden-like setting of the hotel. After doing so much traveling over the past several weeks, it's good to take some time and reflect on all we've seen and experienced in this amazing country. I have to admit, there is some satisfaction to be felt when thinking of all we have encountered, both good and bad, that we would have missed had we not come to India.

Sanchi is only 68 km north of Bhopal, and beyond Bhopal is Ujjain, another very important place of pilgrimage. And though it is tempting to get on the train and head south and go to Ujjain and beyond, this is getting further west than we plan to go for now. So we'll save it for when we tour the western part of India.

When our visit to Sanchi is finished, we take a train north to Gwalior, a city of 450,000. This will be another overnight stop in which we'll arrive in the afternoon, spend a few hours seeing what we came for, and then head out again the next morning. What we want to visit is Gwalior's unused fort that is enclosed by a massive wall and sits on a hilltop that is almost two miles long and rises 330 feet overlooking the town. Though it is not a place of pilgrimage, a paragraph describing it is not unnecessary. The best way to start your tour of the fort is by walking up the southwest road which passes a number of impressive Jain sculptures along the cliffs of the ravine that were carved in the 1400's. The biggest of them is image number 20 of Adinatha, which stands 17 metres tall. As we wander around the fort, some of the things we'll see are the Teli-ka-mandir, a tall Hindu temple that rises 75 feet high and is covered with carvings, and has an unusual design for a temple. There is also the Suraj Kund, a lake that cured Suraj Sen of leprosy after the hermit Gwalipa made Suraj drink from it. The Sasbahu temples are along the east wall, dating back to the ninth century. The larger one was once a Vishnu temple and the interior is especially interesting with pillars and walls covered with carvings. Other old buildings can be found, but the Man Singh palace, or Man Mandir, built from 1486 to 1516, is still in fairly good condition. It has four storeys, two above and two below ground. It has a wide variety of roofs, balconies, ornamental friezes, paintings, and rooms that make it a fascinating place. As you walk through the archway toward the northeast entrance to the fort, you'll here the many voices and sounds of the town below. At first I thought there was a large crowd of people in the palace, but then I realized what it was when I came to the wall overlooking the city. There are some good views from up here. On the northeast side of the fort are other Jain and Hindu sculptures, but they're not as impressive as at the other entrance. At the base of the hill there is the Gujari Mahal that has a museum with a good collection of Jain and Hindu sculptures dating from the first century B.C. to the 11th century A.D., but closed on Mondays.

From Gwalior we go to Agra, which again is not really a pilgrimage center, but many people flock here to see the Taj Mahal. The Taj Mahal was built between 1632 and 1653 by Shah Jahan as a memorial to his wife Mumtaz

Mahal. It is said that as many as 20,000 craftsmen helped work on the building. The tombs of Mumtaz and Shah Jahan are in a lower chamber. The Taj Mahal is an impressive building and many come to see it on the full moon nights. The quietest time to see it is around sunrise. After 9 AM it starts filling up with many tourists, all wanting to stand in the same place to take the same photograph or to see the same thing from the same angle as you. In the summer, however, as can be expected, there are far fewer tourists that visit.

Not far from the Taj is the Agra Fort or Red Fort, which has many buildings inside that had different functions for the Moghul rulers. One of the differences between the Hindu and Moslem rulers is that Hindu rulers would construct great temples that everyone could utilize, while the Moslem rulers constructed big forts simply to show their power and might. Other interesting buildings in Agra include the Itmad-ud-daulah, another tomb, though smaller than the Taj, built between 1622 and 1628. This is a memorial for Mirza Ghiyas Beg and several family members. Guides are willing to take you around the place but some of them have such poor English you can hardly understand a word they say. The building is covered with similar inlay work as the Taj and is considered a prototype.

Nine km north of Agra is Akbar's Mausoleum in the middle of a huge garden at Sikandra. It is a combination of Hindu and Muslim styles of architecture and has four gates that lead to it. One gate is Muslim in design, one is Hindu, one Christian, and one is a mixture that shows Akbar's respect for all religions. Although Akbar had a Muslim background, he had a Hindu guru for a teacher and renounced hunting and tried to adopt a vegetarian diet because of the influence.

Ten km north of Agra is the Dayal Bagh Temple which belongs to the Radah Soami religious sect. Their practices and philosophy are very similar to the path of *bhakti-yoga*. The temple is under construction and looks like it will continue to be for quite a few more years. But two of the three floors are finished and if you want to see some of the most beautiful carved marble and inlay work in India, this is the place to see it. It might not be as big as the Taj, but the quality of work is the best I've seen anywhere.

One place that some people say you should not miss in your visit to Agra is the deserted but well preserved Moghul city of Fatehpur Sikri, 20 miles west of Agra, built between 1570 and 1586. If you like to wander around exploring old buildings and architecture without many restrictions, this is a place where you can let yourself go. The place is divided into two sections. There is the mosque, and there is the residential section. In the mosque, which one enters through the huge gateway on the south side called the Buland Darwaza, or Gate of Victory, buildings include the Dargah Mosque, that is supposed to be a replica of the one in Mecca, and the tomb of Saint Shaikh Salam Chisti, which is visited by many women who want children. This is because the saint foretold the birth of Emperor Akbar's son when the emperor, without heir, went to see the saint in hopes of getting his blessing to have a son. In the back are the tombs of Islam Khan, Shaik Hajji Husain, and other family members. As you leave the mosque on the left side of the main gate you'll find an inscription that refers to the teachings of Christ. It states that the world is a bridge, pass over it but build no residence on it. He who hopes for an hour may hope for eternity. The world endures but an hour. Spend it in prayer, for the rest is unseen.

The city came into existence when Akbar decided to move his capital to Sikri. Akbar spent 12 years building the city and put up a palace for each of his three queens. One was Muslim, one was Hindu, and the other was Christian. Akbar was known for being very liberal towards all religions and even had a Hindu guru. The residential section also included a hall of public audience, a treasury house, a huge sleeping chamber, a swimming pool, a big bath house, a stable for 200 horses, a large outdoor pachisi game board played with slave girls dressed in different colored outfits as the pieces, and a harem of over 600 concubines with a hospital to handle all the pregnant women. But only four years after the city was completed the water went salty and Akbar had little choice but to abandon the place.

If you visit Fatehpur Sikri you may want to hire one of the local guides to take you around to better understand all the buildings and their purpose. It's worth it and actually quite interesting. But the guides always try to sell you things when they show you the shops near the mosque, so be prepared. However, the prices on the marble items are not too bad compared to prices on similar things sold in Agra. You can go to Fatehpur Sikri quite easily by waiting for a bus at the Idgah bus station, but getting back to Agra may be another matter. There's supposed to be a bus every hour between the two towns, but it doesn't quite work that well. The buses are usually overloaded and the people who are waiting to get back to Agra swarm the bus when it pulls in. Tactics to get a seat can get pretty extreme. Aside from the normal pushing and shoving, one thing I learned was to toss something like a water bottle through the window onto a seat to reserve it. Then when you get on the bus you can say it's your bottle and your seat. Or, if it comes to the worst, give a lift to a small Indian man so he can climb through the window into the bus as people are getting off. Then he'll save you a seat as everyone else gets on. Other people just climb on top of the bus for the hour ride back to Agra.

After our visit at Agra we go to Mathura to tour Vrajamandala, one of the most extraordinary and mystical places in all of India. Vraja, which has a perimeter of 168 miles and is composed of many villages and towns, is considered nondiferent from Mayapur (Navadvipa), Jagannatha Puri, and Dwaraka. The same spiritual nature is manifest in all of these places. But Vraja is considered the holiest of all holy *dhams*. In many places in the *shastra* are descriptions of the glories of Mathura and Vrindavan. The glories of Mathura are elaborately explained in the *Varaha Purana*, chapters 152 through 180. One verse states: "A moment in Mathura is worth a thousand years spent in Kashi

(Varanasi)." And simply by bathing in the Yamuna River in Mathura one can be freed from all sins. Residing here for only a few weeks qualifies one for liberation from material existence. And each step taken in Mathura is equal to visiting a holy place elsewhere. It is explained that those who die here attain Vishnu-loka and do not take birth again. The descriptions of the glories of Vrajamandala go on and on, but they are known only to a few rare souls in this world. Only the most fortunate get to hear about it, what to speak of getting the opportunity to visit this holy place.

Many holy men can be seen visiting the temples, walking in the streets, singing or chanting as they go. Though they may seem destitute, they are often very jolly because of their spiritual wisdom and freedom from materialistic problems. Here the holy men and saintly women enter into a higher reality that makes their bodily condition less significant. Many *bhaktas*, sages, and mystics have experienced unimaginable levels of spiritual ecstasy here, though superficially the area may look like any other part of India where people are engaged in the struggle to survive. But as you look deeper, if you are capable of it, you'll find quite another aspect of Vrajamandala that draws pilgrims by the thousands from all over India.

Basically, Vraja is the land of Krishna. If you really want to understand the pastimes of Krishna, you have to know Vraja. And if you want to know the significance of Vraja, you have to understand Krishna's pastimes. Krishna was born in Mathura 5,000 years ago but lived in Gokula for three years, then moved to Chatikara and Vrindavan for 3 years, then lived in Nandagram for three years, and from age 10 to 28 He lived in Mathura. After this He moved to the western coast of India where He lived in Dwaraka for over 96 years. Thus, He stayed in this world for 125 years, but some of His sweetest and most attractive pastimes were performed in Vraja. To fully explain these pastimes and where they took place in this present volume is impossible, unless we wanted to greatly extend the length of this book. But there are some significant sites and temples that I'll try to briefly describe. We'll start out tour at Mathura since that's where we get off the train.

Mathura is the largest city in Vraja with around 150,000 residents. It is a very busy, noisy, and dusty town with a large railroad junction. Nonetheless, it is an important town for pilgrims. Besides being the birthplace of Lord Krishna, Srila Vyasadeva also took birth here at Krishna Ganga Tirtha on the banks of the Yamuna, where there is a small temple to Ganga Devi and many Shiva *lingas*. It was also at Ambarish-tila where the great devotee King Ambarish fasted while waiting for the sage Durvasa Muni to return from being chased by Lord Vishnu's *cakra*, as described in the *Bhagavatam*. Not far from Krishna Ganga Tirtha is Vishrama Ghat, the best known of all the bathing *ghats* on the Yamuna in Mathura. Anyone can direct you to it. It was here that Lord Varaha rested after saving the earth from Hiranyaksha and spoke the *Varaha Purana*. Lord Krishna also bathed and rested here after killing Kamsa, the demoniac king. And

Sri Caitanya also bathed here while visiting Mathura. So many pilgrims come here to perform various rituals and take a purifying bath. You can also watch the *aratika* to the Yamuna river that takes place every evening around seven PM.

The most important temple in Mathura is the beautiful Keshava temple that represents the place where Krishna was born. It stands next to a mosque that the fanatic Muslim Aurangzeb built where the original Keshava temple stood before he tore it down in 1669. The present temple has lovely Radha-Keshava Deities and paintings of Krishna's pastimes covering the walls and ceiling of the large interior. It is said that simply by seeing this Deity of Keshava one is relieved within a second of the sins of one's past seven births and will not take birth again. The real spot where Krishna was born is a few blocks away, represented by a small temple building, past the Potra Kund. The building is not very well kept because it is located on property owned by Muslims. But this may change in the future.

Other important temples in Mathura include the Dwarakadish Mandira which has a small, beautiful black Deity of four-handed Dwarakadish, similar to the Deity in the huge temple at Dwaraka. This temple is quite popular and many people crowd to see the *arati* ceremonies. Nearby is a temple of white Sweta-Varaha, and another of Adi-Varaha which was supposed to have once been Lord Indra's Deity in Swarga, his heavenly abode. The Deity was later taken by Ravana to Sri Lanka and then to Ayodhya by Lord Ramacandra when Rama defeated Ravana. Lord Ramacandra gave it to His brother Satrughna who brought it to Mathura. This story is more fully explained in Chapter 163 of the *Varaha Purana*.

Downstream from Vishrama Ghat is Prayaga Ghat where the ancient temple of Veni Madhava is located. It is said that by bathing here one gets the benefit of bathing at the *sangam* in Prayaga (Allahabad). A little farther is Bengali Ghat where Vasudeva is said to have crossed the river when taking baby Krishna in his arms from Kamsa's prison to Mahavana after His birth. Next there is Dhruva Ghat where there is a temple on a mound called Dhruva Tila which marks the spot where Dhruva performed austerities to get the *darshana* of Lord Narayana, as described in *Srimad-Bhagavatam*.

Across the river from Vishrama Ghat, about 200 metres from the river, is the small village of Isapur. Here you'll find a temple with an image of Durvasa Muni which marks where the great mystic performed many austerities and meditated during Satya-yuga.

Mathura's most popular Shiva temple is the Rangeshwara Mandira, one kilometre south of Vishrama Ghat. This is one of four main Shiva temples of the city, which includes Bhuteshwara to the west near Krishna Janmastan, Pipaleshwara in the east near Vishrama Ghat, and Gokarneshwara in the north. Near the Rangeshwara Mandir is the Keshava temple of the Gaudiya Math where Srila A. C. Bhaktivedanta Swami took *sannyasa*, the renounced order of life. The temple has beautiful Deities of Radha-Keshava and Sri Caitanya.

During the afternoon when the temples are closed you can visit the Government Archeological Museum. It has a good collection of Hindu, Jain, and Buddhist sculptures and art work. Mathura was a major Buddhist center with as many as 20 monasteries when the city was visited by Fa Hian around 401 A.D. and Hiuen Tsang in 634 A.D. But things drastically changed for Hindus and Buddhists alike when the Muslim invaders, like Mahmud of Ghazni, arrived in 1017. After that Buddhism practically disappeared from Mathura.

Another place open all day is Ranga Bhumi, the area which was the wrestling arena of King Kamsa located across from the Main Post Office. On a hill, Kamsa-tila, is where Krishna killed the demoniac Kamsa, and just beyond it is where Krishna crowned Ugrasena as King of Mathura.

Six kilometres south of Mathura is the small town of Gokula next to the Yamuna where Krishna lived during part of His childhood. There are several temples here, such as the Gokulnathji Mandir and the temple in the reconstructed fort, Nanda Qila, of Krishna's father, Nanda Maharaja. Across from the temple are diorama displays of Krishna's Gokula pastimes. These temples are interesting to visit, but the priests simply want to make a business of doing special *pujas* for you and then charge you high prices for them, like 125, 250, 501, or 1001 rupees. So if you don't want this, be sure to tell them you simply came for *darshan* and then leave a small donation you can afford.

Two kilometres south of Gokula is Mahavana where there is the Nanda Bhavan temple on a small hill. Inside are large images of Nanda, Mother Yashoda, Balarama, and baby Krishna. The pillars are said to have come from the original palace of Maharaja Nanda. This is also near the *janma-bhumi* or appearance place of Lord Balarama. Not far away is Yamalarjuna Bhanga where you can see an ancient grinding mortar said to be the one Mother Yashoda tied to baby Krishna which He dragged between two *yamalarjuna* trees and caused them to crash to the ground. When the trees fell, two demigods were freed who had been cursed to live as these trees for offending Narada Muni. Then the demigods were allowed to return to heaven. The *Srimad-Bhagavatam* explains all of these pastimes.

A kilometre further south is Brahmanda Ghat, which is not only a beautiful and serene bathing spot on the Yamuna, but also where Krishna's mother suspected Him of eating dirt. When she looked in His mouth she saw the whole universe. Seven kilometres further south is the Dauji temple. Dauji is the Deity of Lord Balarama that was originally installed 5,000 years ago by King Vajranabha, Krishna's great-grandson. The present temple was built 200 years ago by Shyama Das of Delhi.

Back in Mathura we start toward Vrindavan and soon find the Gita Mandir, a very nice temple built by the Birla family. The temple has a very good standard of worship for the Deities of Lakshmi-Narayana, as well as Sita-Rama. In the courtyard is a column called Gita Stambha that has all the *Bhagavad-gita* verses engraved on it.

Twenty minutes away we find the Pagal Baba temple complex. It has residential facilities and a large temple with many dioramas of the different incarnations of Krishna on the bottom level. As you go to each higher floor there are altars with Deities of Lakshmi-Narayana, Sita-Rama, Vamanadeva, etc. On the top floor you can look out and get a good view of the town of Vrindavan in the distance. Across the road nearby is a path leading to Akrura Ghat, which used to be along the Yamuna River until the river changed its course, as it often does in this area. Akrura Ghat is where Akrura, Krishna's uncle, got to see Krishna and Balarama as Vishnu and Ananta lying on the surface of the Yamuna. Akrura had stopped there to chant the *gayatri mantra* while taking Krishna and Balarama to Mathura. What the vision signified was that Krishna never leaves Vrindavan, He eternally resides there, but Krishna's expansion as Vishnu was going to Mathura.

Now we continue to the most holy town of Vrindavan which has many temples to see. In fact, it's said that there are over 5,000 temples, both large and small, in this town. Out of all of these, I'll describe the most important.

Vrindavan is not a place you go to and expect all its secrets to become easily revealed. It is said that you don't get to Vrindavan simply by purchasing a ticket. Vrindavan is not only a geographical place, but it is a state of spiritual consciousness, without which you'll not comprehend the special nature of the place. Thus, as you become qualified through *bhakti-yoga*, and by receiving the blessings of the resident devotees, Vrindavan will gradually reveal itself to you. I have personally experienced this. Only after staying in Vrindavan for several weeks was I able to find and understand the meaning of certain places and temples that I had been looking for from the time I arrived. Slowly I began to have my own realizations about the spiritual characteristics of this holy town.

The spiritual nature of this place can be very apparent if one is able to perceive it, and some people feel it right away. But there can be plenty of things that can hinder your absorption in such spiritual bliss. Things like misquitoes, noisy monkeys that fight in the night that keep you from sleeping, incredibly hot summers, cold winter nights without central heat, and so on. For the average person it is not an easy place in which to live. That's why it is recommended to keep your visits in Vrindavan short so you do not lose respect for the place and consider it an ordinary, mundane town, and, thus, become critical and offensive. Such an attitude makes one lose all ability to enter into even the most basic level of Vrindavan's spiritual atmosphere. In the proper consciousness, one can perceive that everything about Vrindavan is spiritual.

For me, Vrindavan is my favorite place in all of India. I love to walk around the village visiting the temples and holy places, seeing the beautiful Deities, dealing with the friendly residents, and watching the pilgrims who also tour the temples. Of course, this doesn't mean that you shouldn't be careful as in other places in India. There may still be plenty of *ricksha* drivers and store keepers who are too willing to raise the price on their services and merchandise when they see a foreigner in town. And some tourists are easy prey for such people. But after having done as much traveling as we have throughout the rest of India (unless you've come straight to Vrindavan from Delhi upon your arrival in India), we'll find that Vrindavan is a small and very sweet village that is easy to get to know.

Rupa Goswami explains in his book *Sri Upadesamrta* that Vridavan is spiritually superior to Mathura because this is where Krishna's highly esoteric *rasa-lila* pastimes take place. Rupa Goswami was the top literary disciple of Sri Caitanya Mahaprabhu and chief of the Goswamis who lived in Vrindavan about 500 years ago. He wrote many books about the art of devotional service to Krishna and restored many of the holy places in Vraja, re-establishing its spiritual importance. The *rasa-lila* is the pinnacle of transcendental loving exchange between Krishna and His purest devotees, the *gopis*, as explained in *Srimad-Bhagavatam*. The *rasa* dance is purely spiritual and not easily understood by mundane scholarly interpretations. If one is not a *bhakta* (devotee engaged in *bhakti-yoga*), one cannot comprehend such elevated love of God.

The *rasa* dance took place in the forest of Seva Kunj, which used to be a much bigger area than the small enclosed forest it is today. Nonetheless, it is considered the center of Vrindavan, and is where, according to *shastra*, the *rasa* dance takes place every night. In fact, it's said that Krishna never leaves Vrindavan; the spiritual pastimes are eternal. We'll understand this more clearly as we visit a few of the temples and relate the pastimes connected with them.

There are a number of important temples in this area. Just north of Seva Kunj is Imli Tala. Here we find a very old tamarind tree that has existed since the days of Krishna in the courtyard of a Radha-Krishna temple that was built by Bhakti Saranga Maharaja. Krishna used to sit under this tree and His body would turn golden from ecstatic separation from His dearmost devotee, Srimati Radharani. Five hundred years ago, Sri Caitanya would sit under the tree and due to His love for Krishna His golden body would turn blackish.

Heading east we visit the Radha-Damodar Mandir. The original Deities of Radha-Damodar were installed by Rupa Gosvami in 1542, but were later taken to Jaipur where They are now worshiped. The present Deities are considered equal to the original Deities. There is also a stone or *shila* from Govardhana Hill in the temple that has an actual footprint of Krishna on it. Krishna personally appeared to Sanatana Gosvami to give him the *shila*. He told Sanatana that because he was having difficulty from old age he should stop his daily circumambulation of Govardhana Hill and simply circumambulate the *shila*. The footprint became part of the stone when Krishna stood on it and caused the stone to melt from the sweet sound of His flute playing. Now pilgrims circumambulate the temple four times, which is equal to walking once around the 15 mile path of Govardhana Hill. You can ask the *pujari* (priest) at the temple for Giriraja *darshan* and for two rupees he will bring the Govardhana *shila* for you to see.

On the left side of the Radha-Damodar temple, through a doorway, are the *samadhi* tombs of Jiva Gosvami, Krsnadas Kaviraja Gosvami, Bhugarbha Gosvami, and a *puspa samadhi* of Bhaktisiddhanta Gosvami. Through a door on the right side of the temple is the *samadhi* and *bhajan kutir* of Rupa Gosvami. On the right side of the courtyard are the rooms where Srila A. C. Bhaktivedanta Swami Prabhupada lived for several years from 1959 to 1965 and wrote his commentary on the First Canto of *Srimad-Bhagavatam*, which he later brought to America.

Not far away is the Radha-Shyamasundara temple, which is one of the seven main temples of Vrindavan and has some very beautiful Deities. It was established by Shyamananda Prabhu who was a disciple of Sri Caitanya and a very elevated *bhakta*. In fact, one time he saw Srimati Radharani. He would regularly clean Nidhubana and happened to find an anklebell. He thought it must be Radharani's since he knew Krishna and Radha often spend Their evenings there. When Radharani discovered one of Her anklebells were missing, she sent Lalita to find it. At Nidhubana Lalita saw Shyamananda Prabhu and asked him if he'd found an anklebell. He said he had and asked if it was hers. Lalita said it belonged to her sister and asked to have it. Shyamananda said he would not give it to her but only to her sister. Lalita insisted that he give it to her, and Shyamananda continued to refuse. So Lalita returned to Radharani and Radha decided to personally go for the anklebell Herself. Approaching Shyamananda, Radha asked for the anklebell and he was happy to give it to Her. Radha, being pleased with his service, revealed Her identity to him and by impressing Her anklebell into his forehead personally gave him a *tiloka* mark. Later, the other *bhaktas* criticized him for wearing a new style of *tiloka*. But that night Srimati Radharani appeared to Jiva Gosvami in a dream and told him that She was the one who gave Shyamananda the *tiloka* mark. Then all the devotees went to Shyamananda to ask for forgiveness and accepted that he actually saw Srimati Radharani. This is another story signifying that the eternal pastimes of the spiritual realm are continually taking place in Vrindavan.

A little walk from the Radha-Syamasundara temple is Loi Bazaar, one of the main shopping areas in the village. Here you can find all the necessities for living in Vridavana. Located above the Post Office is the Vrindavan Research Institue which has original leaves with the hand writing of Sanatana, Rupa, and Jiva Gosvamis. Walking through the bazaar we next see the Shahji Mandir which was built in 1876 by Shah Kundan Lal of Lucknow, and has small Radha-Krishna Deities. This is an attractive temple and shows how Shah Kundan Lal, a rich jeweler, appreciated service to Krishna in Vrindavan. To the left of the temple and down a lane is a small but pleasant Krishna temple of the famous poetess Mirabai. On the eastern side of the Shahji Mandir is another enclosed park called Nidhuvana. This is where Radha and Krishna performed many pastimes. Even now it is considered that They still take rest here in the evening. Thus, there is a small temple of Radha-Krishna sleeping on a bed located here.

This was also the place where Haridasa Gosvami found the Deity of Banki Behari, another famous temple in Vrindavan which we will visit shortly.

Another important temple nearby is the Radharamana Mandir, founded by Gopala Bhatta Gosvami. Gopala Bhatta had been worshiping a *shalagrama-shila*, which is a stone form of Krishna that he had gotten while on pilgrimage in Nepal. However, he longed to have a Deity of Krishna to worship and dress. One day the Deity of Radharamana manifested from the *shalagrama-shila*, thus fulfilling Gopala Bhatta Gosvami's desire.

A short walk away is another of the seven major temples, the Radha-Gokulananda Mandir, founded by Lokanatha Gosvami. On the altar of this medium sized temple are the Radha-Vinoda Deities of Lokanatha Gosvami (though his original Deities were moved to Jaipur), Radha-Vijaya Govinda of Baladeva Vidyabhushana, Radha-Gokulananda of Vishvanatha Cakravarti Thakura, and a Sri Caitanya Deity of Narottamadas Thakura. The temple also has a small Govardhana *shila* that was rubbed smooth by Sri Caitanya who used to hold it while chanting Krishna's holy names. The *shila* had been given to Raghunatha Dasa Gosvami. Across from the temple in the courtyard are the *samadhis* of Lokanatha Gosvami, Narottamadas Thakura, and Vishvanatha Chakravarty who were all important Vaishnavas in the Gaudiya line. The Radha-Vamsi Gopala temple is nearby and is where Srila A. C. Bhaktivedanta Swami Prabhupada lived from 1954 to 1962 and wrote his first commentary on *Bhagavad-gita*.

Following the street to the Yamuna River we come to Keshi Ghat where Krishna performed the pastime of killing the Keshi demon. Keshi was a henchman of the demoniac King Kamsa and took the form of a huge horse to terrorize the residents of Vrindavan. Krishna, therefore, killed the demon and then washed Himself in the Yamuna. The *Adi Varaha Purana* establishes that by taking a holy bath at Keshi Ghat brings the results of bathing at all the holy places, and is worth 1,000 baths in the Ganges. Therefore, Keshi Ghat is one of the holiest *ghats* in Vrindavan.

Not far from Keshi Ghat is Bhramar Ghat where Bilvamangala Thakura, the author of *Krishna Karnamrita*, performed austerities years ago. Lord Krishna used to appear in Vrindavan just to serve His great devotee Bilvamangala by supplying him with a cup of milk everyday.

As we head back into the village, not far from the Radharamana temple is the Radha-Gopinatha Mandir. It is another of the seven original temples and was founded by Madhava Pandita. The original Deities were transferred to Jaipur and similar Deities were again installed in this temple. Around the corner is the New Radha-Gopinatha temple with Deities of Srimati Radharani, Gopinatha, and Srimati Jahnava. Jahnava was Lord Nityananda's wife and this Deity of her was brought from Jahnava's native Bengal by a man who said the Deity appeared by Divine Will. This was years after she had left this world. Then Gopinatha appeared to the temple priest in a dream and told him that

Jahnava was actually the elevated gopi Anangamanjari, and that the Deity should be placed on the altar next to His left side. So this is why the Deities in this temple are now arranged in this way.

Farther into the eastern part of town are many other temples; including the large and ornate Lala Babu Mandir with Radha, Krishna, and Lalita Deities; the Gopishwara Mahadeva Shiva temple with a Shiva *linga*, said to have been originally installed by Krishna's great-grandson, Vajranabha; the Tikarirani Radha-Krishna temple; the especially beautiful Thakura Yugala Kishora temple, which has many small cut mirrors embedded in the walls and a sleeping Krishna Deity on a swinging bed; and the large Rangaji temple with its South Indian style *gopurams*. This temple is modeled after the Sri Rangam temple near Trichy in Tamil Nadu. It has three gates you go through to get to the central temple, but Westerners are not allowed past the third gate.

Not far from this temple is Brahma Kunda where the demigod Lord Brahma prayed to Krishna for forgiveness after testing Him to see if He was actually the Supreme. The story is that one time Brahma took away all of Krishna's friends and cows. After a moment he came back to see what Krishna's reaction was and to his amazement saw all of the boys and calves still there. Krishna had expanded Himself into the forms of all the boys and calves. Realizing his insignificant position, Brahma returned all the boys and calves he had taken and prayed for Krishna to excuse his ignorance.

Next is the Radha-Govindaji temple that is another of the seven major temples of Vrindavan. It was established by Rupa Gosvami where he discovered the Gopala Deity. The beautiful temple is made out of red sandstone and was completed in 1590 A.D. The temple is now only two storeys tall but once reached up to seven storeys. The Muslim fanatic Aurangzeb, doing his dirty work once again, dismantled the upper five storeys of the temple. Due to fear of the Moghuls, the original Deities were moved to Jaipur where today many pilgrims go to see Them. (I will describe this and other Jaipur temples in a future book when we go to western India.) The temple now has *prati-bhuh* Deities, or expansions, of the original Radha-Govindaji that are worshiped. The original Govindaji Deity is said to have been installed thousands of years ago by Vajranabha.

A hundred yards northeast of the Govindaji temple is a mound that has the ruins of the Sakshi Gopala temple. You'll remember that we saw the present Sakshi Gopala temple just outside of Jagannatha Puri. Sakshi Gopala had been discovered and installed in the temple in Vrindavan, but walked over 1000 miles to Vidyanagar to bear witness for one of His devotees. From the Radha-Govindaji temple you can follow the road and find many more temples and *ashramas* of Vrindavan.

Back at Seva Kunj, we now head west to the Radha-Vallabha Mandir. This is a temple that is the center of the Radha Vallabha sect founded by Sri Hit Hari Vamsa, a disciple of Gopala Bhatta Gosvami who was known for his poetry about Radha and Krishna. After this we see the Banki Behari Mandir, one of the most popular temples of Vrindavan. Haridas Gosvami found Banki Behari at the bottom of Visakha Kunda in Nidhuvan after Haridas had a dream in which the Deity told him where to look. When you visit the temple you will see that the curtain in front of the Deity is closed for a few seconds every minute. This is because the Deity once walked off the altar and out of the temple to follow a great devotee who had come for *darshan*. When the temple priests found Banki Behari, they placed Him on the altar again but began closing the curtain at short intervals to keep the Deity from getting too attached to any of the visiting devotees.

Not far away, located down a lane, is the Asta-Sakhi Mandir, a lovely eight-sided, dome-topped temple. This temple offers *darshan* of not only Radha-Krishna (Radha-Rasabihariji in this case), but also of eight important *gopis*. They include Rangadevi, Champaklata, Chitra, and Lalita on the left, and Vishakha, Indulekha, Tungavidya, and Sudevi on the right. From this temple you can easily see the old temple of Radha-Madan Mohan to the west.

The Madan Mohan temple, located on a hill near the old river bed of the Yamuna, was established by Sanatana Gosvami. This was one of the first temples erected after Sri Caitanya's visit to Vrindavan. The Deity is said to have been found in the hill by Sri Advaita who gave the Deity to a Mathura priest. The priest treated the Deity like one of his children and when Sanatana Gosvami saw this he criticized the priest for not following the many rules and regulations for Deity worship. Then in a dream Madan Mohan told Sanatana that He was happy with the priest's spontaneous love, but now He was no longer happy with all these rules that were supposed to be followed. So Sanatana went to see the priest who then gave the Deity to Sanatana. At first Sanatana used to keep Madan Mohan in a tree because he had no where else to keep Him. Then one time the Deity asked for some salt with the dried bread that Sanatana offered to Him. Sanatana only said, "I am an old man. What can I do? Please accept it the way it is." Just then a rich merchant was taking a boat loaded with salt down the Yamuna. By Krishna's will the boat got stuck. Madan Mohan changed into a cowherd boy who led the merchant to Sanatana. Sanatana could do nothing to help the merchant, so the merchant prayed to Madan Mohan that if his boat became free he would sell his salt and return to use the money to build a nice temple. After praying, the merchant returned to his boat and found that it was no longer stuck. When the merchant sold the salt, he returned to build the temple. So this is how the temple was erected. Later, this was the Deity from which Krishnadas Kaviraja got the inspiration to write the *Caitanya-caritamrta*.

Unfortunately, in 1670 the original Radha-Madan Mohan Deities were moved to Jaipur, and then again moved to Karauli where a nice temple was built for Them. *Prati-bhuh* Deities were later installed in the Vrindavan temple. You can still see the *bhajan kutir*, or place of worship, of Sanatana Gosvami, along with a well said to have been dug by Krishna Himself for Sanatana's water.

While you are here, you can have a drink from the well. Sanatana Gosvami's *samadhi* is on the hillside behind the temple.

Along the river bed nearby is Kaliya Ghat where the old Kadamba tree is from which Krishna lept into the Yamuna to chastise the multi-headed serpent-demon Kaliya. This is described in *Srimad-Bhagavatam* as is most of Krishna's Vrindavan pastimes. Farther down the trail is Varaha Ghat where Krishna manifested His form as Varaha for the amusement of His friends.

Varaha Ghat is in the area of Raman Reti on the outskirts of the village of Vrindavan. Raman Reti means cooling sands and is where Krishna and Balarama would come and play amongst the large trees, flowers, chirping birds, and peacocks. Raman Reti is where the ISKCON temple of Sri Sri Krishna-Balarama is located. This has become a very popular temple amongst pilgrims who visit Vrindavan. You'll find the most beautiful Deities of Krishna and Balarama on the center altar, with Sri Nityananda and Sri Caitanya on the left altar, and Sri Sri Radha-Syamasundar on the right. The *tamal* tree in the courtyard is said to be the tree under which Srimati Radharani would wait for Krishna to return from herding the cows. The temple was founded by Srila A. C. Bhaktivedanta Svami Prabhupada, and his *samadhi* is in front of the temple.

Some other very holy places are located elsewhere in Vrajamandala, such as Radha Kunda, the bathing place of Radharani and Her most elevated assistants, the *gopis*. Sri Rupa Gosvami explains in verses 9 and 10 of his *Sri Upadesamrta* that out of all the places in Vraja, Radha Kunda is superior to them all because it is flooded with the ambrosial nectar of Krishna *prema*, ecstatic love of God. Therefore, those who live here are the most fortunate in the universe. The *Padma Purana* also explains that just as Radharani is most dear to Krishna, Her bathing place of Radha Kunda is also dear to Him.

Across from Radha Kunda is Shyama Kunda, Krishna's bathing place. Krishna dug Shyama Kunda when Radharani insisted that He purify Himself by bathing in all the holy rivers after He had killed the Aristasura demon who was in the form of a bull. So rather than going to all the sacred rivers, He simply dug His heel into the earth and called the presiding deities of the various holy rivers of India to merge their waters into the pool. After bathing, He explained to Radharani and the *gopis* that the bull was actually a demon, so they should also take a purifying bath to rid themselves of the sin of siding with a demon. Radharani became upset and decided She could also make a *kunda* or lake. Thus, She and the *gopis* broke their bangles and dug a hole, but it remained dry to Krishna's amusement. However, by using water from the Manasi Ganga lake and the waters from the presiding deities of the holy rivers who appeared, Her *kunda* also filled up. Thus, these *kundas* are very special to pilgrims who visit. It is said that anyone who bathes here will get the perfection of Krishna *prema*, which is far beyond mere liberation from material existence. Therefore, Radha Kunda is difficult to attain even for great sages.

To recognize the spiritual significance of Radha Kunda may not be so easy for neophytes. As I said earlier, in order to perceive the spiritual atmosphere in Vrindavan you have to receive the blessings of the resident devotees and become qualified so that Vrindavan reveals itself to you. An example of this was related to me by a friend. When he visited Radha Kunda he met an old *sadhu*, a saintly man who had retired from material life and was now living at Radha Kunda. My friend asked the *sadhu* some questions and at first the man hesitantly explained that he did not work or attempt to maintain himself. He simply depended on Krishna and chanted the holy names at Radha Kunda. How he got his food was that a small boy would come by and give him some food every day. The man explained that as a person becomes more and more spiritual, he will recognize the eternal atmosphere that pervades Vraja, especially at Radha Kunda, and he will not feel the need to take so much care of the body. My friend then asked him if he could actually see the spiritual world or if he had ever seen Krishna at this holy place. The old man said he had not seen Krishna, but sometimes he could here the *gopis* talking with Krishna or discussing amongst themselves how Krishna looked and what He was doing.

My friend then asked the old *sadhu* how it was possible for him to perceive such things? The man then began talking quite readily and convincingly told my friend that Radha Kunda was indeed the spiritual world; you simply had to remove your materialistic vision. Then the old man took my friend's hand and pushed it flat to the ground on the banks of the Radha Kunda and said, "Just touch this land and you can feel the spiritual nature of it." My friend told me that at that moment a charge went up his arm from the ground and he could actually feel the difference, that this was indeed a spiritual place. But before my friend got the blessings of this sage, he could not really feel the difference. And that is what is necessary. Until you can actually perceive it, all you can do is to try to understand with your mind and imagine how Krishna performed so many pastimes here, and how this place is spiritual. But the actual realization of such things goes much further than that. It is a matter of re-establishing your spiritual identity and connection with the spiritual realm. It is the reawakening of your spiritual consciousness and actually perceiving the subtle nature of spiritual reality.

In the area of Radha Kunda are other important places such as Lalita Kunda, some Krishna temples, the small living quarters where Krishnadas Kaviraja wrote the *Caitanya-caritamrta*, and the *bhajan kutirs* of the Gosvamis, Sri Caitanya, and Srila Bhaktivinoda Thakura and Srila Bhaktisiddhanta. These places can be located with the help of local residents, or guides may present themselves to show you around. This is alright, but be sure to establish a price before you accept their service.

Next we see Govardhana Hill which is the hill Krishna lifted with the little finger of His left hand for seven days to shelter the residents of Vraja from the torrential rains that Indra had sent. The hill is also considered a manifestation of Krishna, just as the hill at Barsana is a manifestation of Brahma, the hill at

Nandagram is Shiva, and Charanpari is Sesha. Therefore, many pilgrims circumambulate Govardhana as an act of worship, a route that is about 15 miles and passes near other holy spots. Such places include Kusum Sarovara, a great swimming spot where Radharani used to pick flowers before meeting Krishna at Radha Kunda. Nearby Kusum Sarovara is a temple to Uddhava with a Deity dating back to the days of Krishna. Across the road there is also a temple and *kunda* of Narada Muni where he wrote the *Narada Bhakti Sutras*. Farther along is Manasi Ganga, a lake where Krishna made the Ganges appear. And the Govinda Kunda was made when Indra came to worship Krishna and ask for forgiveness for having sent all the rain to harrass the residents of Vraja.

North of Govardhana is Barsana, 30 miles from Mathura, the town where Radharani grew up and the capital city of her father, King Vrishabanu. We walk up the steps to get to the main temple of the town that looks like a fortress on the hilltop which can be seen from miles away. This is the Shriji or Larily Mandir, a local name for Radha. It is very ornate and the walls of the interior are covered with paintings of Krishna's pastimes. Lovely Sri Sri Radha-Krishna Deities are on the altar. A short walk away is the Radha-Kushal Behari Mandir, another majestic temple on a different peak of the hill. A little farther away is the Mayur Kuti temple that has a painting of Krishna dancing as a peacock for Radha's pleasure. The painting was done by a blind saint who had the divine vision of the pastime as long as he was working on the painting. On another of the hill's peaks is Man Kutir, a temple marking where Krishna made Radharani angry for fun, but She left Him to lament and look for Her.

A few miles from Barsana is Nandagram, another place where Krishna performed many childhood pastimes described in the *Bhagavatam*. On top of the hill is the main temple that has Deities of Krishna, Balarama, Nanda Maharaja (Krishna's father), Mother Yashoda, Srimati Radharani, and two of Krishna's friends. From the top of the walls that surround the temple we can get good views of the area, and someone who is familiar with it can point out other nearby places connected with Krishna's pastimes that we may want to visit.

As I've said, this is by no means a complete description of Vrajamandala and the holy places within it. And there are too many to mention for this discourse. Nonetheless, this description of Vraja will certainly give you a start ffor finding the important places to see if you're ever fortunate enough to visit. It is explained that all the holy places of India are manifest in some way in Vrajamandala. Thus, Rupa Gosvami writes that anyone who leaves Vraja to go to other holy places achieves nothing but the trouble it takes to get there.

When it's time to leave Vrindavan, we'll take a bus or train to New Delhi, where we'll end our tour of the important holy places of east and central India and Nepal. New Delhi, a city of 4.5 million, isn't necessarily a place of pilgrimage, but an innumerable number of people from all walks of life, holy and otherwise, come through this city. New Delhi is also a city that shows how much India has changed through the years, and is perhaps as modern as any part of India we'll find. New Delhi is where we can get most of whatever we need for continuing our travels. There are plenty of travel agencies, tour offices, banks, airline companies, and shops of all kinds for most anything we'll need, including bookstores where we can get additional information on places to see, or photo books on places we've visited to take home. And if you're looking for souvenirs, shops around Connaught Place have art work, sculptures, deities, religious items, carved wood figures, jewelry, etc., from all over India, Nepal, and Tibet. And there is a great deal one can learn about India and its culture just by investigating the many interesting places within the Delhi area. So while we're here, we can spend a few days seeing the sights before taking our flight back to our home country, or before preparing to continue our journey through another part of India.

New Delhi has much history connected with it that goes back 5000 years to the time when the Pandavas, as related in the *Mahabharata*, founded Indraprastha along the Yamuna. The ruins in the area of the Purana Qila are said to be all that remains of the ancient city of Indraprastha. Several other locations also have ruins where different phases of the city's development took place. But aside from ruins, there are many monuments and places of interest that are worth a visit for tourists and pilgrims alike, depending on your own special concerns. New Delhi has something for everyone.

Most of the monuments in the area, however, have an Islamic link. It was the last great empire that held sway over the city before the British rule. There is, of course, the Red Fort along the Yamuna at the end of Chandni Chowk Road. It was built by Shah Jahan and completed in 1648. It is a massive structure and inside is the usual assortment of interesting and decorated buildings that these old Moghul forts have. There are pools, fountains, and inlay work on ornate columns that indicate how opulent was the lifestyle of the emperor. Not far from the Red Fort is the Jami Masjid mosque, also built by Shah Jahan, completed in 1658. It is the largest mosque in India with a capacity of 25,000. You can go in with a camera and for a fee climb one of the minarets that stand 40 metres high. This place can be quite busy at times, especially during Muslim holy days. Not for from the mosque along the river is the Raj Ghat park where Mahatma Gandhi, Jawaharlal Nehru, Indira Gandhi, and, more recently, Rajiv Gandhi were cremated.

Just south of Purana Qila is one of a number of Muslim tombs in the New Delhi area. This one is the tomb of Humayun, the second Moghul emperor, built in the 16th century by his wife, Haji Begum. This is typical of early Moghul architecture with a domed building in the middle of a large garden, entered through large gates, one on each side in the walls that surround it. Across the road is the tomb of the Muslim saint Nizam-ud-din, along with a few other graves, such as that of the Urdu poet Mirza Ghalib. Heading west we find the Lodi tombs, containing graves of some Lodi and Sayyid rulers. All of these monuments are early examples of Moghul architecture that used elements of design that were later refined to the standard found in the Taj Mahal.

Farther southwest of the Lodi tombs is the tomb of Safdarjang, built in 1754 by his son who was the Nawab of Oudh. This is an example of the later styles of architecture before the collapse of the empire. Farther south, 15 km from New Delhi, is the Qutab Minar tower, 73 metres tall, that represents the victory over the last Hindu kingdom in the area. The construction began in 1193 by Qutab-ud-din and was completed a few centuries later. Near the base of the tower is the first mosque built in India, the Quwwat-ul-Islam, or "Might of Islam" mosque. It is said that it was made on the foundation of a Hindu temple and constructed of material and parts gathered by destroying 27 other "idolatrous temples." And if you understand architectural designs, you'll recognize Hindu and Jain elements within the structure of the mosque. There is even a 7 metre tall iron pillar standing in the complex, known for not having rusted after 2000 years of being exposed to the elements, and for being a Garuda *stambha* taken from an ancient Vishnu temple.

Another interesting place is the Lotus temple, which belongs to the B'hai religion. The architecture is totally unique in that it is built to resemble a huge lotus blossom. The B'hai religion is an offshoot of Islam, but they are very open and respectful of all faiths. As with any B'hai temple, anyone can come in to see it or use it for prayer. But this place does not remain very quiet because of the hundreds of people who flow through it. Most of them come simply to see the place. So if you'd like to visit it you must be prepared for the long lines of people who are waiting to get in.

Back in the city there are some fine museums, such as the National Museum on Janpath Road, which I personally feel is one of the best in India. It has some very good exhibits of paintings, costumes, sculptures of wood, bronze, and terra cotta images, and Deities, etc. There is the Nehru Museum on Teen Murti Rd., which was Nehru's residence turned into a museum if you're interested in his life. Not far away is also a Rail Transport Museum if, after riding the trains all over the country, you're interested in India's old trains. There's also a crafts museum on Mathura Road at the exhibition grounds that shows traditional arts and crafts of India. And a doll museum is on Bahadur Shah Zafar Marg with over 6000 dolls from all over the world.

Not far from Connaught Place is a Hanuman temple and a small Shiva-Parvati temple that is regularly visited by local people. They often stop on their way to or from work to pay homage or say prayers. A little walk away is the Jantar Mantar, one of Jai Singh II's unusual observatories. A larger one is found in Jaipur. Though the intruments look peculiar, they are quite accurate in predicting eclipses and plotting the course of stars.

Walking west on Ashoka Road we'll find an important Sikh temple which is very active. There are several Sikh temples in the Delhi area, but this one is called Gurudwara Bangla Sahib. It is named after the bungalow of King Jai Singh where the Eighth Sikh Guru, Harkrishan Ji, stayed during his visit to

Delhi. It is said that, in his concern for the sufferings of common people, he put his feet in a water reservoir and then offered the sacred water to the sick and ailing who got cured of their grief and sorrows. Even today devotees visit the temple and drink the water that is served in a special area just outside the temple. Many Sikhs stop by in the morning and evening to listen to recitations of their holy scripture, the *Granth*, in the temple or over the loudspeakers. The Sikhs are very nice to everyone here, and you can go in, providing you leave your shoes at the stall and wear a cover on your head. In the morning they distribute delicious halava near the temple exit door.

Farther west on Ashoka Road we find the large and beautiful Lakshmi-Narayan temple on Mandir Marg. There are some lovely Deities of Sri Sri Lakshmi-Narayan (Vishnu), as well as Shiva, Ganesh, and others, with a side temple to Buddha. It is another temple built by the Birla family and anyone is allowed in. It is definitely worth a visit.

For Jains there is the Lal Mandir on Chandni Chowk across from the Red Fort. It is a small temple but has a very ornate interior and altars with images of their *Tirthankaras*. At this temple they take care of many sick birds that are brought to them. But they've received some criticism for not giving more help to the local needy people. Farther down Chandni Chowk is the Gauri-Shankara temple dedicated to Shiva, and there are altars with many other demigods and goddesses as well as Lakshmi and Vishnu. Though this temple does not have a fancy exterior, it is very busy with people continually coming and going. Not far from here is another Sikh temple built where the ninth Sikh guru, Tegh Bahadur, was martyred by orders of the fanatic Muslim Aurangzeb because of not adopting to Islam.

What I've given here is just a short description of the major points of interest in New Delhi. Not all of them may be for you, and certainly not all of them may be for those with spiritual interests, so you can take your pick. But there is much that New Delhi can reveal in regards to the history, culture, and spiritual practices of India. So it is worth spending a few days here. Unfortunately, it is one of the most polluted cities in the world. If you take a *ricksha* through the old section of town, the air is so thick with exhaust fumes, dust, and so forth, sometimes you'll hardly be able to breathe. The outskirts of the city are not so bad, but in the summer when it is hot and there is hardly a breeze, it can be horrendous no matter where you go.

Although we started this journey from Madras in the south, we have gradually made our way through many of the most sacred towns in the world. The history, traditions, and culture of these places go back thousands of years. We have seen the birth places of some of the most important spiritual personalities known to man, and have imbibed the atmosphere that exists in the renowned and famous temples and holy sites. Now, with our arrival in New Delhi, we conclude our tour of the major pilgrimage places of the east and central parts of India. It is a tour that has been more than an adventure in geographical or cultural terms. It has been a journey that allows us to look out over that vista that stretches back to the beginning of time and to the edge of eternity. A journey through India is also a journey into our self. And, for some of us, we may have delighted in what we have found. It may have been a journey that has let us better understand our position in this universe and our place in the scheme of things. Of course, maybe not everyone can reach that feeling of inner exhilaration. After all, India does not so easily give its most valued treasures, especially when some of us are new to this sort of travel in countries that may be less than accomodating. We may find ourselves simply trying to survive the challenging circumstances that we encounter, rather than attempting to understand and absorb a different culture. Many people may be only too happy to get on that plane and head for home and return to the surroundings with which they are familiar and comfortable. But for others, India may have provided an experience that will leave them with unforgetable memories, not only of what they saw and experienced, but also of what they realized from within about themselves, the world, and how they fit into all of it. Such realizations of what and who they are may change their whole view of life. Once they return home, their minds will continue to drift back to that dream of India.

PHOTOGRAPHS

PAGE 323: Top, the rock cave temple at Undavalil with a 29 feet long Deity of reclining Vishnu.

Bottom, the Lingaraja temple complex, the most important in Bhubaneswar.

PAGE 324: Top, the great temple of Lord Jagannatha in Jagannatha Puri.

Bottom, building the *ratha* carts on the main road near the temple.

PAGE 325: Top, placed in front of the temple, the carts are ready to receive the Deities for the Ratha Yatra festival.

Bottom, pilgrims start to arrive, some of whom touch their foreheads to the cart in respect of its sacredness. Notice the huge ropes that are used for pulling the carts.

PAGE 326: As huge crowds wait, the temple priests bring the Deities out of the temple to the carts. Only the Deity's headdress can be seen in the doorway.

PAGE 327: Top, the Deity of Lord Balarama being moved to the front of the cart.

Bottom, before the carts are pulled down the main street to the Gundicha temple, the King of Puri sweeps the carts with a gold-handled broom.

PAGE 328: Although some of the facial features, which are outlined in chawk, have been smeared from moving the Deity to the cart, Lord Jagannatha awaits the ride to the Gundicha temple where the Deities will stay for one week and then return to the main temple.

PAGE 329: Top, the huge crowd of people pull one of the three carts down the main road to the Gundicha temple.

Bottom, when the cart is moving it makes a thundering noise, and you either help pull the cart or stay out of the way.

PAGE 330: Top, the town of Puri is also known for being the place where Sri Caitanya Mahaprabhu lived and performed many pastimes. His image is on the wall with the garland. This room is called the Gambhira and is where He resided.

Bottom, in Remuna, the temple of Ksira-cora-gopinatha, the Deity of Krishna who hid the pot of sweetrice (*ksira*) for His devotee Madhavendra Puri.

PAGE 331: Top Left, an image of Durga in a Calcutta temple. This represents her form as Mahishasuramardini when she killed the demon Mahishasura who was in the form of a bull. The demon's human form is seen coming out of the bull.

Top Right, the Dakshineswar Kali temple, one of the most important Kali temples in Calcutta, where Ramakrishna served as a priest.

PAGE 331: Bottom, the picturesque Sitambara Jain temple in Calcutta, dedicated to Sheelnathji, the 10th Jain *Thirtankara*.

PAGE 332: The *yogapitha* in Mayapur, the *nima* tree under which Sri Caitanya Mahaprabhu appeared in this world.

PAGE 333: Top, the wooden Deities of Lord Jagannatha (Krishna) on the right, Balarama (Krishna's brother) on the left, and Subhadra (Krishna's sister). These are the Deities in Mayapur that had been buried under an earthen mound for years until the local residents heard voices coming from within the mound and dug until they found the Deities, unharmed in spite of years of neglect.

Bottom, part of the huge Sri Chandrodaya Mandir (Iskcon) temple in Mayapur, where pilgrims from all over the world visit to learn more about and take advantage of the spiritual process of the Vaishnava tradition. In the background is the Ganges River.

PAGE 334: The Mahabodhi temple in Bodhgaya, one of the important places related to Lord Buddha.

PAGE 335: The gilded image of Lord Buddha inside the Mahabodhi temple.

PAGE 336: The third generation descendant of the original Bo tree under which Buddha was meditating at this spot when he became enlightened, located behind the Mahabodhi temple.

PAGE 337: The main hall of the Tibetan monastery at Bodhgaya.

PAGE 338: Top, the colorful Thai monastery, built like a *wats* from Thailand.

Bottom, the sacred Vishnupada temple in Gaya, which houses a rock slab with the footprint of Lord Vishnu on it.

PAGE 339: Top, inside the Har Mandir in Patna, one of the holiest of Sikh shrines which marks the place where Gobind Singh took birth in 1660. He is the 10th and last of the Sikh gurus.

Bottom, in front of the Pashupatinath temple near Kathmandu, many vendors sell flowers and other articles for offering to the deity of Shiva in the temple.

PAGE 340: The Pashupatinatha temple, one of the most famous Shiva temples in Nepal, viewed from across the Bagmati River.

PAGE 341: Top Left, the image of Shiva on the front of the Pashupatinatha temple.

Top Right, an array of Buddhist metal masks that are used in temple plays, or sold to tourists.

Bottom Left, *thanka* painters making paintings for the tourist trade.

Bottom Right, a girl spinning the prayer wheels at the Buddhist Svayambunatha temple in Kathmandu.

PAGE 342: The Svayambunatha *stupa*, one of the oldest in Nepal, has the watchful eyes of Buddha, and a large *dorje* or thunderbolt sitting in front.

PAGE 343: The Nyatapola temple in Bhaktapur; a good example of Nepalese architecture.

PAGE 344: Maitreya, the Buddha of the future, is about two-and-a-half storeys tall at the Jamchen Lhakhang Monastery near the Bodnatha *stupa*.

PAGE 345: A genuine Buddhist *thanka* painting from the author's personal collection. This is the "Wheel of Life." No Buddhist temple is complete without a copy of this painting. The inner circle contains a rooster, pig, and a snake, which represents desire, ignorance, and hatred. These unwanted qualities force a person to perform actions that cause one to reincarnate through hellish, heavenly, and intermediate types of existences that are represented by the various scenes in the surrounding circles. The outer circle represents the different stages of life, such as birth, growth, school, marriage, old age, and death. Only through enlightenment can one become free from these various levels of existence. The wheel is held by Yama, the Buddhist personification of death, whose teeth signify that he is ready to strike at any moment. All of these concepts are practically the same as those of the Vedic philosophy.

PAGE 346: Paying respects to Kal Bhairav, the Nepali form of the fearful manifestation of Shiva, in Kathmandu.

PAGE 347: Top, vendors near Durbar Square in Kathmandu are ready to sell you anything from religious items, utensils, coins, jewelry, decorated Nepali knives, or other items. Some of these people are refugees from Tibet.

Bottom, the general friendliness of the Nepali people is plainly exhibited by the expressions of these boys on their way to school.

PAGE 348: Top, the Deity of Sleeping Vishnu at Budhanilkantha.

Bottom, the many temples and *ghats* at Ram-ki-Pauri in Ayodhya, the city of Lord Ramacandra.

PAGE 349: Top Left, the most famous Hanuman deity in Ayodhya is found in the Hanuman Ghri temple. No pilgrim visits Ayodhya without stopping at this temple of Hanuman, the monkey servant of Lord Ramacandra. The deity is so thoroughly decorated that all you can see is his eyes.

Top Right, Deities of Lord Ramacandra (in the middle), His wife Sita(on the right), and His brother Lakshmana. The *Ramayana* tells the adventures of Lord Ramacandra.

Bottom, the Babri Masjid mosque. Two of the three rooms in this mosque are used as a Sita-Rama temple, which many pilgrims and devotees visit. It is explained that 500 years ago a Sita-Rama temple stood at this spot, which marks the place where Lord Ramacandra is said to have appeared in this worlld. Then the Muslims came, tore down the temple and built this mosque in its place. There has been trouble and occasional riots here ever since. That is why it is so fortified. There is a strong movement now to build a new Sita-Rama temple at this location.

PAGE 350: Top, in Varanasi, one of the main Shiva temples is the golden Vishvanatha temple, on the left. It was built in 1776 after the original Vishvanatha temple was torn down by the fanatic Muslim Aurangzeb, who built a mosque in its place, on the right. The Vishvanatha temple towers have three-quarters of a ton of gold plating on them. In between the mosque and temple is the Jnana Vapi well (Well of Wisdom). This is said to be where the Shiva *linga* from the original temple was hidden when the Muslims invaded, and it may still be there.

Bottom, Varanasi is especially known for its many temples and bathing *ghats* along the sacred Ganges River. One of the busiest areas is the Dashashvamedha Ghat shown here.

PAGE 351: Top, many people come to the *ghats* to bathe in the Ganges for spiritual purification, cleanliness, or to perform morning worship and meditation.

Bottom, under the large umbrellas people consult with priests over various aspects of life, or perform rituals for particular results.

PAGE 352: Top, another significant *ghat* is the Jalasai Ghat where many cremations take place. This is next to and often considered a part of the Manikarnika Ghat, which is the holiest of all *ghats* in Varanasi. Being cremated at this *ghat* and having one's ashes placed in the Ganges is said to give a person liberation from this world. Oddly, many foreign tourists want to see the cremations as they take place, but photography is not allowed.

Bottom, tourists come to Varanasi from all over the world. In this photo a group tour is packed onto a boat on the Ganges, cameras clicking, video cameras whirring, taking many pictures, much of which they probably have little or no understanding.

PAGE 353: Top Left, many types of people live in Varanasi. Here, a Vaishnava yogi sits in meditation near the Ganges.

Top Right, an old *sadhu* who had recently retired from teaching and moved from Bangla Desh to Varanasi. This is considered the proper use of life in Vedic culture, which is to utilize one's final years of life for spiritual progress.

Bottom Left, an old flower vendor near the Visvanatha temple.

Bottom Right, a typical narrow alley in the old section of town.

PAGE 354: Top, a relaxing boat ride on the Ganges is a must while in Varanasi. Bottom, near Varanasi is Sarnath, a small town with several temples, but is best known for being the place where Buddha gave his first sermon to his five original disciples.

PAGE 355: Top, the *sangam*, confluence of the Ganges, Yamuna, and mystical Sarasvati, where thousands of people come each year to bathe in the sacred waters during the Magh (January-February) Mela festival, and millions visit during the Kumba Mela every 12 years.

Bottom, while some people bathe on the shore, others take a boat out to where the waters of the Ganges and Yamuna mix. The waving flags on the poles mark the small platforms where the pilgrims can get out of the boats and then dip into the water for a sacred bath.

PAGE 356: Top, a small floating shrine for Radha-Krishna may come out to give you further blessings.

Bottom, women drying saris in the wind after a dip in the *sangam*.

PAGE 357: Top, many spiritual *ashramas* or groups from all over India come to the Mela festivals and give discourses on the Vedic texts and philosophy, and people take advantage of such association by listening and asking questions.

Bottom, in other tents or camps they may put on plays or dramas, such as this one on the *Ramayana*.

PAGE 358: Top Left, putting on Vaishnava *tilok* after bathing in the Ganges.

Top Right, the large and ornately decorated Lakshmana temple in Khajurao.

Bottom, the ancient Kandariya Shiva temple, made to look like the Mount Kailas abode of Lord Shiva.

PAGE 359: Top Left, worshiping the Shiva *lingam* at the Duladeo temple, Khajurao. This *lingam* is carved with 999 *lingams* around the sides. So by worshiping or circumambulating it once is equal to 1000 times.

Top Right, the Heliodorus column, or Khamb Baba pillar, in Vidisha, which is the archeological find that proves that knowledge of Vishnu (Krishna) and the stories in the *Puranas* pre-date Christianity by at least 200 years.

Bottom Left, the ornately carved gate to *stupa* number one, Sanchi.

Bottom Right, on the way up to the south-west entrance to the Gwalior hilltop fort you will pass a number of Jain sculptures that were carved into the rock in the mid-1400s, including this 17 metre-tall image of Adinatha, one of the Jain *Thirtankaras*.

PAGE 360: Top, the Man Singh Palace at the hilltop fort, Gwalior.

Bottom, everyone knows the Taj Mahal in Agra, built by Shah Jahan as a tomb in memory of his wife, and completed in 1653. Later, he was also intombed there.

PAGE 361: Top, the modern Keshava Deo temple that represents the birthplace
of Krishna in Mathura. The original Keshava temple was torn
down by the fanatic Muslim ruler Aurangzeb, who built the
mosque in its place.

PAGE 361: Bottom, in the area of Mathura and Vrindavana, called
Vrajamandala, there are many sacred places, such as this water
tank, Kusum Sarovara, that is not only a good swimming spot, but
is also where Krishna and His devoted Radharani would meet.

PAGE 362: Vrindavana is the holy town of Krishna, who plays on His flute and
tends the cows. This Deity is in one of the many temples you can
visit.

PAGE 363: Top Right, the Deity of Radharamana in one of the main temples of
Vrindavana. The Deity belonged to Gopala Bhatta Gosvami and
self-manifested from a *shalagram-shila* stone in 1542. The stone
can still be seen on the Deity's back.

Top Left, the beautiful Deities at the popular Krishna-Balarama
temple in Vrindavana that was established by His Divine Grace A.
C. Bhaktivedanta Swami in 1975. The temple is located in the
Raman Reti area of Vrindavana where Krishna (pictured on the
right) and Balarama used to play as children.

Bottom, the altar at the Radha-Gokulananda temple, one of the seven
main temples of Vrindavan, founded by Lokanatha Gosvami. The
Deities in this temple include Radha-Vinoda of Lokanatha Gosvami
(although the original Deities were taken to Jaipur), Radha-Vijaya
Govinda of Baladeva Vidyabhushana, and Radha-Gokulananda of
Vishvanatha Chakravarty Thakura. On the left is the Sri Caitanya
Deity of Narottama das Thakura.

PAGE 364: Top, one of the main ceremonies in the temples that the devotee
come to see is the *arati* offering to the Deities, as offered here to
Radha-Syamasundara (Krishna) at the Krishna-Balarama temple.

Bottom, lighting candles to offer to the Deities during the month of
Kartika (October-November).

PAGE 365: Top, the older temples of Vrindavana include the Radha-Madan
Mohan temple, erected by Sanatana Gosvami, one of the senior
Gosvamis of Vrindavana and disciple of Sri Caitanya. Near the
temple is a well that was dug by Krishna when He once appeared
to serve His own devotee, Sanatana.

Bottom, one of the most famous temples of Vrindavana is the Radha-
Govindaji temple, erected under the guidance of Rupa and Sanatana
Gosvamis in 1590. The temple stands on a small hill where the
Deity of Sri Govindaji is said to have appeared to Rupa Gosvami.
Finances for the temple were given by Raja Man Singh, a general
under King Akbar, and Akbar is said to have provided the red

sandstone for it. Unfortunately, all that is seen today are two storeys of the original seven storey structure because Aurangzeb could not tolerate the grand architecture of a temple for Krishna and had the upper storeys removed.

PAGE 366: Top, one of the holiest places in the area of Vraja is the Radha Kund, the pond where Krishna's most devoted Radharani bathed, and where the spiritual pastimes continue to this day.

Bottom, throughout Vraja, Vaishnavas and devotees get together in congregational *sankirtana* parties to chant the holy names of Krishna with drums, cymbals, and other instruments.

PAGE 367: Top and Bottom, when a holy man leaves this world, many people come to pay their last respects. In these photos the body of Akhandananda Svami is brought on a palanquin to the Yamuna River where, as he requested, it will be taken in a boat and submerged or buried in the Yamuna. Such water burials are rare, making these photos unique.

PAGE 368: One last look at Vrindavana before we continue our journey; a peaceful sunset over the Yamuna River.

PAGE 369: Top, the Jami Masjid in old Delhi is the largest mosque in India, completed in 1658, and able to facilitate as many as 25,000 people.

Bottom Left, Muslims praying inside the Jami Masjid.

Bottom Right, the Gurudwara Bangla Sahib Sikh temple on Baba Kharak Singh Road in New Delhi. This is a busy temple and many Sikhs come to listen to the *Granth* being recited in the morning and evening.

PAGE 370: Top, the interior of the Gurudwara Bangla Sahib Sikh temple.

Bottom, the Lotus temple of the B'hai faith in New Delhi. Long lines of people continue to move through the temple, mostly to see its unique architecture.

PAGE 371: deities of Shiva, his wife Parvati, and their son Ganesh, in a small temple in New Delhi.

PAGE 372: Top, one of the more popular temples in New Delhi, the Lakshmi-Narayana (Vishnu) temple built by the Birla family.

Bottom, one last look at India, New Delhi at night, from our hotel room before we go to the airport to catch our flight home.

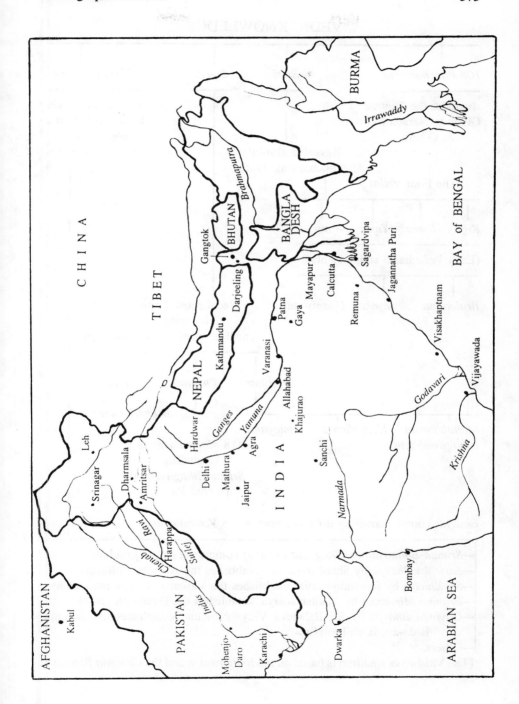

VEDIC KNOWLEDGE

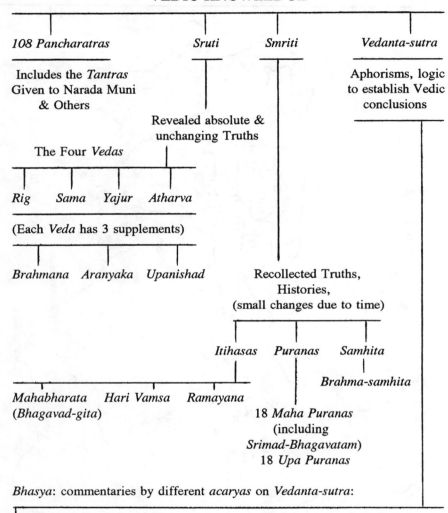

108 Pancharatras   Sruti   Smriti   Vedanta-sutra

Includes the *Tantras*   Aphorisms, logic
Given to Narada Muni   to establish Vedic
& Others   conclusions

                         Revealed absolute &
                         unchanging Truths

The Four *Vedas*

Rig   Sama   Yajur   Atharva

(Each *Veda* has 3 supplements)

Brahmana   Aranyaka   Upanishad   Recollected Truths,
                                          Histories,
                                          (small changes due to time)

                              Itihasas   Puranas   Samhita

                                                     Brahma-samhita

Mahabharata   Hari Vamsa   Ramayana
(Bhagavad-gita)   18 *Maha Puranas*
                                             (including
                                             Srimad-Bhagavatam)
                                             18 *Upa Puranas*

Bhasya: commentaries by different *acaryas* on *Vedanta-sutra*:

—*Srimad-Bhagavatam* (*Bhagavat Purana*) commentary by Vyasadeva.
—*Sariraka Bhasya* by Shankaracarya, establishes the Advaita philosophy.
—*Sri Bhasya* by Ramanujacarya, establishes the Vasistha Advaita philosophy.
—*Brahma Mimamsa* by Madhavacarya, establishes the Dvaita philosophy.
—*Govinda Bhasya* by Sri Baladeva Vidyabhushana, establishes the Achinta
         Beda-abeda philosophy.
—Others.
(The Vaishnava tradition is based on the *Bhagavatam* and the *Govinda Bhasya*.)

APPENDIX ONE

The Significance of Deities and Deity Worship

Deities have been mentioned many times in this volume, but what is the significance of Deities and Deity worship? First of all, I should explain that I make a distinction between deities (with a small d) that are images of the demigods and goddesses, and Deities (with a capital D) of the Supreme Being, who ultimately is established in the Vedic literature as Sri Krishna and His expansions, such as Vishnu, Narayana, Ramachandra, and others. Demigods include Shiva, Brahma, Ganesh, Murugan, Indra, and the demigoddesses, such as Durga, Kali, Sarasvati, Lakshmi, etc. The demigods are the personalities who are agents of the Supreme and are in charge of certain aspects of the universal laws and functions of nature. All the images of the deities in the Vedic pantheon, as found in the temples, are made according to explicit details and instructions found in the Vedic texts. Then they are also installed in an elaborate ceremony wherein the personalities are called to appear in the form of the deity.

Some people, however, do not believe that God has a form. But many verses in the *Puranas* and, particularly, the *Brahma-samhita* establish that the Supreme Being does have a specific form. These texts also describe His variegated features, which include His spiritual form, characteristics, beauty, strength, intelligence, activities, etc. Therefore, it is considered that the authorized Deities of the Supreme that are shaped according to these descriptions provide a view of the personal form of God. (The descriptions concerning the form of God are dealt with more thoroughly in *The Secret Teachings of the Vedas*.)

Those who have no knowledge of God or His form will certainly consider the temple Deities as idols. But this is the effect of their foolishness. They think that the Deities are simply the products of someone's imagination. Of course, there are those who say that God has no form, spiritual or material, or that there is no Supreme Being. Others think that since God must be formless, they can imagine or worship any material form as God, or they regard the image of any demigod as an external manifestation of the Supreme. But images of the demigods are not additional forms of an impersonal God, nor are they equal to

God. All such people who think in the above mentioned ways have resorted to their own imagination to reach such conclusions and are, therefore, idolators. The imaginary images and opinions of God that are formed by those who have not properly learned about, seen, or realized God are indeed idols, and those who accept such images or opinions are certainly idolators. This is because these images or opinions are based on ignorance and are not a likeness of His form.

God is described in the Vedic literature, which explains that God is *sat-cit-ananda*, or complete spiritual essence, full of eternity, knowledge, and bliss, and is not material in any way. His body, soul, form, qualities, names, pastimes, etc., are all nondifferent and are of the same spiritual quality. This form of God is not an idol designed from someone's imagination, but is the true form, even if He should descend into this material creation. And since the spiritual nature of God is absolute, He is nondifferent from His name. Thus, the name *Krishna* is an *avatara* or incarnation of Krishna in the form of sound. Similarly, His form in the temple is not merely a representation, but is Krishna.

Some people may question that if the Deity is made from material elements, such as stone, marble, metal, wood, or paint, how can it be the spiritual form of God? The answer is given that since God is the source of all material and spiritual energies, material elements are also a form of God. Therefore, God can manifest as the Deity in the temple, though made of stone or other elements since He can transform what is spiritual into material energy, and material energy back into spiritual energy. Thus, the Deity can easily be accepted as the Supreme since He can appear in any element. In this way, even though we may be unqualified to see God, who is beyond the perceptability of our material senses, the living beings in this material creation are allowed to see and approach the Supreme through His *arca-vigraha* form as the Deity in the temple.

In this manner, the Supreme Being gives Himself to His devotees so they can become absorbed in serving, remembering, and meditating on Him. Thus, the Supreme comes to dwell in the temple, and the temple becomes the spiritual abode on earth. In time, the body, mind, and senses of the devotee become spiritualized by serving the Deity, and the Supreme becomes fully manifest to him. Worshiping the Deity of the Supreme and using one's senses in the process of *bhakti-yoga*, service to the Supreme, provides a means for one's true essential spiritual nature to unfold. The devotee becomes spiritually realized and the Deity reveals His spiritual nature to the sincere souls according to their evolutionary spiritual development. This can continue to the level in which the Supreme Being in the form of the Deity engages in a personal relationship and performs reciprocal, loving pastimes with the devotee, as has taken place with advanced individuals as previously related in this volume.

At this stage, *darshan* is not simply a matter of viewing the Deity in the temple, but, to one who is spiritually realized, it is a matter of experiencing the Deity and entering into a personal, reciprocal exchange with the Supreme Personality in the form of the Deity.

APPENDIX TWO

The Meaning of the Phrase "God is Love"

The phrase and concept that "God is love" is often used by many people of different religions, but it is hardly ever explained adequately. People may say that God is all-loving, forgiving, or your eternal friend, which is true, but, essentially, this is a fairly shallow explanation of how God is love. So if we are to understand how a person can experience so much spiritual ecstasy that the material pleasures become insignificant, then this is a fitting time to analyze how God is the source of the ecstasy and love and happiness for which we are always seeking. But only in the highest levels of Vedic literature, especially in the Vaishnava tradition, do we find a proper and more complete explanation.

The Vedic literature describes the Absolute Truth as *sat-cit-ananda vigraha*, which means the personal form of eternal knowledge and bliss. And in the *Taittiriya Upanishad* (*Second Valli, Seventh Anuvaka*), the Absolute Truth is described as concentrated *ananda* or bliss. It is understood that this spiritual bliss is the dynamic and personal form of Sri Krishna. The Brahman effulgence, or great white light, is the expansive impersonal glow of that bliss. So the impersonal Brahman originates from the Supreme Personality, who is Sri Krishna, who is also the source of all bliss. The taste or experience of this bliss is dormant or undynamic in the *brahmananda*, or Brahman effulgence. By its very nature, the impersonal Brahman is not something with which you can have a personal relationship. There are no activities or reciprocation in the Brahman. In this way, it leaves unfulfilled those who merge into the impersonal Brahman, or who believe it to be the highest truth. But in the personality of Krishna, the bliss is always expanding and ever-growing to new dimensions in the pastimes and activities Krishna performs. The most sublime taste or experience of the pleasure of this spiritual bliss is called *rasa*, and Krishna is the *rasa*, or the center and source of this ecstatic spiritual experience. In other words, He is the most relishable object. This can also be broadened to mean that Krishna is the most worshipable and lovable object, as well as the ultimate realization and object of all knowledge, religion, yoga, and love. But Krishna is also *rasika*, which means the ultimate enjoyer of *rasa*, the experience of spiritual bliss.

Now we can begin to understand that Krishna is not only the ultimate object of all love, but also is the topmost enjoyer of all loving relationships. Therefore, in the dynamic and expanding form of Krishna, He has unlimited desires to enjoy spiritual loving relationships or pastimes, known as *lila*. To do this He expands Himself into the dual form of Krishna and Radharani, His eternal consort and topmost devotee. In other words, Radharani is the feminine aspect of Lord Krishna and is non-different from Krishna, but together (both the masculine and feminine aspects) They fulfill the purpose of engaging in sublime loving pastimes to exhibit supremely transcendental loving exchanges.

Radha is *bhava*, pure and selfless love personified. Everything Radha does is entirely for Krishna's pleasure. Radha is also *hladini-shakti*, the bliss potency that resides in Krishna. This bliss or pleasure potency within Krishna expands throughout the spiritual and material worlds, and whatever pleasure is felt by anyone is a form of this pleasure potency. But the closer we get to Krishna on the spiritual platform, the more directly we can feel the potency of this pleasure source. And its topmost personified form is Radharani. Therefore, Krishna engages in loving exchanges with Radharani and enjoys the bliss of Her love many millions of times more than the pleasure that comes from His own self. Radharani's love is the selfless love of Krishna's personified bliss potency. In this way, Krishna is the sweetest object of love, while Radha is the sweetest devotee of love.

As Their loving relationship increases, there are more and more devotees who assist in this pastime who also participate in these loving affairs of Krishna. Since all living beings are spiritual in nature, we all have a spiritual relationship with the Supreme Spirit, Sri Krishna. In the spiritual world this loving relationship fully awakens, and everyone feels great bliss because of this. As Krishna's pleasure increases, it expands to all the devotees who feel the ecstasy and reflect it back to Krishna through their devotional exchange. Krishna then reciprocates this love even more, and the loving exchange (*bhakti*) between Krishna and His devotees continues to expand and grow to new and higher levels in never-ending cycles. Thus, everyone is fulfilled in this spiritual love which is completely beyond the boundaries and estimation of material pleasures and relationships.

This is how a person can feel completely fulfilled and satisfied when he or she is engaged in pure Krishna *bhakti*. This is why *bhakti*, which fully manifests as pure love for God, is the real goal of any religion or yoga system. It is both the means and the goal. Therefore, the ultimate end of *bhakti-yoga*, or the devotional process, is not to enter heaven or the spiritual world, but simply to enter *prema*, which is to regain one's spiritual loving relationship with the Supreme regardless of what is our external situation. This is our natural spiritual position. This is the emotional fulfillment and love for which we are always looking. But rarely do we find such love and happiness while we are in the material concept of life, when we think that the temporary material body is our real identity. This sublime loving relationship is desired by all souls as well as the Supreme Being. This love is the gravitational force between us all, but can be fully manifested only on the spiritual level, between the living entities and the Supreme.

This is actually how God is love, all-loving, and the supreme lovable object for whom we all are looking, whether we understand this or not. No matter where we try to look for love, nothing can completely satisfy the soul as much as this spiritual love.

This is why Vaishnavas, worshipers of Lord Krishna, claim no allegiance to any particular religion, but only continue developing pure, unalloyed *bhakti*, love of God, through the practice of devotional service, *bhakti-yoga*. When this fully manifests as *prema*, such a pure relationship becomes so intense that there is no awareness of anything else. In this pure consciousness, there is no question of being Hindu, Muslim, Christian, Jewish, or being effected by any other distinction. There is only God and the lovers of God on the spiritual platform, all of whom are absorbed in sublime and boundlessly ecstatic, loving exchanges.

The Supreme is waiting for us to return to our spiritual position to engage in these spiritual activities. How long it takes for us to return to our spiritual home simply depends on how long we allow ourselves to be influenced or controlled by the material impulses and desires which bind us to this material existence. We should not feel that we are so sinful or fallen that we have no hope for developing our spiritual relationship with the Supreme, for He is always waiting for His lost servants. But we have to begin to show that we want to return to Him by rising above bodily identifications and realizing the science of the soul: our real identity.

The essence of our pure spiritual identity and spiritual experience is our direct and personal loving relationship with the Supreme Being. This spiritual identity is the underlying principle of unity amongst all living entities. Reawakening this identity and love is the ultimate purpose of any true spiritual path. And this is most easily attained through the process of *bhakti-yoga*, the yoga of love of God.

APPENDIX THREE

Spiritual Enlightenment: A Cure for Social Ills

Throughout society most people are absorbed in bodily consciousness. Bodily consciousness means that people think their bodies are the basis of their identity. This usually brings people to think, in various degrees, that the goal of life is to provide as much comfort and pleasure to the mind and body as possible, preferably with as little work as necessary. So what is wrong with that?

In identifying themselves as their body, people look at themselves in terms of their bodily designation. Therefore, they accept themselves to be a man, or a woman, or something more specific like a black African American man, a fat or skinny woman, an oriental or Asian, an Arab, an Englishman, or a liberal Northerner, or a conservative Southerner, etc., etc. Because of this way of seeing themselves, they then become obliged to play a particular role in society. Of course, there may be some people who rebel against any conventional lifestyle. But, generally, people will dress in a certain way, or walk and talk in accord with the bodily identity they assume themselves to be, as well as act in a particular manner because they feel drawn to do so, or because society dictates what is expected.

They will also accept all of their bodily relations as a part of their identity, such as their parents, relatives, or children, their cultural background and heritage, etc. They may also accept particular political or philosophical viewpoints and values, and associate with people who think and feel the same way as they do. And they will often dislike anyone who challenges or threatens their identity or purpose, or may even see them as an enemy. So then there is quarrel and hatred. From there it can escalate into bigger problems and more violent confrontations.

This sort of materialistic, bodily consciousness is like animal consciousness, which causes one to view things with what we might call "animal vision." Any animal will see other living beings in terms of who is its friend or enemy, and who or what may be a source of pleasure or pain. Say, for example, a dog is walking down the street. As it looks at other living beings, it may see a human being or another dog as a potential friend and will approach it in hopes of being petted or for play. If it sees a bigger dog or a person with a large stick, it may feel as though it is being threatened and will run away, or it may bark and be ready to fight. If the dog sees a female dog, it may see her as a potential source of pleasure to be pursued, and then the female will either have sex with the male or have to defend herself. If the dog sees a cat or even a smaller dog, it may feel like exhibiting it's strength and chase after it and try to bite and hurt it, and feel very proud after having done so. If the dog sees a different sort of creature, such as a rabbit or bird, the dog will see them as a source of food to be captured and eaten. And if it is with several other dogs, they will exhibit the gang mentality and often bark at or chase anyone that walks by, or even gang up to fight with smaller dogs for the sport of it. Most of you have no doubt seen this sort of behavior in street dogs at one time or another. But you have also probably seen this kind of activity in other human beings as well.

This is the type of mentality of a person who is absorbed in bodily consciousness, and who sees things with a similar form of "animal vision." To what degree they are fixed on this level of consciousness depends on how far they have or have not progressed in their evolutionary development. As described earlier in this volume, people on the lower levels of consciousness think mostly in terms of how to more perfectly eat, sleep, have sex, defend their positions or ideals, and maintain their economic pursuits. This sort of body consciousness and "animal vision" limits the way we see ourselves and our potential. It also causes us to judge others by their bodily characteristics rather than their intellectual qualities. This is why there is a need for spiritual progress so we can be aware and recognize each others' true spiritual nature. Then we can actually begin to realize that spiritually we are all the same.

Without spiritual advancement, individually and socially, human society becomes like a society of polished animals. We may have so much technology, but we still act and fight on the same order as cats and dogs. But human life is meant for a much higher purpose. Human life is the doorway to other realms of existence, the topmost being the spiritual realm.

In order to rise above "animal vision," we have to become spiritually aware and see beyond the body and its designations, which is merely a temporary covering of the soul, like a shirt or coat. Underneath the bodily covering is the same kind of soul as any other living being. Without this kind of spiritual understanding, there will never be any real solutions to such problems as racial tension, sexual harassment, violent crime, or the problems created by those who try to cheat others for their own selfish gain, such as criminals or slick politicians. Without spiritual progress, you can forget about moral or ethical values. Everyone will simply be concerned about no one but themselves and those who share a similar bodily identity. This kind of concern for "me and mine" will only cause the "animal vision" in society to increase.

This kind of "animal vision" will effect all levels of civilization to the extent to which society is infected with it. This includes the economic system (why the value of money is inflated and not based on intrinsic value), politics (why government passes certain types of legislation that favors particular programs and groups of people, but ignores others), tax laws (why people and businesses have to pay more and more taxes to a government that becomes less and less responsible), sexual harassment and battered wives (why some men see women as objects of pleasure to control or dominate rather than seeing them as individuals to be respected for their personal talents and abilities), racial tension (why some whites and blacks look at each other with disdain), and on and on. In other words, as long as people, including politicians, judges, priests, teachers, etc., are infected with this kind of disease of the consciousness, called "animal vision," there will not be any significant change in society, and the social problems that we have to deal with will only continue, no matter how people try to discuss and resolve such matters.

As long as people's consciousness is centered around their temporary bodily identity, throughout the world you will continue to find quarrels, fights, riots, wars, the tragedy of people starving in Africa and other places because of the politics, and everything else that motivates people to act on the bodily platform because of the superficial differences between races, religions, cultures, sexes, ideals, or political viewpoints. On a more local level, you will continue to see or experience sexual harassment, rape, child abuse, violent crime, drug abuse, unwed mothers, etc., because of the lust and greed that motivates people to cater to their bodily and sensual urges. And with the lust for satisfying the body and senses comes emotions like jealousy, envy, anger, hatred, and so on.

Furthermore, when one's relationship with others is based on the vehicle of the temporary body, it is usually based simply on mutual behavior. This means that the relationship lasts as long as the medium of gratification stays the same. If or when the behavior, ideals, goals, values, political views, etc., change, then the friendship and concern, that once may have seemed so deep, also changes and begins to fade or even disappears. Sometimes it may even give way to opposition and dislike. This is because the relationship has been based on the superficial level.

An enlightened society will naturally be able to work together because they will rise above superficial differences and not let them get in the way. With spiritual enlightenment, there will be real love and concern for others because people will see that we are all in this world together, all working for the same basic needs, and our relationships will be based on our spiritual identity, not our temporary bodily covering. This is what is needed. The bottom line is that only by the spread of genuine spiritual knowledge, far and above fundamental piety, and a progressive change in social consciousness, will there be any real solutions for a troubled or misguided civilization.

REFERENCES

The following is a list of all the authentic Vedic and religious texts that were referred to or directly quoted to explain or verify all the knowledge and information presented in this book.

Agni Purana, translated by N. Gangadharan, Motilal Banarsidass, Delhi, 1984

Atharva-veda, translated by Devi Chand, Munshiram Manoharlal, Delhi, 1980

Bhagavad-gita As It Is, translated by A. C. Bhaktivedanta Swami, Bhaktivedanta Book Trust, New York/Los Angeles, 1972

Bhagavad-gita, translated by Swami Chidbhavananda, Sri Ramakrishna Tapovanam, Tiruchirappalli, India, 1991

The Song of God: Bhagavad-gita, translated by Swami Prabhavananda and Christopher Isherwood, New American Library, New York, 1972

Bhagavad-gita, translated by Winthrop Sargeant, State University of New York Press, Albany, NY, 1984

Bhakti-rasamrita-sindhu, (Nectar of Devotion), translated by A. C. Bhaktivedanta Swami, Bhaktivedanta Book Trust, New York/Los Angeles, 1970

Bhakti-sandarbha sankhya

Bhavisya Purana

Bhavartha-dipika

Bible, New York International Bible Society, 1981

Book of Morman, The Church of Jesus Christ of Latter-day Saints, Salt Lake City, Utah, 1976

Brahma Purana, edited by J.L.Shastri, Motilal Banarsidass, Delhi 1985

Brahmanda Purana, edited by J.L.Shastri, Motilal Banarsidass, 1983

Brahma-samhita, translated by Bhaktisiddhanta Sarasvati Gosvami Thakur, Bhaktivedanta Book Trust, New York/Los Angeles,

Brahma-Sutras, translated by Swami Vireswarananda and Adidevananda, Advaita Ashram, Calcutta, 1978

Brahma-vaivarta Purana

Brihad-vishnu Purana

Brihan-naradiya Purana

Brihadaranyaka Upanishad

Caitanya-caritamrta, translated by A. C. Bhaktivedanta Swami, Bhaktivedanta Book Trust, Los Angeles, 1974

Caitanya Upanisad, translated by Kusakratha dasa, Bala Books, New York, 1970

Chandogya Upanishad

Garbha Upanishad

Garuda Purana, edited by J. L. Shastri, Motilal Barnasidass, Delhi, 1985

Gautamiya Tantra

Gheranda Samhita, translated by Rai Bahadur Srisa Chandra Vasu, Munshiram Manoharlal, New Delhi, 1980

Gitabhasya of Ramanuja, translated by M. R. Sampatkumaran, M.A., Ananthacharya Indological Research Institute, Bombay, 1985

Hari-bhakti-vilasa

How to Know God, The Yoga Aphorisms of Patanjali, translated by Swami Prabhavananda and C. Isherwood, New American Library, 1969

Jiva Gosvami's Tattvasandarbha, Stuart Mark Elkman, Motilal Banarsidass, Delhi, 1986

Kali-santarana Upanishad

Katha Upanishad

Kaushitaki Upanishad

Koran, translated by N. J. Dawood, Penguin Books, Middlesex, England, 1956

The Holy Quran, 'Abdullah Yusaf 'Ali, Amana Corporation, Brentwood, Maryland, 1989

Kurma Purana, edited by J. L. Shastri, Motilal Banarsidass, Delhi, 1981

Linga Purana, edited by J. L. Shastri, Motilal Banarsidass, Delhi, 1973

Mahabharata, translated by C. Rajagopalachari, Bharatiya Vidya Bhavan, New Delhi, 1972

Mahabharata, Kamala Subramaniam, Bharatiya Vidya Bhavan, Bombay, 1982

Matsya Purana

The Law of Manu, [*Manu-samhita*], translated by Georg Buhlerg, Motilal Banarsidass, Delhi, 1970

Minor Upanishads, translated by Swami Madhavananda, Advaita Ashram, Calcutta, 1980; contains Paramahamsopanishad, Atmopanishad, Amritabindupanishad, Tejabindupanishad, Sarvopanishad, Brahmopanisad, Aruneyi Upanishad, Kaivalyopanishad.

Mukunda-mala-stotra

Mundaka Upanishad

Narada-pancaratra

Narada Purana, tr. by Ganesh Vasudeo Tagare, Banarsidass, Delhi, 1980

Narada Sutras, translated by Hari Prasad Shastri, Shanti Sadan, London, 1963

Narada-Bhakti-Sutra, A. C. Bhaktivedanta Swami, Bhaktivedanta Book Trust, Los Angeles, 1991

Narottam-Vilas, by Sri Narahari Cakravarti Thakur, translator unknown.

Padma Purana, tr. by S. Venkitasubramonia Iyer, Banarsidass, Delhi, 1988

Padmottara-khanda

Padyavali

Prema-Vilas, by Nityananda Das

Purana-vakya

Ramayana of Valmiki, tr. by Makhan Lal Sen, Oriental Publishing Co., Calcutta

Hymns of the Rig-veda, tr. by Griffith, Motilal Banarsidass, Delhi, 1973

Rig-veda Brahmanas: The Aitareya and Kausitaki Brahmanas of the Rigveda, translated by Arthur Keith, Motilal Banarsidass, Delhi, 1971

Samnyasa Upanisads, translated by Prof. A. A. Ramanathan, Adyar Library, Madras, India, 1978; contains Avadhutopanisad, Arunyupanisad, Katharudropanisad, Kundikopanisad, Jabalopanisad, Turiyatitopanisad, Narada-parivrajakopanisad, Nirvanopanisad, Parabrahmopanisad, Paramahamsa-parivrajakopanisad, Paramahamsopanisad, Brahmopanisad, Bhiksukopanisad, Maitreyopanisad, Yajnavalkyopanisad, Satyayaniyopanisad, and Samnyasopanisad.

Shiva Purana, edited by Professor J. L. Shastri, Banarsidass, Delhi, 1970

Siksastaka, of Sri Caitanya Mahaprabhu.

Sixty Upanisads of the Vedas, by Paul Deussen, translated from German by V. M. Bedekar and G. B. Palsule, Motilal Banarsidass, Delhi, 1980; contains Upanisads of the Rigveda: Aitareya and Kausitaki. Upanisads of the Samaveda: Chandogya and Kena. Upanisads of the Black Yajurveda: Taittiriya, Mahanarayan, Kathaka, Svetasvatara, and Maitrayana. Upanisads of the White Yajurveda: Brihadaranyaka and Isa. Upanisads of the Atharvaveda: Mundaka, Prasna, Mandukya, Garbha, Pranagnihotra, Pinda, Atma, Sarva, Garuda; (Yoga Upanisads): Brahmavidya, Ksurika, Culik, Nadabindu, Brahma-bindu, Amrtabindu, Dhyanabindu, Tejobindu, Yoga-sikha, Yogatattva, Hamsa; (Samnyasa Upanisads): Brahma, Samnyasa, Aruneya, Kantha-sruti, Paramahamsa, Jabala, Asrama; (Shiva Upanisads): Atharvasira, Atharva-sikha, Nilarudra, Kalagnirudra, Kaivalya; (Vishnu Upanisads): Maha, Narayana, Atmabodha, Nrisimhapurvatapaniya, Nrisimhottara-tapaniya, Ramapurvatapaniya, Ramottaratapaniya. (Supplemental Upanisads): Purusasuktam, Tadeva, Shiva-samkalpa, Baskala, Chagaleya, Paingala, Mrtyu-langala, Arseya, Pranava, and Saunaka Upanisad.

Skanda Purana

Sri Bhakti-ratnakara, by Sri Narahari Cakravarti Thakura

Sri Brihat Bhagavatamritam, by Sri Srila Sanatana Gosvami, Sree Gaudiya Math, Madras, India, 1987

Sri Caitanya Bhagavat, by Sri Vrindavan dasa Thakura

Sri Caitanya Shikshamritam, Thakura Bhakti Vinode, Sree Gaudiya Math, Madras, 1983

Sri Isopanisad, translated by A. C. Bhaktivedanta Swami, Bhaktivedanta Book Trust, New York/Los Angeles, 1969

Srimad-Bhagavatam, translated by A. C. Bhaktivedanta Swami, Bhaktivedanta Book trust, New York/Los Angeles, 1972

Srimad-Bhagavatam, translated by N. Raghunathan, Vighneswar Publishing House, Madras, 1976

Srimad-Bhagavatam MahaPurana, translated by C. L. Goswami, M. A., Sastri, Motilal Jalan at Gita Press, Gorkhapur, India, 1982

Sri Sri Krishna Bhavanamrta Mahakavya, Srila Visvanatha Chakravarti Thakura, completed in 1686

Sri Srimad Bhagavata-Arka Marichimala, Thakura Bhakti Vinode, Sree Gaudiya Math, Madras, 1978

Svetasvatara Upanishad

Taittiriya Upanishad

Tantra of the Great Liberation (Mahanirvana Tantra), translated by Woodroffe, Dover Publications, New York, 1972

Tattva-Viveka, Tattva-Sutra, Amnaya Sutra, Srila Bhaktivinode Thakur, Sree Gaudiya Math, Madras, 1979

Twelve Essential Upanishads, Tridandi Sri Bhakti Prajnan Yati, Sree Gaudiya Math, Madras, 1982. Includes the *Isha, Kena, Katha, Prashna, Mundaka, Mandukya, Taittiriya, Aitareya, Chandogya, Brihadaranyaka, Svetasvatara,* and *Gopalatapani Upanishad* of the Pippalada section of the *Atharva-veda.*

Upadesamrta (Nectar of Instruction), translated by A. C. Bhaktivedanta Swami, Bhaktivedanta Book Trust, New York/Los Angeles, 1975

The Upanishads, translated by Swami Prabhavananda and Frederick Manchester, New American Library, New York, 1957; contains Katha, Isha, Kena, Prasna, Mundaka, Mandukya, Taittiriya, Aitareya, Chandogya, Brihadaranyaka, Kaivalya, and Svetasvatara Upanishads.

The Upanisads, translated by F. Max Muller, Dover Publications; contains Chandogya, Kena, Aitareya, Kausitaki, Vajasaneyi (Isa), Katha, Mundaka, Taittiriya, Brihadaranyaka, Svetasvatara, Prasna, and Maitrayani Upanisads.

Varaha Purana, tr. by S. Venkitasubramonia Iyer, Banarsidass, Delhi, 1985

Vayu Purana, translated by G. V. Tagare, Banarsidass, Delhi, India, 1987

Veda of the Black Yajus School: Taitiriya Sanhita, translated by Arthur Keith, Motilal Banarsidass, Delhi, 1914

Vishnu Purana, translated by H. H. Wilson, Nag Publishers, Delhi

Vishnu-smriti

Vedanta-Sutras of Badarayana with Commentary of Baladeva Vidyabhusana, translated by Rai Bahadur Srisa Chandra Vasu, Munshiram Manoharlal, New Delhi, 1979

White Yajurveda, translated by Griffith, The Chowkhamba Sanskrit Series Office, Varanasi, 1976

Yajurveda, translated by Devi Chand, Munshiram Manoharlal, Delhi, 1980

Yoga Sutras of Patanjali

Other references that were helpful are listed as follows:

A History of India, Hermann Kulke and Dietmar Rothermund, Dorset Press, New York, 1986

The Aryans, V. Gordon Childe, Dorset Press, New York, 1987

Banaras, City of Light, Diana L. Eck, Princeton University Press, Princeton, New Jersey, 1982

Bible Myths and Their Parallels in Other Religions, T. W. Doane, Health Research, Mokelumne Hill, California, 1910

Book of Jasher, Published by The Rosicrucian Order, San Jose, California, 1934

Breakthrough, Clifford G. Hospital, Orbis Books, Maryknoll, New York, 1985

The Cult of Jagannatha and the Regional Tradition of Orissa, edited by A. Eschmann, H. Kulke, and G. C. Tripathi, Manohar Publications, Delhi, 1978

The Daily Practice of the Hindus, Rai Bahadur Srira Chandra Vidyarnava, Oriental Books Reprint Corporation, Allahabad, 1979

Dictionary of Philosophy and Religion, Reese, Humanities Press, Atlantic Highlands, New Jersey, 1980

Egyptian Civilization, L. A. Waddell, Christian Book Club, Hawthorne, CA

Elements of Hindu Iconography, by T. A. Gopinatha Rao, Motilal Banarsidass, Delhi, 1985

Encyclopedia of Witchcraft and Demonolgy, Russell Hope Robbins, Crown Publishers, Inc., New York, 1959

The Gods of India, by Alain Danielou, Inner Traditions, New York, 1985

Harper's Dictionary of Hinduism, by Margaret and James Stutley, Harper & Row, San Francisco, 1917

Hindu Influence on Greek Philosophy, Timothy J. Lomperis, Minerva Associates (Publications) PVT. LTD., Calcutta, 1984

Hindu Samskaras, by Dr. Raj Bali Pandey, Motilal Banarsidass, Delhi, 1969

The Indo-Sumerian Seals Deciphered, L. A. Waddell, Omni Publications, Hawthorne, California, 1980

Inner Reaches of Outer Space, Joseph Campbell, Harper & Row, New York, 1986

In Search of the Indo-Europeans, J.P.Mallory, Thames & Hudson, New York, 1989

Jesus Lived in India, Kersten, Element Book Ltd., Dorset England, 1986

The Jesus Mystery, Bock, Aura Books, Los Angeles, 1980

Jesus the Magician, Smith, Harper & Row, San Francisco, 1978

Kali: The Feminine Force, Moorkerjee, Destiny Books, New York, 1988

Kundalini: The Arousal of the Inner Energy, Mookerjee, Destiny Books, New York, 1982

Lost Years of Jesus, Prophet, Summit University Press, Livingston, MT. 1984

The Makers of Civilization, L. A. Waddell, Hollywood, CA. 1929

Mathura, The Cultural Heritage, edited by Doris Meth Srinivasan, American Insitute of Indian Studies, New Delhi, 1989

Navadvipa Mahatmya, [The Glories of Navadvipa], by Bhaktivinoda Thakur, translated by Banu das

Oriental Mythology, Joseph Campbell, Penguin Books, New York, 1962

Readings From World Religions, Selwyn Champion, Dorothy Short, Fawcett World Library, New York, New York, 1951

Primitive Mythology, Joseph Campbell, Penguin Books, New York, 1959

Puranic Encyclopaedia, Vettam Mani, Motilal Banarsidass, Delhi, 1964

The Religions of Man, Huston Smith, Harper & Row, New York, 1986

The Philosophy and Religion of Sri Caitanya, O. B. L. Kapoor, Munshiram Manoharla, New Delhi, 1977

The Secret Teachings of All Ages, Manly P. Hall, The Philosophical Research Society, Inc., Los Angeles, California, 1962

The Serpent Power, Avalon, Dover, New York, 1974

Seven Systems of Indian Philosophy, by Rajmani Tigunait, Ph.D., Himalayan Publishers, Honesdale, Pennsylvasnia, 1953

The Sumerians, C. Leonard Woolley, W. W. Norton & Co., New York, 1965

The Surya Siddhanta, A Textbook of Hindu Astronomy, edited by Phanindralal Gangooly, Motilal Banarsidass, Delhi, 1860

Tantrism, Walker, Aquarian Press, England, 1982

Tibetan Buddhism, L. A. Waddell, Dover, New York, 1972

Tools for Tantra, Harish Johari, Destiny Books, Vermont, 1986

Vedic Mathematics, by Sri Bharati Krishna Tirthaji Maharaja, Motilal Banarsidass, Delhi, 1965

Vedic Tantrism, [*Rigvidhana of Saunaka*], by M. S. Bhat, Motilal Banarsidass, Delhi, 1987

Vedic Cosmography and Astronomy, by Richard L. Thompson, Bhaktivedanta Book Trust, Los Angeles, 1989

Vijnanabhairava or Divine Consciousness, A Treasury of 112 Types of Yoga, by Jaideva Singh, Motilal Banarsidass, Delhi, 1979

What the Great Religions Teach, Health Research, Mokelumne Hill, California, 1958

World Religions, From Ancient History to the Present, Parrinder, Facts on File Publications, New York, 1971

Yantra: The Tantric Symbol of Cosmic Unity, Madhu Khanna, Thames and Hudson, London, 1979

ABBREVIATIONS

Bhagavad-gita is abbreviated in this book as *Bg*.

Caitanya-caritamrita is *Cc*.

Manu-samhita is *Manu*.

Srimad-Bhagavatam or *Bhagavat Purana* is *Bhag*.

Vishnu Purana is *VP*.

GLOSSARY

A

Acarya--the spiritual master who sets the proper standard by his own example.

Acintya-bhedabheda-tattva--simultaneously one and different. The doctrine Lord Sri Caitanya taught referring to the Absolute as being both personal and impersonal.

Advaita--nondual, meaning that the Absolute is one with no difference between His form and Himself. The philosophy taught by Sankaracharya.

Agni--fire, or Agni the demigod of fire.

Agnihotra--the Vedic sacrifice in which offerings were made to the fire, such as ghee, milk, sesame seeds, grains, etc. The demigod Agni would deliver the offerings to the demigods that were referred to in the ritual.

Ahankara--false ego, identification with matter.

Ahimsa--nonviolence.

Akarma--actions which cause no *karmic* reactions.

Akasha--the ether, or etheric plane; a subtle material element in which sound travels.

Ananda--spiritual bliss.

Ananta--unlimited.

Apara-prakrti--the material energy of the Lord.

Aranyaka--sacred writings that are supposed to frame the essence of the *Upanishads.*

Arati--the ceremony of worship when incense and ghee lamps are offered to the Deities.

Arca-vigraha--the worshipable Deity form of the Lord made of stone, wood, etc.

Aryan--a noble person, one who is on the path of spiritual advancement.

Asana--postures for meditation, or exercises for developing the body into a fit instrument for spiritual advancement.

Asat--that which is temporary.

Ashrama--one of the four orders of spiritual life, such as *brahmacari* (celibate student), *grihastha* (married householder), *vanaprastha* (retired stage), and *sannyasa* (renunciate); or the abode of a spiritual teacher or *sadhu.*

Astanga-yoga--the eightfold path of mystic yoga.

Asura--one who is ungodly or a demon.

Atma--the self or soul. Sometimes means the body, mind, and senses.

Atman--usually referred to as the Supreme Self.

Avatara--an incarnation of the Lord who descends from the spiritual world.

Avidya--ignorance or nescience.

Aum--*om* or *pranava*

Ayodhya--the town of Lord Rama in East India.

Ayurveda--the original wholistic form of medicine as described in the Vedic literature.

B

Babaji--wandering mendicant holy man.

Badrinatha--one of the holy places of pilgrimage in the Himalayas, and home of the Deity Sri Badrinatha along with many sages and hermits.

Betel--a mildly intoxicating nut.

Bhagavan--one who possesses all opulences, God.

Bhajan--song of worship.

Bhajan kutir--a small dwelling used for one's worship and meditation.

Bhakta--a devotee of the Lord who is engaged in *bhakti-yoga*.

Bhakti--love and devotion for God.

Bhakti-yoga--the path of offering pure devotional service to the Supreme.

Bhang--pronounced bong, a sweet mixed with hashish.

Bhava--preliminary stage of love of God.

Bidi--an Indian cigarette.

Brahma--the demigod of creation who was born from Lord Vishnu, the first created living being and the engineer of the secondary stage of creation of the universe when all the living entities were manifested.

Brahmacari--a celebate student who is trained by the spiritual master. One of the four divisions or ashramas of spiritual life.

Brahmajyoti--the great white light or effulgence which emanates from the body of the Lord.

Brahmaloka--the highest planet or plane of existence in the universe; the planet where Lord Brahma lives.

Brahman--the spiritual energy; the all-pervading impersonal aspect of the Lord; or the Supreme Lord Himself.

Brahmana or brahmin--one of the four orders of society; the intellectual class of men who have been trained in the knowledge of the *Vedas* and initiated by a spiritual master.

Brahmana--the supplemental books of the four primary *Vedas*. They usually contained instructions for performing Vedic *agnihotras*, chanting the *mantras*, the purpose of the rituals, etc. The *Aitareya* and *Kaushitaki Brahmanas* belong to the *Rig-veda*, the *Satapatha Brahmana* belongs to the *White Yajur-veda*, and the *Taittiriya Brahmana* belongs to the *Black Yajur-veda*. The *Praudha* and *Shadvinsa Brahmanas* are two of the eight *Brahmanas* belonging to the *Atharva-veda*.

Brahmastra--a nuclear weapon that is produced and controlled by *mantra*.

Brahminical--to be clean and upstanding, both outwardly and inwardly, like a *brahmana* should be.

Brijbasi--a resident of Vraja, Vrindavan.

Buddha--Lord Buddha or a learned man.

C

Caitanya-caritamrta--the scripture by Krishnadasa Kaviraja which explains the teachings and pastimes of Lord Caitanya Mahaprabhu.

Caitanya Mahaprabhu--the most recent incarnation of the Lord who appeared in the 15th century in Bengal and who originally started the *sankirtana* movement, based on congregational chanting of the holy names.

Caranamrita--the water that has been used to bathe the Deity and is offered in small spoonfuls to visitors in in the temple.

Chakra--a wheel, disk, or psychic energy center situated along the spinal column in the subtle body of the physical shell.

Candala--a person in the lowest class, or dog-eater.

Causal Ocean or Karana Ocean--is the corner of the spiritual sky where Maha-Vishnu lies down to create the material manifestation.

Cit--eternal knowledge.

Chhandas--sacred hymns of the *Atharva-veda*.

D

Darshan--the devotional act of seeing and being seen by the Deity in the temple.

Deity--the *arca-vigraha*, or worshipful form of the Supreme in the temple, or deity as the worshipful image of the demigod. A capital D is used in refering to Krishna or one of His expansions, while a small d is used when refering to a demigod or lesser personality.

Devas--demigods or heavenly beings from higher levels of material existence, or a godly person.

Devaloka--the higher planets or planes of existence of the devas.

Devaki--the devotee who acted as Lord Krishna's mother.

Dham--a holy place.

Dharma--the essential nature or duty of the living being.

Dharmashala--a shelter or guesthouse for pilgrims at temples or holy towns.

Diksha--spiritual initiation.

Dualism--as related in this book refers to the Supreme as both an impersonal force as well as a person.

Durga--the form of Parvati, Shiva's wife, as a warrior goddess known by many names according to her deeds, such as Simhavahini when riding her lion, Mahishasuramardini for killing the demon Mahishasura, Jagaddhatri as the mother of the universe, Kali when she killed the demon Raktavija, Tara when killing Shumba, etc.

Dvapara-yuga--the third age which lasts 864,000 years.

Dwaita--dualism, the principle that the Absolute Truth consists of the infinite Supreme Being and the infinitesimal individual souls.

E

Ekadasi--a fast day on the eleventh day of the waxing and waning moon.

G

Gandharvas--the celestial angel-like beings who have beautiful forms and voices, and are expert in dance and music, capable of becoming invisible and can help souls on the earthly plane.

Ganesh--a son of Shiva, said to destroy obstacles (as Vinayaka) and offer good luck to those who petition him.

Ganges--the sacred and spiritual river which, according to the *Vedas*, runs throughout the universe, a portion of which is seen in India. The reason the river is considered holy is that it is said to be a drop of the Karana Ocean that leaked in when Lord Vishnu, in His incarnation as Vamanadeva, kicked a small hole in the universal shell with His toe. Thus, the water is spiritual as well as being purified by the touch of Lord Vishnu.

Gangapuja--the arati ceremony for worshiping the Ganges.

Gangotri--the source of the Ganges River in the Himalayas.

Garbhodakasayi Vishnu--the expansion of Lord Vishnu who enters into each universe.

Gaudiya--a part of India sometimes called Aryavarta or land of the Aryans, located south of the Himalayas and north of the Vindhya Hills.

Gaudiya *sampradaya*--the school of Vaishnavism founded by Sri Caitanya.

Gayatri--the spiritual vibration or *mantra* from which the other *Vedas* were expanded and which is chanted by those who are initiated as *brahmanas* and given the spiritual understanding of Vedic philosophy.

Ghat--a bathing place along a river or lake with steps leading down to the water.

Godasa--one who serves the senses.

Goloka Vrindavana--the name of Lord Krishna's spiritual planet.

Gompa--Buddhist monastery.

Gopuram--the tall ornate towers that mark the gates to the temples, often found in south India.

Gosvami--one who is master of the senses.

Govinda--a name of Krishna which means one who gives pleasure to the cows and senses.

Grihastha--the householder order of life. One of the four *ashramas* in spiritual life.

Gunas--the modes of material nature of which there is *sattva* (goodness), *rajas* (passion), and *tamas* (ignorance).

Guru--a spiritual master.

H

Hare--the Lord's pleasure potency, Radharani, who is approached for accessibility to the Lord.

Hari--a name of Krishna as the one who takes away one's obstacles on the spiritual path.

Haribol--a word that means to chant the name of the Lord, Hari.

Harinam--refers to the name of the Lord, Hari.

Har Ki Pauri--the holy bathing ghats in Hardwar where the Ganges leaves the mountains and enters the plains. It is at this spot where the Kumbha Mela is held every twelve years.

Hatha-yoga--a part of the yoga system which stresses various sitting postures and exercises.

Hiranyagarbha--another name of Brahma who was born of Vishnu in the primordial waters within the egg of the universe.

Hrishikesa--a name for Krishna which means the master of the senses.

I

Impersonalism--the view that God has no personality or form, but is only an impersonal force.

Impersonalist--those who believe God has no personality or form.

Incarnation--the taking on of a body or form.

Indra--the King of heaven and controller of rain, who by his great power conquers the forces of darkness.

ISKCON--International Society for Krishna Consciousness.

J

Jai or *Jaya*--a term meaning victory, all glories.

Japa--the chanting one performs, usually softly, for one's own meditation.

Japa-mala--the string of beads one uses for chanting.

Jiva--the individual soul or living being.

Jivanmukta--a liberated soul, though still in the material body and universe.

Jiva-shakti--the living force.

Jnana--knowledge which may be material or spiritual.

Jnana-kanda--the portion of the *Vedas* which stresses empirical speculation for understanding truth.

Jnana-yoga--the process of linking with the Supreme through empirical knowledge and mental speculation.

Jnani--one engaged in *jnana-yoga*, or the process of cultivating knowledge to understand the Absolute.

K

Kala--eternal time.

Kali--the demigoddess who is the fierce form of the wife of Lord Shiva. The word *kali* comes from *kala*, the Sanskrit word for time: the power that dissolves or destroys everything.

Kali-yuga--the fourth and present age, the age of quarrel and confusion, which lasts 432,000 years and began 5,000 years ago.

Kalpa--a day in the life of Lord Brahma which lasts a thousand cycles of the four *yugas*.

Kama--lust or inordinate desire.

Kama sutra--a treatise on sex enjoyment.

Kapila--an incarnation of Lord Krishna who propagated the Sankhya philosophy.

Karanodakasayi Vishnu (Maha-Vishnu)--the expansion of Lord Krishna who created all the material universes.

Karma--material actions performed in regard to developing one's position or for future results which produce *karmic* reactions. It is also the reactions one endures from such fruitive activities.

Karma-kanda--the portion of the *Vedas* which primarily deals with recommended fruitive activities for various results.

Karma-yoga--the system of yoga for dovetailing one's activities for spiritual advancement.

Karmi--the fruitive worker, one who accumulates more *karma*.

Kirtana--chanting or singing the glories of the Lord.

Krishna--the name of the original Supreme Personality of Godhead which means the most attractive and greatest pleasure. He is the source of all other incarnations, such as Vishnu, Rama, Narasimha, Narayana, Buddha, Parashurama, Vamanadeva, Kalki at the end of Kali-yuga, etc.

Krishnaloka--the spiritual planet where Lord Krishna resides.

Kshatriya--the second class of *varna* of society, or occupation of administrative or protective service, such as warrior or military personel.

Ksirodakasayi Vishnu--the Supersoul expansion of the Lord who enters into each atom and the heart of each individual.

Kumbha Mela--the holy festival in which millions of pilgrims and sages gather to bathe in the holy and purifying rivers for liberation at particular auspicious times that are calculated astrologically. The Kumbha Mela festivals take place every three years alternating between Allahabad, Nasik, Ujjain, and Hardwar.

Kuruksetra--the place of battle 5,000 years ago between the Pandavas and the Kauravas ninety miles north of New Delhi, where Krishna spoke the *Bhagavad-gita.*

L

Lakshmi--the goddess of fortune and wife of Lord Vishnu.
Lila--pastimes.
Lilavataras--the many incarnations of God who appear to display various spiritual pastimes to attract the conditioned souls in the material world.
Linga--the phallic symbol of Lord Shiva.

M

Mahabhagavata--a great devotee of the Lord.
Mahabharata--the great epic of the Pandavas, which includes the *Bhagavad-gita,* by Vyasadeva.
Maha-mantra--the best *mantra* for self-realization in this age, called the Hare Krishna *mantra.*
Mahatma--a great soul or devotee.
Mahat-tattva--the total material energy.
Maha-Vishnu or Karanodakasayi Vishnu--the Vishnu expansion of Lord Krishna from whom all the material universes emanate.
Mandir--a temple.
Mantra--a sound vibration which prepares the mind for spiritual realization and delivers the mind from material inclinations. In some cases a *mantra* is chanted for specific material benefits.
Martya-loka--the earth planet, the place of death.
Maya--illusion, or anything that appears to not be connected with the eternal Absolute Truth.
Mayavadi--the impersonalist or voidist who believes that the Supreme has no form.
Mitra--the deity controlling the sun, and who gives life to earth.
Mleccha--a derogatory name for an untouchable person, a meat eater.
Moksha--liberation from material existence.
Murti--a Deity of the Lord or spiritual master that is worshiped.
Murugan--means the divine child, the Tamil name for Subramaniya, one of the sons of Shiva and Parvati, especially worshiped in South India.

N

Narayana--the four-handed form of the Supreme Lord.
Nirguna--without material qualities.

Nirvana--the state of no material miseries, usually the goal of the Buddhists or voidists.

O

Om or *Omkara--pranava*, the transcendental *om mantra*, generally referring to the attributeless or impersonal aspects of the Absolute.

P

Pan--a concoction of ground betel nut and spices that acts as a mild stimulant or intoxicant. It is very popular and often leaves the teeth stained red.

Pandal--a large tent where religious gatherings are held.

Paramahamsa--the highest level of self-realized devotees of the Lord.

Paramatma--the Supersoul, or localized expansion of the Lord.

Parampara--the system of disciplic succession through which transcendental knowledge descends.

Parvati--Lord Shiva's spouse, daughter of Parvata. Parvata is the personification of the Himalayas. She is also called Gauri for her golden complexion, Candi, Bhairavi (as the wife of Bhairava, Shiva), Durga, Ambika, and Shakti.

Patanjali--the authority on the *astanga-yoga* system.

Pradhana--the total material energy in its unmanifest state.

Prajapati--deity presiding over procreation.

Prakriti--matter in its primordial state, the material nature.

Prana--the life air or cosmic energy.

Pranayama--control of the breathing process as in *astanga* or *raja-yoga*.

Pranava--same as *omkara*.

Prasada--food or other articles that have been offered to the Deity in the temple and then distributed amongst people as the blessings or mercy of the Deity.

Prema--matured love for Krishna.

Puja--the worship offered to the Deity.

Pujari--the priest who performs worship, *puja*, to the Deity.

Purusha or *Purusham*--the supreme enjoyer.

R

Raja-yoga--the eightfold yoga system.

Rajo-guna--the material mode of passion.

Ramachandra--an incarnation of Krishna as He appeared as the greatest of kings.

Ramayana--the great epic of the incarnation of Lord Ramachandra.

Rasa--an enjoyable taste or feeling, a relationship with God.

Rishi--saintly person who knows the Vedic knowledge.

S

Sacrifice--in this book it in no way pertains to human sacrifice, as many people tend to think when this word is used. But it means to engage in an austerity of some kind for a higher, spiritual purpose.

Shabda-brahma--the original spiritual vibration or energy which the *Vedas* are composed of.

Sac-cid-ananda-vigraha--the transcendental form of the Lord or of the living entity which is eternal, full of knowledge and bliss.

Sadhana--a specific practice or discipline for attaining God realization.

Sadhu--Indian holy man or devotee.

Saguna Brahman--the aspect of the Absolute with form and qualities.

Samadhi--trance, the perfection of being absorbed in the Absolute.

Samsara--rounds of life; cycles of birth and death; reincarnation.

Sanatana-dharma--the eternal nature of the living being, to love and render service to the supreme lovable object, the Lord.

Sangam--the confluence of two or more rivers.

Sankhya--analytical understanding of material nature, the body, and the soul.

Sankirtana-yajna--the prescribed sacrifice for this age: congregational chanting of the holy names of God.

Sannyasa--the renounced order of life, the highest of the four *ashramas* on the spiritual path.

Sarasvati--the goddess of knowledge and intelligence.

Sattva-guna--the material mode of goodness.

Satya-yuga--the first of the four ages which lasts 1,728,000 years.

Shaivites--worshipers of Lord Shiva.

Shakti--energy, potency or power, the active principle in creation. Also the active power or wife of a deity, such as Shiva/Shakti.

Shastra--the authentic revealed scripture.

Shiva--the benevolent one, the demigod who is in charge of the material mode of ignorance and the destruction of the universe. Part of the triad of Brahma, Vishnu, and Shiva who continually create, maintain, and destroy the universe. He is known as Rudra when displaying his destructive aspect.

Sikha--a tuft of hair on the back of the head signifying that one is a Vaishnava.

Smaranam--remembering the Lord.

Smriti--the traditional Vedic knowledge "that is remembered" from what was directly heard by or revealed to the *rishis*.

Sravanam--hearing about the Lord.

Srimad-Bhagavatam--the most ripened fruit of the tree of Vedic knowledge compiled by Vyasadeva.

Sruti--scriptures that were received directly from God and transmitted orally by
    brahmanas or *rishis* down through succeeding generations.
    Traditionally, it is considered the four primary *Vedas*.
Sudra--the working class of society, the fourth of the *varnas*.
Svami--one who can control his mind and senses.

T

Tamo-guna--the material mode of ignorance.
Tapasya--voluntary austerity for spiritual advancement.
Tilok--the clay markings that signify a person's body as a temple, and the sect
    or school of thought of the person.
Tirtha--a holy place of pilgrimage.
Tirthankaras--the person who is the spiritual guide or teacher in Jainism.
Treta-yuga--the second of the four ages which lasts 1,296,000 years.
Tulasi--the small tree that grows where worship to Krishna is found. It is called
    the embodiment of devotion, and the incarnation of Vrinda-devi.

U

Upanishads--the portions of the *Vedas* which primarily explain philosophically
    the Absolute Truth. It is knowledge of Brahman which releases one
    from the world and allows one to attain self-realization when received
    from a qualified teacher. Except for the *Isa Upanishad*, which is the
    40th chapter of the *Vajasaneyi Samhita* of the *Sukla* (*White*) *Yajur-veda*,
    the *Upanishads* are connected to the four primary *Vedas*, generally
    found in the *Brahmanas*.

V

Vaikunthas--the planets located in the spiritual sky.
Vaishnava--a worshiper of the Supreme Lord Vishnu or Krishna and His
    expansions or incarnations.
Vaishnava-*aparadha*--an offense against a Vaisnava or devotee, which can negate
    all of one's spiritual progress.
Vaisya--the third class of society engaged in business or farming.
Vanaprastha--the third of the four *ashramas* of spiritual life in which one retires
    from family life in preparation for the renounced order.
Varna--sometimes referred to as caste, a division of society, such as *brahmana*
    (a priestly intellectual), a *kshatriya* (ruler or manager), *vaisya* (a
    merchant, banker, or farmer), and *sudra* (common laborer).
Varnashrama--the system of four divisions of society and four orders of spiritual
    life.

Vedanta-sutras--the philosophical conclusion of the four *Vedas*.

Vedas--generally means the four primary *samhitas;* the *Rig, Yajur, Sama,* and *Atharva.*

Vidya--knowledge.

Vikarma--sinful activities performed without scriptural authority and which produce sinful reactions.

Virajanadi or Viraja River--the space that separates the material creation from the spiritual sky.

Vishnu--the expansion of Lord Krishna who enters into the material energy to create and maintain the cosmic world.

Vrindavana--the place where Lord Krishna displayed His village pastimes 5,000 years ago, and is considered to be part of the spiritual abode..

Vyasadeva--the incarnation of God who appeared as the greatest philosopher who compiled all the *Vedas* into written form.

Y

Yajna--a ritual or austerity that is done as a sacrifice for spiritual merit, or ritual worship of a demigod for good *karmic* reactions.

Yamaraja--the demigod and lord of death who directs the living entities to various punishments according to their activities.

Yantra--a machine, instrument, or mystical diagram used in ritual worship.

Yoga--linking up with the Absolute.

Yoga-*siddhi*--mystic perfection.

Yuga-avataras--the incarnations of God who appear in each of the four *yugas* to explain the authorized system of self-realization in that age.

INDEX

DISCLAIMER

ABOUT THE AUTHOR

Stephen Knapp grew up in a Christian family, during which time he seriously studied the Bible to understand its teachings. In his late teenage years, however, he sought answers to questions not easily explained in Christian theology. So he began to search through other religions and philosophies from around the world and started to find the answers for which he was looking. He also studied a variety of occult sciences, ancient mythology, mysticism, yoga, and the spiritual teachings of the East. After his first reading of the *Bhagavad-gita*, he felt he had found the last piece of the puzzle he had been putting together through all of his research. Therefore, he continued to study all of the major Vedic texts of India to gain a better understanding of the Vedic science.

It is known amongst all Eastern mystics that anyone, regardless of qualifications, academic or otherwise, who does not engage in the spiritual practices described in the Vedic texts, cannot actually enter into understanding the depths of the Vedic spiritual science, nor acquire the realizations that should accompany it. So, rather than pursuing his research in an academic atmosphere at a university, Stephen directly engaged in the spiritual disciplines that have been recommended for hundreds of years. He continued his study of Vedic knowledge and spiritual practice under the guidance of a spiritual master. Through this process, and with the sanction of His Divine Grace A. C. Bhaktivedanta Swami Prabhupada, he became initiated into the genuine and authorized spiritual line of the Brahma-Madhava-Gaudiya *sampradaya*, which is a disciplic succession that descends back through Sri Caitanya Mahaprabhu and Sri Vyasadeva, the compiler of Vedic literature, and further back to Sri Krishna. Besides being *brahminically* initiated, Stephen has also been to India several times and traveled extensively throughout the country, visiting most of the major holy places and gaining a wide variety of spiritual experiences that only such places can give.

Stephen has been writing *The Eastern Answers to the Mysteries of Life* series, which so far includes *The Secret Teachings of the Vedas* and *The Universal Path to Enlightenment*. He has also written a novel, *Destined for Infinity*, for those who prefer lighter reading, or learning spiritual knowledge in the context of a fictional, spiritual adventure. Stephen has put the culmination of over twenty years of continuous research and travel experience into his books in an effort to share it with those who are also looking for spiritual understanding.

If you have enjoyed this book, you will also want to get Volume One of this series:

The Secret Teachings of the Vedas

This book presents the essence of the ancient Eastern philosophy and summarizes some of the most elevated and important of all spiritual knowledge. This enlightening information is explained in a clear and concise way and is essential for all who want to increase their spiritual understanding, regardless of what their religious background may be.

The topics include: what is your real spiritual identity; the Vedic explanation of the soul; scientific evidence that consciousness is separate from but interacts with the body; the real unity between us all; how to attain the highest happiness and freedom from the cause of suffering; the law of karma and reincarnation; the karma of a nation; where you are really going in life; the real process of progressive evolution; life after death--heaven, hell, or beyond; a description of the spiritual realm; the nature of the Absolute Truth--personal God or impersonal force; recognizing the existence of the Supreme; the reason why we exist at all; and much more. This book provides the answers to questions not found in other religions or philosophies, and condenses information from a wide variety of sources that would take a person years to assemble. It also contains many quotations from the Vedic texts which show the knowledge the Vedas have held for thousands of years, and explains the history and origins of the Vedic literature. This book has been called one of the best reviews of Eastern philosophy available.

There is also a special section on traveling to the major historical holy sites of South India with over 75 photographs of art work, sculptures, deities, architecture, and some of the most amazing temples you will see anywhere. This section elaborates on the many ancient legends connected with these important places and what it is like to travel and see them today.

To get your copy, order it from your local bookstore (ISBN:0-9617410-1-5), or simply send $14.95, plus $2.50 for postage and handling ($6.50 for overseas orders) to:

The World Relief Network, P. O. Box 15082, Detroit, Michigan, 48215, U. S. A.